The Emerging Technological Trajectory* of the Pacific Rim

This book directly confronts the notion that the twenty-first century will indeed be the "Pacific Century." It discusses in depth the new patterns of manufacturing and technology transfer that are emerging as Japanese companies seek to harness Asia's technological resources and to utilize these resources to compete both regionally and globally.

This book is being published under the auspices of the
Center for Technology and International Affairs
at the Fletcher School of Law and Diplomacy, Tufts University.

The Emerging Technological Trajectory of the Pacific Rim

Denis Fred Simon
Editor

An East Gate Book

M. E. Sharpe Inc.
Armonk, New York
London, England

An East Gate Book

Library of Congress Cataloging-in-Publication Data

The Emerging technological trajectory of the Pacific Rim /
Denis Fred Simon, editor
p.   cm.
"An East Gate Book."
Includes index.
ISBN 1-56324-196-X (c.)—ISBN 1-56324-197-8 (p.)
1. Technology—Pacific Area.
2. Technology transfer—Pacific Area.
3. Technology and state—Pacific Area.
I. Simon, Denis Fred.
T30.A1E45   1993
338.9507—dc20
93-31103
CIP

Printed in the United States of America

The paper used in this publication meets the minimum requirements of
American National Standard for Information Sciences—
Permanence of Paper for Printed Library Materials,
ANSI Z 39.48-1984.

BM (c)	10	9	8	7	6	5	4	3	2	1
BM (p)	10	9	8	7	6	5	4	3	2	1

Contents

About the Editor and Contributors

Denis Fred Simon is associate professor of international business and technology at the Fletcher School of Law and Diplomacy at Tufts University. He also directs the Center for Technology and International Affairs.

Dipo Alam is the S&T coordinator at PAPITEK (The Center for Analysis of S&T Development) under the Indonesian Institute of Sciences (LIPI).

Anuwar Ali is dean of the faculty of economics at University Kebangsaan, Malaysia.

Yasunori Baba is a member of the faculty at RACE (Research into Artifacts, Center for Engineering) at the University of Tokyo.

W. Michael Denny is senior lecturer, department of computer science, City Polytechnic of Hong Kong.

Jingping Ding is deputy director of the Institute of Industrial Economics at the Chinese Academy of Social Sciences.

Hamzah Kassim is a senior staff member responsible for technology management at SIRIM (Standards and Industrial Research Institute of Malaysia).

Fumio Kodama is professor of policy studies at Saitama University in Japan.

Winston Liang is chief executive officer, Hong Kong Industrial Technology Center Corporation.

Karen Minden is associate professor of policy studies in the Center for Higher Education Research and Development at the University of Manitoba.

David O'Connor is senior researcher at the OECD Development Center, Paris.

Chatri Sripaipan is director of the S&T Development Program at the Thailand Development Research Institute.

Richard P. Suttmeier is professor of political science at the University of Oregon.

Charles Weiss is president of Global Technology Management in Bethesda, MD.

Poh-kam Wong is director of the Center for Management of Technology at the National University of Singapore.

Soichi Yamashita is professor of economics at Hiroshima University.

Seongjae Yu is professor of international business and technology at Chung Ang University in Seoul, Korea.

Zhou Yuan is director of regional studies at the National Research Center for S&T for Development in Beijing.

Acknowledgments

The editor wishes to thank the National Science Foundation for providing financial support (Grant #s: SRS-8719232 and SRS-8813941) to find this entire project, including the conference held at the Fletcher School of Law & Diplomacy at Tufts University. In addition, I also would like to thank EG&G Corporation, the Beijing office of the Ford Foundation, the Xerox Foundation, Fujitsu Corporation, and the Hitachi Corporation for providing funding to facilitate the implementation of this project and the book publication. In addition, I want to convey my appreciation to the authors and discussants who attended the Fletcher conference and provided the intellectual capital that made our three-day conference a major success. Finally, I would like to express my appreciation to Karin McMaster, Jessica Daniels, and Laura Conti for their hard work and for making all the arrangements that allowed this project to occur without even the slightest appearance of a problem.

Introduction

Beginning in the early 1980s, the world began to witness a fundamental transformation in the global political economy, driven, in large part, by the rapid emergence of the economies of the Asia-Pacific region as key players in global and regional markets. As these economies have pushed ahead with their own industrialization and have put in place, albeit gradually but steadily, a well-developed, well-articulated manufacturing and S&T (science and technology) infrastructure, a new architecture of cooperation and competition has appeared, manifested in the growing salience of Asia's production and research and development (R&D) capabilities in key industries ranging from microelectronics and computers to biotechnology and new materials. As a recent study in *Science* magazine concluded, these economies have the talent and the energy to engage in world class science and technology research.[1] Accordingly, the economies of the Asia-Pacific region are no longer simply passive actors in an economic game defined by firms or governments from the United States, Japan or Western Europe. Rather, their growing prowess in all facets of manufacturing and research has helped to reshape and redefine the boundaries of once stable markets and technological hierarchies.

The changes engendered in the global political economy by the rise of the Pacific Rim economies has led many observers of the region to rethink their projections about the structure and design of the intra-Asian as well as inter-Asian economic, financial, and most important, technological relationships.[2] A new technological trajectory for Pacific Rim economies is being posited by the chapters in this volume, one that departs in a number of significant ways from the previous scenarios that were being discussed in the 1960s and 1970s. As the chapters by Fumio Kodama (chapter 2), Greg B. Falker and Charles Weiss, Jr. (chapter 18), and several others show, the concept of a "trajectory" can be a difficult one to pin down. The term "trajectory" was chosen because it connotes a "path or direction" that is being followed without necessarily raising questions about the nature or orientation of that path. As a metaphor, it appears to provide us with a simple framework upon which to capture developments on a country or regional level. The majority of chapters in the book, however, raise critical questions about the drivers and sources of technological advance in the region; some of the chapters even raise political questions about the degree to which forces external to the ASEAN economies or the Asian NIEs are shaping and influencing this new technological trajectory. Japan, for example, through the foreign investment activities of its large and small-medium firms, is exerting a significant and sometimes undesirable impact on the new architecture that is being forged—though it may be premature to think in terms of long-term Japanese predominance in the region, especially given recent developments in the People's Republic of China. In fact, as the chapter by Richard P. Suttmeier (chapter 17) suggests, if present trends continue, it may turn out to be China rather than Japan that is the real catalyst for change and restructuring across the Pacific Rim.

In essence, to raise the question of a new technological trajectory in the Asia-Pacific region is to bring to the surface a number of alternative scenarios about the future orientation and cohesion of the Pacific Rim. To begin with, it is probably appropriate to ascertain whether putting forth the concept of a "technological trajectory" implies merely one such path for the entire region or whether it is possible that various countries will end up moving, albeit at different rates, along a range of different, perhaps parallel paths, some of which may be complementary, while others may portend future competition or conflicts. Clearly, at the present time, even when taking into account present and future processes of technological and economic leveling, there seemingly appears to be little value in thinking about a single trajectory for the region as a whole. As the chapters by Anuwar Ali (chapter 6) and Karen Minden (chapter 15) reveal, despite bilateral and multilateral efforts to promote greater regional cooperation and collaboration, there have been only a limited number of major successes. Very little formal regional orchestration seems possible or desirable by the key actors in the region, other than that provided by the market. It is important to remember, however, that this could change if the world were to fragment into three formal trading blocks; the economies of the Asia-Pacific would, of necessity, find themselves forced to march together in a way that necessitated greater technological cohesion and coherence among the various players.

Based on the chapters presented in this book, it also is useful to start off by considering whether or not the unit of analysis when discussing technological trajectories should, in fact, be countries. Given the activist role of government in several of the Pacific Rim nations, especially with respect to S&T development, countries would seem to be a relevant starting point for discussing trajectories—including the eventual points, if any, of competition. In fact, most of the chapters in this book adopt a country orientation. Yet, from another perspective, it may be more relevant to think about a technological trajectory with reference to specific industries. The chapter by Denis Fred Simon (chapter 1), which deals with globalization and regionalization trends, would seem to suggest that there are a series of more comprehensive forces at work in the international system that makes industry-level analysis a legitimate starting point for any discussion of alternative technological paths and possibilities. The present variable nature of competition across industries—even taking into account the increased emphasis on both time and technology—highlights the fact that so-called emerging pockets of excellence in some sectors within the Asian NIEs, for example, may be drawn into the mainstream of global competition, while other sectors remain largely "local" in orientation. This would imply that the roles and tasks performed by individual countries in the playing out of different industrial trajectories will likely be primarily sectoral rather than comprehensive in character. The key point is that in thinking about various scenarios regarding technological trajectories in the Pacific Rim, a number of forces are likely to influence the range of paths; governments will have a modicum of control over some of these forces, but in other cases, the forces at work will moderate the impact that any one set of government policies may have.

Does this then suggest that the idea of a regional technological trajectory is of limited value? After all, if what we mean by a technological trajectory is no more than the sum of the actions of individual countries or firms in the region, then there is probably not much utility to the concept. Yet, if the idea were to connote something more substantial, then it might prove to be an interesting lens through which to view the total consequences of those government policies, corporate strategies, multilateral initiatives, and private associations that have been initiated over the last several years. And, in fact, this is precisely why the metaphor was adopted—to provide an analytic vehicle for calculating, not simply in arithmetic terms, the dynamic changes that have come about from the unique synergies and forms of joint articulation across countries and industries. Positing a new technological trajectory on a regional scale would seem to warrant proof of some sort of paradigmatic change in the way the actors in the region relate to one another both at the public sector and private sector levels. Many of the chapters in this book, in fact, suggest that such a paradigmatic change is occurring—though how it is being orchestrated and where the locus of control lies are points on which there appears to be only modest agreement.

The new technological trajectory in the Pacific Rim is being driven by four key forces. First, it is being driven by the results of the massive investments in infrastructure, education, and new institutions that have been going on in Asia since the end of the postwar period. The economies of the Pacific Rim all seem to agree about one basic proposition, namely that science and technology progress is an important building block for sustained economic development. One merely has to review the size of the investments, in aggregate, as well as the level of effort that has been expended by the respective governments and private actors in the region, to recognize the substantial gains over the past three decades in terms of greater efficiency, productivity, and innovativeness. Most important, these gains are not some sort of aberration that can simply be attributed to an exotic facet of the Asian culture. Rather, they reflect concerted and explicit attempts to create new sources of national competitive advantage where these did not previously exist, especially through strong state-oriented policies designed to mobilize both public and private sector resources. Spending on R&D, for example, has been increasing at a 15 to 20 percent rate on average across the region over the last decade or more. As the chapter by David O'Connor (chapter 3) indicates, the Korean effort in microelectronics and the Taiwan program for creating a modern informatics industry were designed to enhance the position of indigenous firms vis-á-vis companies from the advanced industrialized nations. While it is true that government-led programs have had heterogenous outcomes, they generally have been highly homogenous in intent.

The second factor driving this new Pacific Rim trajectory have been the rapid and sustained changes taking place in the realm of manufacturing and R&D. The move towards flexible specialization and away from the once sacrosanct Fordist model of production has helped to bring into greater prominence the major talents and specialized capabilities of the Asian economies. While high-volume, high-quality, low-cost production may have been the vehicle that opened the door for Japan and the Asian NIEs to enter world markets, the nature of the game has changed insofar as the rules and focus of competitiveness are concerned. Today, in many industries, there is greater emphasis on customization of products; companies around the world are being admonished to think globally, but act locally. This trend has led to a greater emphasis on small batch production runs that reflect greater sensitivity to the specific needs of individual end users or customers. Expand and improved coordination—sometimes very direct and explicit—between developers and producers, on the one hand, and end-users or customers, on the other hand, has become not simply desirable, but a vital ingredient in sustaining market share.

There also has been a greater emphasis on time in the realm of global competition. Companies can no longer rest on their past laurels because numerous competitors are hot on their heels with new, innovative products and production processes. Customers, whether consumer or industrial, want to work with suppliers who are highly responsive and have the infrastructure in place to offer the type of participation in design and production noted above—all within an increasingly shorter and shorter time frame.

The microelectronics revolution has been the technological underpinning for much of what is happening in this regard; the re-programmability feature that is now an integral part of most modern manufacturing systems has meant that the small size of firms is not necessarily the disadvantage it once was thought to be in the era when economies of scale were the primary game. As the chapter by Poh-kam Wong (chapter 5) shows, this has allowed firms from Singapore and several other Asian economies to play a more central role in the new architecture of production that has been created by Japanese, American, and EC companies.

The stress is now on entry into the higher valued-added segments of the international division of labor; the watchwords are knowledge-intensive and skill-intensive industries, where time and technology are the critical success factors.

The revolution in information technologies also has helped to stimulate the onset of this emerging trajectory by providing the infrastructure for a new global and regional production and R&D architecture. Information technologies have shifted the emphasis away from control in terms of corporate governance and management; instead, we now see greater focus on coordination. Already, this has translated into added new opportunities for firms from the Pacific Rim as they become part of the new transborder networks being formed in all parts of the region. Suppliers, assemblers, and sub-assemblers are being connected in ways that few thought possible or viable in the past; horizontal communications among units from different countries as well as vertical communications with headquarters are now facilitated by the linkages that have been engineered using various types of modern telecommunications and computer technologies. Even firms from China are joining these networks, with more potentially to be invited to participate in the future.[3]

The third force driving the new technological trajectory has been the return of appreciable numbers of scientists and engineers to the region, many of whom had been part of the brain drain in the 1960s and 1970s. Taiwan, for example, has witnessed a dramatic reversal of the brain drain; more and more persons who were born on Taiwan, but were trained in the United States, are now returning to become high-tech entrepreneurs. Similar developments are taking place with respect to Korea and Singapore as well. Many of these individuals have well-established professional networks in the United States or other countries, and can plug into these networks to obtain necessary information or even capital to launch new initiatives in places such as the Hsinchu Science and Industrial Park on Taiwan. The big unknown in this regard is the People's Republic of China; it remains unknown just how many Chinese scientists and engineers trained in the West or Japan will return to mainland China in the immediate future.

Some persons in China seem worried about this issue, but others such as Dr. Xie Xide, former President of Fudan University in Shanghai, seem less concerned because of what has been happening most recently with regard to the brain-drain reversals Taiwan, Korea and other countries are experiencing. A growing number of PRC scientists and engineers are going to Singapore or Hong Kong, where they have greater independence and better facilities to conduct their research; their links with mainland China, however, have not been ignored and could further stimulate more rapid technological advance in China as well as other Pacific Rim nations. As the chapter by Zhou Yuan (chapter 10) implies, an improved climate for intellectuals as well as for commercially driven innovation, has already helped to produce a number of successes in China and could help to attract large numbers of badly needed high-quality scientific and technical personnel back to the PRC.

The fourth force driving this new trajectory revolves around the growing sense that cooperation and competition can go hand in hand. Most of the Asia-Pacific nations have come to realize that the world's leading companies will not take them seriously until they have something to bring to the table in the form of technological assets. Samsung in Korea, for example, was not taken very seriously by its Japanese competitors in the semiconductor memory field until it was able to produce, on a commercial basis, the first 16 megabyte DRAM memory chip ahead of Toshiba and other Japanese companies. Once that occurred, more and more Japanese companies began to see the virtues in developing a range of serious collaborative ties with the Koreans. Today, we have started to witness a proliferation of strategic alliances, joint ventures, and other collaborative arrangements—a growing percentage of which is taking place on an intraregional basis. As the chapter by Yasunori Baba and Tokio Suzuki (chapter 13) points out, this increased emphasis on intraregional cooperation rather than simply interregional cooperation could generate an entirely new set of technological synergies that many had not considered before.

All of this is not to suggest that there no longer is a technological gap between the industrialized West and the economies of the Pacific Rim. As the chapters in this volume acknowledge, there are enormous strides that must be made before parity can be achieved or claimed. The pattern of technological advance remains uneven within and across countries. This is clearly reflected in the respective chapters on Indonesia by Dipo Alam (chapter 9) and Thailand by Chatri Sripaipan (chapter 7). Resources—financial and human—are not unlimited; nor are the channels for technological exchange or collaboration entirely open. As both Kodama and Soichi Yamashita (chapter 16) show in their respective chapters, technology transfer is still something difficult to accomplish when viewed from the perspective of a potential Japanese supplier firm. Still, few can deny what has become obvious to most of the authors who contributed to this volume: Something fundamental is happening in the region and the framework that was used in the past, which seemed to place definable limits on the pace and extent of Pacific Rim technological growth, has proven inadequate to capture overall developments and their implications.

The chapter by Simon focuses on the ways in which globalization and regionalization has affected the "value" of Asia's manufacturing and R&D capabilities. As suggested earlier, Simon's chapter provides a context for understanding those larger forces that have led to the appreciation of Asia's production and S&T assets. It is against this backdrop that the chapters analyzing each of the S&T development efforts occurring across the region shed light on the broader consequences hinted at above. The chapter by David O'Connor, for example, presents the development experience of the Asian NIEs. O'Connor reminds us that the successes of the Asian NIEs must be viewed not simply from the perspective of the specific policies formulated for dealing with science and technology affairs. Rather, O'Connor stresses that we must always be cognizant of the larger picture, which includes exchange rates, trade policies, education policies, and

macro-economic policies. The NIEs have been able to transcend a certain technological threshold that has opened up a new range of opportunities in terms of
cooperation and collaboration, though more limited access to technology and
other related factors could constrain future opportunities for rapid advance.[4]

In the final analysis, the future evolution of the various economies in the
region as well as of the entire region itself, particularly in technological terms,
would seem to be caught up in a new kind of strategic triangle—a type of
technological triangle—involving Japan, the United States, and more recently,
China. The role of Japan in the region remains an issue of great debate and
conjecture; as the chapter by Tran Van Tho and Shujiro Urata (chapter 14)
suggests, Japanese firms appear embarked on a new type of strategic thrust in the
Pacific Rim. Viewed from the perspective of traditional economics, with its
focus on exchange rates and comparative costs, the growth of the Japanese
presence in the region is a response to an appreciating yen, rising wages and
costs at home, and intense domestic competition. Viewed from the perspective of
a different set of factors—the need to plug into and harness Asia's growing
reserve of technological assets to sustain or enhance their share of regional and
global markets—the expansion of Japanese capital (private and public) and technology in the Asia-Pacific raises many questions about the forces shaping the
technological trajectory of the region as well as various individual economies.
While there does not appear to be any reason to fear Japanese economic or
technological hegemony in the region, one does have to ask what the overall
impact of a more activist Japan will mean in the Pacific Rim, even if this
activism is largely private-sector driven and is being conducted via open, yet
fierce competition among Japanese firms themselves as they vie for new sources
of competitive advantage against their competitors at home and abroad. As the
chapter by Hamzah Kassim (chapter 8) on Malaysia asks, what will be the
bottom line for that country's economy if foreign firms, especially from Japan,
continue to define the technological agenda and set the tone for the path of
economic development?

In a world of intense global competition, the growing interest among Japanese
companies in the region would seem to be ample reason to spur the United States
to take a closer look at what is happening in the Asia-Pacific. Suttmeier, in his
chapter on the position of the United States in the new technological trajectory of
the Pacific Rim, seems to imply that while United States industry as well as the
country as a whole has strategic economic interests in maintaining strong links to
the region, the fact is that American policy towards Asia is ambiguous and
unfocused. The Clinton Administration's emphasis on cleaning up the problems
within America would seem to preclude an aggressive stance towards Asia; an
aggressive stance might involve a more activist diplomatic thrust plus a more
well-defined agenda of bilateral and multilateral issues that the United States is
willing to tackle through partnerships with the countries of the Pacific Rim.
Clinton's willingness to become involved in the APEC initiatives in Seattle

during a time of intense domestic pressures regarding health care and crime seemed to provide a ray of hope that Asia would indeed assume a place high on the agenda of the administration. The substance, however, has proven hard to find in the aftermath of a tremendous amount of rhetoric. Accordingly, it is unlikely that the U.S. government will be the architect of a new U.S. policy toward Asia.

The role of the American business community, therefore, would seem to provide the next logical alternative—perhaps even a better alternative given the fact that Pacific Rim regionalism is being driven largely by private actors responding to growing opportunities in the expanding Asian marketplace. Suttmeier is less precise here about what the expectation ought to be, though it is clear from reading the pages of such publications as *Electronic Business Asia* and the *Asian Wall Street Journal* that American companies, including Apple, Hewlett Packard, and Motorola have committed themselves to take advantage of the rapid development in the quality of technological and human resources. One merely has to visit the production facilities of some of the above-mentioned firms in places such as Singapore and Hong Kong to recognize that the onset of a new technological trajectory in Asia has not gone unnoticed by many important U.S. companies.

Companies as well as governments based in the economies of the Pacific Rim clearly like doing business with the Americans. In fact, as the chapter by Yamashita indicates, they seem to prefer the U.S. mode of technology transfer over the Japanese mode. Nonetheless, despite the demand for a larger U.S. economic and business presence in the region, in many instances, the U.S. presence is skewed towards a few selected industries or is conspicuous by its near absence. Fortunately, given the open-ended questions that remain about the United States and Japan, the economies of the region have not had to depend merely on the United States and Japan for capital and technology. The Asian NIEs, for example, have become important foreign investors in countries such as Malaysia, China and most recently Vietnam. Add to this the evolving interest of European firms in Asia and it becomes readily apparent that the competition for access to the region's technological assets and associated partnerships, consumer and industrial markets, and even for political favor will only intensify in the years ahead.

As for China, this is indeed the big question mark. Yet, one thing is clear; that is, the complexion of economic and technological life in the Asia-Pacific region has been profoundly altered by the growth and opening up of China's economy. Both the chapters by Jingping Ding (chapter 11) and Zhou, respectively, indicate that China is not sitting by idly as the rest of the players in the region continue to invest in upgrading their human and technological resources. In fact, the Chinese are simultaneously building up their manufacturing capabilities and R&D system at the same time. Programs such as the technical transformation of enterprises on the production side and the "Torch plan" on the R&D side would seem to indicate that China intends not simply to be an active player in regional markets, but also to assume a leading position in the world market through its enhanced technological capacity. If one has any doubts about the shape or character of the technological trajectory of the Pacific Rim, they just need factor into the equation a technologically adept China and the picture of the future begins to reveal itself quite clearly. Add to China's resource base the financial clout and dexterity of Hong Kong in 1997, as discussed by Liang and Denny in chapter 12, and the market knowledge and sensitivity of Taiwan, and the picture achieves even greater clarity. China's potential impact at both the sector level as well as at the regional level in aggregate is something easy to underestimate if we take a freeze frame of the PRC today; looked at from a more dynamic perspective, including the rapid technological advances that have occurred since the reforms were launched in 1978, it is more likely that the full implications of China's emergence will be appreciated.

Of course, the interesting thing about triangular models is that they provide ample fodder for speculation about all sorts of possible collaborative alignments. In this case, where we are focused on the technological trajectory of the Pacific Rim, we need not come to any definitive conclusions about possible permutations to identify from where the sources of Asian technological dynamism are to come. Japanese firms, driven by the imperatives of global competition are building manufacturing and R&D networks in the region that are more open in terms of local content and more forthcoming in terms of technology transfer. This new posture will clearly blunt some of the reticence about cooperation with Japan, especially if U.S. firms remain aloof and the only evidence of U.S. presence are the frequent visits of the Asia desk officer of the Office of the U.S. Trade Representative (USTR). Japanese networks in Asia include those networks being built by firms such as Toshiba and Hitachi in China. Thus, Japanese companies, through the competitive drivers of the market, are pulling China into the mainstream of Asia's evolving manufacturing and R&D infrastructure.

At the same time, China continues to act as a magnet for foreign capital, production knowledge, and management skills. As the key firms in the global automobile industry have already determined, China will become a key player in a vast array of global industries. The adage first put forth by Kenichi Ohmae that "in order to be considered a true global firm, your company had to have a presence in each of the key Triad markets—the US, Europe and Japan," has now had to be modified to include China. As the Chinese leverage their market for access to foreign technology, this will mean that China will likely be drawn into the world marketplace at a faster pace then any other country in history. Moreover, it will do so as it is being fed a steady diet of foreign technology—software and hardware. The question is not whether China will be a force in technological markets, but rather what will be the terms upon which U.S., Japanese and European as well as other Asian companies link up with the PRC.

At the outset of this essay, the question was raised about whether the idea of a "path" or "trajectory" to explain the course and direction of technological development was a useful tool. In its most narrowest, theoretical sense, as Kodama shows, it may not be as the concept tends to raise more questions than it provides answers. Looked at in a broader sense, however, the concept does, in fact, have value. It allows us to draw a visual picture or map that highlights the points of convergence and divergence, of parallelism and competition, of synergy and fragmentation, and of conflict and complementarity as each of the economies in the region marches forth on its own path of technological development. Overlaid on this map, however, is another map that looks at those macro level forces that are affecting the way these paths have been defined and the degree of control each country has in selecting a path for itself—whether on an industrial sector or national basis. The issue of control is an extremely sensitive one as access to those precise technologies needed to embark upon a certain path for new market entry or greater competitiveness could be denied directly and indirectly. The chapter by Seongjae Yu (chapter 4), which suggests that Japanese companies have withheld critical semiconductor equipment from potential Korean competitors—whether true or not—highlights how even the perception of unequal control and unfair constraints can produce dissatisfaction and conflict.

Nonetheless, it is important to remember that while the processes of globalization and regionalization are multilevel and uneven, they do serve as an important starting point for understanding why the idea of a new technological trajectory in Asia is not just an abstract, analytic construct. These forces have opened new market opportunities, new channels of access to technology, and new forms of cross-border collaboration, which when taken together, have revised the way many of the key players in the world economy think about competition and cooperation. This being the case, the economies of the Asia-Pacific region are doing nothing much more complex than responding to the new incentive structures and requirements in the world economic arena and technological marketplace. If this has led them to forgo former inhibitions and to embrace a range of new initiatives by Japan, China, and others, then the way that the region relates to the rest of the world in both technological and economic terms may already have begun to change. Whether this portends a new technological trajectory may not be fully clear right now to some, though after reading the various chapters contained here, the possibility of one should seem more probable if not highly likely.

Notes

1. See the special issue entitled, "Science in Asia," *Science*, Volume 262, October 15, 1993.

2. The terms "Pacific Rim," Asia-Pacific region, and Asia-Pacific economies or nations are used interchangeably throughout this book to refer to the economies that are located on the Western edge of the Pacific Ocean. The United States is often included when terms such as the Pacific Rim are used because of its participation in organizations such as APEC, the PECC, and PBEC.

3. Denis Fred Simon, *The Technology Strategy of Japanese Firms Towards the Pacific Rim* (Cambridge: Cambridge University Press, 1995 forthcoming).

4. Sanjaya Lall, "Policies for Building Technological Capabilities: Lessons from Asian Experience," *Asian Development Review*, Volume 11, Number 2, 1993, pp.72–103.

Part I
Overview

1

Globalization, Regionalization, and the Pacific Rim

Denis Fred Simon

Substantial changes are taking place in the world economy, so much so that one author (Toffler, 1990) has suggested we are embarked on a major powershift—one that promises to alter the existing relationships among nations. We can see the manifestations of this powershift in a number of critical areas. Since the onset of the so-called "electronics and materials revolution," for example, the rapid and sustained pace of technological change throughout the world has had a significant impact on the structure and operation of the international technology market (Wriston, 1993). Traditional patterns of R&D activity have been altered by the global diffusion of technology. In particular, R&D activities are no longer simply concentrated in the United States, Japan, and Western Europe. As a result, the agglomeration patterns for technology development and commercialization that existed for much of the postwar period have been gradually, albeit steadily, transformed as new centers of excellence have begun to appear. As Bruce Merrifield (1991, p. 226) has suggested, "in a hypercompetitive global marketplace 'comparative advantage' no longer results primarily from low-cost labor and natural resources, arable land, or from close access to markets. Rather, comparative advantage now derives from value-added technology that creates new products, processes and services together with flexible automated manufacturing systems" (see also Muroyama and Stever, 1988).

One of the most potent factors underlying the changes in the international technology market has been the rapid emergence of the Pacific Rim economies as new sources of technology competence and capability (Elegant, 1990). Led by Japan and the so-called "four dragons"—Taiwan, South Korea, Hong Kong, and

Singapore—these economies have become important players as far as the current restructuring of the international division of labor is concerned. Through a combination of assertive government science and technology promotion policies and aggressive behavior on the part of private sector firms in the realm of R&D and technology acquisition, the so-called "East Asia edge" now includes a critical technological dimension (Ernst and O'Connor).

The Pacific Rim economies have also become significant sources of increasing demand for high-value consumer products as well as for sophisticated, high-quality components and production inputs for equipment (see "Power of Asia," 1991; see also Pacific Economic Cooperation Council, 1992). As the world enters the 1990s, the locus of trade for North America has shifted from the Atlantic to the Pacific. United States–Pacific trade since 1980, for example, has averaged 9 percent-plus growth while U.S.–Atlantic trade has grown at a 7 percent rate. And, in 1989, U.S. trade with the Pacific Rim stood at US$297 billion, almost 50 percent more than the United States' trade with Europe. As a recent Japanese publication has suggested, by upgrading their production and trade structures, the Asian nations have emerged as a new growth axis, transforming the global economy's orientation away from a mono-axis dominated by the United States, to more of a multiple axis. There is little doubt that any corporation that seriously professes to have a global posture must have a significant presence in the region, a presence that will provide strategic advantages in terms of access to sophisticated technological resources as well as intraregional and interregional market position.

In fact, with their skilled labor force, their strong communications and transport infrastructure, and their dynamic research and manufacturing capabilities, the economies of the Pacific Rim have become the new center of attention in terms of international business and technology strategy among the largest multinational corporations in the world. It is probably not too far afield to suggest that we are now witnessing what might be best called the "globalization of the Pacific Rim," and that this process of globalization is not a temporary phenomenon in terms of the evolving structure of the global economy. Both as a market and as a source of increasingly advanced R&D and production outputs, the economies of the region have assumed a key role in the playing out of the competitive dynamics in high-value-added segments of both traditional and high-technology industries.

At the same time, we are also witnessing the "regionalization of the Pacific Rim" (Palmer, 1991). This process of regionalization is being driven by several forces, all of which have served to foster greater intraregional trade and technology exchange (see Suh and Rao, 1990). The economies of the Pacific Rim are beginning to focus more on the complementarities among themselves than their differences, especially in the technology area. Japanese firms, in particular, are beginning to alter the basic design of their technology development strategy, moving gradually from one largely centered in Japan to one that increasingly incorporates the growing technological assets of the Pacific Rim economies.

These regional imperatives provide an interesting counterinfluence to the forces of globalization.

This chapter provides a discussion of how the forces of globalization and regionalization are influencing the international technology marketplace, with special emphasis on the role of the Pacific Rim economies. It is argued that we have begun to witness a fundamental change in the direction and pattern of innovation as the number of linkages among the Asian economies has increased, especially those involving Japan and the so-called four dragons. A number of recent examples of intraregional technology collaboration are highlighted in industries such as microelectronics, computer software and hardware, and biotechnology. Based on some of the information presented here, it is suggested that given the intensive push to promote S&T development among the countries in the region, there may be more substantive evidence than most scholars have heretofore believed to support the proposition that the locus of technological dynamism in the world may be shifting from the Atlantic to the Pacific.

Characteristics of the International Technology Market

Unlike the situation with respect to the trading of goods and services across national boundaries, some might argue that the parameters of the so-called "international technology market" remain vague and ill defined. At times, it is hard to pinpoint who are the main actors in the market as well as the main principles and operating mechanisms by which the technology market functions. In fact, instead of speaking about one holistic market, it is probably more accurate to speak about the existence of multiple technology markets insofar as there are critical differences among industries such as semiconductors and aerospace. Yet, despite the differences between what occurs in the realm of international trade *and* technology exchange, the fact is that there are a number of features that characterize the evolving structure of the global technology market.

First, the international technology market is characterized by the "transnationalization" of the R&D process (Pearce, 1992). Neither technology exploration nor commercialization is simply within the purview of one nation; various aspects of the processes, along with various elements of the manufacturing process, are taking place in multiple countries and are being coordinated as if the world were one big "technological" chessboard. This process of transnationalization is somewhat different from the process of internationalization that has been occurring since the 1950s. As more and more R&D activities have become diffused, so have the patterns of R&D concentration, thus altering the agglomeration patterns that existed in the 1960s and 1970s (Casson, 1990).

Second, the international technology market is characterized by the movement of technologies overseas at an earlier point of their life cycle, thus invalidating many aspects of the traditional product life cycle. Unlike the situation in the past when most technologies moved overseas only after they had reached their mature stage, today we are witnessing a greater willingness on the part of both large and small firms to share or license their know-how at a significantly earlier time (Guile, 1987). Multiple reasons account for this change in practice, including the steadily increasing costs and risks of undertaking large, expensive R&D projects on a unilateral basis. This has led to the end of the so-called "individual enterprise" and the formation of a multiplicity of networklike organizations whereby R&D, manufacturing, and even distribution activities are carried out on the basis of varied relationships—some of which are equity-based and others that occur on a nonequity, contractual basis.

Moreover, as the intensity of technology competition has increased, the process of commercialization has been shortened as firms striving for market leadership push to bring their research results from the laboratory to the market in a shorter period of time. With the compression of the product life cycle and the more rapid movement of new technologies overseas, the effective global management of technology assets has taken on strategic importance. Some have suggested that we have now entered a stage in the world economy characterized not only by an emphasis on technology-based competition, but also, and perhaps more importantly, by "time-based" competition.

Third, within the international technology market there has been a proliferation of technology transfer mechanisms as well as a general trend toward greater openness in terms of transborder technology flows. Aside from the traditional vehicles by which technology was transferred in the past, including licensing and foreign investment, a host of similarly important mechanisms has emerged in the form of government-to-government S&T exchanges, student and scholar exchanges, international conferences, university–industry liaison programs, international consulting, and technical service agreements. More technology and know-how is flowing on the international level than ever before in history. This is the case despite the fact that there continue to be complaints, especially among Third World nations, about the unwillingness of multinational corporations to make their latest technology available (Dunning, 1988).

Of course, this increasing movement of people and know-how across national boundaries should not lead us to ignore another important development, namely, that we are also witnessing a net increase in "technonationalism" as well. In fact, it has become quite evident that as the intensity of global competition has increased, so too has there been a tightening up in selected, but critical, areas of technology transfer. To begin with, greater attention has been paid to the protection of intellectual property rights among companies from the industrialized world, especially in the software field. In a similar fashion, firms from South Korea report difficulties in acquiring critical semiconductor manufacturing and testing equipment from Japan as part of an alleged effort by Japanese firms to delay Korean progress in the microelectronics field. Finally, apprehension about technosecurity issues in the post–Cold War era have led to renewed thinking in the United States and elsewhere about foreign acquisition of firms associated with the development of critical dual-use technologies.

And fourth, in spite of the emergence of the Asian NIEs, as well as countries such as Brazil and India, as increasingly important players in the international technology market, the fact is that this market is becoming more and more bifurcated (see UNCTAD, 1990). In other words, the gap between the technological haves and have-nots is growing wider, leading to the marginalization of many Third World nations with respect to the mainstream of global economic and technology affairs. Within the context of the current world economic environment, it seems clear that to get "new" technology, a country already has to possess considerable technological assets itself. Accordingly, it appears that two different games are being played simultaneously—the paramount game of global competition primarily involving firms from the major industrialized and newly industrialized nations *and* the subordinate game of development—primarily involving international organizations and a select number of large corporations. While the actors involved in the former game are becoming increasingly interdependent and their technology activities more and more integrated, the actors involved in the latter game remain, for the most part, in a state of long-term technological inequality and dependence vis-à-vis the major sources of innovation in the world.

While these trends within the international technology market do not make one particularly sanguine in terms of the potential for growth and development in much of the Third World, they do highlight the fact that, for those with the appropriate technological assets and capabilities, new opportunities are emerging —opportunities that serve as a catalyst to stimulate further movement along the axis of indigenous technological progress (Lee and Proctor, 1991). The Pacific Rim economies have been engaged in an effort to respond to these emerging opportunities by investing, respectively, in the buildup of a more effective and responsive domestic S&T infrastructure. What remains to be answered, however, is the question of which forces—globalization, regionalization, or technonationalism —will predominate in determining when, where, and how their newly acquired technological resources will be harnessed.

Globalization of the Pacific Rim

The increasing globalization of the Pacific Rim economies is the product of several forces. First, it is the result of what Ted Levitt (1983), former editor of the *Harvard Business Review*, and Kenichi Ohmae (1990), head of the McKinsey Japan, have called the "globalization of markets." According to this perspective, we are witnessing a homogenization of demand among consumers in the United States, Europe, and Asia. In general, tastes and product requirements are converging, as is evidenced by the rapid proliferation of fast-food chains such as McDonalds and Kentucky Fried Chicken throughout the Asian region as well as in other parts of the world. Linked to the homogenization of demand is the growing saturation of home markets, along with an intensification of competition for new markets. Market saturation is hardly a permanent phenomenon in this era of rapid technological change. Nonetheless, as it becomes more and more difficult to acquire and sustain market shares in everything from consumer to industrial products, the search for new and possibly virgin markets has encouraged Asian firms as well as Western multinational corporations, in particular, to develop a more "global" perspective regarding their business development activities.

Second, changes in the nature of the manufacturing process as well as in the delivery of services have made both more susceptible to scale economies, while at the same time allowing for "mass customization" (Hayes et al., 1988; see also Pine, 1993). In both instances, firms are seeking, and are now able, to centralize certain facets of their businesses as a way to promote greater efficiency. They are also engaged in the establishment of global networks to assist with the sourcing of raw materials and components (UNCTC, 1992). The Ford Escort is made in the United Kingdom by an American firm with parts from eleven different countries. Apple computers and Boeing airplanes are also global products in the sense that no one nation or firm is responsible for designing, manufacturing, and marketing these products in their entirety. The information technology revolution has helped to provide the infrastructure to meet the communication and coordination requirements associated with the need to move large quantities of people and resources around the world to different spots simultaneously. The same could be said for rationalization of distribution channels as efforts are underway to consolidate these activities. Trans-shipment points such as Singapore and Taiwan take on added value in seeking to support such a global distribution network.

Third, globalization is being driven by technological change and the rising costs and risks of undertaking large-scale research and development projects. The R&D processes themselves have become globalized as the potential success of the processes of technological discovery and commercialization are becoming more and more dependent on the pooling of specialized resources as well as the sharing of the costs. The search for what David Teece (1987) called "complementary technological assets" in terms of laboratories, equipment, and personnel defines the nature of innovation as we see it developing today. These changes have proven critical for Japan in its relations not only with the United States and Western Europe, but also with Taiwan, Korea, Singapore, China, and even Hong Kong—where sustained efforts are underway to strengthen domestic R&D capabilities and create new technological hothouses to participate in the global technological revolution (see Simon, 1990).

A fourth force for globalization has been the general move toward liberalization and privatization across the globe. Many of the formal and informal trade barriers that remained in place in spite of the initial successes of the GATT regime have now been broken down as a combination of economic imperatives and political pressures have dictated greater openness among most countries. Today, more goods, services, people, and technology flow across national boundaries than ever before. Similarly, the move toward privatization, especially with respect to such industries as telecommunications, has helped to bring about much more trade and investment linked to these high-value industries to the benefit of consumers in all countries.

All of these factors that have fostered the globalization of markets and industries continue to make themselves felt in various parts of the world. The impact of globalization on the Pacific Rim appears to be highly significant; for the nations of the Pacific Rim, globalization has been a catalyst that has fostered a number of critical changes. These changes are manifested in the following developments, many of which are of fairly recent vintage.

Responses to Globalization in the Pacific Rim

First, the impact of globalization can be seen in the expanded global spread of companies from the region. A look at the *Global 500* reveals that Japanese companies comprise 111 of the biggest firms; they are joined on this list by 11 South Korean and 10 Australian companies as well as by one company each from Taiwan and Malaysia (*Fortune*, July 22, 1992; see also "Top 500," 1991). Japanese banks are playing a key integrating role in establishing a broad-based financial network throughout the world. Just as significant, however, is the expansion of direct investment by firms from the region. Much publicity has been given to the sharp increases in Japanese investments in the United States over the last few years. Interestingly, Japanese firms have been followed by firms such as Tatung and Formosa Plastics from Taiwan *and* Samsung and Goldstar from South Korea—all of whom are seeking to gain closer proximity to their customers as well as to get behind potential trade barriers. The impetus behind the rapidly expanding overseas investments of the Asian NIEs is linked not simply to trade frictions but more fundamentally to the restructuring going on within their respective economies. This restructuring is, for the most part, characterized by an emphasis on higher value-added manufacturing[1]. Not far behind will be multinationals from Malaysia selling automobiles and from China selling computers and precision instrumentation.

Ironically, the model of the global firm that most Japanese and other Asian multinationals want to emulate is America's IBM Corporation. IBM, which runs one of the most successful foreign ventures in Japan, operates as if the world were its playing field, with manufacturing or research facilities in the United States, Switzerland, Japan, and elsewhere. Japanese firms are seeking to evolve in this same direction by reducing some of their traditionally inward-looking attitudes. According to the *Japanese Economic Journal* (October 5, 1991, p. 12), Matsushita has already made some headway, taking some of its eighty-eight overseas factories and rearranging them to supply four major consumer centers in North America, Europe, Japan, and the rest of Asia. Similar changes are underway in companies such as Hitachi, NEC, and Fujitsu.

A further testament to the global spread of firms from the region, however, is probably best revealed by looking at the rapid pace at which Japan, Korea, and Taiwan firms have attempted to expand into Eastern Europe and the countries of the former USSR (see *International Herald Tribune*, May 11, 1992, p. iv). Recognizing the tremendous opportunities that perhaps lie ahead as these countries divest themselves of the vestiges of socialism, it is becoming increasingly clear that the next battleground for the playing out of competition among firms from Asia will be the reformed socialist world. South Korean firms ranging from Jindo (furs and pelts) to Hyundai construction have sought out key market positions. Taiwan companies such as Acer and Mitac see tremendous opportunities in the computer business; Eastern Europe and the countries of the former USSR are hungry for low-priced, reliable computers to bring them into the modern world of informatics. The potential in these markets is especially significant given the pressures being placed on many of these Asian countries to diversify their trade and redirect their exports away from the United States and European Economic Community (EC). Firms from Asia would appear to have a distinct advantage in Eastern Europe and the former USSR, especially in the area of consumer electronics, since there are few suppliers in the United States (if any) and Western Europe to service these markets.

Along with hoping to gain access to the potential markets in this part of the world, Asian firms are also interested in access to technology and scientific personnel. Korea, Taiwan, and Japan, for example, are all anxious to recruit Russian scientists and engineers, many of whom possess world-class knowledge in their specific fields. Similarly, Asian firms also want to tap into Russia's R&D establishment. Samsung, for example, has imported advanced plastics materials technology from V.A. Kargin Polymer Research Institute in Novgorod. Samsung's Advanced Institute of Technology developed a digital video disc recorder using Russian laser technology. All of these cases point to the value of having a global reach and presence (see *Korea Times*, March 16, 1993, p. 8).

The second manifestation of globalization in the Pacific Rim is the growing technological interdependence of the various actors. For years, the United States has been considered the global technological leader; few nations had the physical, financial, or personnel resources to compete with the U.S. scientific and engineering community. Even today, overall U.S. spending on R&D almost tops that of Western Europe and Japan combined. Still, the fact remains that we are witnessing more of a two-way flow of technology.[2] Whereas a few years ago, corporate America was complaining about alleged Japanese efforts to "buy" their way into America's source of basic R&D by providing various forms of financial support for U.S. colleges and universities (*Business Week*, September 24, 1984), today we find that a new crop of American scientists—some with Japanese-language skills—are anxiously seeking entry points into the Japanese R&D

establishment. While the numbers are still comparatively small—1,500 compared with over 8,500 Japanese working in the U.S. labs—there is clearly a trend afoot. Since 1984, for example, Hitachi Ltd. has hosted over seventy foreign researchers for extended stays at its Central Research Laboratory. Japanese firms are also in the process of exchanging personnel with their U.S. and European counterparts. A good example involves the case of Ford and Mazda. The two firms will engage in an exchange of marketing and engineering design personnel. Through this exchange, Ford will gain some of Mazda's automobile development expertise, while Mazda will gain knowledge regarding the marketing of cars in the United States.

Currently, Japan has about 500,000 engineers, most of whom are employed in industry—which supplies about 80 percent of Japanese funding for R&D. As of 1989, Japan overtook Germany as the country with the world's highest ratio of expenditure on R&D to GNP, thus giving added impetus to the expansion of this two-way flow (*Asahi Shimbun*, December 16, 1990, p. 3). Upjohn Pharmaceuticals, which opened a US$113 million R&D facility because, as one Upjohn official suggested, "the level of Japanese science in pharmaceuticals has reached a point where it can't be overlooked," has been joined by Du Pont, Eastman Kodak, and several other leading multinational firms. In the 1980s, American companies licensed or otherwise bought more technology from Japan than any other country except the United Kingdom; in 1990 the United States spent US$491 million to license technology from the Japanese, up from US$89 million in 1982 (see Table 1.1). By setting up R&D facilities in Japan, American firms hope to learn of Japanese technological advances earlier than they might have if they were situated just in the United States (*Fortune*, May 25, 1991, p. 85).

Technological interdependence, however, also extends to other countries in the region, many of which are becoming more important as partners in the global technological race. In the computer and electronics industries, for example, Taiwan's technological assets are going to assume an increased importance in the playing out of global competition in the years ahead; Taiwan has already become the sixth-largest producer and exporter of information technology products in the world (*Far Eastern Economic Review*, January 14, 1988, pp. 467; see also August 31, 1989). This has already occurred to some extent with the agreements between Acer and Texas Instruments and Vitelic and Hualon to manufacture sophisticated computer memory chips. In the case of the former agreement, this is part of a larger effort underway in Taiwan to enter the global semiconductor competition; by 1995, Taiwan hopes to supply approximately 4–5 percent of the world's demands for chips—which would put it in the position of leapfrogging every European producer and making the island the fourth-largest producer behind Japan, the United States, and South Korea (*Far Eastern Economic Review*, October 10, 1991, p. 59; see also December 13, 1990, pp. 623). In the case of the latter, Vitelic will provide its advanced processing technology—some of

Table 1.1

American R&D in Japan

Company	Location	Technology sector
IBM	Tokyo/Yokohama	Computers
Hewlett-Packard	Tokyo	Photonics, ICs
Dow Corning	Yokohama	New materials
Bristol-Myers Squibb	Yokohama	Pharmaceuticals
Du Pont	Yokohama	New materials
Digital Equipment	Yokohama	Computers
Eastman Kodak	Yokohama	Electronics
Proctor & Gamble	Osaka	Soaps, detergents
Pfizer	Nagoya	Pharmaceuticals
Monsanto	Tsukuba	Agricultural chemicals
Intel	Tsukuba	Semiconductors
Upjohn	Tsukuba	Pharmaceuticals
Texas Instruments	Tsukuba	Semiconductors
Medtronic	Chitose	Medical devices
American Cyanamid	Tahara	Agricultural chemicals
W.R. Grace	Atsugi	New materials
Dow Chemicals	Gotemba	Chemicals
Corning	Kakegawa	New materials
Applied Materials	Narita	Semiconductor manufacture

Source: Adapted from *Fortune*, May 25, 1991, p. 85.

which comes from Japan's OKI Corporation—in exchange for Hualon's capacity. The ability to entertain such a grandiose development scheme is based on the fact that the number of local firms engaged in the critical process of wafer fabrication and etching will increase from two (prior to 1988) to six or more during the 1990s. Of course, the task will not be an easy one, especially since it is one thing to survive and prosper in the world of small-batch customized chips (which is Taiwan's present position) and to survive and prosper in the world of mass production of low-cost, standardized chips (which is the segment where the United States has felt the brunt of Japan's competitive challenge).

In addition, Taiwan's Industrial Technology Research Institute, with the support of the government, has been the driving force behind the creation and successful operation of a $US206 million project to establish a VLSI (very large-scale integrated circuit) company (Taiwan Semiconductor Manufacturing corporation [TSMC]) that manufactures both domestic and foreign-designed "application-specific" ICs as well as some of the more general types of chips (*Free China Journal*, February 3, 1986; see also February 9, 1987). ITRI is an nonprofit corporation established in 1973 to promote generic technology development that it believes Taiwan industry requires. Approximately 45 percent of its revenues come from contract research, which reflects the fact that unlike the giant, vertically integrated firms in Korea, most Taiwan companies cannot afford to spend large sums on R&D. In general, the links between ITRI and Taiwan industry are very close, the most important example being when after ITRI successfully absorbed advanced integrated circuit technology from RCA of the United States and then licensed it at a below-market rate to the new startup (UMC).

The TSMC project represents the largest investment ever made in the domestic electronics industry. The major foreign partner is Philips of Holland, which owns 27 percent of the equity. TSMCs main activities are focused on IC manufacturing. Its success can be attested to by the fact that its directors are already considering a huge expansion project to establish up to three full manufacturing lines. This project is complemented by the establishment of a national laboratory at National Chiao Tung University dedicated to the development of submicron integrated circuit technology. The government's aim is to ensure that this project becomes a vehicle for private commercialization of R&D.

The government on Taiwan is the chief force behind the move to enhance domestic technological capabilities, although R&D spending as a percentage of GNP reached only 1.65 percent in 1990 (*Free China Journal*, September 17, 1991, pp. 3, 7). Taiwan's overall goal is to become a global production base for advanced components—which explains the emphasis on automation engineering, automobiles, and industrial machinery. The core of Taiwan's high-technology program is the government-orchestrated Hsinchu Science and Industry Park, which was founded in 1980 (*Tien Hsia*, 1990). The park constitutes Taiwan's engine for growth in the twenty-first century in much the same that the island's export-processing zones fueled economic growth from the mid-1960s to the early 1980s. At present, there are 134 companies in operation in the park, employing 20,000 persons, 60 percent of whom have at least a junior college education. There are over 4,000 engineers in the park, 60 percent of whom are graduates of nearby universities. One of the unique features of the park is the close cooperation among the private sector, research institutions, and the Taiwan government. R&D spending (as a percentage of sales) by firms located in the park exceeds that of most local firms by a ratio of 5 to 1.[3] Many of the firms in the park have been startups with investments from engineers and scientists, some of whom were employed by organizations such as ITRI and others who have returned from the United States as a part of the "reverse brain drain." In addition, many of the ideas for new products, among other things, come from small Taiwan-invested companies located in Silicon Valley in the United States; these firms serve as an important vehicle for "technology intelligence."

The park also has become an attraction for the transborder movement of overseas Chinese engineers, many of whom left Taiwan in the 1950s and 1960s for education and employment in the United States and elsewhere. Approximately one-half of the firms in the Hsinchu Park are operated by overseas Chinese; over 600 returnees now hold positions in enterprises and institutes based in the Hsinchu Park. This type of "brain drain" is a critical aspect of Taiwan's prevailing global linkages.

In South Korea, similar things are happening that also reinforce the techno-logical interdependence of the Pacific Rim with the rest of the world (see "East Asia's Power Crescent," 1991). Korea has put forth a multifaceted program for technological upgrading, the bulk of which is coordinated through three agencies —the Ministry of Science and Technology, the Ministry of Industry and Trade, and the Economic Planning Board. R&D spending in Korea as a percentage of GNP reached the 1.91 percent mark in 1990; Korean S&T officials hope to reach the 3 percent mark sometime in the early twenty-first century. Indicative of the importance attached to technology advance by the government was the plan announced in early 1991 to spend about US$2.1 billion in grants and loans over five years to help industries develop new manufacturing technologies. Along with increased government support, the number of private research cen-ters operated by Korean firms also has been steadily increasing, having reached over 1,000 by early 1991. These R&D centers employ over 30,000 persons. Overall, Korea has 16.4 scientists and engineers per 10,000 population. The total R&D spending by the private sector in Korea was approximately 1.98 percent of sales, which, while lower than that of Japan, reflects a substantial increase from the situation in 1980—when there were only 54 such R&D centers in the country.[4]

Perhaps there is no industry that better exemplifies South Korea's determina-tion to be a major player in the high-technology field than microelectronics in general and semiconductors in particular (*Business Korea*, 1991; see also Mody, 1991). Korea's drive into semiconductors was pioneered in the 1970s by Goldstar's two key subsidiaries: Goldstar Company and Goldstar Semiconduc-tor, a joint venture with AT&T that also manufactures electronic switching sys-tems. As of 1992, South Korea ranks third in the world in the production of semiconductors, although it only accounts for about 10 percent of total world production (which will climb to 13 percent by 2000). Firms such as Samsung Electronics, which is now able to produce 1 MB and 4 MB DRAMs—the former at a rate of 5–7 million per month—have joined the ranks of leading global players such as Toshiba—whose monthly production is estimated to be about 9 million DRAMs. In 1994, Korea overtook Toshiba in terms of its share of the global DRAM market, accounting for a 13,6 percent share versus 12.8 percent for Toshiba (see *Korea Economic Weekly*, 1993, p. 1; see also Electronics Indus-try Association of Korea, 1992). The growing intensity of the Korean commit-ment to microelectronics can be seen in the evolution of the industry from the 1960s when the focus was mainly on manufacturing, assembly, and packaging of discrete devices by multinationals through the 1970s when integrated circuit manufacturing and packaging were the predominant activities and into the 1980s when the country entered into VLSI design and production. Total production in electronics exceeded US$25 billion in 1992, with US$20.8 billion in exports.

Perhaps the best evidence attesting to Korean progress in microelectronics can be seen in two examples. The first involves the decision of Hitachi to enter into a joint venture with Goldstar Electronics in June 1989 for the production of 1 MB DRAM chips.[5] The agreement marked the first major involvement of a Japanese firm in Korea's high-technology drive. Goldstar officials therefore were naturally pleased when Hitachi decided to provide the firm with assistance for the manufacture of 4 MB and 16 MB DRAM chips. This agreement also complements another important joint venture, namely, the cooperative arrangement between Hewlett Packard and Samsung for the manufacture of an advanced computer workstation that HP hopes will give it a competitive advantage in the U.S. domestic market as well as abroad. The second example is linked to the announcement by Samsung that is has been able to master the manufacture of a 16 MB memory chip (*Electronic Business*, 1991, p. 68). As one Samsung engineer suggested , it was after this announcement that Japanese and American semiconductor firms began to take Korean efforts seriously. Samsung Electronics, which was founded in 1974, spends about 3 percent of its US$1.3 billion semiconductor revenue on R&D. Korean firms are aiming at the manufacture of more sophisticated, high-profit-margin semiconductors, such as the reduced-instruction set computing microprocessors (RISC) that are used in computer workstations.

Regionalization and Technonationalism in the Pacific Rim

The globalization of the Pacific Rim takes on added significance when looked at in conjunction with recent developments in the European Economic Community and the U.S.–Canada trade pact. Some observers of the world scene have suggested that we are witnessing a sort of dialectical process, with the emergence of two parallel, but potentially opposing, forces—regionalization and globalization. There are those who believe that regionalization is the predominant force in international affairs today, reflecting a combination of both political and economic/technological factors. Under this scenario, the world may be moving toward the emergence of three major trading blocs: North America, Europe, and Asia. The formalization of the EC 1992 initiative may, in the eyes of some, be seen as a sort of supranationalistic response to the rising economic and technological power of Asia, especially of Japan. When combined with Europe's traditional concerns regarding American economic and technological hegemony, however, regionalization may not simply be a feature of globalization, but in reality, in one of its forms, it may be an anathema to it. According to this interpretation, the Europeans, unwilling to allow the imperatives of global efficiency to determine the viability of industries such as microelectronics and computers within their own regional boundaries, have banded together, among other reasons, to create a competitive edge in the face of the growing technological competence of both the United States and Asia.

One good example involves the percentage of local content required by the EC versus the United States from Japanese color TV and integrated circuit producers manufacturing in both locations. For the 3.2 million color TV sets built in Europe in 1988 by Japanese companies, 71.9 percent of the electronics content came from European suppliers. Within the integrated circuit industry, the percentage of European local content was 69.8 percent. This can be sharply contrasted with the United States, where out of 18 million color TVs built in the United States by five Japanese-owned companies, an average of only 29.8 percent of the electronics content came from European suppliers. The percentage for integrated circuits produced in the United States was smaller than 1 percent.[6]

The trend toward regionalization is being fed and abetted by a number of forces. Heretofore, the most important force behind regionalization may be the shift away from comparative advantage and a new emphasis on competitive advantage. Michael Porter, a professor at the Harvard Business School and author of *The Competitive Advantage of Nations* (1990), suggests that despite the growing attention to globalization at the level of the corporation, industrial policy and technology targeting are still forces that are driving the behavior of the nation-state. In this sense, regionalization may even be seen as a form of "supranationalism" rather than as a subset of globalization. Unlike Ohmae and others, who contend that we are on the verge of becoming a borderless world, citing the experience of countries such as South Korea and Singapore, Porter stresses that the nation-state is not dead and that creating country-based competitive advantage is the paramount game being played on the global chessboard.

From this perspective, regionalization is not simply an impediment to globalization, it is also a form of what Robert Reich (1988, p. 27) of Harvard's Kennedy School has called "technonationalism." The U.S. case provides the best example of technonationalism in its most traditional, parochial form. U.S. efforts to sustain American technological advantage through the provisions of the 1988 Omnibus Bill that apply to intellectual property protection and the prevention of corporate acquisitions by foreign firms for alleged national security reasons reflect anything but a global perspective regarding technology. When the U.S. government made all sorts of noises about Fujitsu's intended acquisition of Fairchild Industries, forcing Fujitsu's withdrawal from the deal, even though it only used the "threat" of acting as a deterrent, it signaled to the world that the United States was not about to accept the buyout of its electronics industry by foreign concerns. In a similar vein, various companies from South Korea report that they are having an increasingly difficult time finding potential technology transfer partners as Japanese, U.S., and European firms fear the so-called "boomerang effect."[7] Even China, which has been given steadily expanding access to advanced Western technologies through a relaxation of export controls and COCOM controls, found itself in the aftermath of the Tiananmen incident being forced by the U.S. government to sell its newly acquired shares in a medium-size aeronautics components firm on the west coast of the United States because of pressure by the U.S. government. And, more recently, the U.S. government refused, temporarily, to approve the export of U.S. satellite components to China as a protest against Beijing's weapons sales to the Middle East (*Financial Times*,

February 6, 1990, p. 6; see also *Los Angeles Times*, February 9, 1992, p. 5).

As suggested, the U.S. experience is perhaps indicative of the "protectionist" side of technonationalism; this dimension of technonationalism is most clearly manifested in the continued belief that one nation can still achieve and maintain a significant level of "national technological self-reliance." It also is manifested in continuing discussions about the role of "economic intelligence" in the post–Cold War era, especially in the United States, where the responsibilities of organizations such as the CIA appear to be shifting away from traditional national security concerns and into such areas as "competitive analysis." More recently, this concern about self-reliance has been "regionalized" in the case of the EC in the form of such programs as Eureka, Jessi, and the like. These technology-oriented projects reflect the concerns of individual European nations about falling behind in the global technological race (see Steinberg, 1990). As such, they also reflect the realization that no one nation in Europe alone can successfully take on the challenge posed by Japan and/or the United States.

Still, it must be recognized that the United States and the EC do not stand alone in wanting to sustain some form of "national" and "transnational" technology progress over time. The ambitious programs that are being implemented in Singapore, Taiwan, South Korea, and China—not to mention Japan—all highlight the fact that indigenous technological advance is viewed as the only way to stay active in the game of global competition. In this respect, they lack the defensive "protectionist" character of the U.S. response, though it is still too early to know whether it will be through regional or global channels that these economies will make their technological influence felt in the future. South Korea and Taiwan, in particular, have both orchestrated extremely focused programs to encourage new high-technology industries designed to draw their economies further into the high-end sphere of global competition (*Taiwan Industrial Panorama*, 1991, pp. 12). Both economies, for example, have begun highly ambitious programs in the field of aerospace; aside from the obvious national security dimensions of these programs, they are primarily designed to help local companies qualify as key component suppliers to the leading defense and civilian aerospace companies around the world. It was this desire to make a great leap into the global aerospace industry that prompted the idea of a strategic alliance between Taiwan Aerospace Corporation and McDonnell Douglas in 1991–1992—an idea that has since been aborted. The Taiwan program is seeking to build on the R&D and advanced manufacturing capabilities of the Chungshan Institute of Science and Technology—the key government research unit in the defense sector—and the government-sponsored ITRI in the civilian sector. The Korean program, which is being led by Samsung Aerospace and Daewoo Heavy Industries, reflects much more of a private-sector initiative fueled with significant government support. While differences in industrial structure and the nature of government-business relations have led these respective programs to develop along somewhat dissimilar lines, they still share one common feature—they are viewed as strategic national imperatives, and as such their success is viewed as essential to the future prosperity of these economies.

The Future Global Orientation of the Asia Pacific Region

Where does East Asia stand in the midst of these seemingly countervailing forces, particularly with respect to the prevailing structure of the international technology market *and* the pattern of innovation in the region (see United Nations Economic and Social Commission, 1990). How will East Asia's advancing technological capabilities be deployed globally and regionally? It has become quite clear that while there are those who continue to view the rise of the Pacific Rim and the emergence of the Pacific Century with a great deal of trepidation, the majority of the international business community and government policy makers see the growth and prosperity of the region as a tremendous opportunity (U.S. Congress, 1991). Plugging into Asia's technological assets, in particular, would seem to represent a tremendous opportunity for companies both inside and outside the region. Many of these synergies have already begun to occur, leading to the appearance of a host of new "strategic alliances" that differ from traditional joint ventures in that they are characterized by the two-way or "bilateral" flow of technology rather than the unilateral flows of the past (Mytelka, 1991). In many cases, former competitors are entering into cooperation agreements as each seeks a "win–win" outcome rather than pursuing a zero-sum game as in the past. These new relationships tend to be less hierarchical and more complementary than previous joint ventures in terms of ownership and management, though in practice, resolution of such issues is not always so clear. Some good examples would include the recent Motorola–Toshiba agreement, the FSX project involving General Dynamics and Mitsubishi Industries, National Semiconductor and Singapore Semiconductor to design and produce VLSI CMOS application-specific integrated circuits, Thompson CSF and Daewoo for development of ceramics, and IBM's agreement with NDC of Taiwan for computer hardware and software. Even in the airline industry, new linkups such as that between Singapore Airlines and Swissair promise to alter the nature of international business as we know it today.

Obviously, as of the mid-1990s, Japanese firms constitute the leading edge as far as the globalization of East Asian technology is concerned ("Asian Ambitions," 1992; see also *Forbes*, November 23, 1992, p. 108). According to the *Nihon Keizai Shimbun* (May 21, 1991, p. 27), since the mid-1980s, along with the internationalization of Japanese investment and manufacturing activities, the establishment of overseas bases for R&D has also rapidly increased. In general, Japanese companies have expanded both the number of overseas R&D bases as well as the scale of R&D operations conducted outside Japan. As of 1991, approximately 10 percent of the manufacturing companies listed on the stock exchange (with a capitalization of over ¥1 billion) have established some form of R&D facilities abroad, including the United States and Western Europe. In many cases, the Japanese firms have transformed what were basically "information collection bases" in the 1970s into "development and design bases" starting in the mid-1980s and "research bases" in the late 1980s. In the case of the former, these are closely tied to Japanese factories to assist with market responsiveness; in the case of the latter, efforts are underway to create independent technology centers and basic research operations. Eventually, these multiple activities will be linked together within a broad-based global technology network, thus allowing for both the horizontal and vertical movement of information and technical knowledge within specific Japanese companies across the globe. The key tasks facing Japanese firms will be finding appropriate partners and systematically coordinating R&D and related manufacturing activities.

According to some preliminary research conducted on strategic alliances, it seems that Japanese firms have shifted their technology strategy away from licensing and have begun to focus on acquisition (National Research Council, 1992). Japanese firms have recognized that sharing technological assets may be the only way to gain access to U.S. and European know-how in this world of intense economic competition. While some in the West see Japanese moves in this direction as a kind of "Trojan horse" phenomenon, the reality is that costs and risk make it necessary for Japan's companies to approach these ventures in a more collaborative fashion if they want these opportunities to continue to exist. The semiconductor industry represents the sector where these new technology-based alliances have been the most significant. Whatever their outcome, they show that Japanese firms have not been able to resist the forces of globalization (see Table 1.2).

Within Asia itself, these types of relationships are also beginning to emerge, reflecting a transformation in the regional division of labor. It is here in the realm of technology where the one popular so-called "flying geese" analogy is perhaps becoming less relevant (*Financial Times*, July 15, 1991, p. x). Japanese companies are recruiting software engineers from the PRC to assist the development of Japan's still fledgling software industry. Since the beginning of 1991, no less than ten leading Japanese computer and software makers have set up joint ventures in China with enterprises, universities, and research institutes (*Nihon Keizai Shimbun*, May 14, 1991, p. 13; see also May 22, 1991, p. 11). According to Japan's Information Service Industry Association, these ventures will aid Japanese firms to overcome the increasing shortage of computer engineers in the Japanese labor market, a shortage that could grow to over 970,000 by the turn of the century. A good example is the joint venture between Kawasaki Steel Systems and Beyike Information Processing Corporation in Beijing. Beyike, which is an institute under the Beijing Academy of Science and Technology, developed the software used by China to support the 1990 Asian Games.

The main objective of the cooperative venture is to develop office automation software, computer-aided design and computer-aided manufacturing software, and control systems for the Japanese market. Kawasaki hopes to use the relationship with China to recruit software engineers and establish a base in China.

Table 1.2

U.S.–Japanese Alliances in Semiconductors

U.S. firm	Japanese firm	Focus of alliance
Motorola	Toshiba	Manufacturing jv/Tech exchange involving DRAM tech & microprocessor technology
Texas Instruments	Hitachi	Joint tech development/exchange involving 16 MB DRAMs
AT&T	NEC	Tech development/exchange involving custom chip tech
Advanced Micro Devices	Sony	Joint development/exchange involving process tech for next-generation chips
LSI Logic	Kawasaki Steel	Manufacturing jv involving ASICs
INTEL	NMB Semiconductor	Licensed production focused on flash memory chips
National Semiconductor	Toshiba	Design, manufacture & marketing of flash memory chips

Source: Adapted from *Business Week*, June 17, 1991, p. 97.

Chinese officials fully support the venture because of the potential for training, but also because of the general emphasis on manufacturing-related technologies. The joint venture is capitalized at ¥100 million, with Kawasaki holding 5 percent of the equity. Other examples include a joint venture for software development between Alpine Electronics, a car audio maker, and the Northeast China Engineering Institute in Sheyang, a joint venture for software development between Japan's Sodick Company, a major Japanese maker of numerically controlled electrodischargers, and the Shanghai Jiaotong University, and a factory automation system engineering company with participation from Mitsui Engineering and Shipbuilding Company Limited and Omron Corporation in Dalian.

In a somewhat similar vein, Taiwan companies are engaging in a sometimes low-profile, but nonetheless substantial, process of technology transfer vis-à-vis the China mainland as it moves some of its lower-end manufacturing operations to such places as Xiamen and Shenzhen. Hong Kong companies are using Chinese design engineers as a means to revitalize such industries as textiles. In fact, the application of new CAD/CAM technologies to such traditional Hong Kong industries has been facilitated by the use of PRC engineers who can work together with the Hong Kong counterparts in an effective and efficient fashion. Such collaboration has spread to other sectors as well. In early 1990, for example, the Shangai branch of the Chinese Academy of Sciences and the Hong Kong Institute of Biotechnology established a joint development center.[8] The main function of this center is to coordinate biological R&D between HK and Shanghai, and most important, to use Hong Kong's global links to help Shanghai's biotechnological products enter world markets. A similar agreement was signed in June 1990 involving the Yunnan Provincial Commission of Science and Technology; this agreement is also aimed at the commercialization of biotechnology for international markets. The potential for technological synergies within so-called "Greater China" (the PRC, Hong Kong, and Taiwan) has grown appreciably as economic and investment links among the three "Chinese-based economies" have expanded.

As suggested earlier, Japan, which for a long time was ostracized for its limited contributions in the form of technology transfer, has now changed and has clearly adopted a more forthcoming set of policies to promote technology transfer. Canon, for example, has begun to shift production of the majority of its single-lens reflex cameras overseas (*Japan Economic Journal*, January 26, 1991, p. 16; see also *Tokyo Business Today*, January 1992, p. 245). This includes the establishment of a high-end production facility in Taiwan along with facilities for manufacture of less sophisticated cameras in southern China. Between 1988 and 1990, Canon set up five plants in the Asian region, installing the same types of machine tools they used at home—reflecting the belief within Canon that these countries can handle the tasks involved in manufacturing sophisticated products for Japan and the world economy. In a similar fashion, Sony announced plans in May 1991 to manufacture precision parts for its video cameras in Singapore. This marks the first time that Sony has made such components outside of Japan.

Relatedly, Japanese companies have begun to regard highly skilled technician personnel from throughout the Pacific Rim. In many respects, this is in response to what some claim is a serious crunch facing graduate schools in Japan. Compared with other countries, Japan has the fewest graduate students on a per capita basis (per 1,000 people, Japan has 0.7 graduate students, compared with 7.1 in the United States, 2.9 in France, and 1.6 in the United Kingdom). Seiko Epson, for example, has begun recruiting technicians from Taiwan for R&D work concerning electronics equipment such as semiconductors. Seiko's recruitment efforts in Japan have faced an uphill struggle because of the location of its main development center—far away from major Japanese cities where local technicians and engineers prefer to live.[9] In the late 1980s, Japan launched a program known as the "Asian brain" that is designed to expand training and financial support for residents of the Asia Pacific region. This program has started to bring capable individuals from around the region to Japan for both temporary and permanent employment in high-skilled jobs in both manufacturing and research (*Forbes*, November 23, 1992, p. 108; see also Romm, 1992).

It is even more significant that Japanese companies have begun to develop R&D facilities overseas in Asia for the first time as part of their shift away from reliance on regional locations for cheap labor, warehouses, or sales outlets. Today there is an increased interest on the establishment of local R&D facilities as a means to respond more quickly to shifts in the regional and global marketplace. With the new emphasis on time, flexibility, and responsiveness as sources of competitiveness, these facilities should yield big payoffs. A good example involves NKK Corporation, a major Japanese steelmaker, which has signed an agreement with Macronix International of Taiwan to develop one, two, and four megabit flash electrically erasable programmable read-only memories (EEPROMs) (*Japan Times*, September 13, 1991, p. 10; see also *Nihon Keizai Shimbun*, April 13, 1991, p. 10). These chips will be used in hard disk drives and memory cards. Another example involves Matsushita, which has set up several R&D facilities in East and Southeast Asia. In Taiwan, the Matsushita Institute of Technology is linked to that company's 5,300-person joint venture. The main aim of the project, according to Matsushita officials, is to perform design work for new product development through the use of local R&D personnel on the island. Taiwan officials have indicated that they have also been approached by Hitachi, Sony, and Sharp about the creation of similar R&D activities (*China Economic News Service*, August 6, 1991; see also *Japan Economic Journal*, July 1, 1989, p. 4). The Matsushita R&D facility in Malaysia is for conducting design and testing R&D for home air conditioners. Matsushita built a state-of-the-art facility that opened in 1992 with the expectation that this R&D center will eventually become the primary site for the company's overall home air conditioning research.

It is difficult to say whether or not the Pacific Rim will emerge as a regional technology bloc in much the same way as the EC 1992 appears to be developing; organizations such as the Asia Pacific Economic Cooperation (APEC) and the Pacific Economic Cooperation Council (PECC) would like to encourage the formulation and implementation of several regional technology projects, although it is unlikely that these will assume the same characteristics of the majority of technology projects in the EC. Much may depend on the posture adopted by Japan, and the response of the countries of the region to any formal or informal Japanese initiatives (*Japan Times*, December 2, 1991, p. 10; see also *Nikkei Weekly*, October 19, 1991, p. 6; "Asia and Japanese Business," 1992). And, while few would disagree that the Pacific Rim has grown in overall importance in terms of technology capabilities as well as trade flows and international business, there is still no firm consensus as to whether the rise of the Pacific Rim portends a fundamental shift in the center of dynamism in the international technology marketplace. For some, the rapid and sustained growth of the Asia Pacific region suggests that we are indeed in the midst of a global shift, one that promises to alter the global "balance of power" in economic and technological terms as we enter the twenty-first century. For others, however, the trend lines are still not so clear. The various global and regional scenarios that have been postulated are indeed quite provocative, and whether or not any will come to pass may, in the long run, be less important than the fact that technological change is ubiquitous in the world and East Asia continues to be at the cutting edge of those changes.

The Pacific Rim will continue to lie at the heart of these two seemingly contradictory processes: globalization and regionalization. That we are witnessing the globalization of East Asia, with many of the economies of the region being drawn into the mainstream of global competition, few can deny. There is both a "push" and a "pull" dimension to this process—the push coming from the desire of many of the larger multinational firms to ally with Asia's steadily growing R&D and manufacturing capabilities. The globalization of the Pacific Rim will also continue to be driven by concerns about technological as well as trade protectionism. As indicated, these concerns have led firms from the Pacific Rim to expand their investment in R&D, diversify their markets, and seek out more stable and secure relationships in some of the new emerging markets around the globe. It is said that the successful companies of the future will be those that "think globally, but act locally." Given present trends in the development of robotics, flexible manufacturing systems, and telecommunications, sustaining technology progress, though very important, will not be the major challenge that the Pacific Rim nations must overcome.

The test of whether the nations of the Pacific Rim will discard their penchant for participating in a globalized economy as a full player will be the degree to which regionalization in Europe and North America becomes a significant constraint on their ability to acquire technology and compete in various local settings. There are numerous signs that the countries of the Asia Pacific region do not favor the fragmentation of the global economy into regional blocks. No less an authority than Lee Kuan Yew, former prime minister of Singapore, noted in his speech to the 1990 Davos *World Economic Forum*, "in an interdependent world, economic growth is determined more by global than regional factors." The future prosperity of the Pacific Rim depends on a liberal world trading system and technology market. These themes regarding "open regionalism" have been echoed in APEC, the PECC, and Pacific Basin Economic Cooperation (PBEC) as well—the three main multilateral organizations created to facilitate more intraregional cooperation.

At the same time, however, there are also signs that the process of regionalization in the Pacific Rim has significantly moved ahead over the last few years. Here again, there are no definite indications that this regionalization is of a "protectionist" sort. Intraregional trade and investments are steadily increasing, with corporations from Taiwan and South Korea joining Japan as major sources of capital and technology transfer. According to a study done by Japan's Nomura Research Institute, intraregional export trade as a percentage of total exports grew from 31 percent in 1986 to 43 percent in 1991; the share of exports to the United States fell from 34 percent to 24 percent over the same period (*Business Times*, April 7, 1991, p. 5). Even China has assumed a pivotal regional role as it emerges out from under the events of the Tiananmen incident in June 1989. In this regard one cannot ignore the tremendous financial clout and capacity of the expanding network of overseas Chinese business interests—a network that ties together the entrepreneurial Chinese communities in Southeast Asia, Hong Kong, and Taiwan with the PRC.[10] Moreover, in spite of domestic financial constraints, the PRC's high-technology development programs known as the

Table 1.3

The Evolution of Japanese Overseas R&D in East Asia

Industry Name	Information Collection Base	Development/ Design Base	R&D Base
Electrical applicances	Early 1970s	Mid-1980s	Since 1988
Primary Drivers	Market needs standards, data	Support of local factories, politics	New tech concepts
Automobiles	Early 1970s	Mid-1980s	Mid-1990s
Primary Drivers	Regulations, data, market needs	Support factories & local demand	Regional markets & global sourcing
Pharmaceuticals	Mid-1970s	Mid-1980s	1987
Primary Drivers	Standards, tech info, data	Establish standard R&D system	Utilize local technicians
Software	Late 1980s	Early 1990s	Mid-1990s
Primary Drivers	Local skills assessment	Domestic labor shortages	Harness "Asian" brainpower

Source: Adapted from *Nihon Keizai Shimbun*, May 2, 1991, p. 27.

"Torch Plan" and the "863" program are moving ahead quite rapidly; China's growth is clearly having a catalytic affect on the region insofar as the PRC is attracting capital, technology, and related resources from throughout the Pacific Rim. If present trends continue, suggests a recent World Bank study, the growth of the Greater China economy could outstrip the United States by early in the twenty-first century (*Nikkei Weekly*, May 3, 1993, p. 19; see also *Asian Wall Street Journal*, May 10, 1993, pp. 1, 16).

Thus, while a yen-dominated trading bloc will be hard to create, there is ample reason to expect that some *modus vivendi* could be worked out if the political and economic circumstances warrant. How sustainable this could be over time remains to be seen, raising all sorts of questions about which countries or regions would be the winners if regionalization were pushed too far, too fast anywhere on the globe. As Arthur Dunkel, former Director-General of GATT, has remarked, "Asia has high stakes in ensuring that the multilateral trading system remains open, liberal, and secure" (*Far Eastern Economic Review*, May 27, 1993, p. 23). Nonetheless, there is little doubt that from a regional perspective the emerging technological trajectory of the Pacific Rim will be an important area of study if we are to fully appreciate the dynamics of change and competition in the global economy (see Table 1.3). As one study has concluded, given the pace and thrust of economic change in the region and the extremely rapid buildup of indigenous advanced manufacturing and R&D capabilities among the countries in East and Southeast Asia, the global balance of technological power is being reshaped—leading perhaps to a new locus of influence in business and perhaps even political affairs ("Asia's High Tech Quest," 1992, p. 126; see also *Asian Wall Street Journal Weekly*, May 17, 1993, p. 1).

Notes

1. Interestingly, as the *Asian Wall Street Journal* has noted, "contrary to the common perception, industrial upgrading in the region isn't limited to the electronics sector," but also includes such sectors as petrochemicals and clothing, e.g., South Korea. See "Asian Industrialization Enters Its Second Phase" (1991, pp. 1, 22).

2. Of course, from the U.S. perspective, this two-way flow is not always to the advantage of both sides. Today, for example, several of Japan's leading scientific researchers received their advanced training as part of AT&T's Bell Laboratories. These include Dr. Hiroshi Kamimura, chairman of the Physics Department of the University of Tokyo, Dr. Michiyuki Uenohara, NEC Senior Executive Vice-President, and Dr. Izuo Hayashi, director of the Tsukuba Laboratory at the Optoelectronics Technology Research Corporation.

3. Figures derived from interviews conducted by the author in Taipei in April 1992.

4. Data obtained from the Ministry of Science and Technology in Seoul, 1992.

5. *Far Eastern Economic Review*, October 31, 1991, pp. 66–69. Another major event in the Korean electronics industry occurred when Goldstar bought 4.97 percent of Zenith in the United States in 1991.

6. See *The Economist*, March 12, 1988, p. 66. For an overview of the European technology situation, see Steinberg, 1990.

7. From interviews conducted by the author in Seoul, Korea, April 1992.

8. Interviews by author conducted in Hong Kong, October 1991 and March 1992. See also *Economic Daily* (Taipei), May 6, 1991, p. 2.

9. Interviews by author conducted in Tokyo, March 1992. See also *Ekonomisuto*, September 3, 1991, pp. 58–61.

10. *Nikkei Weekly*, May 24, 1993, p. 28. There are over 55 million overseas Chinese; the 1990 GNP of Asia's 51 million overseas Chinese, plus Taiwan and Hong Kong, was US$450 billion—25 percent more than China's stated GNP. See also *Straits Times*, July 27, 1992, p. 1, L2/3.

References

Asahi Shimbun. December 16, 1990.
"Asia and Japanese Business." *Tokyo Business Today* (June 1992).
"Asian Ambitions." *Business Tokyo* (July 1992): 10–15.
"Asian Industrialization Enters its Second Phase." *Asian Wall Street Journal Weekly* (June 3, 1991), 1, 22.
Asian Wall Street Journal Weekly. May 10, 1993.
Asian Wall Street Journal Weekly. May 17, 1993.
"Asia's High Tech Quest." *Business Week* (December 7, 1992).
Business Korea. October 1991, pp. 81–5.
Business Times. April 7, 1993.

Business Week. September 24, 1984.

Casson, Mark. *Global Research Strategy and International Competitiveness.* London: Basil Blackwell, 1990.

China Economic News Service (Taipei). August 6, 1991.

Dunning, John. *Multinationals, Technology and Competitiveness.* London: Unwin Hyman, 1988.

"East Asia's Power Crescent." *IEEE Spectrum* (June 1991): 26–66.

Economic Daily (Taipei). May 6, 1991.

The Economist. March 12, 1988.

Ekonomisuto. September 3, 1991, pp. 58–61.

Electronic Business. May 10, 1991.

Electronics Industry Association of Korea (EIAK). *Statistics.* Seoul: EIAK, 1992.

Elegant, Robert. *The Pacific Destiny.* New York: Crown, 1990.

Ernst, Dieter, and O'Connor, David. *Technology and Global Competition.* Paris: OECD, 1989.

Far Eastern Economic Review. January 14, 1988, pp. 46–7.

Far Eastern Economic Review. August 31, 1989, pp. 47–51.

Far Eastern Economic Review. December 13, 1990, pp. 62–3.

Far Eastern Economic Review. October 10, 1991, p. S9.

Far Eastern Economic Review. October 31, 1991, pp. 66–9.

Far Eastern Economic Review. May 27, 1993.

Financial Times. February 6, 1990.

Financial Times. July 15, 1991.

Forbes. November 23, 1992.

Fortune. May 25, 1991.

Fortune. July 22, 1992.

Free China Journal. February 3, 1986.

Free China Journal. February 9, 1987.

Free China Journal. September 17, 1991, pp. 3, 7.

Guile, Bruce, ed. *Technology and Global Industry.* Washington, DC: National Academy of Engineering, 1987.

Hayes, Robert, et al. *Dynamic Manufacturing: Creating the Learning Organization.* New York: The Free Press, 1988.

International Herald Tribune. May 11, 1991.

Japan Economic Journal. July 1, 1989.

Japan Economic Journal. January 26, 1991.

Japan Economic Journal. October 5, 1991.

Japan Times. September 13, 1991.

Japan Times. December 2, 1991.

Korea Economic Weekly. May 3, 1993.

Korea Times. March 16, 1993.

Lee, Thomas, and Reid, Proctor, eds. *National Interests in an Age of Global Technology.* Washington, DC: National Academy of Engineering, 1991.

Levitt, Theodore. "The Globalization of Markets." *Harvard Business Review* (May–June 1983).

Los Angeles Times. February 9, 1992.

Merrifield, D. Bruce. "Value-Added. The Dominant Factor in Industrial Competitiveness." *International Journal of Technology Management, Special issue on the Role of Technology in Corporate Policy* (1991).

Mody, Ahoka. "Institutions and Dynamic Comparative Advantage in the Electronics Industry in South Korea and Taiwan." *Industry of Free China* (August 1991), 1–25.

Muroyama, J., and Stever, H. G. *Globalization of Technology*. Washington, DC: National Academy Press, 1988.

Mytelka, Lynn, ed. *Strategic Partnerships in the World Economy*. London: Pinter, 1991.

National Research Council. *U.S.–Japan Strategic Alliances in the Semiconductor Industry*. Washington, DC: National Academy Press, 1992.

Nihon Keizai Shimbun. April 13, 1991.

Nihon Keizai Shimbun. May 2, 1991.

Nihon Keizai Shimbun. May 14, 1991.

Nihon Keizai Shimbun. May 22, 1991.

Nikkei Weekly. October 19, 1991.

Nikkei Weekly. May 3, 1993.

Nikkei Weekly. May 24, 1993.

Ohmae, Kenichi. *The Borderless World*. New York: Harper Business, 1990.

Pacific Economic Cooperation Council (PECC). *Pacific Economic Outlook, 1992–93*. San Francisco: Asia Foundation, 1992.

Palmer, Norman. *The New Regionalism in Asia and the Pacific*. Lexington, MA: Lexington Books, 1991.

Pearce, Robert. *Globalizing R&D*. New York: St. Martin's Press, 1992.

Pine, B. Joseph, II. *Mass Customization: The New Frontier in Business Competition*. Boston: Harvard Business School Press, 1993.

Porter, Michael. *The Competitive Advantage of Nations*. New York: The Free Press, 1990.

"Power of Asia." *Fortune* (October 17, 1991), 119–29.

Reich, Robert. "Technological Barriers Won't Help Us." *Japan Economic Journal* (February 27, 1988).

Romm, Joseph. *The Once and Future Superpower*. New York: Morrow, 1992.

Simon, Denis Fred. "Technology Policy on the Pacific Rim." *Forum for Applied Research and Public Policy* (Fall 1990), 67–72.

Steinberg, Michael, ed. *The Technical Challenges and Opportunities of a United Europe*. College Park, Maryland: Barnes and Noble Books, 1990.

Straits Times. July 27, 1992.

Suh, J. W., and Rao, J. B., eds. *Asia-Pacific Economic Cooperation: The Way Ahead*. Seoul: Korea Institute for International Economic Policy, 1990.

Teece, David J., ed. *Competitive Challenge*. Cambridge, MA: Ballinger, 1987.

Taiwan Industrial Panorama. December 1991.

Tien Hsia [Commonwealth Magazine]. December 1, 1990, pp. 62–6.

Toffler, Alvin. *Powershift*. New York: Bantam Books, 1990.

Tokyo Business Today. January 1992.

"Top 500: Asia's Leading Companies." *Tokyo Business Today* (September 1991), 24–32.

UNCTAD. *Transfer and Development of Technology in Developing Countries*. New York: United Nations, 1990.

UNCTC. *The World Investment Report, 1992: TNCs as Engines of Growth*. New York: United Nations, 1992.

United Nations Economic and Social Commission for Asia and the Pacific. *Restructuring the Developing Economies of Asia and the Pacific in the 1990s*. New York: United Nations, 1990.

U.S. Congress, Office of Technology Assessment. *Competing Economies: America, Europe, and the Pacific Rim*. Washington, DC: Government Printing Office, 1991.

Wriston, Walter. *The Twilight of Sovereignty*. New York: Scribners, 1993.

2

Emerging Trajectory of the Pacific Rim: Concepts, Evidences, and New Schemes

Fumio Kodama

The unique features of the Pacific Rim can be described in several ways. First, this area includes almost all types of countries: advanced, newly industrialized, and developing. Second, almost all aspects of the science and technology spectrum are represented: technologies for economic development, technology transfer, high technology innovation, and creation of new scientific advances.

What is most interesting, however, is that this region is the most rapidly growing area in the world, due mainly to the emergence of the newly industrialized economies. Further, the participation of these economies in the world market has coincided with the emergence of high technologies. This chapter therefore focuses on the transfer process of high technologies. The concept of "natural trajectory" will be used as an analytical tool.

There are many problems in this region that are waiting to be solved, and technology development is a key to finding the necessary solutions. This means that a new perspective on technology development is in order. The process of development of high technologies can best be analyzed by the concept of "demand articulation." We will apply this concept in order to formulate problems in terms of technology development.

The Pacific Rim has also been responsible for the creation of new scientific advances. A sentiment, however, of "technonationalism" has prevailed throughout the world. There is no conceptual scheme of international cooperation that might accommodate an ideal of technoglobalism. On the basis of understanding the dynamic nature of innovation, therefore, a new scheme for international scientific cooperation is proposed here.

Conceptual Framework of Technology Transfer

Key Concept: Natural Trajectory

The economics of innovation point to the fact that innovation occurs when it pays, thus highlighting the cost-effectiveness side of innovation. Since this analytical framework is static and retrospective, it produces no implications for technology policy that addresses the dynamic and action aspects of innovation.

Some economists, however, pay attention to the intrinsic dynamics of technology development. Nathan Rosenberg (1976, pp. 109–25) concludes that *backward linkage* has been an enormously important source of technical change in the Western world. He discusses the manner in which the demand for new techniques emerges and is perceived; he argues that the ordinary messages of the marketplace are general and not specific enough to indicate the directions in which technical change should be sought. Therefore, he argues, besides the marketplace, there must be forces pointing emphatically in certain directions. Rosenberg offers the concept of *technological imperatives* that guide the evolution of certain technologies: bottlenecks in connected processes and obvious shortcomings in products form clear targets for improvement.

On the other hand, as Nelson and Winter argue, the directions taken seem "straighter" than Rosenberg's emphasis on the shifting focus of attention would suggest. They term these paths *natural trajectories* (Nelson and Winter, 1982, pp. 254–62). The interpretation of trajectories within classes of technology is useful for organizing thinking about certain irregularities in the pace and pattern of technical progress. These authors also point out that within any of these classes of technology, technological advance may follow a particular trajectory. At any given time, all R&D may be focused on one class of technologies, for instance, while no attention is paid to other technologies because of lack of knowledge in that area.

This concept of natural trajectory stresses the continuity of technological evolution, and is thus helpful for our understanding of the importance of incremental innovation. On the other hand, we can interpret this concept as explaining radical changes as a shift in trajectory, that is, newly emerging trajectory. In other words, by emphasizing a possible discontinuity, we can understand the unique features of high technologies that are bringing about several phenomena that might be beyond our understanding based on existing common knowledge.

Although the concept of "trajectory" was developed to analyze the process of technological innovation, it can be extended to the process of technology transfer. A remarkable economic growth which can be observed among Asian NIEs (newly industrialized economies) indicates that they might be following a new trajectory due to technology transfer. We therefore review here the debate on technology transfer between developed and developing nations, and then challenge the accepted argument of technology transfer.

Product Cycle Theory

The well-known product cycle theory by Raymond Vernon (1966) states that technological innovation takes place in wealthy countries (those with high wage levels), and that production technology is steadily transferred to countries where wage levels are low, depending on the maturity of the technology. According to this theory, production bases are transferred from developed countries to semi-developed countries, and from there to developing countries, according to the stage of technology. However, the expansion of the multinational enterprises' international operations calls for a modification of this line of product cycle theory.

Some Japanese firms are producing new VCR models at their overseas factories in Asia within about two years of the new models' development while in Malaysia these firms are building nineteen-inch television sets on a highly automated manufacturing line that uses some equipment so advanced, it has yet to be installed in their older plants in Japan (*New York Times*, 1991).

The speed at which new technologies are spreading overseas is much faster now. We are observing a growing number of cases where decisions regarding the most suitable area for production are based less on technology or wage levels in the target area, and more on the overall corporate strategy of the manufacturing company. The transition to a borderless economy has progressed in such a way that companies have stepped beyond the product cycle theory and developed what can be called a *simultaneous world production structure*.

Appropriate Technology

The appropriate technology concept specifies the kinds of technologies with which developing countries should begin their technological advancement, based on the idea that developing countries face a wide range of problems in the process of assimilating technology. It states that the best form of technology that developed countries can transfer to developing countries is that which technical experts in the developing countries can manage, for the transfer of the latest technology can create many lasting problems (Schumacher, 1973).

This view might be valid for modernization of domestic industries that use resources and traditional technology. In view of the limited size of the domestic markets, however, export promotion is becoming an effective measure in the industrialization of the East Asian countries. And exporting requires the development of products that are internationally competitive. Accordingly, East Asia's technological development appears to indicate that the growth trajectories for developing countries are quite distinct from those put forward in the appropriate technology theory.

Even in the case of domestic development, the concept of "appropriate technology" seems less relevant. In fact, a number of projects based on this approach have been attempted, but almost all have failed. The reason is simple. The appropriate technology approach is guilty of fundamental errors regarding the concept of technology itself.

In developing countries, technology must be adapted to an economy that lacks the massive infrastructural systems taken for granted in the developed countries. This places far more stringent criteria on technologies for use in the developing nations than would exist in developed countries. The theory of technology holds that the more stringent the criteria, the higher the level of technology needed to resolve a given problem. It is not surprising, then, that the concept of appropriate technology, which moves in exactly the opposite direction, has generally ended in failure.

Technology as Tacit Knowledge

Few can deny that technology is not a physical substance but embodied in information. Very few scholars, however, had ever seriously asked the fundamental question of whether or not it is codified information. In the past, developing countries were very wary of overseas direct investment from developed countries: they feared it might lead to economic domination by the developed countries. In other words, they tried to separate technology from direct investment. This strategy, however, is based on the premise that technology is codified information.

Since production technology is very specific to the company that owns it and is yet not easily codifiable, it is fundamentally difficult to transfer and put that technology into effect outside the company. Among Japanese firms, the opinion is widely held that developing countries are having difficulties in comprehending technical information completely because they are unable to experience for themselves the trial-and-error process that led to the development of that technology, and that, consequently, they lack the know-how that can only be acquired by such first-hand experience.

If we take into account such difficulties experienced by developing countries in introducing technology, direct investment that transfers technology to subsidiary companies in the investment area can be looked upon in a positive light. It is not greatly influenced by the level of technology in the recipient country, and the technology is of a form that can be transferred easily.

During the late 1970s and early 1980s, many East Asian countries discarded their cautionary postures toward the inflow of overseas investment. Indeed, many adopted policies and measures that would attract foreign capital. Malaysia recently reversed course, creating huge tax incentives for foreign investment. Now, more than 800 Japanese manufacturers are in Malaysia, and their presence has transformed the economy: 59 percent of Malaysia's exports in 1990 were manufactured goods (*New York Times*, 1991).

Technical Change and Technology Transfer

In general, case studies are the most effective means of elucidating the newly emerging trajectory based on technology transfer. For this reason, we conducted

case studies of color television and camera manufacturing, where overseas production is well advanced in East Asia.

In order to understand the dynamic interaction between technology change
and transfer, first of all, we investigated the characteristics of technical progress
in color television and camera manufacture. Innovation in color television has
been characterized by the development of transistors and ICs (integrated circuits), functional upgrading of various electronic parts, and emphasis on automation and saving labor in the assembly process. Innovation in camera technology
has been characterized by a greater use of electronic parts, use of plastic materials, grouping of the assembling process into blocks, automation of individual
parts production, and the use of computers in design.

Product Innovation

In order to understand the product innovations that occurred in color televisions,
we used the "product tree"—that is, the chart that illustrates the relationship between
the final product and its parts in the shape of a tree, as shown in Figure 2.1.

As the figure reveals, the end product—for example, the television—is placed
on the left, and spreading out to the right are its parts. At the top are console-
related parts; in the center is the cathode-ray tube; and at the bottom are the various
electronic circuits. In order to make the technical change process clear, the dotted
line is used to show parts that were used a quarter-century ago. Today, these
parts have been replaced by the parts shown in the accompanying parentheses.

Color Televisions

From the figure, we can see vividly that the old vacuum tube has been replaced
by the transistor, and the numerous electronic circuits replaced by ICs (integrated
circuits); fourteen-inch color televisions utilize from six to ten ICs (the television
shown in the figure uses eight ICs). Each IC has a specific function; it replaced
circuits that had comprised dozens of elements (shown by the dotted line in the
figure). Moreover, electronic wires that connected parts and circuits were replaced by printed circuit boards. Thus, when advanced technology was introduced into television parts, it simplified the parts structure considerably.

Cameras

Through the introduction of electronics technology, many of the old precision
metal parts have been replaced by ICs and other electronic circuits. Hardly any
electronic circuits were used in the old cameras. Nowadays, however, electronic
parts in the recent compact camera account for 40 percent of all parts, and 50
percent of the total value of parts.

In response to improvement of the strength and appearance of plastic materi-

Figure 2.1. **Product Tree of Small Size Television**

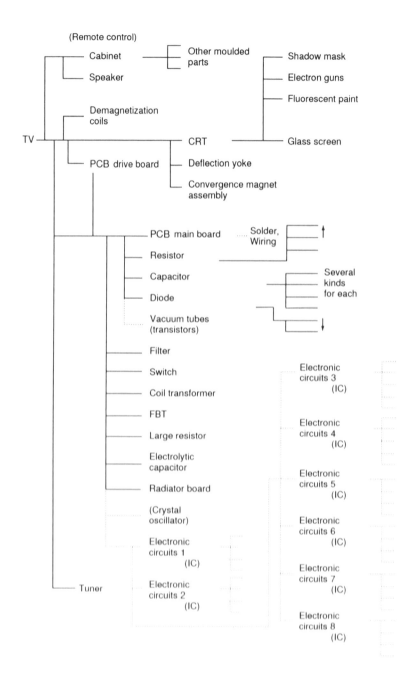

als and to progress in molding technology, molded plastics have been used for console parts of the camera since around 1965. Plastic was later used for the camera body and internal parts, and is now widely used for lenses as well. Since plastics can be molded into various complex configurations with relative ease, it is helpful in reducing the number of parts.

However, the latest cameras incorporate many more functions than their predecessors, and the number of parts for these functions have increased accordingly. Compared with the product of twenty years ago, today's cameras have not seen a significant reduction in the number of component parts.

Process Innovation

Color Televisions

In color television production, the automation of the assembling process is an example of a major change. In the 14–15-inch models, several thousand electronic parts are grouped and soldered onto a printed board at very high speed by an automatic mounting device.

In the past, this mounting operation was conducted with simple machinery and required a considerable number of workers. Because the performance of the automatic mounting devices has improved and parts configuration has been standardized, more than 90 percent of electronic parts are being mounted by automatic machines, all of which has resulted in substantial labor saving. The emphasis in the assembling process has shifted to automatic machinery operation, maintenance checks, and the reliable supply of electronic parts for mounting.

Through the simplification of circuits and the shift to automatic mounting brought about by standardization of many elements, the number of assembling processes and the amount of inspection work have been reduced and the overall process has become much simpler.

Meanwhile, as electronic parts production became more automated and high-volume supply became possible, further automation of assembly occurred. At the same time, overseas production progressed in parallel to such development. We can, therefore, assume that this technical progress has had the effect of facilitating the production of high-quality goods overseas as well.

Cameras

In camera manufacturing, the widespread use of plastic molding technology gave rise to the simplification of the parts production process, as shown in Figure 2.2. Metal processing is diverse and complex: it involves casting, stamping, cutting, grinding, finishing, surface treatment, plating and painting. These processes are no longer necessary for parts made of plastic and the work involved in camera production has decreased steadily as the percentage of plastic parts has in-

Figure 2.2. **Process Innovation of Camera Manufacturing**

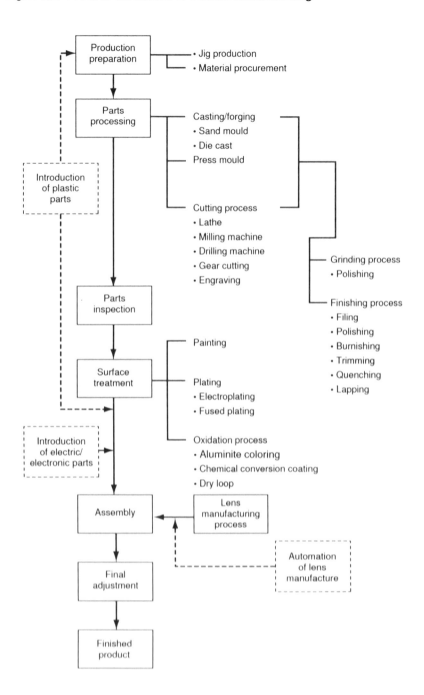

creased. The use of plastics, thus, has led to a simplification of the assembling process through a reduction in the number of parts involved.

The widespread use of electronics also brought about significant changes in the production process. In the past, cameras consisted of precision machine parts, but the use of the automatic exposure function, which links the exposure meter and the shutter, and of electronic shutters, has progressed. Today, almost all major control functions have been replaced by electronic circuits.

Previously, parts production, ranging from preparatory work to processing and then to surface treatment, was carried out at main factories, subsidiary companies, or affiliated factories. But electronic parts are now purchased externally, and then merely mounted on a printed board; the amount of time saved is striking. Manufacturing of electronic circuits is now located outside the main business range of almost all camera manufacturers, who instead commission domestic electronics manufacturers to produce the circuits. However, it is necessary to develop parts that suit the particular technical specifications of the camera, such as a need for compactness or signal processing using a weaker electrical current. Therefore, camera manufacturers have been putting a great deal of effort into joint development with electronic manufacturers.

Production automation has progressed through the introduction of NC (numerically controlled) machine tools for mechanical parts, as well as high-speed polishers for optical parts. The lens has a major effect on the performance of a camera. In the past, a great deal of work went into its design, and craftsman-like skills were essential for its production. Production efficiency, however, improved dramatically with the use of computers for lens design and with the move toward automatic production processes.

As for the assembling operation, automation and rationalization have been achieved by dividing the process into several blocks, thus shortening the final assembling process and eliminating the need for inspection. Through these developments the overall efficiency of the assembling process has been enhanced remarkably.

Transfer Mechanism of High Technologies

The kinds of technical progress described above might have a substantial influence on technology transfer. We will, therefore, analyze the transfer mechanism of high technologies by examining their pros and cons in terms of transferability.

First, we can find a negative aspect of high technologies. All accumulated know-how with regard to design is contained in ICs, so the transfer of production technology for highly advanced electronic parts is becoming difficult.

Second, we can find a positive side of high technologies. The development of engineering plastic is witnessing its substitution for metal parts, and this leads to a simplification of the parts manufacturing processes. It is becoming cost-effective to transfer plastic parts production technology overseas. Engineering plastics is also a primary factor in the simplification of the parts structure of various products. They are facilitating assembling works, and help make overseas assembly worthwhile.

Overall, upgrading the functions of ICs and other electronic parts has changed the product part structure remarkably. It has led to a reduction in the amount of assembly work, that is, requiring fewer manufacturing processes and inspections. Consequently, with supplies of ICs from advanced countries, assembly work could easily be carried out overseas, thus contributing positively toward transferring assembly technology overseas.

Third, technical progress in high technologies is changing conditions upon which an international division of labor structure will stand, and the newly emerging international division of labor will promote technology transfer. The development of automatic assembling machinery, and its prerequisite conditions, such as standardization, mass production, and increased reliability, have played a large part in automating assembling works. The fact that the assembling process requires less skilled labor works in favor of the transfer of its technology.

Fourth, there are cases where the basic technology is not suitable for transfer. Engineering plastics requires the technology to manufacture precision molds. Since it is the technology that demands precision and skill, it is not easily transferred from advanced countries.

In conclusion, through the shift to high technology, the essence of technology has been incorporated into parts or machinery. Sales of these parts and machinery has raised technology's potential for circulation. And if parts or machinery can be easily procured, high-technology goods that use these parts or machinery can be easily produced anywhere. Such technological change has not only increased the overseas move by companies of advanced countries, but has also helped to raise production levels of the locally capitalized companies in the Asian NIEs.

This fact, however, has become the chief cause of problems with industrialization in the countries of East Asia. Even though assembly technology can be and has been transferred to these countries, structural problems have arisen as a result of the slow progress of production technology.

Measuring Technology Transfer

For a scientific analysis of the emerging technological trajectory in Asia, an attempt to measure technology transfer via case studies is indispensable. Therefore, an investigation of Japan's direct investment in East Asian countries was conducted by the National Institute of Science and Technology Policy (NISTEP). We surveyed major color television and camera manufacturers that have established companies in East Asia, with regard to their respective places of procurement for major parts when operating overseas assembling factories. Countries included in our survey were: South Korea, Taiwan, Hong Kong, Singapore, Thailand, and Malaysia. Specific products chosen were small color televisions with screen sizes ranging from fourteen to eighteen inches, and compact cameras.

For the survey, we chose *eleven* color television parts, and *sixteen* camera parts[1]. For each of these parts, we asked the manufacturer about the country where it was produced, and the nationality of the company that produced it. In other words, for each Japanese overseas assembly factory, we found out the country where the parts were procured. However, as far as the volume of procurement was concerned, we were unable to get the entire picture because many companies treat such transactions as confidential. Instead of asking the volume, therefore, we asked the assembly factories to list the places of procurement in descending order, based on the percentage of parts procured.

We then estimated the volume of procurement from each country by using the following formula: in cases where there were two places of procurements, the one ranked higher was given a value of two-thirds, while the other was given a value of one-third; for three places of procurement, the largest is given a value of four-sevenths, the second largest a value of two-seventh, and the third a value of one-seventh. In other words, the order was weighted on the basis of a geometric progression, and the sum of the values became, of course, one.

Results of Measurements

Following this formula, we calculated the degree of parts procurement from Japan and from the East Asian countries specified above. The results of the overseas assembling operation for two Japanese color TV manufacturers is depicted in Figure 2.3. The upper, hatched portion shows procurement from countries other than Japan, while the lower, blacked-in portion shows procurement from Japan. The parts listed below the graph are, from left to right, in descending order of degree procured from Japan.

As the figure reveals, the shift of parts supply away from Japan to these East Asian countries has made progress. Rough calculation shows that the average degree of parts procurement from Japan has been reduced to as low as 43 percentage points (by quantity).

There is also a marked difference in procurement of parts. In descending order, all the ICs and almost all transistor diodes were procured from Japan, while procurement of such items as tuners, high-voltage transformers (FBTs), and deflection yokes was decreasing. The majority of such items as CRTs (cathode-ray tube), printed boards, capacitors, resistors, coils and capacitors were being procured from countries other than Japan. As far as cabinets are concerned, nothing was procured from Japan.

In the same manner, an estimate of the degree of procurement by three Japanese camera manufacturers in their overseas operation is shown in Figure 2.4. Compared with the number for the color TV, the percentage of camera parts

Figure 2.3. Parts Procurement from Japan in Overseas Production of Color Televisions (Two Major Japanese Companies)

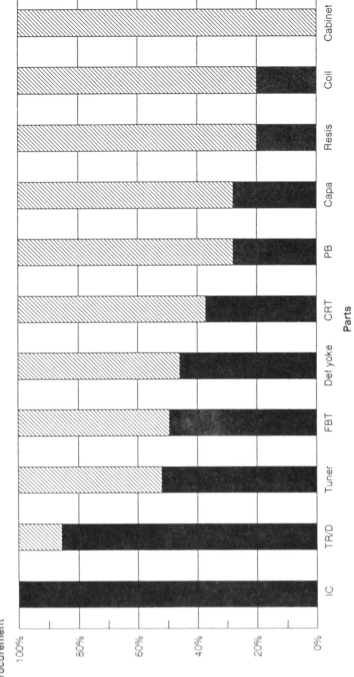

■ Procurement from Japan

▨ Procurement from countries other than Japan

Figure 2.4. **Parts Procurement from Japan in Overseas Production of Cameras** (Three Major Japanese Companies)

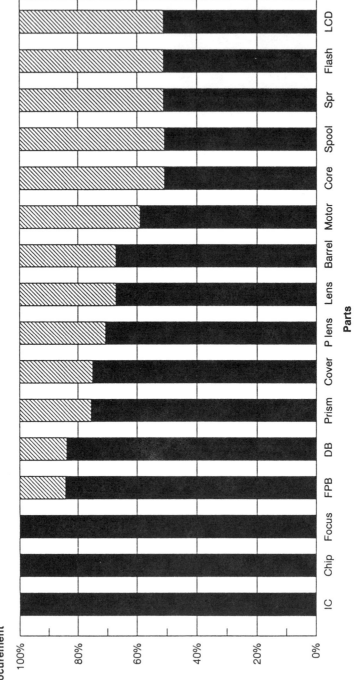

supplied from Japan was higher: the average degree of procurement from Japan was as high as 71 percentage points.

As for the differences in parts categories, all of the ICs, chip parts, and focusing sensors were procured from Japan. The majority of flexible printed circuit boards, diaphragm blades, prisms, and lens barrels were supplied from Japan. However, almost half of the procurement of such items as plastic cores, sprockets, spools, flash units and LCD panels, was supplied from countries other than Japan.

Toward a New Theory of Technology Transfer

By comparing these two case studies—the color television and the camera—we can draw the following three lessons concerning the dynamics of technology transfer.

First, the percentage of camera parts procured from countries other than Japan is lower than that of color television. This difference can be assumed to be due mainly to the difference between electronics and mechanical industries. By assuming that electronics products are "naturally" more high-technology than mechanical products, we can better understand the perplexing paradox that the progress toward high technology is making technology transfer easier.

There also might be several reasons more specific to these two products. Because of higher level skill requirements imposed on camera parts manufacturing, parts suppliers tend to be smaller. This makes it difficult for them to establish factories overseas. Because of the precision-oriented nature of the camera, manufacturers often confront design changes. This again makes overseas manufacturing more difficult.

Second, further investigation into the place of procurement in terms of the ownership of the company (Japanese-owned companies or not), shows an overwhelming tendency for parts to be supplied from Japanese-owned companies. Movement toward procuring parts for locally owned companies has not yet progressed very much. This is a reflection of the uncodified nature of manufacturing technologies: the *uncodifiable information* can only be transmitted within an organization. The dual relationship between product and process innovation, which becomes evident in a high-technology area, should also be studied from the viewpoint of the organizational theory of technology transfer.

Third, a very high degree of procurement from Japan of electronics parts such as the transistor diode for color televisions, and of chip parts and focusing sensors for cameras, is common in these case studies. Since these two products are typical high-technology products, we might make the following generalization: by keeping the innovation capacity of critical parts at home, we free ourselves from the fear of the *hollowing phenomena*. We can speculate that the development of high technology is facilitating a corporate strategy in which the competitive edge is maintained by keeping and concentrating on the R&D activity of critical parts in the home country and by locating manufacturing activities in individual places close to individual markets.

In fact, the *New York Times* speculates,

> For the Japanese, Asia is the critical cog in the machine, a cure for Japan's shortage of talented labor and inexpensive land, a way to free up Japan's resources for more profitable, research-oriented work at home.
>
> If the move was driven by economics, it was accelerated by Japanese-American trade politics. Goods built in Malaysia or Thailand are not included in Japan's trade accounts with the United States, even if they contain largely Japanese components. So Japan can still make television sets and VCRs and send them to American stores without further enlarging the American trade deficit with Japan because of what amounts to an accounting shell game that no one has yet been able to quantify accurately. [1991]

In conclusion, all three lessons described above allude to a fundamental difference in the technology transfer pattern between high technologies and conventional technologies. However, only by serious efforts in both empirical and quantitative studies can we establish a new theory of high-technology transfer.

Problem Solving by High Technologies: A Think Experiment

Key Concept: Demand Articulation

When one ponders the vast issue of technology's role in civilization, one can't avoid the issue of what technological approach would be the most worthwhile as we seek to resolve the world's problems. In the high-tech era, the key technology-policy issue has become not how to break through technological bottlenecks, but how to put existing technology to the best possible use. Accordingly, a day of reckoning has come for technology policy, which has traditionally emphasized the supply side of technology development. What we need now is a technology policy that works from the demand side.

As we develop new policies to meet this need, the most important element is the process in which the need for a specific technology emerges and the R&D effort is targeted toward developing and perfecting it. We call this "technological *demand articulation*" (Kodama, 1991, pp. 75–109). According to *Webster's Dictionary*, the word "articulate" comes from the Latin *articulare*. Among other things, this word has the following two conflicting meanings: (1) to draw up in *separate* articles: and (2) to put *together* by joints. Articulation therefore can be interpreted as encompassing the two opposite concepts: analysis and synthesis, or decomposition and integration. In fact, both are necessary in technology development, and the heart of the problem concerning technology development is how to manage those two conflicting tasks.

We, therefore, define demand articulation as *a dynamic interaction of technological activities that involves integrating potential demands into a product con-*

cept and decomposing this product concept into development agendas for its individual component technologies.

The best example of a dynamic interaction of the two kinds of technological activity can be found in the development of liquid crystal technology. The process of integrating potential demands into a product concept can be illustrated by the development of Japanese-language word processors. And the process of decomposing a product concept into development agendas for component technologies can be demonstrated by the development of the home-use VTR (video tape recorder).

In the case of liquid crystal technology, what turned out to be the correct technological choice was made by the more specialized manufacturers who limited their applications to displays for calculators and watches—applications that had a specific need for a reduced energy requirement. In other words, they were the only manufacturers that achieved demand articulation vis-à-vis liquid crystal technology.

In the case of Japanese-language word processors, the first attempt with ideas of direct analogy from English typewriters ended in failure. Manufacturers were forced to return to fundamental research, starting from the basic principles of linguistics. The result was the birth of a new product concept: the Japanese-language word processor, which embodies a primitive version of artificial intelligence (AI) technology.

In the case of home-use VTR, a long-term commitment to a specific product concept made possible a consistent demand articulation. This in turn allowed the successive development of new technologies to meet specific technological needs. In retrospect, these achievements would have been inconceivable through a mere extrapolation of existing technologies.

In endeavors of this sort of technology development, Nelson and Winter's metaphor of "alternatives out there waiting to be found" is somewhat forced (Nelson and Winter, 1982, pp. 254–62). As far as sources of innovation are concerned, however, some parts may be drawn off the shelf of existing technologies, while some parts may be drawn from the scientific pools or sometimes beyond them. In fact, this range of technology development may cover the majority of technology development.

As the above examples demonstrate, demand articulation worked at the company level. The question that remains, however, is whether demand articulation works at different levels of problems. An example of such a problem on the international level is global environmental problems, such as global warming. Within national boundaries, the question remains as to whether demand articulation can be applied to the public sector, such as in social and urban development. In order to illustrate a kind of new approach through demand articulation, we will conduct a "think" experiment.

Third World Development: Holistic Technology

At the top of the list of global concerns sits the issue of Third World development; that is, narrowing the gap between rich and poor nations. This then leads us to the question of what sort of technology would best address this issue, and how that technology should be applied

The term "high technology" represents a well-known technological concept. But when we look for a policy to address the needs of developing countries, we need a totally new concept of technology. The concept that would best meet the technological needs of Third World development is "holistic technology," which permits autonomous economic growth.

The concept of "appropriate technology" has long been held up as an effective means of promoting development. This concept focuses on the specific circumstances of the developing countries, and argues that it would be better to provide the developing nations with simpler, less advanced technology than that used in the developed countries. As described before, however, intellectually, this concept is almost collapsing, mainly because it imposed more stringent criteria on technologies for the Third World than would exist in developed countries. In the developing countries, the lack of extensive infrastructure necessitates the use of autonomous, decentralized systems. This points squarely to the concept of holistic technology.

One example that embodies this technological concept is the "solar battery." A key problem for developing countries is that, because of a lack of electric power, as well as other forms of infrastructure, development projects often cannot be carried out except in major urban centers. Building up extensive energy supply systems like those in the developed countries, however, will take a tremendous amount of time. Solar batteries, however, do not require a massive network of transmission lines. A supply of electricity can be secured as long as the sun is shining.

Another example of holistic technology is "radio-chemistry," which can be used to preserve food. A number of food-producing regions in the developing countries suffer periodically from food shortages, in spite of adequate sunshine and rain. The problem is that, although sufficient food is produced, proper storage technology is lacking. As a result, much of the food eventually spoils.

Traditional chemical technologies for preserving foodstuffs, however, require an extensive supporting infrastructure. Sophisticated radio-chemistry technology can prevent food from spoiling simply through the application of radiation. This technology is therefore more easily adapted to situations in the developing countries. Here, as well, it is not necessarily best to follow the technological systems of developed nations.

The key point is that holistic technology does not require extensive infrastructure. When developing countries attempt to industrialize with limited infrastructure, it is often inappropriate for them to adopt the technological systems of the developed countries. In short, they do not necessarily have to follow the same *trajectory* that advance countries had followed in developing their economies.

But, as the developing countries actually begin to establish holistic technologies, difficulties emerge in terms of personnel and economic feasibility. For example, while India turns out a large force of highly skilled scientists and engineers every year, many of them end up moving to the United States. One reason is the greater opportunity to work on the cutting edge of advanced technology, which is the ultimate aim of most scientists and engineers. This desire cannot be fulfilled by the simpler tasks involved in appropriate technology.

Holistic technology, as noted in the above examples, encompasses the most advanced forms of technology, and can be applied within developing as well as developed countries. Accordingly, holistic technology would help mobilize for development the talent nurtured by the developing countries' own education systems.

With regard to economic feasibility, holistic technologies such as solar batteries must compete in the developed countries with technologies for which sufficient infrastructure already exists. This renders the holistic technologies more costly and more difficult to utilize. For example, solar batteries will not necessarily be readily adopted in the developed countries, where extensive electric power networks are already in place. But the utilization of such forms of high technology in the developing countries is considerably less expensive than the construction of large projects for new infrastructure. From the demand side as well, it is a highly rational technology.

Over the long term, the development of this sort of technology is also highly desirable for Japan, even though it is a developed country. For example, Japan's security is seriously threatened by the potential for an oil crisis that could cut off supplies of raw materials. A situation may well develop in which solar batteries would be crucial to Japan's survival.

In a broader sense, development of this technology could also contribute to Japan's security by improving relations with the developing countries. In this way, holistic technology offers the dual benefits of contributing to Third World development while promoting Japan's own national security interests.

Japan Problem: Threshold Technology

The lexicon of Japanese political and economic observers had recently come to include the term "intermestic," which combine the words "international" and "domestic." The term is used to highlight the highly domestic character of the international issues confronting Japan. In other words, it is argued that Japan can contribute most to resolving world problems by resolving its own domestic problems. From this standpoint, undoubtedly the greatest problem for Japan is the excessive concentration of people and economic activity in the city of Tokyo.

As a means of addressing this problem, I propose the concept of "threshold technology," which would make it possible to reverse the excessive concentration in Tokyo and to promote decentralization. Particular attention is focused on high-definition TV (HDTV) and the linear motor car as concrete examples of this new technological concept.

Prior to the oil crises of the 1970s, the National Land Agency issued a new comprehensive national development plan which sought to end excessive concentration in Tokyo and promote development in the provinces. The agency cited advances in communications and transportation technology as factors that would make this decentralization possible.

But the communications technology on which its plan was based was the telephone, while the transportation technology it counted on was the Shin-Kansen bullet train. These technologies, while the most advanced of that time, were not sufficient to support a decentralization of economic activity into the provinces.

As a comparison with the facsimiles machines in use today make clear, the telephone alone is capable of transmitting only small amounts of information. Even while it has made communications with the provinces somewhat more convenient, it was still insufficient. This insufficiency, moreover, served only to intensify the concentration in Tokyo.

And the bullet train, the pinnacle of transportation technology of its time, nevertheless takes three hours to travel from Tokyo to Osaka. This means that a round trip would constitute nearly a full day's work. Such technology could not be expected to contribute significantly to decentralization. Rather, it merely made it easier for employees to make business trips from the provinces to Tokyo, with the ultimate result of further concentration in the capital.

A more important cause of the concentration, however, was the transformation of Japan's industrial structure. At the time of the Land Agency's national plan, Japan's industrial structure was centered around heavy industry and large-scale production facilities. Accordingly, the technological regime of the time required vast industrial areas. It was predicted that, without decentralization away from the crowded Tokyo area, Japan's economic growth could not last.

This prompted a debate over decentralization into the provinces. But with the advent of high technology, the industrial structure was transformed into one of smaller products and production facilities with a higher degree of value added. The concentration of information in Tokyo attracted more people and businesses, further exacerbating the problem of Tokyo-centrism. In this way, the insufficiency of technology, combined with changes in the industrial structure, promoted further concentration in Tokyo and gave rise to a number of urban problems.

This brings us to technologies such as HDTV, which make it possible to transmit images of greater resolution than the average human eye can perceive. Accordingly, any images that could not be seen through HDTV could also not be perceived by the human eye. As a technology, HDTV has passed a threshold value; it permits precise communication regardless of distance. But HDTV cannot replace face-to-face communication. As a result, it is ultimately necessary to develop the linear motor car.

If travel time between Tokyo and Osaka were cut to one hour, a business trip could be completed in only half a day. One could go to Osaka in the morning, conduct one's business, and be back in Tokyo before noon. This also represents the passing of a key threshold value, since business is generally conducted in units of half-days. Any further reduction in travel time would be of little significance.

The above analysis indicates that any attempt to decentralize economic activity, if carried out without sufficient technology, would merely address the symptoms rather than the causes of the problem. But the adoption of technological innovations such as HDTV and the linear motor car based on the concept of threshold technology would produce a breakthrough in policy.

In terms of urban development policy, Japan has experienced at least two major failures since the end of the Second World War. The first instance occurred when Japan was rebuilding itself from the ashes of the war. It failed to make use of ideas seen in West Germany and elsewhere, where streets were built wider and electricity lines were laid underground. The second failure took place in the 1970s, when an effort to apply industrial technology to social development was thwarted by two oil crises.

But from a technological standpoint, these failures occurred at times when there were neither facsimiles nor HDTV, and absolutely nothing was known about superconductivity. Accordingly, if a great push had been made toward social development using rather old technology, the result would have been forced. It certainly would not have brought an ultimate resolution to the problem.

Legislators and policy makers, however, must be aware of one important feature of technology. While technological progress is continuous in nature, the application of technology is not. It becomes possible to enter a whole new domain of technological applications only when the capabilities of a given technology recipient cross a certain threshold.

As Japan's industrial structure shifted from high energy consumption to energy conservation, and from heavy industry to high-tech, Japan was able to overcome the oil crises of the 1970s and achieve the highest per capita gross national product in the world. Now, in the 1990s, technology to support drastic decentralization is coming within reach. This is the best chance to tackle the problem in earnest.

Toward a Theory of External Demand Articulation

Through our "think" experiments, we have learned that demand articulation is theoretically conceivable even at different levels of problem solving. A major difference can be formulated as "external" versus "internal" demand articulation. However, when it comes to implementation, we have to confront a different set of problems.

The first problem is whether demand articulation is necessary and/or effective in technology development in international and public arenas. The structure of external demand articulation might be quite different from that of internal demand articulation. Who is the beneficiary of the development of those technologies? Who pays the cost of their development? Is there any mismatch between those two agents?

The second problem is determining if the process of external demand articulation is different. Even if external demand articulation is effective for technology development, the decision-making process for adopting new technologies is different. For social and urban development, actors in decision making include citizens, developers, and local government. For global environmental problems, national governments, regional organizations and international organizations are the decision makers.

The third problem is determining who the external demand articulation agent is. It might be local government and international organizations in urban development and global environment respectively. Those agents, however, do not own the technical capability for demand articulation. What is important is how they can mobilize and organize the technical capability needed for demand articulation.

In terms of political science, these problems could be formulated as the difference between "control" and "influence." To answer these challenges, therefore, the research community of science and technology policy research might have to be extended to include other disciplines. In fact, how best to organize these needed disciplines is a challenging subject.

A New Scheme for International Scientific Cooperation

Key Concept: Fluid Pattern

International cooperation has traditionally been dominated by the notions of "cost sharing" and "task sharing." Both refer to dividing up costs and tasks among participating nations in order to pursue an option that has already been selected. They also emerged for purely economic reasons.

These concepts, in other words, have not derived from the logic of science and technology itself, which appears to have been left thoroughly out of the equation. This fact highlights the need for a new concept of international cooperation based on an understanding of the dynamics of science and technology.

W. Abernathy studied patterns of industrial innovation and found that two distinct patterns exist: one is the "fluid" pattern in the early stage of innovation, and the other is the "specific" pattern which arises in the later stage of innovation:

> One pattern of technological innovation can be seen in the important changes that occur in established high- volume product lines, such as incandescent light bulbs, rolled steel, refined gasoline, and auto engines. The markets for such goods are well defined; the product characteristics are *specific* and often standardized.
>
> However, major new products do not seem to be consistent with the first pattern of incremental change. A more *fluid* pattern of product change is associated with the identification of an emerging need or a new way to meet an existing need; it is an entrepreneurial act.

When a major product innovation first appears, performance criteria are typically vague and little understood. In this second pattern of innovation, the diversity and *uncertainty* of performance dimensions for major new products might be expected to require a more flexible organization and technical approach and a greater degree of external communication than in the first pattern.

These patterns are not independent of one another, however. It is apparent in several industries that products currently represented by the specific pattern were much more like the fluid one at the time of their origin. [Abernathy, 1978, pp. 68–85]

As Abernathy describes, in the early stage, everything is fluid both in the performance and in the technology dimensions. Therefore, the major task at this stage is to reduce the fluidity in identifying both the performance criteria and the technical approach to meet these criteria.

As far as the government policy implications of these fluid characteristics are concerned, R. Nelson studied the supersonic transport (SST) program of the 1960s and the liquid metal fast breeder reactor (LMFBR) of the Atomic Energy Commission (AEC) during the same period, and came to the conclusion that it is not just that the particular proposals were not cost-effective, but also that the form of the proposed subsidy was generally unwise.

In *The Moon and the Ghetto*, Richard Nelson argued that the organizational model for the SST and LMFBR programs was the Manhattan Project. "The style," says Nelson, "involves a willingness to make large early bets on particular technological options, and force these through at very high cost." Unlike the Manhattan Project, however, these latter programs foundered: "[T]he early batting average has been dismal. . . .[T]here has been a tendency to stick with the game plan despite mounting evidence that it is not a good one" (Nelson, 1977, p. 105).

Left to themselves, Nelson doubts that contractors would have kept with the original game plan: "The heart of these programs was early commitment of government funds to a particular design. In the case of the supersonic transport, it is highly unlikely that Boeing would have persisted so long in pushing its swing-wing SST design had the bulk of funds been its own, and had it the ability to make that decision on its own." Nelson continues, "[T]he AEC was persisting in R&D on a design long after evidence had accumulated that the route was not an attractive one," and "[T]he AEC has been very sticky about initiating work on new concepts" (Nelson, 1977, p. 105).

One of the pitfalls in a government's aggressive support of technological projects is the "early commitment of governmental funds to a particular design," in the stage where both the performance criteria and the technological approach are still very fluid. Therefore, the policy problem for the government is how to avoid this kind of pitfall.

Although it was not intended, the importance of this fluidity was illustrated by the recent development of space programs. While the United States had sought unification of space transportation through the Space Shuttle, the ESA's (European Space Agency) Ariane Space went in a different direction and commercialized expendable vehicles. The availability of ESA's services contributed to vitalization of the world space activities which would otherwise have been long depressed by the Challenger accident (Morino and Kodama, 1990).

Deficiency of Conventional Scheme

The intrinsic deficiency of international technology cooperation, which is conducted on the basis of the old scheme such as cost/task sharing, can be most clearly illustrated by the recent controversy over joint Japan–U.S. development of the FSX fighter aircraft, which climaxed with a U.S. congressional resolution in opposition to the project.

The issue stirred such widespread controversy not only because the project involved military technology, but also because the form of the joint development effort was substantially different from what had prevailed in the past. The U.S. congressional resolution, while imposing various limitations on the transfer of technology from the United States to Japan, allegedly required that Japanese corporations transfer to U.S. corporations their carbon fiber technology, developed in Japan's civilian sector, without condition and without payment for the technology.

In fact, in the past, most attention focused on the transfer of technology from the United States to other countries. It could be easily said, therefore, that a new scheme of cooperation has become necessary to accommodate the ideal of equal partnership among advanced countries. However, we should go further than just talking about a rhetoric such as equal partnership.

As described above, in their early stages, research and development projects, especially those identified as national projects, are characterized by a high degree of fluidity. No individual or country can be certain about the proper standards for evaluating the performance of a certain technology or judging which alternative is best. It is therefore very important to preserve as much diversity as possible.

Recently, news about cold fusion grabbed the world's attention. Before that the central topic was superconductivity. Both these examples make it clear that as we strive to achieve a certain goal, such as securing new sources of energy, science and technology present us with a variety of different options.

In the instance of cold fusion, development of the next generation of energy supplies can follow at least two distinct routes. One would bring an increase in energy supplies by developing a new form of nuclear power. The other would take advantage of superconductivity to eliminate energy loss during the transmission of electric power.

Option Sharing Scheme

The cases described above serve as a stunning reminder that science and technology progress entail a vast array of options and alternatives. A thorough search of all possible options, therefore, should be made the chief aim of future international cooperation.

In this regard, the dividing up of responsibilities for pursuing all possible alternatives would represent an effective and constructive role for international cooperation. Conversely, only through international cooperation would it be possible to pursue all potential options. Through this form of option sharing, moreover, it becomes possible to resolve the inherent tension that exists between international cooperation and national autonomy (Kodama, 1990).

This cooperation scheme should not permit one country to force on other countries the specific alternative it has selected. Each country would have the right to choose which alternative it wishes to pursue. Given the need to ensure that all possible alternatives are covered, however, there would also have to be a certain amount of compromise and adjustment of each country's interests. In addition, information about which alternative is best must be shared openly among all participating nations. Determining the most desirable alternative is possible only if all the alternatives are tested and compared.

This sharing of information could be assured by allowing a free flow of researchers across national borders. Specifically, researchers from each country would freely choose the alternative they wish to pursue, in accordance with their own views, convictions, and career objectives, and would participate in the project of the corresponding country. After the best alternative has been determined, the researchers would return to their respective countries. The participation of researchers from various countries in each project would ensure that, once the researchers have returned home, the information on the alternative ultimately selected would be automatically disseminated throughout the participating countries.

At present, there are growing fears that moves in the direction of technological protectionism will turn into a zero-sum game for the world as a whole. It can be said that only through option sharing can a win-win game be assured. In a world where "technonationalism" is seemingly the prevailing mood, international cooperation through option sharing may offer the conceptual breakthrough that can make "technoglobalism" the new reality.

Postscript

The collapse of one communist regime after another in Eastern Europe over the past few years marks an important chapter in world history. Moreover, the dissolution of the Soviet Union into independent republics has generated a substantial impact on the world order. This dissolution implies that the center of gravity among the former Soviet socialist republics will move toward the East, thus they will inevitably become members of the Pacific Rim. Whatever new dimensions this new movement will bring into the Pacific Rim, I would like to believe that only through thoughtful development and careful application of high technologies will it be possible to construct a peaceful new order in the

Pacific Rim. The idea of a new technological trajectory in the Pacific Rim could take an even greater meaning if there was to be a joining of the technological assets—human and physical—between these former Soviet Far East and the Asia-Pacific economies.

Note

1. The parts chosen for color television sets were: integrated circuits (IC); transistor/diode (TR/D); tuner; fly-back transformer (FBT); deflection yoke (Def yoke); cathode-ray tube (CRT); printed board (PB); capacitor (Capa); resistor (Resis); coil/transformer (Coil); and cabinet. For cameras, the parts were: integrated circuits (IC); chip parts (Chip); focusing censor (Focus); flexible printed board (FPB); diaphragm blades (DB); prism; outer cover (Cover); plastic lens (P lens); lens; lens barrel (Barrel); motor; plastic core (Core); spool; sprocket (Spr); flash unit (Flash); and LCD panel (LCD).

References

Abernathy, W. *The Productivity Dilemma*. Baltimore: Johns Hopkins University Press, 1978.

Kiba, T., and Kodama, F. *Measurement and Analysis of the Progress of International Technology Transfer*. Report no. 18. Tokyo: National Institute of Science and Technology (NISTEP), April 1991.

Kodama, F. "Technological Entropy Dynamics: Towards a Taxonomy of National R&D Efforts." In J. Sigurdson (ed.), *Measuring the Dynamics of Technological Change*. London: Pinter Publishers, 1990, pp. 146–67.

———. *Analyzing Japanese High Technologies: The Techno-Paradigm Shift*. London: Pinto Publishers, 1991.

Morino, Y., and Kodama, F. "An Analysis of Space Commercialization in Japan." IAA–90–614. Paper presented to the 41st Congress of the International Astronautical Federation, Dresden, October 6–12, 1990.

Nelson, R. *The Moon and the Ghetto*. New York: W.W. Norton, 1977.

Nelson, R., and Winter, S. *An Evolutionary Theory of Economic Change*. Cambridge, MA: Belknap Press of Harvard University Press, 1982.

New York Times. December 5, 1991.

Rosenberg, N. *Perspectives on Technology*. Cambridge: Cambridge University Press, 1976.

Schumacher, E.F. *Small Is Beautiful*. New York: Harper Collins, 1989. [Japanese trans. by Shiro Saito, Yugakusya: 1976].

Vernon, R. "International Investment and International Trade in the Product Cycle." *Quarterly Journal of Economics 80*, 2 (1966): 190–207.

Part II

The Newly Industrialized Economies

3

Technology and Industrial Development in the Asian NIEs: Past Performance and Future Prospects

David C. O'Connor

Introduction: The Issues Summarized

The Asian newly industrializing economies (NIEs)—Korea, Taiwan, Hong Kong, and Singapore—have been unsurpassed in economic growth over the last few decades. By now, sufficient research has explored the causes of their success to instill caution in all but the most intrepid systematizers against facile generalizations. Few today would attempt to defend the proposition that unfettered market forces lie at the heart of the East Asian success story. While a growing literature (cf. Wade, 1990) points to the importance of the state in "governing the market," state intervention as such is not a major differentiating characteristic of the Asian NIEs.

There is still considerable debate about what role the government has played in the industrial transformations of the Asian NIEs. Neoclassical economists have generally argued that the Asian NIEs come closest of all developing countries to conforming to the Smithian ideal of government—that is, providing a stable currency, protecting property rights, enforcing contracts, defending the country's borders, investing in public health and education, and providing certain basic infrastructure. The neoclassical version of the Asian success story is succinctly stated by Little (1979), who argues in the case of Taiwan that its 1963–73 industrial boom can be explained by four key factors: the creation of a virtual free trade regime for exports, conservative government budgeting, high interest rates, and a free labor market. When confronted with evidence of extensive government intervention in the economy, those most strongly wedded to the "neoclassical parable" are inclined to respond that government "meddling" has slowed down the Asian NIEs—that they could have grown even faster had their governments resisted such temptations. While arguable in specific contexts, such as the Korean government's heavy-industry drive of the late 1970s, as a general proposition it begs the question why, even with such intervention, those economies were able for decades to grow faster than the rest of the world.

On the other side are those who would attribute the Asian NIE success to the strategic visions and effective policies of "strong states."[1] There can be little doubt that competent government and economically informed policy making have contributed to the strong Asian NIE performance. One would not want to generalize too far about the advantages of a "strong state": the Philippine experience should remind us how easily a strong state can run an economy to ruin with the wrong sorts of vision and policies. In the current jargon, "policy failure" can be at least as serious a cause of resource misallocation as "market failure."

While granting that specific policy mistakes have been made in the Asian NIEs, the intriguing question is what has enabled those countries to avert systemic policy failure. In general, policies appear to have been effective in promoting economic growth, though whether the least-cost policies were always chosen is likely to remain a matter of dispute. In this paper we are particularly interested in the role that science and technology (S&T) policies have played in the development of the Asian NIEs. It is not especially enlightening, however, to focus exclusively on S&T policies, since they represent a small part of a large picture that also includes macroeconomic, exchange rate, and trade policies, as well as industrial, labor, and educational policies. While we cannot treat these exhaustively, it is important to bear in mind that the collective weight of these other policies in explaining at least the early industrialization of the Asian NIEs is probably much greater than that of S&T policies per se. Nevertheless, S&T policies pursued from an early date in many of the Asian NIEs have been instrumental in laying the foundation for the difficult transition to a new stage in their industrial development.

The structure of this paper is as follows. The next section touches on the central role that technological change plays in the process of industrialization. The concept of "technological catch-up" provides a useful lens through which to view the experiences of late industrializers. The third section provides a broad overview of the industrialization strategies, policies, and experiences of the four Asian NIEs. Especially noteworthy are the pressures for restructuring which have built up over the course of the last decade, intensifying since 1985.

The fourth section reviews the science and technology (S&T) policy experience of the Asian NIEs, with two objectives: to understand the contextual factors that help explain the direction S&T policy has taken in a particular country and to evaluate the effectiveness of such policy to date. The final section lays out the challenges the Asian NIEs face in the 1990s as they seek to sustain their high rates of per capita income growth. Of particular interest is what those new challenges imply for the future direction of S&T policies.

Technological Catch-up: The Challenge for Late Industrializers

One might legitimately ask why a country needs a science and technology (S&T) policy.[2] Those inclined toward laissez-faire might view such a policy as merely another excuse for the government to interfere where it does not belong. Yet, even neoclassical economic theory has come to recognize a place for government encouragement of science and technology development. The question then is not whether there is a government role but what that role should be. Judging from the Asian NIE experience, the appropriate government role changes as a country moves through different stages in its industrial development, and it also depends on such factors as the prevalent industrial structure. Thus, generalizations about "correct policy" are bound to be conditional.

Broadly conceived, S&T policies can be defined to include all those measures that seek to strengthen a country's capacity to acquire, apply, adapt, and develop technologies. That technology is critical to economic development hardly needs mention in the present day and age. Even neoclassical economists have come belatedly to accept that a large share of growth must be ascribed to technological improvements. Technology can be viewed in the broadest terms as consisting of improved methods of doing things, in particular, of providing useful goods and services. It may permit a more efficient transformation of inputs into outputs, or the production of a wholly new product or range of products. The improvements may be in "hardware"—for example, in capital equipment—but they may also involve organizational innovations or improvements in the quality of human capital.

Traditionally, the literature on technology development has distinguished three "moments" in the life of a technology: invention, innovation, and diffusion. The first refers to the initial discovery of a new and useful product or process; the second consists of the successive incremental improvements on the basic design that bring it to the point of technical feasibility and commercial applicability; the third is the transmission of the innovation throughout the community of potential users/beneficiaries. This highly schematic view is certainly a simplification—and perhaps even a distortion—of how technological change occurs in practice, since it downplays possible feedback effects from diffusion to innovation and from both to invention.

For our discussion, it is useful to begin with the assertion that the Asian NIEs, in the first few decades of their industrial development, were concerned principally with accelerating the diffusion process. They played a relatively minor role in either invention or innovation. The challenge they faced was one of "catching up" with the technology leaders, for the most part the OECD countries. New process and product technologies were first introduced in the latter countries, then more or less quickly found their way into the hands of those lagging behind the technological frontier. Shortening the diffusion lag was the primary objective of early Asian NIE technology policy.

Whether as a result of explicit policy or of structural features of their economies, the evidence demonstrates that NIEs have been quite effective in catching up technologically, although in many areas they remain behind the frontier. A study by Dollar (1991) points to technological catch-up in the case of Korea. Comparing total factor productivity (TFP) growth in Korea and Germany, Dollar finds that, between 1966 and 1978, TFP in the former converged most rapidly to that in the latter in those industries where Korea's relative TFP was initially low. In other words, the lower relative TFP, the more an industry stands to gain by borrowing disembodied technology from a more advanced foreign counterpart. Dowrick and Gemmell (1991) attempt a more general test of the "catch-up hypothesis" for a large sample of countries, divided between high-income (mostly OECD) countries (the leaders) and middle-income countries (the followers). They find strong convergence in industrial total factor productivity levels between the two country "clubs," suggesting that catch-up is occurring. At the same time, evidence for a third "club" of the poorest countries suggests that they are falling further behind the industrial technology leaders. This suggests that not all countries can benefit equally from technology spillovers from more advanced countries. For a country to be able to catch up, Dowrick and Gemmell argue, it needs first to cross a "structural poverty threshold"—to be able to generate savings and investment and perhaps to moderate population growth. Several of the Asian NIEs began their industrialization drives with low savings/income ratios. In 1965, for example, in Korea gross domestic savings represented only 8 percent of GDP and in Singapore only 10 percent (World Bank, 1991); in Taiwan gross national savings constituted only 15 percent of GNP in 1962 (Council for Economic Planning and Development, 1990). The three countries adopted different approaches to overcome this low savings barrier—from foreign borrowing to domestic financial liberalization to heavy government taxation of income. In all four Asian NIEs, by 1989 savings constituted well over 30 percent of income.

Other structural factors can also be important preconditions for successful technological catch-up. For example, it helps if domestic consumption patterns create demands for those products and production processes in which technological advance is rapid. For example, if incomes are too low to generate a sizable demand for automobiles or consumer appliances, a country may not be able to support their domestic manufacture; in such a case there is no basis to benefit from technological advances in car or appliance manufacture in leading countries.

Two other critical thresholds need to be crossed for a country to sustain improvements in total factor productivity. The first is the establishment of an efficient physical infrastructure; the second is the creation of a supply of high-quality human capital. The latter is absolutely essential to foster technological learning and rapid absorption of imported technologies. The Asian NIEs placed heavy emphasis from an early date on investments in human capital formation.

Korea's school enrollment rates increased dramatically. In 1965 the secondary enrollment rate was 35 percent and the tertiary rate only 6 percent; by 1988 the former had risen to 87 percent and the latter to 37 percent (World Bank, 1991). In the case of Taiwan, the proportion of the population above the age of six with a tertiary education rose from only 2.3 percent in 1965 to over 10 percent by 1989; the proportion with a secondary education rose from 15.2 percent to 45 percent (Council for Economic Planning and Development, 1990).

It is worth emphasizing that, while we have referred to structural preconditions for (or impediments to) technological intervention (e.g., financial policy reforms to encourage savings, investments in education, etc.), these factors may be necessary, but not sufficient to promote technological upgrading.

The role of trade policy in promoting export industries in the Asian NIEs has been extensively noted. Apart from the familiar argument about relieving the external financing constraint, there is another sense in which exports have mattered a good deal to the Asian NIEs. Once they began to put their economies on an export footing, the pressures to catch up technologically intensified. For, as Baumol (1986) notes, with an increasing export/GNP ratio, sustaining economic growth comes to depend increasingly on maintaining international competitiveness. Put differently, the social opportunity costs of failing to catch up (or keep up) technologically rise the more trade-dependent an economy becomes. As the Asian NIEs have expanded manufactured exports, a growing range of their industries has come to confront industrialized country competitors head-on in world markets. Thus, if an industry in an OECD country benefits from a significant innovation, the competing industry in an Asian NIE comes under strong pressure to gain access to the innovation, or an imitation or substitute, as quickly as possible so as not to lose market share. Catch-up becomes imperative for the survival of the firm and the growth of the economy.

The Asian NIEs: Growth and Structural Transformation in Manufacturing

The economic success of the Asian NIEs has understandably engendered admiration and the desire for emulation in other developing countries. No single factor can explain their phenomenal economic performance. The economies and polities of the Asian NIEs need to be seen as dynamic, evolving systems that have managed to combine a variety of institutions, policies, and practices in ways that reinforce the competitiveness of their industrial sectors, thereby enabling them to challenge the dominance of OECD countries in a growing range of manufactures.

The Beginnings of Industrial Development in the Asian NIEs

Development Strategy and Policy Framework

Those who would attribute the success of the Asian NIEs to their high degree of openness to world markets tend to gloss over the early years of their industrial development. With the exception of Hong Kong, the others passed through a period of import-substituting industrialization (ISI) before embarking on their export-oriented growth paths. The early impetus to Hong Kong's industrial development arose from the decline of the entrepot trade with the change of government on the mainland in 1949 and the U.N. embargo of China resulting from the Korean war, combined with the large influx of entrepreneurial talent, capital, and skilled labor to the British colony (Chen, 1989). The trade regime was already very liberal and the colonial government did little to protect nascent industries from import competition. Given the small size of Hong Kong's domestic market, exports were almost essential to the survival of most manufacturing enterprises from the very beginning. Moreover, the possibility of obtaining imported inputs at world prices made for low manufacturing costs.

During the colonial era, Singapore emerged as a regional base for large international companies engaged in the extraction of natural resources from neighboring Malaysia and Indonesia. It developed early on a strong infrastructure to serve financial and commercial transactions, and this has continued to be a major attraction for multinational corporations in the service sector. Despite its very small domestic market, Singapore pursued an import-substitution strategy for the better part of a decade after self-government was granted in 1959. Following separation from Malaysia in 1965, import restrictions continued to be imposed for a couple of years on the expectation that a common market would soon be formed between the two countries. When that failed to materialize, the Singaporean government looked to export markets to promote its industries. Corporate income tax rates were drastically cut with the Economic Expansion Incentives Act of 1967. Foreign direct investment was actively encouraged (Lim and Pang, 1991).

Korea had pursued an import-substitution strategy following the Korean war, which resulted in the highest growth rates in the world of both light and heavy industry from 1953 to 1958. Nevertheless, by the end of the decade Korea still faced severe balance-of-payment problems. With first-phase import substitution having run its course, the government had to choose between pursuing the more difficult second phase or promoting manufactured exports. Park Chung-Hee, the president at the time, decided to pursue the latter strategy. In 1961, the won was devalued against the U.S. dollar, from 62.5 to 130 won/dollar; a further devaluation from 130 to 265 won/dollar occurred in 1964. Especially following the second devaluation, import restrictions were gradually liberalized and export incentives introduced. Those incentives included tariff and tax concessions on raw material imports by exporting firms, accelerated depreciation, and export credit subsidies. Export targets were set for particular firms or industries, with access to incentives made contingent in many cases on meeting the targets. In some cases, if meeting export targets lowered profitability on export sales, the government provided protection in the domestic market to compensate.

From 1951 to 1957, the Taiwan government also pursued strict import-substitution policies. Import controls were accompanied by a multiple exchange rate system. The policies clearly had an effect: manufacturing output doubled during this period. Over the period from 1955 to 1960, import substitution is estimated to have contributed as much as one-third to manufacturing sector growth. Taiwan's import substitution was possibly even more extensive than Korea's (Wade, 1990). As early as 1955 the government offered rebates on raw material import duties and certain other taxes for exported products. From 1958 to 1960, a number of policy changes were introduced that moved manufacturing toward greater export orientation. The multiple exchange system was gradually collapsed into a single rate; the official rate of the New Taiwan dollar was devalued from 24.8 to 36.4/U.S. in 1958, then to 40.0/U.S. in 1961. Commodity import quotas were abolished and rates of nominal protection generally reduced, with the steepest reductions on export-competing products. The government also offered various export incentives, including the establishment of three export-processing (or free trade) zones—in Kaohsiung, Nantze, and Taichung—subsidized by credit to exporters, export insurance, and promotion by government organizations (Chen, 1989).

Industrial Structure in the Early Growth Phase

In all the Asian NIEs, labor-intensive light manufacturing was an important feature of early industrial growth. For three of the four (Singapore was an exception), this meant that the textile and clothing industries played a predominant role. In Hong Kong, the immigration of textile entrepreneurs from Shanghai put the textile and clothing industries on a firm foundation from an early date. Indeed, textile and clothing exports were probably the major stimulus to economic growth following the decline in entrepot trade with the mainland. In 1952, textiles and clothing accounted for 27 percent of Hong Kong's total merchandise exports; by 1958 they accounted for 40 percent of exports and by 1962 43 percent, remaining in that neighborhood for the next decade and a half (Census and Statistics Department, Hong Kong, 1969, 1989).

In Singapore, the industrial structure at the onset of rapid industrialization reflected to a large degree its dual function as processing center for raw materials coming from Malaysia and Indonesia and as regional base for international trading and finance companies. In 1961, for example, food and beverage processing accounted for almost 30 percent of industrial value added (excluding rubber processing, which contributed half as much again). Printing and publishing, to support the large service sector, was also a major contributor to manufacturing value added. In 1967, the combined share of food, beverages, and tobacco represented 24 percent of industrial value added; petroleum refining had emerged in the meantime as a major industrial activity, contributing 15 percent of industrial value added by 1967; printing and publishing remained important, while other sectors that had grown significantly included timber processing and fabricated metal products (Department of Statistics, Singapore, 1983). Singapore also developed a sizable shipbuilding and repair industry (in which the state sector took a large stake), which (combined with oil rig construction) contributed 14.6 percent of industrial value added in 1970.

Taiwan's manufacturing sector experienced strong growth as early as the 1950s, with private sector manufacturing output rising an average of 17.3 percent a year from 1953 to 1960. Food processing was the fastest-growing sector, accounting for one-fourth of manufacturing sector growth from 1954 to 1961 (Kuo, Ranis, and Fei, 1981). From an early date, the state played an important role in manufacturing, especially in such heavy industries as chemicals, steel, and shipbuilding. In effect, public sector investment was used as a form of industrial targeting.

In the 1960s, manufacturing growth accelerated significantly. Between 1961 and 1968 the average annual growth of private sector manufacturing production was 23.2 percent. In the public sector, growth averaged only 9.5 percent, so over the course of the 1960s the relative importance of the public sector in manufacturing declined steeply, from 39 percent to 23 percent of production value (Executive Yuan, 1969). Exports contributed significantly to manufacturing sector growth. Exports as a share of GNP rose from 11.3 percent in 1960 to 29.7 percent in 1970; at the same time, manufactured exports rose as a share of the total from 28.2 percent to 76.7 percent (Mutoh et al., 1986). The major growth sectors over this decade (in descending order) were electrical and electronics products, clothing, textiles, and transport equipment. In the electronics industry, production of transistor radios exploded, from 487,000 in 1964 to over 4 million by 1968, while television production rose from only 31,000 units in 1964 to 650,200 units by 1968 and almost 950,000 units by 1969. During this period, Taiwan's production of machinery used in key manufacturing sectors also began to accelerate. For example, after 1966, production of sewing machines rose steeply, increasing from 124,591 units in that year to 519,277 units by 1969 (Executive Yuan, 1970).

In most of the export-oriented industries that emerged during this decade, the average size of enterprise was small. As of 1971 there were some 44,054 manufacturing establishments in Taiwan, 68 percent of which employed fewer than twenty workers, with another 23 percent employing up to fifty workers. Small firms predominated in such sectors as textiles, clothing, leather goods, wood and bamboo products, basic metals, metal products, and machinery (Myers, 1986).

In Korea, the manufacturing sector's contribution to GNP doubled (from 6 to 12 percent) between 1953 and 1962. Growth during this phase was based largely on import substitution, with exports increasing only marginally as a share of GNP (from 1 to 2 percent) (Hong, 1979). During the 1960s the manufacturing sector grew rapidly, especially after 1965. From 1965 to 1969, it registered average growth of 21.6 percent a year in real terms (Kwack 1986). Manufacturing's contribution to GNP increased to one-fourth by 1972, while exports as a share of

GNP increased to 18 percent. Still, this export share is low by present standards and it should be borne in mind that import substitution continued to contribute significantly to Korea's manufacturing sector growth during much of the 1960s.

In the early 1960s, processed food represented Korea's single most important manufactured export (accounting for 36 percent of the total in 1961). Textiles quickly came to surpass food and by 1965 represented 41 percent of all manufactured exports. Preferential loans, tax and tariff exemptions, and other forms of government support helped the Korean textile industry compete in world markets against Japan which, despite higher wages, was still highly competitive during this period. Other labor-intensive industries that expanded rapidly during the 1960s include clothing, footwear, electrical/electronics machinery, and wigs and false beards. The iron and steel industry also began its ascent during the latter half of the 1960s, with heavy public sector involvement (Hasan, 1976).

It is common knowledge that the industrial structure on which Korea's export drive was built differed dramatically from that in Taiwan. While earlier data are not available, 1977 concentration ratios for the two economies paint a clear picture. While in Taiwan the 100 largest companies accounted for 22 percent of total shipments, in Korea the top 100 accounted for 45 percent (Lee *et al.*, 1986). The large, diversified *chaebol* (Korean conglomerates) have excelled in standardized mass production; they have also tended toward a higher degree of vertical integration than is the case with the average Taiwan firm. The more successful Taiwan exporters have grown rapidly but the size discrepancy between them and the *chaebol* persists: for example, in 1985, Tatung, Taiwan's largest electronics producer, had a capitalization only one-tenth that of Goldstar, Korea's second largest (Schive, 1990).

The Acceleration of Export Manufacturing in the 1970s

The strategy and policy shifts that took place in the Asian NIEs in the 1960s had clearly begun to bear fruit by the 1970s. From 1971 to 1980, GDP rose in those economies an average of 9.2 percent a year; value added in industry grew during the same period by 14.2 percent a year in Korea, 12.8 percent a year in Taiwan, and 9.8 percent a year in Singapore (Asian Development Bank, 1991). These growth rates look especially impressive when one considers that the world economy was beset by two oil price shocks during the decade, and the Asian NIEs are all heavily dependent on imported oil.

Hong Kong's industrial structure underwent considerable change during this decade. While in absolute terms the textile and clothing sectors continued to grow, their relative importance declined. In 1973 those two sectors contributed 48 percent to manufacturing census value added; by 1978 their contribution had declined to 42 percent. (At the same time, a major shift occurred in the relative contributions of textiles and clothing, the former shrinking from 28 percent to 16 percent while the latter grew from 20 percent to 26 percent. This was probably attributable in large part to the incentive provided by the physical quota restrictions under the Multi-Fibre Arrangement to maximize value added to unit exports.) The industrial sectors that gained most during this decade included electronics and electrical products (whose share of MVA rose from 9 percent in 1973 to 12 percent in 1978) and metal, products, and machinery (which increased from 15 to 17 percent of MVA) (Census and Statistics Department, Hong Kong, 1981).

The changes in Hong Kong's industrial structure are reflected in manufactured exports. Textiles and clothing remained the most important export items throughout the decade, but their share in total domestic exports peaked in 1975 (at 54 percent), then declined to 41.8 percent by 1981 (Lin and Ho, 1984). Meanwhile, two categories of manufactures, electrical/electronic equipment and precision instruments, increased their export shares significantly. In the former case, exports rose from 11.2 percent of domestic exports in 1971 to 17.57 percent by 1981; in the latter case, from 1.99 percent to 10.26 percent. The overwhelming share of precision instrument exports is accounted for by watches and clocks. Plastic toys and dolls also represented a large export item during the decade, but the share declined slightly, from 8.6 percent in 1971 to 8.1 percent in 1981.

The geographic pattern of exports also shifted during the decade of the 1970s. The shares of domestic exports accounted for by North America and Western Europe both declined slightly: in the former case from 43.5 percent in 1972 to 39.2 percent in 1981; in the latter case from 33.4 percent to 29.5 percent. Japan's share increased only marginally, from 3.1 to 3.7 percent. The most dramatic increase occurred in the portion destined for the rest of Asia, China accounting for the lion's share. Hong Kong's domestic exports to China represented only 0.14 percent of the total in 1972; by 1981 they had risen to 3.6 percent, with almost all the increase occurring after the initiation of China's "open door" policy in 1979 (Census and Statistics Department, Hong Kong, 1982).

Singapore's industrial economy underwent a rapid transformation beginning in the late 1960s. From one heavily dependent on primary commodity processing, it became increasingly oriented toward labor-intensive assembly activities, notably electronics. Radios, televisions, semiconductors, and other electronics goods production rose dramatically, from 3.4 percent of industrial value added in 1967 to 11.6 percent in 1970. By 1975 the contribution of electronics/electrical machinery to industrial value added had reached 16.2 percent and by 1980 it stood at almost 24 percent. Another sector that expanded significantly over the decade of the 1970s was nonelectrical machinery (more than doubling its contribution to industrial value added, from 4 percent in 1971 to 8.7 percent in 1980). Unlike the other three Asian NIEs, Singapore never came to depend heavily on textiles and clothing. In 1970 the two sectors combined contributed only 4.3 percent to industrial value added; in 1975 the share was only marginally higher (5.0 percent) and it remained the same in 1980 (Department of Statistics, Singapore, 1983).

Singapore's economic growth over this decade was clearly driven by exports, which rose an average 30 percent a year from 1970 to 1980. Electrical and electronics products led the export growth, with a 42 percent annual rate of increase. By 1980 electronics/electrical exports accounted for 17 percent of total exports (30.8 percent of exports excluding petroleum products). The market orientation of Singapore's industrial exports also changed somewhat during the decade of the 1970s, with the importance of the European market declining slightly and that of the North American market increasing significantly. In 1970, Western Europe absorbed 15 percent of Singapore's exports and North America 11.8 percent. By 1980 the Western European share of Singaporean exports was only 14.4 percent while the North American share had risen to 15.6 percent. Singapore's exports to Northeast Asia had also increased over the decade, from 20 to 25 percent of total exports, with the other three NIEs and China accounting for all of the increase (Japan's share actually declined very slightly). Perhaps most significant was the steep decline in the share of Singapore's exports bound for its ASEAN neighbors, from 38.1 percent in 1970 to only 17 percent in 1980 (Department of Statistics, Singapore, 1983). As its exports became more technology-intensive, the OECD and Asian NIE markets absorbed a growing share.

During the 1970s Taiwan began to experience a shift in the structure of its manufacturing industries away from unskilled labor-intensive ones like textiles and clothing in the direction of more skill- and capital-intensive ones. This decade was one in which a sustained export drive was accompanied by a concerted effort at secondary import substitution. While textile production grew strongly (at an average rate of 26.4 percent per year) from 1969 to 1973, its growth was matched by chemicals and rubber products and vastly exceeded by electrical/electronics machinery (43.5 percent a year growth). Much of the upstream chemical industry growth was aimed at supplying synthetic fibers and yarns to the textile sector (Schive, 1990). (Import substitution in this sector was more complete in Taiwan than in Korea.) By the latter half of the decade, the growth of the textile sector had slowed markedly, to only 8.3 percent a year between 1976 and 1980. While growth in other sectors also slowed, the leading growth sectors during this period were chemicals (18.4 percent per annum), electrical/electronic machinery (17.6 percent per annum), and basic metals (16.3 percent per annum). By 1978, chemicals, petrochemicals, and rubber products accounted for 27 percent of industrial value added. Feedstocks for the plastics industry became readily available, supporting a variety of plastics end-user industries, from toys to electronics. The electrical/electronics sector was rapidly closing in on the leading export position of textile products; by the end of the decade the former's exports were roughly two-thirds of the latter's, up from only 40 percent at the beginning.

Korea experienced a similar sort of industrial restructuring to Taiwan's during the 1970s. In particular, its industrial mix became more heavily weighted toward capital- and skill-intensive industries. The heavy and chemical industry group (which includes consumer electronics) accounted for a rising share of both manufacturing output and merchandise exports during the 1970s. To a significant degree this was the result of explicit government policy. In June 1973 the government targeted six industries for promotion: steel, petrochemicals, nonferrous metals, machinery, shipbuilding, and electronics. Most are secondary import-substituting industries, but significantly by the end of the decade several had also emerged as competitive export industries. The promotion of these heavy industries was in part motivated by an "export pessimism" which questioned the sustainability of an export drive based on labor-intensive manufactures, given rapidly increasing wage rates in the early 1970s (Kim, 1991) and growing protectionism of OECD countries against labor-intensive developing country exports such as textiles and clothing.

From 40.5 percent in 1971, the contribution of the heavy and chemical industries to manufacturing output rose to 56.3 percent by 1980; their contribution to merchandise exports rose over the same period from 13.7 percent to 39.9 percent. Within this industrial sector, the chemical industry share of output and exports declined somewhat over the decade while the export share of basic metals (notably iron and steel) rose significantly (from 26.5 percent to 36.6 percent of total merchandise exports) (Amsden, 1989). The growth of the machinery industry lessened Korea's dependence on imported capital goods: from 29.7 percent in 1970 the import share fell to 23.0 percent by 1980 (Schive, 1990, p. 273). Even with the rapid growth in heavy industry, however, by the end of the decade textiles and clothing sill represented by far the largest export category.

Structural Changes in Asian NIE Manufacturing from the 1980s

The first half of the 1980s did not bring major changes to the growth patterns of the Asian NIEs. Their export drives continued. Korea raised its share of exports in GDP from 27.3 percent in 1979 to 37.5 percent in 1984; Taiwan raised its export/GDP ratio by 4.1 percentage points over the same period. (In the other two Asian NIEs the shares were already very high due to their entrepot functions.) The result of the sustained export boom was that, by 1984, Korea's trade account was roughly in balance and Taiwan had a trade surplus equal to 11.6 percent of GDP (Bradford, 1990). By 1985, Hong Kong was also enjoying a small merchandise trade surplus (Census and Statistics Department, Hong Kong, 1989). While Singapore's trade account remained in deficit, by 1985 its current account was virtually balanced (IMF, 1990).

One of the most noteworthy features of the first half of the decade is the growing prominence of the electronics industry. While in Singapore it had already assumed the role of leading manufacturing sector during the 1970s, in Taiwan it overtook textiles and clothing as leading exporter during the early 1980s, while in Korea it quickly narrowed the gap. In 1984, Taiwan's exports of electrical/electronics machinery reached U.S.$6.6 billion, exceeding for the first time textile exports (at U.S.$6.1 billion) (Council for Economic Planning and Development, Taiwan, 1988). In Korea, whereas in 1981 electronics/electrical exports were only 38 percent as large as textile and clothing exports, by 1985 they were two-thirds as large (Economic Planning Board, 1986). In Hong Kong, textiles and clothing still represented by far the largest export sector at mid-decade, with exports twice as large as those of electronics/electrical products. Electronics nevertheless was the second-largest export sector.

When electronics first took root in the Asian NIEs, it was still a semiskilled labor-intensive industry. Undoubtedly the low labor costs in those countries during the 1960s and 1970s contributed to their competitiveness. Over time, and especially beginning in the early 1980s, the skill and capital intensities of the industry have increased. Even so, the Asian NIEs generally strengthened their competitive positions in electronics during this period. As the importance of skilled engineering and technical labor has increased relative to semiskilled production labor, the relative abundance of engineers and technicians in the Asian NIEs has proven a critical advantage. For example, Korea's supply of R&D scientists and engineers per million population stood at over 1,100 in 1985, on a par with Italy's and well ahead of Spain and Portugal (UNESCO, 1989). Increasing automation of the industry has raised capital intensity significantly, but capital has become far more readily available in the Asian NIEs during the 1980s than it was during previous decades. It is no longer a relatively scarce factor.

For a variety of reasons, pressures for restructuring of the Asian NIEs' industrial sectors were mounting by the mid-1980s. First, their export success was creating widening trade surpluses in both Korea and Taiwan, especially vis-à-vis the United States and the European Economic Community (EEC). This was beginning to cause trade frictions and pressures on those countries to revalue their currencies. Second, labor shortages were worsening, causing real wage increases to outstrip productivity gains in three of the four economies. In Taiwan, real wages rose an average 6.6 percent a year between 1979 and 1984 while productivity rose only 4.8 percent a year; in Korea the corresponding increases were 4.1 percent and 3.9 percent; in Singapore 6.5 percent and 4.6 percent (OECD, 1988).[3] Third, rapid growth over the previous few decades had also raised other domestic costs, especially real estate prices, making expansion of space-intensive increasingly difficult.

The 1985 Plaza Accord of the G–7 countries marked a turning point for the Asian NIE economies. The main outcome of the accord was a realignment of the major world trading currencies, with the Japanese yen revalued steeply against the U.S. dollar (from 238.5 yen/U.S. dollar in 1985 to 144.6 yen/dollar by 1987). The immediate effect on the Asian NIEs was generally positive in that their exports gained in competitiveness vis-à-vis Japanese exports in the U.S. market. Yet, the positive effects were smaller and shorter-lived than the Asian NIEs might have liked. Smaller because the revaluation of the yen dramatized their own dependence on Japanese intermediate products for their manufacturing sectors. Their component imports became more expensive, partially offsetting the competitive gains of a relatively cheaper currency. Shorter-lived because the revaluation of the yen was merely the prelude to the revaluation of their own currencies against the U.S. dollar. The Korean won went from 881.5 to the dollar in 1987 to 671.5 to the dollar by 1989. The New Taiwan dollar rose from 39.9 to the U.S. dollar at end–1985 to 26.2 to the U.S. dollar at end–1989. The Singapore dollar climbed from 2.2 to the U.S. dollar in 1985 to 1.95 to the U.S. dollar in 1989.

Meanwhile, Japanese manufacturers responded quickly and decisively to their own reduced competitiveness by extensive restructuring. This involved a combination of greater automation of domestic production and the large-scale transfer of low-value-added, labor-intensive product lines to lower-wage countries, especially in Southeast Asia. Export manufacturers in the Asian NIEs found themselves challenged for market share in low-end markets that they had considered secure from competition by high-cost Japan-based manufacturers. Thus began the massive outflow of investment from the Asian NIEs to the ASEAN countries (and China) which, combined with the influx of Japanese investment, launched the latter countries on their current growth trajectories.

A Review of Science and Technology Policies in the Asian NIEs

Science and technology policy is just one of a number of "levers" that governments may use to try to raise an economy's productivity. What sort of policy is most adequate to this task depends in part on how far behind the technological frontier a country is at a given time. In the early days, the Asian NIEs lacked the capacity to catch up technologically across a broad front. While governments invested in human capital formation, infrastructure development, and other preconditions for a broader advance, they selectively promoted the development of "strategic" technologies and industries. This "mission-oriented" approach (Ergas, 1987) has been most evident in Korea and Taiwan. It involves identifying critical technological bottlenecks and targeting R&D resources at overcoming them. In some cases the technologies can be developed locally, but in most cases the preferred approach—to save time and money—has been to study, then imitate or adapt imported technologies.

As the industrial and technological capabilities of the Asian NIEs have evolved, government R&D targeting has diminished in relative importance. Private sector resources devoted to R&D have increased substantially and technological catch-up is proceeding along a much broader front than in the past. In Taiwan, for example, private domestic R&D expenditures increased more than fourfold (in current dollar terms) between 1980 and 1988 (Council for Economic Planning and Development, 1990). Nevertheless, even as the Asian NIEs draw nearer the technological frontier, OECD industries continue to forge ahead. Moreover, as competition intensifies between leaders and ever closer followers, the former have sought to tighten their control over critical technologies that confer on them temporary competitive advantages and innovation rents. The Asian NIEs thus find themselves confronted with barriers to technology acquisition in a number of leading technologies.

In electronics, for example, Korean and Taiwanese firms have been attempting to move from low-end segments of the consumer and computer markets into more differentiated and technologically sophisticated products. This has brought them into more direct competition with U.S. and especially Japanese firms. The latter have maintained fairly tight control over several key component technologies, such as ink-jet print heads, laser printer engines, liquid crystal displays (LCDs), and charge-coupled devices (CCDs) for use in camcorders. In most cases oligopolistic control is exercised by a few Japanese firms, who can charge noncompetitive prices not only to Asian NIE competitors but even to other Japanese firms.[4] The difference is that the Asian NIE firms are less able to pass on higher component costs to customers, since they are in a weaker position to trade on their brand names.

The concern that major export industries could be held hostage to Japanese or other foreign component suppliers has catalyzed Asian NIE governments and firms into action. In Korea, individual companies have initiated R&D projects to develop subsystems of products central to their competitive strategies. In 1984, for example, Goldstar began developing its own laser printer engine, consulting Japanese firms for engineering know-how on two key components, the laser scanning unit and the drum. After several years it finally announced a workable product in 1989. More recently, Taiwan's Mechanical Industry Research Laboratories (MIRL), a division of the government-sponsored Industrial Technology Research Institute (ITRI), announced the development of its own laser printer. The Electronics Research and Service Organization (ERSO), also part of ITRI, is developing liquid crystal display (LCD) technology in an effort to lessen the local personal computer industry's dependence on Japan for this critical component of laptop computers.

Korea's S&T Policy

Korea's first five-year plan for the promotion of science and technology was formulated in the early 1960s; then, in close succession the government founded the Korea Institute of Science and Technology (KIST) in 1966 and the Ministry of Science and Technology (MOST) in 1968. As Lee (1991) notes, this represented an exceptional commitment to S&T development on the part of a country whose per capita income was only around U.S.$100 at the time. KIST was established as a quasi-university with government financial support yet with relative autonomy from bureaucratic influences. While KIST was interdisciplinary, in the 1970s it spun off a second generation of more specialized research and development (R&D) centers, in areas like electronics and telecommunications, chemistry, shipbuilding, and mechanics. This was followed in the 1980s by a third generation of R&D organizations, this time in-house units set up by private sector enterprises. Currently, some 1,000 firms are undertaking their own R&D (Lee, 1991).

Prior to the 1980s, the government still represented the dominant force in R&D. Over the decade of the 1980s the balance steadily shifted toward private-sector R&D. From 59 percent in 1981, government's share of R&D expenditures declined to only 25 percent by 1989. Meanwhile, overall R&D expenditures increased almost tenfold and their share in GNP rose from 0.64 percent to 1.92 percent. This shift toward private sector R&D reflects the heavy investments required to establish strong competitive positions in R&D-intensive industries such as semiconductors, computers, telecommunications, and fine chemicals. While Korean firms have made enormous strides in these fields, their hard-won international market shares are by no means secure. Escalating cost pressures and currency appreciation in the late 1980s have highlighted the continued vulnerability of Korean industry. Dependence on imports of critical components and sophisticated capital equipment remains high, as the deteriorating trade balance attests.

At least as important an influence on Korea's early industrial development as formal S&T policies were policies regarding foreign direct investment (FDI), foreign licensing, and other types of regulations impacting on technology imports. As Amsden (1989) argues, Korea's industrialization was based largely on borrowing and learning from the use of foreign technologies. The Korean government opted for a strategy that deemphasized FDI and relied instead on extensive technology licensing (from 1962 to 1971 there were 318 approved technology-licensing agreements, two-thirds with Japan—Amsden, 1989, p. 233) and temporary hiring of foreign technical assistance (epitomized by the "moonlighting" Japanese engineer who spends his weekends sharing secrets in Seoul). The country still needed to import large quantities of capital equipment, but chose to rely principally on foreign loans rather than on equity investment.[5] Korean firms insisted on thorough training and skills transfer by foreign capital goods suppliers, a large proportion of whom were Japanese. Such a strategy could only succeed with a well-educated cadre of engineers and technicians able to master the imported technology and know-how in a short time frame.

The approach to technology acquisition in Korea differed markedly across industrial branches during the early catch-up phase. Data on labor productivity in Korea and Germany from 1966 to 1978 point clearly to rapid convergence in productivity levels (Dollar, 1991). The source of labor productivity convergence differs by sector, however: in the case of heavy industries, capital deepening lies behind it, while in the case of light industries, total factor productivity convergence is the main explanation. In other words, Korean heavy industry relied on importing technology already embodied in capital equipment, which significantly raised the capital–labor ratio and boosted labor productivity. In contrast, light manufacturers relied much more extensively on disembodied technology imports in the form of licensing and hiring of technical assistance. Improvements in the quality and skill level of the labor force no doubt also contributed to boosting labor productivity. Another important factor is that, as the economy became more export-oriented over this period, small firms were able to grow rapidly on the basis of a vastly expanded market and in the process were able to reap economies of scale. As firms reorganized to cope with the need to produce on a larger scale, there was almost certainly some borrowing of organizational know-how from industrialized countries with longer mass production traditions.

Taiwan's S&T Policy

Like its Korean counterpart, the Taiwan government has played an important role in shaping the country's industrial and technological capabilities. For the most part, Taiwan firms have not enjoyed the same degree of import protection as in Korea, in part perhaps because the smaller domestic market could not be expected to play as effective a role in helping firms realize scale and learning economies. Taiwan's industrial structure has also evolved along very different lines from Korea's; partly as a result of government's high real interest rate policy, private industrial enterprises have tended to be smaller and more labor-intensive than in Korea. The diffuse industrial structure and small average firm size deterred entry by private entrepreneurs into capital-intensive industrial sectors such as petrochemicals and steel. In the case of petrochemicals, Chu (1991) observes that "the government itself undertook . . . the most capital-intensive part of the operation, i.e., naphtha cracking, at a time when private capital was still unable to do it alone."

Beyond investing in heavy industry, however, the Taiwan government's role in industrial development has generally been more indirect. In the 1960s the government established several research and service organizations to promote technological upgrading in industry. Significantly, government-sponsored R&D institutions in Taiwan have always had a strong "service" orientation, with the result that their activities have seldom lost touch with industry needs. In 1963 the Metal Industries Development Center was founded to demonstrate improved production and quality control methods in the metal-working sector. In 1965 the China Data Processing Center was established to promote the introduction of computers into industry. Other research institutes established during the 1960s covered chemicals, mining, energy, glass, textiles, and food processing (Wade, 1988).

Then, in 1973, the government set up the multidisciplinary Industrial Technology Research Institute (ITRI), whose principal function is to undertake applied R&D. Presently, 60 percent of operating funds still come from the government, though there is a growing emphasis on private contractual research. Once technologies are developed to the precommercial stage, they are normally licensed at relatively low fees to private firms. Besides spawning technologies, ITRI has in many instances spawned the firms that commercialize them, as ITRI scientists and engineers strike out to become entrepreneurs. In some cases, as with the semiconductor wafer fabrication industry, ITRI as an institution may take an equity stake in a new venture. This "incubator" function is by no means the least important one ITRI performs.

There are six laboratories and three research centers within ITRI, employing a total of 4,000 people, 60 percent of whom hold university degrees in science and engineering. The Mechanical Industry Research Laboratory (MIRL) was mentioned above. Union Chemical Laboratories (UCL) is another division; it employs some 600 people on a wide range of research projects, including a small team studying alternatives to chlorofluorocarbon (CFC)-based technologies for use in refrigeration and air conditioning, solvent cleaning, and foam blowing (O'Connor, 1991). Others include: The Energy and Mining Research/Service Organization, which has done work in solar energy and pollution control technologies, among others; Materials Research Laboratories, which does research in casting, forging, and powder metallurgy, high-polymer and composite materials, second-generation semiconductor materials, and fine ceramics; Electro-Optics and Peripherals Development Center, which has developed prototypes of hard disk drives and designed a laser printer engine and a servo system for optical disk drives (Dahlman and Sananikone, 1990). Perhaps the best-known and certainly one of the most important divisions of ITRI is the Electronics Research and Service Organization (ERSO) (mentioned above), which has been instrumental in the development of several key technologies used by the local electronics industry. One of its earliest endeavors was the refinement of the semiconductor process technology known as C-MOS (complementary metal oxide-on-silicon), which has become the technology of choice for most integrated circuits (IC) used in personal computers. ERSO was also responsible for developing a local version of the basic input-output system (BIOS) for an IBM PC AT-compatible computer. In 1982 the BIOS was licensed to several local firms that have since become leading personal computer export manufacturers. Finally, ERSO has developed a number of communications ICs and chipsets for use in personal computers, and it is currently developing a RISC (reduced instruction set computing) chipset for use in a leading make of computer workstation.

In Taiwan more so than in Korea, the government continues to perform the critical function of developing key generic technologies, reflecting the limited capacity of small and medium enterprises in Taiwan to cross the steep R&D thresholds involved in much "high technology" research. Given economies of scale and scope in R&D, small firms may get higher returns to their R&D investments if they rely on centralized laboratories like those at ITRI to undertake their R&D on contract rather than investing in their own in-house R&D. During the 1980s, there was no clear-cut trend in Taiwan, as there was in Korea, toward the private sector assuming a growing share of the R&D burden. The government still accounted for 57 percent of R&D spending in 1988, while private domestic firms accounted for 43 percent (Council for Economic Planning and Development, 1990).

Perhaps because government industrial R&D still plays such a prominent role in Taiwan, with the democratic transition there has been a growing demand for accountability on the part of government-supported research institutions such as ITRI. A major study is in progress to evaluate the effectiveness of ITRI's research programs. Industry has also become more active in trying to shape ITRI's research agenda. For example, ERSO has recently had to address concerns that its semiconductor R&D program is not sufficiently responsive to rapidly evolving technology needs in a highly competitive industry.

S&T Policy in Singapore and Hong Kong

Singapore and Hong Kong have adopted quite different technology policy approaches from Korea and Taiwan. In Singapore, the government has played a role in S&T planning, but its direct role in supporting R&D has been far more limited. Its main strategy has been to create conditions conducive to investment in R&D by international high-technology firms. The major element of this strategy has been heavy investment in scientific and technical education and training. Unlike Hong Kong and more like Korea and Taiwan, the Singaporean government has on occasion provided generous financial and fiscal incentives to promote investment in "strategic" industries. A clear example of this is its policy toward the semiconductor industry. Early on, in 1970, it withdrew "pioneer" status (which confers a multiyear tax holiday) from pure assembly operations (Haggard, 1990). In the early 1980s, in an effort to induce multinational firms with assembly plants on the island to integrate backward into wafer fabrication, the government offered generous financial packages to the first few firms to build such facilities. Then, through a state-owned corporation, it invested with two U.S. semiconductor firms, National Semiconductor and Cypress Semiconductor, in a joint venture "silicon foundry" (Chartered Semiconductor) to make application-specific integrated circuits (ASICs). The silicon foundry is in difficult financial straits at present—largely due to the computer industry's prolonged slump—and owes its survival in no small measure to the largess of the Singaporean government.

Very recently, the Singaporean government has taken another step toward strengthening the local command of microelectronics technologies through the establishment of the Institute of Microelectronics (IME). The top management of IME consists largely of veterans of stints in R&D laboratories of leading U.S. semiconductor firms; several, for example, have worked at AT&T Bell Labs while one hails from Intergraph Corp. Most of IME's divisions are seeking out technology partners among international electronics firms based in Singapore: for example, NEC Corp. has formed a partnership with the IC Failure Analysis and Testing Services Division while it is possible that Toshiba Corp. will share VSLI CAD logic design technology with IME's VLSI CAD Division. It is also expected that the Silicon Process Technology Division will help develop process modules for the partially government-owned Chartered Semiconductor (Boys-Merritt, 1991).

The primary emphasis in both Singapore and Hong Kong has been on diffusion of advanced technologies throughout their economies. Their large service sectors—especially financial services but also commerce and transport—have been leading adopters of advanced information and communication systems. At the same time, given chronic labor shortages and rising labor costs, both countries place a premium on labor-saving technological innovations in their manufacturing sectors as well. To a certain degree such pressures have been relieved by the growing economic integration between Hong Kong and southern China on the one hand and between Singapore, southern Malaysia, and northern Indonesia on the other. The transfer of low-skill, labor-intensive jobs to those neighbors has allowed Hong Kong and Singapore to restructure their own economies toward more highly skilled forms of employment. Even those, however, can benefit, in terms of enhanced productivity, from new information technologies—such as computer-aided software engineering (CASE) and computer-aided design (CAD) tools. Singapore has already progressed quite far in its use of CAD systems on a per capita basis.

Recently the government of Hong Kong—traditionally averse to anything like technology or industrial targeting—decided to support the establishment of a center devoted to the training of engineers in the computer-aided design of application-specific integrated circuits (ASICs). Government policy makers apparently concluded that a laissez-faire approach is one factor explaining why Hong Kong's electronics industry has been lagging behind those of the other three Asian NIEs. Still, rather than supporting electronic component producers, it has chosen to stimulate greater demand for ASICs by helping system engineers acquire the skills needed to design innovative features into their products.

This last example gets to the heart of a policy debate raging not only in the Asian NIEs but even more so in the OECD countries, that is, to what extent and in what way should government support an industry whose products are essential components in almost all modern machines, whether for home, road, office, or factory use? There can be little question that, in the present day and age, any industry aiming to devise innovative products or production processes must possess some familiarity with the microelectronics and information technologies on which so much innovation has come to depend. If those technologies are really critical to maintaining competitiveness, should governments be content to take a laissez-faire attitude in the expectation that the private firms know best what they need and can obtain the necessary resources to acquire it?

Future Technological Prospects of the Asian NIEs

Is the future of the Asian NIEs as bright as the past? Growth rates are almost certain to slow as the Asian NIEs approach industrial maturity, though they may well remain above average OECD levels through the next decade. As labor productivity levels in the Asian NIEs converge toward those of certain more advanced OECD countries, so too will per capita income levels. The narrowing or elimination of the technology gap across a widening spectrum of industries will make further improvements in total factor productivity more difficult to achieve.

If the Asian NIEs cannot expect to become technology leaders in any but a few fields, at least they need to remain close followers. Yet, a close follower strategy is not without its risks. In high-technology fields characterized by rapid technological change and short product generations, those who follow by more than a short distance can suffer heavy losses. The market for computer memory chips dramatically highlights the dilemmas followers face. A new-generation production facility (for 4 MB DRAMs) can cost as much as U.S.$500 million. A delay of a year or less in bringing such a facility into production can spell the difference between tremendous profits and potentially disastrous losses. The technological and financial hurdles to be crossed in entering the commercial production of liquid crystal displays (LCDs) are perhaps even more formidable.

Each of the four Asian NIEs faces a different set of challenges in the coming decade. In Korea, the large *chaebol* have taken over the initiative in R&D on semiconductors, computers, fine chemicals, and numerous other technologies. Their large size and deep pockets have served them well until now. Yet strains are evident. There is a clear danger that they may be spread dangerously thin, that the diversification that served them so well in the past may be a hindrance in mastering sophisticated technologies, each of which demands enormous human and financial resources. How can they focus their product strategies and at the same time exploit synergies? As Simon suggests in this volume, one answer seems to be to rely more on strategic alliances with other firms whose technological strengths can complement their own. Meanwhile, the government is trying to redefine its own R&D role in this new environment. Should it be supporting more basic research or continuing to develop generic technologies, with a view to helping small and medium-size firms build up their own technological capabilities?

In the case of Taiwan, one concern is how the average firm can command the resources to cross the R&D and investment thresholds to compete in many areas of advanced electronics. While the government is working to develop LCD technology, it is not clear who can afford to commercialize it. Almost certainly the government would need to take a sizable equity stake and shoulder some of the risks. In the case of the fast-changing semiconductor business, can Taiwan's still relatively small firms muster the financing to invest in developing new product generations early enough to make an adequate return on their investments? Can they afford to rely on the government's R&D efforts to provide them with technologies that may be obsolete by the time they leave the labs? Teaming up with foreign technology partners has been one solution to the problem, but this normally requires that the local partner be cash-rich. In the case of computers, there is a danger that firms without strong R&D capabilities may remain stuck in the low-end PC market, where they are finding it increasingly difficult to compete with lower-cost suppliers elsewhere in the region. In short, Taiwan's greatest challenge would seem to be how to ensure that a sizable number of technology-based firms can afford the investments in R&D needed to compete in higher value-added, more innovative products. As industry becomes more R&D-intensive, industrial structure is bound to change, but Taiwan does well to avoid an overly top-heavy industrial structure and retain much of the flexibility afforded by its many small and medium-size enterprises.

Hong Kong's government is being forced to reexamine its laissez-faire philosophy in the face of evidence from its neighbors that government direction and support can make a difference in the degree of technological dynamism of electronics and other leading industries. How can the government strengthen the competitiveness of local industry without interfering excessively with the workings of the market? It has chosen to focus on training, technical information diffusion, and testing and analytical services rather than on direct industrial targeting. Hong Kong must cope with some of the same problems as Taiwan, that is, its relatively fragmented industrial structure with many small enterprises, but without the benefit of the government's commitment to undertake generic R&D on their behalf. Upgrading management skills has been identified as one priority area, with a focus on technology management and the use of management information systems and other new management tools. A number of technology areas are identified (Liang and Denny, this volume) as having competitive importance for the island's economy; these include information and telecommunications technologies to support the service sector; advanced manufacturing technologies for use in key industries like garments, plastics, and electronics; the proper use and handling of advanced materials in the plastics, textile, and electronic component industries; biotechnology for use in food processing and waste treatment; and large-scale urban environmental technology. The government is likely to play principally a supportive, facilitative role in the private sectors' acquisition of the relevant technologies.

Finally, in the case of Singapore, the problems of small population and market size are most stark. The island has been drawing heavily in recent years on neighboring countries not only for production but also for engineering and technical personnel. Is this an adequate long-term solution? Perhaps a more vexing question is how to cope with the legacy of an industrialization strategy that, to a far greater extent than any of the other three Asian NIEs, has depended on attracting foreign direct investment. To an extent, the government has succeeded in recent years in convincing foreign firms to establish R&D and software centers in Singapore, principally to serve the regional market. Still, local industrialists have not yet fully emerged from the shadow of the larger and technologically more sophisticated multinational subsidiaries. The government's Science Park and its resident incubator have gone some way to encourage local "high-tech" entrepreneurship, but there is still some way to go.

To address the challenges of the coming decade, the government has formulated a new National Technology Plan (NTP). Announced in September 1991, the five-year plan seeks to raise R&D expenditures from the current level of 1% to 2% of GNP by 1995 and to increase the number of research scientists and engineers per 10,000 labor force from the current 28 to 40. The National Science and Technology Development Board (NSTB), formed at the beginning of 1991, is to oversee the implementation of the plan, including the establishment of a new research center to support Singapore's large disk drive industry and an Institute of Manufacturing Technology to undertake research on factory automation. While a national plan for the diffusion of information technologies already exists, a new National IT Plan (called IT2000) is in preparation, which should emphasize higher value added, design- and innovation-oriented IT applications (see Wong, this volume).

Competitive Rivalry and Complementarity among the Asian NIEs

A comparison of the "strategic technologies" and "strategic industries" considered vital to the future competitiveness of the Asian NIEs would turn up broad similarities: advanced manufacturing technologies, information technologies, advanced materials, biotechnology, environmental technologies would be included on most if not all countries' lists. Not surprisingly, perhaps, these are largely the same technology groups that would appear on a similar "strategic" listing by most OECD member countries and, for that matter, by less technologically advanced Asian countries like Malaysia and Thailand (see, e.g., Malaysia's Action Plan for Industrial Technology Development). One of several possible conclusions could follow: (1) many of these fields could become overcrowded, with intense competition leaving few if any entrants profitable; (2) some countries may fail to acquire (or maintain) a comparative advantage in any of these advanced technology areas; (3) a division of labor may emerge among countries, both within and across technology areas. For example, one country may be relatively strong in a specific biotechnology application like genetic engineering of plants and animals, while another may be strong in bioengineered pharmaceutical products. One may be strong in the design and development of advanced information systems, while another may be especially effective in the application of advanced manufacturing technologies. In general, however, there are likely to be complementarities in use of various technologies. A country with strong information technology capabilities is likely also to possess strong manufacturing automation capabilities. The reason for such complementarities is that subsets of the technologies share a common generic knowledge base. To the extent, therefore, that a country has laid the proper scientific and technical foundations, it should have the potential to compete in a range of technology-intensive industries. Still, country-specific factors such as industrial history and structure or domestic market characteristics are likely to shape relative performance in different market niches, spelling the difference between those in which the country's industry is a market leader and those in which it is just one of the pack. As long as governments lay the proper foundations—build the science and engineering faculties of universities and the technical training institutes; develop the broadly skilled human resources; create an environment conducive to innovative activity, R&D investment, and risk taking; and ensure high technology entrepreneurs do not lack financing—they should be able to let competitive international markets decide which firms and industries survive and thrive and which perish.

Notes

1. For analyses that place heavy emphasis on the role of "strong" (in some instances authoritarian) states, see Haggard (1990) and Wade (1990).
2. While we refer throughout to S&T policy, we tend to place more stress on the "T" than on the "S." This reflects the reality that technology development has been the highest priority for the Asian NIEs during the first few decades of their industrialization.
3. Singapore's wage increases were partially policy-induced. The government tried prematurely to force an industrial restructuring (in the name of a "Second Industrial Revolution") in the direction of more technology-intensive industries with more demanding skill requirements. In June 1979 the National Wages Council recommended an average 20 percent wage increase (Haggard, 1990). The labor shortage of the late 1970s and early 1980s turned to glut toward the middle of the decade when the semiconductor, computer, construction, and oil industries all went into recession.
4. Sony, for example, may have difficulty reducing prices on its new CD-I (compact disk-interactive) Entertainment System because it does not produce its own color LCDs, which are a sizable portion of total product cost. This represents a rare instance in which Sony depends on outside suppliers for such a critical component (*Far Eastern Economic Review*, 1991, p. 90).
5. From 1961 to 1975 Korea borrowed some U.S.$11,797 million abroad; from 1962 to 1976 total FDI amounted to only U.S.$625 million (Choi, 1983).

References

Amsden, Alice H. *Asia's Next Giant: South Korea and Late Industrialization.* New York, Oxford University Press, 1989.

Asian Development Bank. *Asian Development Outlook 1991.* Manila: ADB, 1991.

Baumol, William J. "Productivity Growth, Convergence, and Welfare: What the Long-Run Data Show," *American Economic Review* 76–5 (December 1986): 1072–1085.

Boyd-Merritt, Rick. "IME Ready for Tech-Transfer Deals," *Electronic World News* December 16, 1991: 2.

Bradford, Colin I. Jr. "Policy Interventions and Markets: Development Strategy Typologies and Policy Options." In Gary Gareffi, and Donald L. (eds.), *Manufacturing Miracles: Paths of Industrialization in Latin America and East Asia.* Princeton: Princeton University Press, 1990.

Census and Statistics Department, Hong Kong, *Hong Kong Statistics 1947–1967.* Hong Kong: 1969, 1989.

———. *Hong Kong Social and Economic Trends: 1970–1980.* Hong Kong: 1981.

———. *Hong Kong Annual Digest of Statistics.* Hong Kong: 1982, 1989.

Chen, E. K. Y. "Trade Policy in Asia." In Naya, S., M. Urrutia, S. Mark, and A. Fuentes (eds.), *Lessons in Development: A Comparative Study of Asia and Latin America.* San Francisco: International Center for Economic Growth, 1989, pp. 55–76.

Choi, Hyung Sup. *Bases for Science and Technology Promotion in Developing Countries.* Tokyo: Asian Productivity Organization, 1983.

Chu, Wan-Wen. "The Use of Import-Substitution Policy in Export-Led Growth: A Study of Taiwan's Petrochemical Industry," Preliminary draft of paper prepared for presentation at Western Economics Association Annual Meeting, Seattle, 1991.

Council for Economic Planning and Development, Taiwan. *Taiwan Statistical Data Book.* Taiwan: CEPD, 1988, 1990.

Dahlman, Carl J., and Sananikone, Ousa. *Technology Strategy in the Economy of Taiwan: Exploiting Foreign Linkages and Investing in Local Capability*, preliminary draft. Washington, DC: World Bank, December 1990.

Department of Statistics, Singapore. *Economic and Social Statistics: Singapore 1960– 1982.* Singapore: 1983.

Dollar, David. "Convergence of South Korean Productivity on West German Levels, 1966–78," *World Development 19*, 2/3 (February/March) 263–273.

Dasgupta, Partha, and Stoneman, Paul (eds.) *Economic Policy and Technological Performance.* Cambridge: Cambridge University Press, 1987.

Dowrick, Steve and Gemmell, Norman. "Industrialisation, Catching Up and Economic Growth: A Comparative Study across the World's Capitalist Economies."*Economic Journal 101* (March 1991): 263–75.

Economic Planning Board, Republic of Korea. *Korea Statistical Yearbook 1986.* Seoul: National Bureau of Statistics, 1986.

Ergas, Henry. "The Importance of Technology Policy." In Dollar, David. "Convergence of South Korean Productivity on West German Levels, 1966–78," *World Development 19*, 2/3 (February/March) 51–96.

Executive Yuan, Council for International Economic Cooperation and Development. *Taiwan Statistical Data Book 1969.* Taipei: 1969.

Executive Yuan, Directorate-General of Budgets, Accounts and Statistics. *Statistical Abstract of the Republic of China, 1970.* 1970.

Far Eastern Economic Review 19 (September 1991).

Gereffi, Gary and Wyman, Donald L. *Manufacturing Miracles: Paths of Industrialization in Latin America and East Asia.* Princeton: Princeton University Press, 1990.

Haggard, Stephan. *Pathways from the Periphery: The Politics of Growth in the Newly Industrializing Countries.* Ithaca: Cornell University Press, 1990.

Hasan, Parvez. *Korea: Problems and Issues in a Rapidly Growing Economy.* Baltimore: Johns Hopkins University Press, 1976.

International Monetary Fund. *International Financial Statistics.* Washington, DC: IMF, September 1990.

Kuo, Shirley; Ranis, Gustav; and Fei, John C. H. *The Taiwan Success Story: Rapid Growth with Improved Distribution in the Republic of China, 1952–1979.* Boulder, CO: Westview Press, 1981.

Kim, Kwang Suk. "The Economic Development of the Republic of Korea, 1965– 1981." In L. J. Lau (ed.), *Models of Development: A Comparative Study of Economic Growth in South Korea and Taiwan.* San Francisco: Institute for Contemporary Studies (ICS) Press, 1986.

Lee, Chong-Ouk. "Stages of Economic Development and Technology Policy: The Experience of Korea." *Science and Technology Policy* (August 1991): 219–24.

Lee, K.-U.; Urata, S., and Choi, I. "Recent Developments in Industrial Organizational Issues in Korea," Mimeo, Korea Development Institute (KDI) and World Bank, Washington, DC [cited in Amsden, 1989].

Liang, Winston W., and Denny, W. Michael. "The Upgrading of Hong Kong's Technology Base." In Denis F. Simon (ed.), *The Emerging Technological Trajectory of the Pacific Rim*. Chapter 12, this volume.

Lim, Linda Y.C., and Fong, Pang Eng. *Foreign Direct Investment and Industrialization in Malaysia, Singapore, Taiwan, and Thailand*. Paris: Development Centre Study, OECD, 1991.

Lin, T. B., and Ho, Y. P. "Industrial Restructuring in Hong Kong." Asian Employment Programme Working Papers, ILO-ARTEP, Bangkok, December 1984.

Little, Ian M. D. "The Experience and Causes of Rapid Labour-Intensive Development in Korea, Taiwan, Hong Kong and Singapore; and the Possibilities of Emulation." ILO-ARTEP, WPII–1, Bangkok, February 1979.

Mutoh, H.; Sekiguchi, S.; Suzumura, K.; and Yamazawa, I. eds. *Industrial Policies for Pacific Economic Growth*. London: Allen and Unwin, 1986.

Myers, Ramon H. "The Economic Development of the Republic of China on Taiwan, 1965–1981." In L. J. Lau (ed.), *Models of Development: A Comparative Study of Economic Growth in South Korea and Taiwan*. San Francisco: Institute for Contemporary Studies Press, 1986.

O'Connor, David C. *Strategies, Policies, and Practices for the Reduction of CFC Usage in the Electronics Industries of Developing Asia*. Paris: OECD Development Centre, June 1991.

OECD. *The Newly Industrialising Countries: Challenge and Opportunity for OECD Industries*. Paris: OECD, 1988.

Schive, Chi. "The Next State of Industrialization in Taiwan and South Korea." In Gary Gareffi, and Donald L. Wyman (eds.), *Manufacturing Miracles: Paths of Industrialization in Latin America and East Asia*. Princeton: Princeton University Press, 1990.

UNESCO. *Statistical Yearbook*. Paris: UNESCO, 1989.

Wade, Robert. "State Intervention in 'Outward-Looking' Development: Neoclassical Theory and Taiwanese Practice." In Gordon White, ed., *Developmental States in East Asia*, London: Macmillan, 1988, pp. 30–67.

Wong, Poh-Kam. "Singapore's Technology Strategy." In Denis F. Simon (ed.), *The Emerging Technological Trajectory of the Pacific Rim*. Chapter 5, this volume.

World Bank. *World Development Report, 1991*. Washington, DC: Oxford University Press for the World Bank, 1991.

4

Korea's High-Technology Thrust

Seongjae Yu

After three decades of phenomenal economic growth, Korea seems to have reached a critical juncture at which it either takes a course leading to an advanced and competitive industrial country or stays on a stagnant course not unlike the so-called Latin American countries syndrome. Korea has been forced to face such a juncture, on the one hand, by the internal sociopolitical dynamics recently experienced during the democratization process. On the other hand, Korea has had to confront powerful international forces characterized by the globalization and the regionalization of the world economy which is suspected to have been influenced to a large extent by dynamic changes in the characteristics of technological development and by their roles in affecting competitive relations in international trade (Simon, 1991).

From the competition perspective, technological change has dual roles. It can be an equalizer, eroding the competitive advantages of even well-entrenched firms and countries and propelling others to the forefront. Or it can be a powerful instrument for consolidating firms' competitive position in the market (Ernst and O'Connor, 1989). Korea has benefited greatly by the former role during the past three decades of industrial development. But now there is a growing sense of crisis in Korea that the latter role of the technology changer is being played by the advanced industrial countries (AICs) such as Japan, the United States, and the EC countries. There are many unmistakable signs that the emerging technological trajectory in the Pacific Rim is likely to push Korea away from becoming a major competitor in the world market.

The purpose of this paper is to discuss Korea's strategic moves in high-technology development in response to the challenges Korea currently faces in the domestic and international market environment. The paper is structured as follows: the next section discusses the nature of the challenges Korea faces with particular views on the competitiveness in the world market. The third section presents the rationale for Korea's choice of the course of high-technology development. The fourth section discusses strategies Korea has adopted to push high-technology development. Here, most of the discussions concern the government strategies made known to industry, whereas the strategies of private firms are yet to be revealed, perhaps because they are still in an early stage of adjusting to new challenges and thus have no stable patterns of response. In the fifth section, the role of government in developing high technology is discussed. The final section presents some thoughts on the question of whether the "high-tech" strategy is the best option Korea has at the moment.

Disturbing Signals

In a span of one generation Korea has been transformed from one of the poorest agricultural countries to a viable industrial economy. The meager 1960 GNP of $1.95 billion has grown to $225.5 billion in 1990 (in current prices) and is projected to grow to $321 billion by the end of 1992, becoming the twelfth-largest economy in the world. Total exports in 1960 were only $33 million, consisting mostly of primary products. By 1990 exports had grown to $65 billion and were supported by industrial products. Transformation from an underdeveloped rural economy to an industrially developed one entails multifaceted development of the socioeconomic fabric: it requires sound economic and industrial policies and strategies as well as development of its educational system and industrial infrastructure. It also requires managerial and entrepreneurial skills and technological capabilities.

Succinctly put, Korea's economic development may be characterized as guided by export-oriented industrialization strategy. A country without natural resources to speak of, Korea had very limited options available to escape poverty. One of the viable options was to drive exports and to use the foreign currencies earned from export activities to import raw materials to process further and export again. In the process, jobs and value added were created and the expansive motion of the industrialization process was set. From this process the Korean economy has grown impressively, sixteen times in real terms during the thirty-plus years since 1960. Double-digit annual growth rates in exports have been a routine phenomenon and even a double-digit GNP growth was not infrequent. Though many factors are put forward to explain the impetus behind this remarkable growth, perhaps the most important one is Korean firms' entrepreneurial ability to maintain *competitive advantage* acquired through a combination of *low wages* and imported *technologies* in a favorable investment environment induced by various government policies.

This force of competitive advantage in the world market seemed invincible, and it looked plausible that the export-driven Korean economy could sustain its

Figure 4.1 **Export Growth Rate**

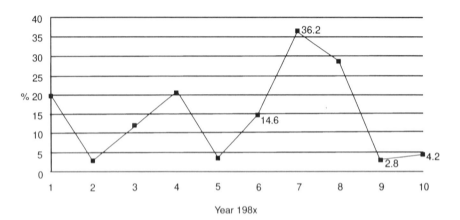

Year 198x

high-growth path well into the 1990s. However, the optimism came to a sudden halt in 1989, when the export machinery started to falter, registering only 2.8 percent growth—a precipitous decline from the 28.4 percent growth of the previous year. The situation did not change in 1990 when exports again registered only 4.3 percent growth (Figure 4.1). The predicament of the Korean economy can be seen even more dramatically in the trade balance: a trade surplus of $8.8 billion in 1988 shrank to a meager $912 million in 1989 and turned into a deficit of $4.8 billion in 1990. By the end of 1991, the cumulative trade deficit for the year was $8.8 billion (see Fig. 4.2).[1] This is despite the opening of new markets in Eastern European countries and China, hitherto inaccessible to Korean products.

The problems Korea currently faces seem formidable, caused by the interplays of various internal and external forces emerging in the past several years. Since 1988 Korea has been undergoing a significant transitional process. Politically, the authoritarian government was replaced by rather genuine democratic governments in the late 1980s and early 1990s, suddenly resulting in a pluralistic, divergent society where self-interest-seeking groups make cacophonous political demands. Economically, an unprecedented trade surplus ballooned from 1986 to 1988, bringing the Korean people higher profits, more spending, higher wages, and a greater tolerance for a rise in inflation. Socially, the explosion of labor disputes, aggravated by the newly acquired political freedom and the economic confidence engendered by the trade surplus, increased social unrest as well as wage levels far above those in competitor countries such as Hong Kong, Singapore,

Figure 4.2 **Trade Balance, 1981–1991**

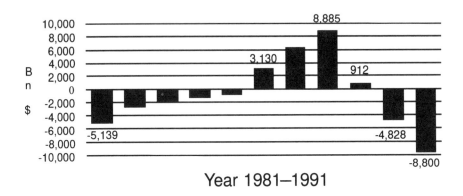

Year 1981–1991

and Taiwan. The average Korean family, once praised for its traditionally frugal life-style, has rapidly yielded to a more comfortable form of consumerism (see "Too Rich Too Soon," 1991), which has caused the nation's savings ratio to fall below the annual investment requirements.

In addition to these domestic problems, which were already formidable enough, the external forces of the international economies have been pushing Korean industries into an even more difficult position. A new international economic realignment has been emerging through the dynamics of the regionalization of economic superpowers and the globalization of multinational enterprises. The underlying forces of these dynamics were the Uruguay Round of the GATT system, the market-opening pressure from the Super 301 of the U.S. Trade Act, and the emergence of regional economic blocs represented by the North American Free Trade Agreement (NAFTA) and the integration process of a single European market by 1992. Moreover, a tightened intellectual property regime has been developing under the emerging new international technology order triggered by trade disputes between economic superpowers.[2]

Any of these domestic or international events alone would be a major challenge to Korean industries to adjust their business strategies. The combined effect of these events has been the loss of competitive advantage in the world market Korean firms once enjoyed. The nation's economic community and the government are caught in a crisis psychology. Criticisms and diagnoses have abounded, various policies and measures have been tried, and new ones are always being suggested.

Choice of the High-Technology Path

The Korean government recognized from an early date the role of science and technology as a crucial underpinning of industrial development. Technology in particular was perceived as a means to compensate for the country's poor endowment of natural resources. The Korea Institute of Science and Technology (KIST), established in 1966, was the first manifestation of this perception and it, together with other research institutions established subsequently, has faithfully performed its catalytic role in reversing the brain drain and developing and diffusing technologies necessary for industrial development progress. The development of an indigenous capability through local research organizations in technology absorption, adaptation, and innovation has been the central theme of science and technology policies. The assumption was that the fusion of indigenous technological capability with imported technologies would generate very powerful results with synergic effects. This policy has been duly supported in resource allocations in the series of five-year economic development plans of the Korean government. Along with the growth of technological capability, Korean export competitiveness has also grown impressively, thus reinforcing the belief that the investment in science and technology development has been wise.

The government plan documents (MOTI, 1989, MOST, 1989, 1991a) show a number of rationales for developing "high-technology" industries as Korea's strategic choice for further industrial development from both positive and negative perspectives. From the positive point of view, the government planners claim that high technology will be (a) a major competition factor in the world market in the coming decades; (b) the main engine transforming Korea into an advanced industrial society; (c) an important factor to keep the Korean economy on a high-growth track; (d) a means to build competitive advantage; and (e) the key to creating the information society.

From the negative perspective, the planners argue that the costs of not developing high technologies are prohibitively high, including: (a) the cost of missing wide opportunities in emerging "high-tech"-based industries; (b) the cost of losing competitive advantage through new products and productivity in existing industries; (c) the cost of maintaining ineffective industrial structures; and (d) excessive royalty payments to overcome access barriers to high technology.

These arguments sound rational; some are even convincing. Government planners now use these rationales as if they were factually proven. But in fact they are neither empirically proven nor necessarily logical. Some are claimed on the basis of possibility rather than probability. Some are simply the same arguments expressed with different emphases and from different perspectives.

Perhaps more convincing arguments why Korea has adopted a "high-technology" strategy should be sought in environmental factors. First of all, the perception generally shared by the Korean industrialists regarding the country's current predicament is that their products are losing competitive advantage fast in the international market and that technology has much to do with the loss. Flattened export growth rates during the past three years (Figure 4.1), when other Asian competitors (e.g., Taiwan, Thailand, Malaysia, and China) have registered a healthy export growth, are cited as evidence of this loss of competitiveness. No empirical study has yet identified the causes for the recent decline in the Korean export growth rate. The factors that once made Korean manufactured goods competitive in the world market are still there: Korea has a skilled labor force, competitive wage rates, entrepreneurial leadership, a well-trained class of managers, government support, good work ethics, industrial infrastructure, appropriate technologies, and so on. Many of these factors have a certain degree of inertia, which makes the shift of competitiveness rather gradual. But two factors that could adversely affect competitiveness rather quickly have recently surfaced: labor cost and technology. An increase in wage rates has a direct and immediate effect on price competitiveness. But the effect of high labor costs cannot be the only reason, since it can be compensated through an increase in productivity. Though the Korean wage level is high compared with competitor NIEs, it is still about one-fourth of the level of the AICs; as long as the country can increase productivity in relation to the change in labor costs, relative competitiveness can be maintained.

A more important reason suggested by industrialists for the recent downturn of Korean competitiveness is the technology factor. It is generally believed that technology increasingly has become the critical factor in the export market: it is a key to a productivity increase; it is the underpinning factor for the ever-shortening product life-cycle; it is the differentiating factor between high-value-added products and low-value-added; it affects product quality through the design and manufacturing method; and, above all, mastery of technology is the key to producing innovative products that sell. As Korea moves up the ladder of industrial development, the level of technology it requires becomes increasingly sophisticated. While the AICs make steady advances in high technologies and transform them to their competitive advantage in the world market, Korean manufacturers have been unable to obtain easy access to high technologies, either through acquisition from foreign sources or by local development. Overcoming the barrier to high technology becomes even more critical as Korea's industrial gravity shifts toward sophisticated products such as automobiles, computers, state-of-the-art memory chips, machine tools, electronic switching equipment, and the like, most of which require high-technology supports.

Furthermore, Korean industrialists realize that they are trapped between the AICs and the emerging NIEs, and that the only way out of this difficult position is through the development of high technologies. The market for high-value-added products is dominated by the advanced countries, which increasingly raise the entry barrier against competitors from NIEs. The market for low-value-added products where Korean industries have traditionally been competitive is increasingly challenged by the emerging NIEs, bolstered by low wages and modern product assembly technologies. There could be a number of different strategies to escape from the trap. But a general consensus among industrialists and government planners is that Korea should pursue high technology. One of the important arguments behind this suggestion is that high technology would be a double-edged instrument that Korea could use: it is effective in, on the one hand, in overcoming the entry barrier to the club of AICs, and, on the other hand, in outdistancing challenges from the emerging NIEs such as Thailand, China, Malaysia, and Indonesia. It is argued in Korea that high technology is perhaps the only effective tool, particularly for meeting the challenges from the NIEs. The challenge these countries impose on Korea lies in high-quality, low-priced products manufactured with state-of-the-art assembly technology supported by Japanese multinational enterprises. The critical parts and components of high value added are supplied by multinational enterprises (MNEs) directly to the assembly operations in the offshore factories equipped with modern assembly technologies. Korean industrialists perceive that the Japanese MNEs control both high- and low-end products: high end through direct manufacturing from plants in Japan, and low end through offshore factories. Of the wide range of the "high-tech"-based products (e.g., electronic products), the low-end products are generally the area in which the Korean manufacturers traditionally compete in the international market. Though Korean manufacturers have been successful in some "high-tech"-based products, it is felt, with some trepidation, that unless Korea strives to develop an indigenous capability in high technology, the country will soon be derailed from becoming a competitive power in the world market.

The reasons discussed above are reactive in nature in the sense that the "high-tech" strategy is triggered by threats in the market. But perhaps a more positive reason why the country has adopted a "high-tech" strategy is the recent successful experience in "high-tech" products, which have contributed to building the nation's confidence that Korea, too, can handle certain high technologies, with enough effort. Two well-publicized examples are the 4 MB and 16 MB DRAM memory chips and a large-scale digital switching system (code-named TDX 10). TDX 10 is a main component for building an "integrated services digital network" (ISDN), a future integrated telecommunications system. Both developments require state-of-the-art technologies and are produced only in AICs. So far, no other NIEs have been able to produce such advanced products. Both developments are sufficiently complicated to grant Korean industrialists a glimpse of what the development of high technology is like. And, more important, they have helped instill national confidence that Korea, too, can emulate AICs in certain high-technology areas. If so, these are some cultural implications in terms of Korea's projected technological trajectory.

Definition of High Technology

The term "high technology" is vague, but seems generally related to intensity of R&D activities. One way of measuring such intensity is in terms of R&D expenditure in relation to sales turnover. However, in a country like Korea where the level of science and technology is not as advanced as in AICs, a simple ratio of R&D expenditures to sales may not conjure up the real meaning of high technology. A Korean company may spend a significant amount of R&D money in a bid to obtain a technology simply because it is not available in Korea, but the technology may not be considered high technology in AICs.

In Korea, high technology is defined by describing its generally, if vaguely, known attributes. Two definitions of high technology are common: one advanced by the Ministry of Science and Technology (MOST), and the other by the Ministry of Trade and Industry (MOTI). Each definition serves the research objectives demanded by the mandates of the respective ministry.

MOST (1989) defines high technology in terms of the following attributes: (a) recent technology based on new theory or discovery, expected to create new industries; (b) generic in nature, dynamically applicable to various phases of existing industries; (c) knowledge-intensive with the strong attribute of the ability to create competitive advantage when applied to existing products; and (d) technology associated with national security and public welfare systems. MOST identifies ten generic technologies that fall under this definition:

1. information technology;
2. mechatronics technology;
3. new materials technology;
4. biotechnology;
5. fine chemical and process technology;
6. new energy technology;
7. aerospace and oceanology technology;
8. 21st-century transportation technology;
9. medical and environmental technology;
10. other basic core technologies.

MOTI (1989), on the other hand, defines high technology from market perspectives, with the following attributes: (a) fast technology innovation with a short life-cycle; (b) high-intensity technology contents; (c) ability to create high value added; (d) high capital requirement and high risk; (e) low price elasticity and high income elasticity; (f) ability to contribute solutions for pollution problems and preserve scarce resources; and (g) high diffusion effects on conventional industries. MOTI identifies the following eight industries that fit this definition:

1. microelectronics industry;
2. mechatronics industry;
3. new materials industry;
4. fine chemicals industry;

6. biotechnology industry;
7. aircraft industry;
8. any other industry designated by presidential order

These two definitions respectively reflect characteristics of each ministry's mission. MOST sees high technology from the science and technology perspective whereas MOTI defines it from a market perspective. The orientation of their respective missions leads MOST to emphasize the downstream technologies of product applications. To describe the target, MOST uses the term "technology" (e.g., mechatronics *technology*) whereas MOTI uses the term "industry" (e.g., mechatronics *industry*). Naturally, the approaches of the two ministries complement each other by emphasizing generic and specific technologies of the same target (e.g., mechatronics). In five areas, the definitions of the two ministries coincide. The differences in the other areas on their respective lists may be attributed to the different priorities required by the individual ministry's missions and development goals.

Development Strategies

A dual approach has been pursued by the Korean government in its efforts to promote science and technology (S&T): one is an indirect approach in which the government tries to create a general condition conducive to the diffusion of S&T (i.e., diffusion-oriented policies); the other is a more direct approach, in which the government guides and facilitates the development of specific projects through short- and long-term plans and programs (i.e., mission-oriented policies). Each approach complements the other. The former is to make the S&T soil fertile so that the mission-oriented R&D investment can harvest the result of research effectively. The latter approach is, of course, directly to obtain needed technologies but the consequence of its success also enhances the general level of the nation's research capability.

The "high-technology development" policy has followed the same dual policy framework. In what follows we will discuss diffusion-oriented policies and mission-oriented policies in terms of high-technology development in Korea. But these policies are not necessarily exclusively applicable to the development of high technology.

Diffusion-Oriented Policies

There are many S&T policies that are considered diffusion-oriented. They may be classified into four categories: (1) R&D institution building; (2) supply of R&D manpower; (3) supply of financial resources; and (4) legislative support. Each of these includes a number of policies and measures administered by the government with certain specific objectives.

R&D Institution Building

One of the first efforts the Korean government made toward building an indigenous technological capability was to establish a series of modern research organizations. From this effort came the Korea Institute of Science and Technology (KIST), born in 1966 with assistance from the United States, and in 1967 the Ministry of Science and Technology was established. During the ensuing quarter century, a rather respectable network of R&D institutions, with KIST at its apex, has been established. Many of these institutions are now clustered in the Daeduk Science Town (DST), located 120 miles south of Seoul. DST now has within its boundary fifteen government-supported R&D institutions, three private R&D organizations, and three educational institutions, including the Korea Advanced Institute of Science and Technology (KAIST). By the end of 1992, DST was expected to have eleven additional government-supported organizations and twenty-seven private R&D institutions fully operational. In parallel with the establishment of these research organizations, the government has created a number of Science Research Centers (SRCs) and Engineering Research Centers (ERCs) at various universities throughout Korea primarily to encourage research in basic and upstream technologies that would be linked to the research activities in the government-supported R&D institutions.

Recognizing the importance of R&D efforts in the private sector, since around 1980 the government has introduced incentive schemes to encourage private enterprise to set up their own R&D centers. As a result, the number of private R&D institutions has grown from 53 in 1981 to over 1,000 in 1991. The government also encouraged the establishment of as many R&D consortia as possible, involving both public and private sector parties.[3]

Supply of Research Manpower

Research manpower is considered the key element in developing high technologies. It has been long accepted in Korea that manpower is the only medium through which technology is indigenized, and that only when a nation has indigenous technological capability can it become an industrialized country. Since around 1970 the government has vigorously pursued S&T manpower supply policies. As a result, the number of researchers in the country has increased from 5,628 in 1970 to 70,503 in 1990. Of this number, 25 percent hold doctoral degrees and 30 percent hold master's degrees. Though impressive in growth, this still represents only 16.4 researchers per 10,000 population, which is less than half the rate of 38 researchers in the United States and Japan. It should be noted, however, that as recently as the early 1970s in Japan and Germany there were only 14 to 18 researchers per 10,000 population, and in the late 1970s in France and the United Kingdom about 15. The government (MOST 1992) plans to further increase the number to as many as 30 by the year 2000, with the specific intention of bringing Korea up to the level of the AICs within a decade. The number of researchers was met by scientists and engineers repatriated from the United States. The government expects that in the future the mainstay of the high-caliber researchers will be supplied from local elite graduate schools, such as Seoul National University and the Korea Advanced Institute of Science and Technology. KAIST, for example, is expected to expand its enrollment and to produce as many as 3,600 engineers and scientists with doctoral degrees by 1996.

Supply of Financial Resources

Funds in Korea for research activities, as in any other developing country, have not been sufficient. The ratio of R&D expenditures to GNP was 0.58 percent in 1980 and it has been increased to 1.92 percent in 1989 (see Appendix). This ratio is respectable when compared with other developing countries, where it mostly falls in the area of less than 1 percent. Though the Korean figure does not appear unfavorable vis-à-vis other countries, the actual amount in dollar terms is still small because the GNP base itself is not large. The total amount of research expenditures in 1989 was only $3.98 billion (see Appendix), which was roughly equivalent to the amount spent for R&D by a single U.S. corporation such as IBM or General Motors. It has been argued among the Korean science and technology planners since the 1980s that for Korea to be a serious contender in high technology the magnitude of R&D expenditures should be viable in absolute amount and that it is therefore necessary to further increase the ratio to 5 percent by the year 2001. The 5 percent target is certainly very ambitious. No other nation, not even the United States and Japan, let alone a developing country, has spent that much for R&D investment. Whether Korea will ever be able to invest that much for R&D remains to be seen. But at least this indicates how serious the government is about the development of science and technology.

Of the nation's investment in R&D, the proportion shared by the government and public sector has declined from 70.3 percent in 1970 to 17.1 percent in 1989. Although the comparable ratio in Japan was also 17.1 percent in 1989, back in 1970 it was already as low as 25.2 percent. The burden of R&D investment may have been shifted to the private sector in Korea too early and too soon. Reflecting this concern, the government (MOST, 1991a) plans to increase the public-sector ratio up to 35 percent by the year 2000.

Legislative Support

A panoply of legislative measures have been developed to institutionalize the research support mechanism. Most of the measures are designed to strengthen the science and technology infrastructure and to facilitate resource allocations to the science and technology sector. Generally, the laws aim at institution building, credit channeling, incentives, and devices intended to reduce the risk involved in R&D activities. Representative laws are:

- Science and Technology Development Promotional Law (for private sector R&D institutes);
- R&D Consortium Law for Industrial Technology Promotion;
- Government-supported R&D Institutes Law;
- Special Provisional Law for Structural Adjustment and Management Stability of Small and Medium Business;
- Industry Development Law (for support of basic industrial technology).

Mission-Oriented Policies

A developing country with limited resources, Korea has followed the target approach in developing strategic industries. The same approach has been adopted in developing technologies. The government has promulgated short- and long-term plans and programs (i.e., mission-oriented policies) that would guide and facilitate the development of specific industries and/or technologies. Until the early 1980s, most of the missions with which the government had been concerned were directly related to industrial development. Focus had been on industry per se rather than on technology. The target industries often were supported by special laws such as the "Electronics Industry Promotion Law," and the "Textile Industry Promotion Law." Technology was an integral part of the overall industrial development strategy. Most of the required technologies were obtained through technology transfer and/or technology-imbedded equipment and machineries from foreign sources.

Since the mid-1980s, however, government policies have shifted their focus from industrial development to technology development. Having obtained a viable basis in most industries, Korea was now ready to move to the next rung of the industrial ladder. This required higher technological support from the domestic research systems. Demand for research support from domestic sources has been accentuated as the intellectual-property-rights regime has increasingly been tightened by AICs and the fear of technonationalism has loomed large in the minds of government planners and industrialists. As better-defined plans and more specific technologies are required, a number of technology development missions have been identified and promoted. More powerful and effective support has come in the form of legislation; for example:

- Substitute Energy Development Promotional Law;
- Software Development Promotional Law;
- Genetic Engineering Promotional Law;
- Aerospace Industry Development Promotional Law;
- Basic Law for Oceanology Development.

These laws are aimed at treating the target technologies differentially from the others in terms of fiscal and financial support. They also have provisions that require government ministries and agencies to execute certain functions to expedite development.

The HAN Project

The most recent mission-oriented policies pertaining to technology development are the "HAN Project." In April 1991, President Rho Tae Woo revealed before the Korean Press Club his vision of enhancing Korea's science and technology capability to join the ranks of the most advanced countries. His announcement was subsequently finalized into a national plan labeled the "Science and Technology Development Plan to Join the Rank of the 7 Most Advanced Countries,"[4] which is commonly referred to as the "G–7 Project" or the "HAN Project"[5] (MOST, 1991c).

The HAN Project is basically a strategy focused on a limited number of high-technology projects that have the greatest viability to make Korea competitive in the international market by around the year 2001. It consists of two project groups: (a) Product Oriented Technology Development Projects; and (b) Base Technology Development Projects.

Product Oriented Technology Development Projects. Seven high-technology products are identified as targets for Korean development; these are expected to be in the growth or maturity stage of the product life-cycle sometime between the years 1997 and 2000. They should be those products that Korea can develop with domestic resources and can use to attain competitive advantage in the international market. They include the following development plans in seven categories:

1. For the electronics industry, develop 256 megabit DRAM chips by 1996 and 1 gigabit DRAM chips by 2000.
2. For the telecommunications industry, develop an ISDN using the ATM digital switching system.
3. For the consumer electronics industry, develop HDTV receiver technology by 1993 and also develop flat panel display technology by 1997.
4. For the automobile industry, develop a battery-operated passenger car by 1966.
5. For the computer industry, develop an artificial-intelligence-based computer capable of performing two-way voice translation by 2000.
6. For the fine chemical industry, develop one or two new antibiotic materials by 1997.
7. For the mechatronics industry, develop a computer-integrated manufacturing (CIM) system by 1996, and also develop an intelligent manufacturing system (IMS) by 2000.

Base Technology Development Projects. This section of the HAN Project deals with some base technologies that are generic in nature and necessary to increase the quality of life in general. The development of specific projects is not expected but at least the ability to apply the technologies to specific problems by local scientists and engineers is expected. These projects include the following seven technologies:

1. In the new materials area, acquire technologies related to electronics, information, and energy.
2. In the machinery area, acquire technologies related to transportation, machinery and critical parts, and components.
3. In the bioengineering area, acquire base technologies related to functional biomaterials.
4. In the environmental area, acquire base technologies related to environmental control and preservation.
5. In the energy area, acquire base technologies related to highly efficient, clean energy systems that will affect the industrial structure.
6. In the atomic power area, acquire base technologies related to the next-generation nuclear reactor that will be used for the supply of stable energy, replacing fossil materials.
7. In the human engineering area, acquire "high touch" technologies that will enhance the quality of life in postindustrial society.

The HAN projects are to involve all relevant government ministries and agencies as well as government-invested enterprises and private sector corporations. Furthermore, the project plan is to promote international collaborative research where necessary. The total estimated budget is 4.9 trillion won (about $6.8 billion), to be expended between 1992 and 2001. The share of government support is planned to be around 50 percent of the total budget and the remainder is to be borne by the private sector.

Role of Government

The Korean government maintains the position with respect to high-technology development that its role is not to be directly involved in research activities of a commercial nature but only actively to encourage and facilitate R&D activities by the respective role players through the market mechanism. The government clearly states (MOST, 1989) that its role is to be promoter and coordinator among participants such as the government-supported R&D institutes, universities, and private sector corporations. It encourages competition among private firms to develop technologies of a proprietary nature but at the same time also encourages collaboration (e.g., R&D consortia) in certain instances. The government's role is to show industry a vision related to high technology through medium- and long-term plans and to create conditions conducive to high-technology development by private firms. Government activity includes the supply of high-caliber research manpower, infrastructure, and information, as well as promotion of international cooperation.

The government is reluctant to involve itself directly in developing high technology of commercial value for several reasons (MOST 1989). First, it fears that direct assistance to or involvement with private firms would likely create the appearance of unfair practice in the eyes of competing countries, resulting in trade conflict, particularly with the United States. Second, if the government were to choose to be an active research partner with private firms, it would tend to favor large conglomerates that possess the resources and capability to develop high-technology products. It then would invite criticism on the grounds that it was helping further economic concentration in the hands of *chaebols*, which are already criticized for being too large. Third, the government is all too well aware of the negative experience of market distortions and problems it created during the 1970s, when it did involve itself in the development of heavy and chemical industries.

The government reluctance to become directly involved in high-technology research is manifested in the magnitude of the government R&D budget, which accounts for only 17.1 percent of the nation's total R&D expenditure. This does not mean, however, that the government stays away totally from active participation in high-technology development. Rather, the government can and will become an active player under the following conditions: (a) there is a high externality effect with implications of public interest; (b) the field involves technology with high risk and high investment, where private firms show no interest; (c) there is risk of market failure, and (d) there is high R&D cost beyond the capability of most private firms. Recently, the government's announcement of the HAN Project (MOST, 1991c), which identified seven high-technology-based products and seven generic high technologies, showed its willingness to exercise active leadership. This active leadership, however, does not imply that the government will take the driver's seat in executing research activities. It means that the government will deploy resources and administrative power to ensure that the projects with specific development targets achieve national objectives. To facilitate development, a government ministry is designated as the coordinating agency for each project that requires support from several government ministries and agencies; and the ministry is responsible for seeing that the project receives necessary resources and support.

Is High Technology a Panacea or Illusion for Korea?

All the government policies and signals indicate that Korea has opted to go "high technology" in selected areas as a means of steering the country into the highly competitive international market and ultimately to guide it into the club of AICs. Three questions emerge: First, can Korea, with its present level of technology, successfully develop high technologies? Second, if the answer to the first question is yes, can the high technologies developed in laboratories be transformed into new manufacturing industries that will be competitive in the world market?

Third, does the allocation of scarce resources invested in the development of high technologies justify the opportunity costs?

To address the first question, many negative reasons have been discussed why Korea should not endeavor to develop high technology yet. Many of these reasons are familiar arguments generally found in developing countries. One convincing argument is that Korea cannot afford the cost of developing high technology when the R&D budget for the whole of Korea is no larger than that of just one large corporation in the United States or Japan. An even more disturbing fact is that Korean firms are far behind in playing such critical strategies as technology alliance and R&D globalization, which many of the large Japanese and U.S. firms use to their advantage (Simon, 1991; Baba and Suzuki, 1991; Yamashita, 1991). These are strategies designed not only to complement and/or supplement local technology talents and thus increase the probability of success, but also to share the risk associated with volatile high technologies. Under the circumstances, it looks optimistic to expect that Korean researchers, lacking sufficient funds and the collaboration with foreign counterparts, can produce high technologies that will technologically and commercially outperform the AICs.

But Korea also has many positive factors conducive to success. Though the present level of science and technology is not considered highly advanced compared with the United States and Japan, Korea has perhaps accumulated enough critical mass in R&D capability to try to develop high technologies in limited areas. Three major factors are believed to contribute to the critical mass: (a) there is a good supply of high-caliber researchers, many of them trained abroad; (b) there are large numbers of private sector R&D organizations and many good public research institutes such as KIST and ETRI; and (c) there are the strategic development programs supported by the government. The force of the critical mass will be further intensified by the government's visionary R&D investment target, which is to increase from the present 2 percent of GNP to 5 percent by the year 2000. The efforts to develop high technologies are well coordinated by various short- and long-term plans and strategies structured in a systems approach. Perhaps more important is that the force of the critical mass and the related efforts are to be synergistically amplified by the "can-do" mentality implicit in the perceptions of the government officials, entrepreneurs, and researchers, which is derived from the powerful inertia associated with the country's phenomenal success in industrialization during the past few decades.

Second, when a "high-tech" product is developed successfully in a laboratory, can it be made into a large-scale commercial venture and ultimately expand into a viable "high-tech" industry in Korea? Obviously many factors are involved in making an innovative high technology into a commercial success. Even if the demand for the high-technology product is assured, at least three important factors require attention from a strategic perspective: (a) the general technological capability of local industries related to manufacturing of the new "high-tech" product; (b) the ability to source technology from foreign countries for critical parts and components, as well as certain production know-how necessary for large-scale manufacturing, which is not available from local sources; and (c) countermoves by foreign competitors who will attempt to keep the Korean companies from becoming serious competitors in the international market.

In general, Korean industry is still in the fledgling stage, particularly in such high-technology industries as biotechnology, electronics, new materials, mechatronics, machine tools, computers, and telecommunications. Korea produces and exports some high-tech products. The critical parts and components, however, as well as the manufacturing equipment and facilities necessary for the manufacture of the products, are still imported, mostly from Japan. This is clearly manifested in the trade statistics with Japan. The more Korea exports in "high-tech" products, the more it has to import from Japan.[6] There are too many gaps within Korea in the technology chains that collectively support a country's advancement in industrial development. What this implies is that even if a new "high-tech" product were developed in a laboratory ahead of other competitive countries, it might never be transformed by Korean industry alone into a large-scale commercial manufacturing technology, or else the time it takes to develop might be prolonged enough to jeopardize the timely introduction of the new product in the market. For example, in 1984, KIST discovered a new aramid pulp that was claimed to be stronger than DuPont's famous Kevler. KIST successfully acquired patents from the United States, Japan, West Germany, and other AICs, and decided to develop the manufacturing technology in Korea in collaboration with the Kolon Group, one of the *chaebols*. After eight years, the project was still in a pilot-plant stage and far from commercial production. Alternatively, the missing technologies could have been supported either by joint research with foreign firms or by technology transfer from AICs. But sourcing the "high-tech"-related technologies from AICs is increasingly difficult in these days of technonationalism.

In the case of Korea, the problem of sourcing from foreign firms may have become even more difficult; this is largely the result of inept moves by the Korean government. As discussed earlier, the government announced the so-called G–7 Projects, which have been highly publicized and must unwittingly have invited attention from potential competitors in Japan and the United States. Thus, it will be unlikely that Japanese and American firms will willingly support Korean firms trying to develop high technology. Sourcing necessary technologies and technology-imbedded equipment from AICs would still be available but only at a very high price, high enough to preclude the Korean firms from entering the world market competitively on a timely basis. Obviously, forming a technology alliance would firms in AICs is a viable option for Korean firms. But given the level of Korean technology, the likelihood is that the terms of alliance would be unequal, with Korean firms most probably becoming junior partners with limited benefits or compelled to pay high access fees.

Even when the Korean firms successfully develop high-technology products on a commercial scale, profitability is not assured: marketing becomes another hurdle to overcome. The countermoves by existing producers in the AICs effectively prohibit the new Korean entrants from becoming effective competitors even in the Korean market, let alone in the international market. Recently, the Korean government sent an official memorandum to the Japanese government threatening to impose countervailing duties unless dumping practices by Japanese firms in sixteen products exported to Korea were rectified. Most of the products are related to high technologies in electronics and petrochemicals, which the Korean firms have successfully localized recently. For example, when Samsung Electronics, after six years of development effort and 36 billion won (about $50 million) investment cost, started in 1990 to produce THP, a core part used in facsimile machines, Kyocera of Japan reduced the export price from 14,400 yen per unit to a mere 4,320 yen to maintain the market share in Korea. Another example is the small high-precision ball bearing used in video cassette recorders: the unit price charged by the Japanese companies fell by 13 percent when localized in Korea (*The HanKook Ilbo*, April 11, 1992). This kind of pricing strategy used to meet the new competitors in the international market is perhaps a legitimate business practice. The lesson emphasized here is that cracking the secret of high technology is a necessary but not sufficient condition for a developing country to create an economically viable new industry based on that high technology (Ernst and O'Connor, 1989). It is worth noting that the United States, which possesses the most advanced high technologies in almost all areas, does not necessarily enjoy a competitive edge against Japan. In this regard, Korea's recent successes in high technology (e.g., the 4 MB and 16 MB DRAM chips and the large scale digital electronic switch systems, TDX10), may have been temporary aberrations rather than repeatable achievements.

The third question raised earlier was whether the scarce resources invested in the development of high technologies justify the opportunity costs. This question has never been seriously discussed in Korea at the national-economy level. The need for high technology is accepted almost *a priori* by both government planners and entrepreneurs in Korea. It is partly because any attempts to calculate such opportunity costs at the national-economy level would require too many variables and alternative than any planners can possibly comprehend. However, individual firms investing in high technology do perform feasibility studies and try to calculate investment returns. Considering the difficulties and problems discussed above, however, many firms will never actualize what they set out to achieve. Perhaps Korea's experience along the learning curve in industrialization is simply too short to enable Korean firms to challenge the high technologies of AICs. Nevertheless, many entrepreneurs, encouraged by the government, will continue to attempt the challenge; they may not, however, bring about the desired returns within the time frame the entrepreneurs have planned.

The real returns may come to the national economy in the form of spinoff or fallout effects, which are not specifically measurable but are collectively real and substantive. The efforts will gradually fill the gaps in the technology chains that currently exist in Korea, and will also broaden the basis relevant to high-technology industries. Furthermore, they will help effectively shorten the time to cover the "high-tech" learning curve. Once that stage is reached, the reward will be realized cumulatively, just as the Japanese firms reap the reward exponentially these days after so many years of meticulous and continuous development and application of high technology.

Appendix

Table 4.1

R&D Expenditures and Government budget (million US$)

Year	R&D Exp. (A)	(A)/GNP %	Government S&T Budget	R&D Ratio to Govt. Budget		
				Korea	U.S.A.	Japan
1970	33	0.38	31	2.2	8.2	3.3
1971	29	0.31	33	1.9	7.5	3.3
1972	30	0.19	27	1.7	7.1	3.3
1973	39	0.29	33	2.0	7.0	3.2
1974	79	0.5	32	2.2	6.7	3.2
1975	88	0.42	63	2.0	6.0	3.2
1976	126	0.44	138	3.1	5.8	3.2
1977	224	0.61	166	2.9	5.8	3.1
1978	315	0.64	180	2.5	5.7	2.9
1979	360	0.57	276	2.6	5.7	3.0
1980	321	0.58	278	2.8	5.5	3.0
1981	418	0.64	310	2.6	5.5	3.0
1982	611	0.88	315	2.5	4.9	2.9
1983	782	1.01	324	2.4	4.7	2.9
1984	1,008	1.19	340	2.5	5.1	2.9
1985	1,298	1.48	397	2.8	5.1	2.9
1986	1,768	1.68	489	2.0	5.4	3.0
1987	2,370	1.78	712	2.4	5.5	3.1
1988	3,431	1.86	998	2.9	5.6	3.0
1989	3,980	1.91	1,111	2.4	5.5	2.9
1990		1.91	1,577	2.9		

Source: Korea Industrial Research Institutes (1991).

Table 4.2

R&D Expenditure by Type of Research (unit: current won in million)

Year	Total R&D Expenditure	Basic Research (%)	Applied Research (%)	Development Research (%)
1984	833,894	16.99	28.70	54.31
1985	1,155,156	16.85	29.18	53.96
1986	1,523,279	16.64	26.72	56.64
1987	1,877,965	16.63	19.60	63.77
1988	2,347,415	15.56	19.81	64.63
1989	2,705,104	14.95	18.20	66.85
1990	3,210,486	16.04	24.02	59.95

Source: MOST (1992).

Table 4.3

R&D Expenditures as Percent of Sales

Year	Korea Industry	Korea Manu-facturing	U.S.A. Industry	U.S.A. Manu-facturing	Japan Industry	Japan Manu-facturing
1976	0.34	0.39	—	—	1.42	1.64
1977	0.99	1.02	—	3.10	1.48	1.57
1978	0.60	0.72	—	3.00	1.57	1.82
1979	0.31	0.33	—	3.00	1.49	1.71
1980	0.47	0.50	—	3.10	1.48	1.73
1981	0.54	0.67	—	3.10	1.62	1.91
1982	0.58	0.65	—	3.70	1.78	2.15
1983	0.66	0.80	—	3.80	1.97	2.31
1984	1.03	1.30	—	3.80	1.99	2.34
1985	1.12	1.51	—	4.20	2.31	2.69
1986	1.35	1.63	—	4.20	2.31	2.69
1987	1.52	1.83	—	4.60	2.59	3.14
1988	1.61	1.88	—	4.80	2.60	3.15
1989	1.74	2.01	—	—	2.72	3.29

Source: Korea Industrial Research Institutes (1991).

Notes

1. The magnitude of this trade deficit in the Korean economy is equivalent to a $200 billion deficit in the context of the U.S. economy. At this rate, even the United States would have turned into a debtor country.

2. It is feared that a tightened intellectual property rights regime may be exploited by some countries under the disguise of a "neomercantilism" of technology.

3. The successful development of 4 MB and 16 MB DRAM semiconductor memory chips and TDX10 digital switching systems was the outcome of R&D consortia established between the Electronics and Telecommunications Research Institute (ETRI), a government-supported institute, and *chaebols*, conglomerates in the private sector.

4. Though the plan does not specify the names of the seven advanced countries, it seems implicitly to refer to the governments of the seven Western countries having the economic summit; hence the name G–7 Project.

5. Initially the name "G–7 Project" was used for domestic consumption, i.e., for publicity purposes, to draw the attention of the Korean people and entrepreneurs. But later, realizing the negative effects of the excessive claims implied in the name "G–7," the government started to call it the "HAN Project," which stands for Highly Advanced National Project. Incidentally, the word HAN also is used to refer to "the people of Korea."

6. The trade deficit with Japan for 1992 is projected to reach $10 billion, if the current trade pattern is allowed by the government to continue.

References

Baba, Yasunori, and Suzuki, T. "Japan's Evolving Strategies for Science and Technology: Toward the 21st Century." Chapter 13, this volume.

Choi, Hyung Sup. *Springboard Measures for Becoming a Highly Industrialized Society.* APCTT/UN ESCAP.

Council for Hi-Tech Industry Development. *Hi-Tech Industries and Intensification of Industrial Structure: Development Strategy for the Present and Future.* Seoul: Korea Institute of Economy and Technology (KEIT), 1989.

Ernst, Dieter. "Global Competition, New Information Technologies and International Technology Diffusion—Implications for Industrial Latecomers." Paper presented to the OECD Conference on "Technology and Competitiveness," Paris, June 24–27 1990.

Ernst, Dieter, and O'Connor, David. *Technology and Global Competition: The Challenge for Newly Industrializing Economies.* Paris: Development Center, OECD, 1989.

Hong, Yoo Soo. "Interactions of Economic, Industrial and Technology Policies in Korea." In *Role and Perspectives on Science and Technology Policy of the Government, University and Industry.* Proceedings of the Conference organized by CSTP/KIST and the University of North Carolina at Greensboro, 1989, pp. 89–105.

Lee, Hong Koo. "A Proposal for Investment Increase and Efficiency for Technology Development." Discussion paper. Seoul: Korea Development Institute, 1991.

Ministry of Trade and Industry (MOTI). *Five Year Plan for High-Tech Industry Development: 1990–1994.* Seoul: MOTI, Government of Korea, 1989.

Ministry of Science and Technology (MOST). *Twenty Years of Science and Technology Administration* (in Korean). Seoul: MOST, Government of Korea, 1987.

———. *High-Technology Development Basic Plan: 1990–1996.* Seoul: MOST, Government of Korea, 1989.

————. *The 7th Five Year Economic and Social Development Plan—1992–96: Science and Technology Sector* (draft). Seoul: MOST, Government of Korea, 1991a.

————. "Measure for Technology Intensification of Industry." Policy paper. Seoul: MOST, Government of Korea, 1991b.

————. "The Promotion Plan for the Development of Leading Technologies Required to Make Entry to an Advanced Country in the 2000s." *Report to Integrated Council for Science and Technology.* Seoul: MOST, Government of Korea, 1991c.

————. *Science and Technology Year Book 1991.* Seoul: MOST, Government of Korea, 1992.

Porter, Michael. *The Competitive Advantage of Nations.* London: Macmillan, 1990.

Rhee, Yung Whee; Ross-Larson, Bruce; and Pursell, Gary. *Korea's Competitive Edge: Managing the Entry into World Markets.* A World Bank Research Publication. Baltimore: Johns Hopkins University Press, 1985.

Simon, Denis F. "Globalization, Regionalization, and the Pacific Rim." Chapter 1, this volume.

Song, Byung-Nak. *The Rise of the Korean Economy.* Hong Kong: Oxford University Press, 1990.

"Too Rich Too Soon." *Newsweek* (November 11, 1991): 12–16.

UNESCO. *OECD Science and Technology Indicators Report: No. 3, R&D, Production and Diffusion of Technology.* Paris: UNESCO, 1989.

"The World in Figures: Countries," *The World in 1992.* London: *The Economist,* December 1991, p. 87.

Yamashita, Shoichi. "Japan's Role as a Regional Technological Integrator in the Pacific Rim." Chapter 16, this volume.

5

Singapore's Technology Strategy

Poh-Kam Wong

As one of the four Asian dragons, Singapore has achieved remarkable economic growth and technological development over the last three decades. As in other Asian NIEs, a major contributing factor to Singapore's past economic success has been its strategic emphasis on, and effective policies for, the development of human resources and supporting infrastructures. Unlike Taiwan and especially Korea, however, Singapore's rapid technological development has, until recent years, been achieved largely through its ability to attract investments from multinational corporations (MNCs), which bring in increasingly sophisticated technologies and know-how, rather than through indigenous technological development efforts.

While this strategy of emphasizing technology absorption through MNC investment has served the country well, Singapore by the late 1980s had achieved a level of economic development whereby further sustained growth would call for a much higher emphasis on proactive technological development. Consequently, the Singapore government's technology strategy in recent years has been evolving in the direction of encouraging greater R&D and innovation intensity. In addition, the strategy of achieving technology transfer through MNCs is continuously being refined and modified to further enhance its effectiveness in the face of growing competition by other NIEs and second-rung NIEs. Finally, the existing manpower development strategy is being intensified and supplemented by a more concerted program to attract overseas talent.

The objective here is to present an account of how the Singapore government's technology strategy has evolved over the years, and to identify the emerging issues and policy responses for the next few years. The organization of the chapter is as follows: in the next section, we present a framework for analyzing

the strategic issues of technological development in the context of newly industrializing economies. The third section then applies this framework to examine
the historical evolution of Singapore's S&T strategy; it first provides an overview of Singapore's evolving economic development strategy over the last two
decades, setting the context for identifying the changing patterns of technological development. We then briefly discuss the performance of Singapore's technology development, and highlight the potential biases of traditional indicators
of S&T performance. In the fourth section, we examine the emerging technology
strategy that the Singaporean government is pursuing as part of its new economic
development strategy for the 1990s. The final section concludes by highlighting
the problems and prospects that Singapore faces in pursuing this strategy.

Technological Development in Newly Industrializing
Economies: Strategic Issues

Technological development involves two basic thrusts: creation of new technological know-how and absorption or deployment of existing technological know-
how through various diffusion or transfer processes. Within each of these
strategic thrusts, a variety of activities can be pursued (Figure 5.1). For example,
creation can be done through R&D activities in private firms, universities, or
government laboratories, while absorption can be achieved through internalized
transfer from parent multinational enterprises (MNEs) to their subsidiaries, new
technology adoption and imitation by private firms, interfirm movement of staff,
and returning students from overseas. For a newly industrializing economy, the
major sources for technology absorption are likely to be foreign rather than local.
Different countries, however, may emphasize different means of international
technology acquisition.

In general, the overall extent to which a nation can effectively exploit technology as a source of competitive advantage in the marketplace depends not only on
the relative mix of resource allocation in technology creation versus absorption,
but also on the efficiency of such resource investments and their effective linkages. While technology creation and the selling of know-how is an important
source of economic power, the ability to exploit existing technology as inputs to
value-added activities may be even more important, as the rapid rise of Japan as
an economic power illustrates. Moreover, too early an emphasis on technology
creation may be socially inefficient if the infrastructure for diffusion and the
capacity for absorption and commercialization are not well developed.

In addition to this issue of investment in technology creation versus absorption, there is also the issue of public versus private sector involvement, and the
relative efficiency of each. The usual justification of public sector involvement is
that of externalities and other forms of market failures. To the extent that much
basic research, manpower training, and infrastructural support for technology
diffusion has a public good characteristic, they create significant positive exter-

nalities that cannot be easily appropriated by the investing party; consequently, the private sector would tend to underinvest compared with what is socially desirable. Another usual justification is the failure of the capital market in allocating finance and pooling risks for major R&D projects involving high fixed costs and great uncertainty. On the other hand, public sector involvement may also be socially inefficient due to agency problems, rent seeking by special interest groups, and other sources of government failure. In addition, many government macroeconomic, industrial, and social policies, even though they are not designed with technology development in mind, may nonetheless have a significant effect on the propensity and efficiency of private sector investment in technology development. Thus, government policies can affect technology development both directly as well as indirectly.

Countries at different stages of industrial development generally will need to emphasize different resource allocation choices. In particular, for relatively late-industrializing countries that are confronting other more industrialized nations in the marketplace, they will typically need to pursue a strategy of "follower" that emphasizes building up absorption capacity—the effectiveness of learning, assimilating, and possibly improving upon available technology created by others to gain competitive advantage. The public sector may need to play a significant role in this absorption-capacity-building stage. As the country moves up the technological ladder over time, the emphasis can then shift toward creating new technological know-how. Because the resource inputs and policy environments differ significantly between technology absorption and creation, it is important that policies and institutions established for an earlier period do not become entrenched and counterproductive in a later period.

A "follower" strategy need not preclude a "niche" strategy of focusing resources on technology creation in a small number of highly selected areas that may be relatively neglected even by more advanced countries, or where unique circumstances imply that technological leadership in those niche areas may confer disproportionately significant advantages. In this regard, the strategic fit between government investment in technology development and industrial policy is critical.

Singapore's Evolving S&T Strategy

As one of the newly industrializing economies, Singapore has basically pursued a "fast follower" strategy that seeks to absorb and exploit technology more efficiently and at a faster speed of diffusion than other developing countries, thereby gaining competitive advantages over them. In addition, being extremely small and open, Singapore is much more constrained by basic resources as well as highly vulnerable to the external environment. Consequently, the need for flexibility and to find particular niches on which to focus resources becomes even more critical for Singapore than it is for Korea or Taiwan.

While outward orientation, a liberal trade regime, and free-market competition have been a cornerstone of Singapore's economic success, government intervention has also played a very important role. As emphasized by Wade (1991), the two are not inconsistent; it is the *kind* of public sector intervention, not public intervention per se, that affects economic performance. This observation is particularly true in the case of government intervention in the area of technology development. Our basic argument is that the Singapore government's interventionist role in science and technology (S&T) development has been highly positive, and, moreover, has been flexibly evolved over time to serve the changing needs for economic development over the years.

To provide the historical context for understanding how Singapore's approach to S&T has evolved over time, it is useful first to review how Singapore's economic development strategies have evolved over the last three decades since colonial rule.

Phases of Economic Development

In a nutshell, Singapore's rapid economic growth over the last thirty years has involved a major transformation of the economic structure from a labor-surplus, entrepot-trade–based urban mercantile center within a largely rural, regional hinterland into a labor-short, modern regional business hub involving high-value-added manufacturing, transportation, trading, and services within one of the fastest-growing hinterland regions (ASEAN) in the world (see appendix A). In achieving this remarkable transformation, government development strategy has evolved over the years as circumstances changed. To facilitate discussion, we can divide this transformation process into three phases.[1]

Phase I: Early Industrialization (1959–1960s)

In the early period from independence in 1959 to the late 1960s, the Singapore government's most pressing concern was with employment creation. This was tackled through a concerted effort in attracting foreign investment in export-oriented manufacturing activities that created jobs. To make Singapore attractive for such investments, the government embarked right from the start on a program of infrastructural developments, including industrial estate, public utilities, and seaport facilities. At the same time, the government recognized correctly that the major bottleneck at that early stage of economic development is not skilled workers, but experienced managers, plant engineers, and supervisory/maintenance technical manpower. Consequently, a liberal policy of free immigration of foreign managers and technical staff is introduced to allow MNC investors to bring in the necessary personnel from overseas.

Phase II: Technological Upgrading (1970s–Early 1980s)

The foreign investment promotion program was highly successful and attracted major investments by MNCs, especially in the electronics sector. At the same time, the good location of Singapore also started to attract major investments in ship repair and maintenance and petroleum refining. With more manufacturing activities being attracted to Singapore, labor surplus turned into labor shortage, and an increasing demand for local supporting industries in machining, mould and die making, and precision engineering developed. To meet the rising demand for skilled workers, technicians and technically competent supporting industries, the government embarked on a massive program in industrial training to upgrade the skill levels of the workers and to increase the supply of technicians and engineers. Infrastructural investments were also intensified.

By the late 1970s, Singapore economy has experienced significant labor shortage. To meet this challenge, the government initially drew upon a ready supply of labor from Malaysia. However, as the amount of foreign labor became too large, the government embarked on a program to restrict foreign worker inflow and to introduce a deliberate high-wage policy to force firms to upgrade and phase out the lower-skilled, labor-intensive activities

*Phase III: Industrial Restructuring and Economic
Diversification (early 1980s–late 1980s)*

The industrial restructuring and high-wage policy that started in late 1970s were continued over the first half of the 1980s. At the same time, the financial and business services sectors were being emphasized as part of the industrial restructuring exercise to move the economy away from too high a dependence on manufacturing.

Partly as a result of slowdowns in the global and ASEAN regional economies and partly exacerbated by firms' failure to achieve productivity growth in line with the high wage policy and the rapid increase in land cost, the Singaporean economy lost competitiveness compared with other Asian NIEs and experienced a sharp recession in 1985. This prompted a major review of existing government policies and the formulation of a new economic development strategy to further diversify the economy and to improve its resilience (MTI, 1986). The high wage policy was moderated and a flexi-wage system put into practice. The industrial restructuring exercise that started in the late 1970s was continued, but with greater emphasis on government programs and policies to help local enterprises, especially the small and medium enterprises (SMEs), to grow and upgrade their technological capability. Business growth and technology transfer through linkages between local SMEs and the large foreign MNCs were also given greater emphasis. The concept of strategic business partnership was promoted to encourage long-term commitments by MNCs to operate in Singapore through continuous upgrading. New technology-intensive industries such as aerospace and printing and publishing were promoted, while the business services and transportation/logistics support sectors were given greater emphasis to strengthen Singapore's infrastructural competitive advantage.

Emerging Phase: Total Business Center, Knowledge-Intensive
Industrialization and Internationalization (1990s–   )

The end of 1990 saw the transition of political leadership from Mr. Lee Kuan Yew, who had been at the helm since independence, to a new and younger generation of political leaders headed by Mr. Goh Chok Thong. This transition helped crystallize the explicit formulation of a more coherent, comprehensive vision for the long-term strategic development directions of Singapore. Called the "Next Lap," this new vision for Singapore is to attain the status and characteristics of a first-league developed country within the next thirty to forty years (Government of Singapore, 1991). To achieve this vision, a Strategic Economic Plan (SEP) has recently been prepared by the Ministry of Trade and Industry (MTI) to chart the key economic development policies for the 1990s and beyond (MTI, 1991). The key elements of the SEP include: positioning Singapore as a global city or total business hub in the Asia Pacific region at par with other leading global cities in the world; emphasis on attracting high-tech, knowledge-intensive industries and promoting high-value innovative/creative activities; investment in enhancing human resources; promoting teamwork and cooperation between labor, business, and government; and internationalization of local firms as a means to transcend the constraints of small size and to achieve better access to overseas markets and technology.

Singapore's Approach to S&T under Different Development Phases

Singapore's approach to science & technology (S&T) development can be best characterized by its flexible and pragmatic adaptation to the requirements of economic development. Indeed, unlike many developing countries, Singapore until very recently did not have a well-developed and specialized institutional structure for formulating and implementing S&T policies. In 1968, a Ministry of Science and Technology was formed, but it never played an important role in development strategy, and was dissolved in 1981 with the bulk of its S&T functions taken over by the Singapore Science Council (SSC) which had existed since 1967. It was not until 1991, when the SSC was revamped to become the National Science and Technology Board (NSTB) under the Ministry of Trade and Industry (MTI), that an integrated, organizational framework was put in place to deal with S&T strategy formulation and implementation.

Similarly, until very recently, Singapore had no formal policy on S&T as spelled out in a plan or blueprint (Chng et al., 1986). It is true that, as part of its industrial restructuring plan initiated in 1979, the Ministry of Finance did formulate an indicative long-term R&D plan in conjunction with other interested agencies such as the Ministry of Trade and Industry (MTI), the Singapore Institute for Standards and Industrial Research (SISIR), and the Science Council. Similarly, in 1986, when the "New Directions" document was prepared by the

Ministry of Trade and Industry to help guide the Singaporean economy out of the 1985 recession, there was significant focus on specific S&T-related policies. Nonetheless, these indicative plans and policies were always regarded as part of an overall economic development strategy, and a multiagency framework was always adopted to implement the various policies.

Because of the constantly evolving nature of Singapore's technology development policies, it is somewhat misleading to talk in terms of a single set of policies or approach to technology development that is applicable throughout the past economic development phases. Nonetheless, in examining how Singapore's government policies and programs have changed over the years, one can analytically identify certain key, generic components of technology development that have always been emphasized by the Singapore government, even though the specific forms of policies and programs have varied significantly over the years. These components can be identified as:

- reliance on DFI as vehicle for technology transfer;
- flexible and responsive manpower development programs and policies;
- heavy commitment to infrastructure development to support technological deployment;
- rapid deployment of technology in the government sector;
- gradual increase in emphasis on R&D.

Policies to Encourage Technological Upgrading of MNC Operations and to Attract New "High-Tech" Investments

Throughout all phases of economic growth, a major contributing factor to the growth in technological sophistication of Singapore's economic base has been the significant inflow of foreign technology through capital-embodied know-how and expatriate technical expertise and managers.

As pointed out earlier, in the early phase of industrialization, Singapore concentrated on attracting investments that were labor-intensive. Generous tax incentives through pioneer status schemes were introduced to encourage such investments, in addition to the heavy investments by the government in public infrastructures. Over time, as the economy approached full employment, the government switched to attracting investments that would bring higher-valued contents. Existing MNCs were encouraged to upgrade their operations in order to continue to enjoy tax incentives, while preferences were given to new investments that had higher technological contents.

A pragmatic, market-oriented approach appeared to have been taken with regard to what constituted investments with higher technological contents. Basically, MNCs made the decisions about what new technologies to bring into Singapore, with the Singapore government responding (or anticipating through proactive planning and consultation) by providing the necessary skilled manpower in consultation with the MNCs. In many instances, it is the speed and flexibility of government response that gave Singapore the competitive edge compared with other competing host countries. In particular, the boom in investment in offshore production by MNCs in the electronics industry in the 1970s and early 1980s created a major opportunity by ensuring that all the enabling supporting industries, transport and communications infrastructures, as well as relevant skills training programs were available to attract these industries to Singapore. This concentration of resources helped Singapore to achieve significant agglomeration economies and hence first-mover advantage for many electronics-related industries. An example is the disk-drive industry, where all the major U.S. disk-drive makers have located their assembly plants in Singapore. These industries demanded not only electronics components and PCB assembly support, but also various precision engineering-related supporting industries such as tool and die, plastic injection moulding, electroplating, and others. These supporting industries were actively promoted by the government as part of a "clustering" approach (Porter, 1990) to ensure the competitiveness of the downstream industries.

By the late 1980s, labor and land costs in Singapore had risen so much relative to other ASEAN countries that many MNC manufacturing operations in Singapore had become uncompetitive. Consequently, many have started to relocate some of their operations to Malaysia, Thailand, and Indonesia. Rather than try to delay such redistribution with incentives, the Singapore government used the opportunity to encourage these MNCs to reconfigure their operations on a regional basis, making Singapore their regional administrative headquarters and/or regional marketing/distribution/services/R&D centers to support their manufacturing and sales operation in the ASEAN and Asia-Pacific region.

To promote such reconfiguration, new incentives such as the regional headquarter (RHQ) scheme, international procurement office (IPO) scheme, international logistics center (ILC) scheme, and the approved international trader (AIT) scheme are introduced. In addition, since 1990, the Singapore government has actively promoted the concept of a "Growth Triangle" comprising Singapore, the southern state of Malaysia (Johor), and the Riau islands of Indonesia.[2] MNCs are encouraged to invest in the triangle on an integrated basis, with more land- and labor-intensive operations located in Johor or the Indonesian islands. Overseas investment promotion is conducted jointly by the three countries concerned, while labor, material, and capital movement among the three areas is being simplified. Singapore also offers to assist the triangle counterparts to improve their infrastructures.

While most of the above-mentioned policies toward foreign investment are not explicitly related to technology development, they have been very important in enabling foreign firms to maintain their presence in Singapore through operational upgrading, even when some of their existing activities are being redistributed to other countries in the region.

Promotion of MNC Technology Transfer to Locals

While no detailed statistics are available, various indirect evidence suggests that there has been a very high rate of technological know-how gains by local staff working in the various MNC operations in Singapore. While these gains were derived mainly through know-how transfer in the form of supervised learning in the initial stages, increasingly, the gains are made simply through having the opportunities of learning by doing. Indeed, in some instances, the manufacturing process know-how of these MNCs no longer resides in their parent companies, but among the engineering and technical staff working in their production facilities in Singapore. This is evident from the fact that process engineers from Singapore have been sent to help in the initial set-up and subsequent process improvements of other plants in the parent country or elsewhere.[3] There has also been an increasing number of instances of senior engineers and managers leaving these MNC operations to start their own businesses, although the absolute number of such cases is still low.

In addition to the sizable transfer of know-how to local staff employed in the various MNC operations in Singapore, there has been considerable technology development induced among local firms by the presence of MNCs in Singapore (see Wong, 1991a). In particular, many local SMEs in the various electronics supporting industries have benefited not only through direct and indirect technology know-how transfer while working as subcontractors to the MNCs, but in many cases, they have also been induced to invest in technological development at a faster pace as a result of their long-term relationship with the MNCs. Through a program called Local Industry Upgrading Programme (LIUP), the Singapore government has actively promoted this technological transfer mechanism through MNC linkages to stimulate the technological development of local subcontracting firms.

Manpower Development Programs

Like Taiwan and Korea, Singapore made a major investment commitment in human resources development right from the start of industrialization. While the forms and emphasis of training have changed tremendously over the years, the guiding principle has always been that the kinds of training and skill formation must be made relevant to the economic development requirements of the country. Indeed, it is the flexibility and nimbleness by which Singapore has been able to adapt its manpower development programs that have contributed to the relatively high effectiveness of its investments in training.

In the early industrialization phase, the government concentrated attention on general industrial training to inculcate good work attitudes and industrial discipline among the mass of relatively unskilled workers available at the time. Bottlenecks in experienced managers were overcome through a liberal policy of allowing foreign firms to bring in the necessary expatriate staff. In retrospect, this policy has been very important in getting the industrialization process started (Soon, 1991). Through this inflow of key personnel, the learning period was substantially reduced, thereby shortening the critical path for project development and profitability. At the same time, it facilitated the training and development of young engineers and managers by allowing them to work with more experienced staff. This "quick start" approach is further enhanced by an industrial development scholarship scheme by EDB whereby financial assistance was provided to MNCs to send their local employees abroad for in-plant, apprenticeship training.

As the economy approached full employment in a relatively short time, the government's industrial training emphasis switched to more skill-specific training, especially at the technician level. The training of engineers was also emphasized. Besides expanding tertiary training through the two polytechnics and the national university, overseas industrial training institutes were started for high-skill occupations requiring a long apprenticeship period, such as tool and die making, computer numerical control (CNC), computer-aided design (CAD), and other precision engineering skills. The innovative feature of these institutes is that they were invariably organized as joint ventures between the government and MNCs or reputable overseas training institutes, and that workers were paid an allowance while in training to provide added incentives. The participation of foreign reputable partners provided quality assurance as well as technology transfer to local administration and training staff. To encourage firms to invest in skill training, a skill development fund (SDF) was also established through a levy on firms, which is used to subsidize various approved training and productivity/quality improvement programs.

Since the mid-1980s, when a National Information Technology (IT) Plan was launched to greatly expand the IT infrastructure of the country, a massive training program for industrially relevant IT professionals was implemented. In addition, a program to train office workers in the basic use of office automation software and equipment has also been implemented to raise white-collar productivity.

In more recent years, the emphasis on training has shifted to highly specialized professional manpower, especially in the information technology-related industry. These include new postgraduate programs in knowledge engineering, advanced computer communications, and computer-integrated manufacturing (CIM).

Besides the increasing sophistication of industrial manpower training, the general primary and secondary educational system of the country has also undergone restructuring away from the British system to incorporate certain features of the German system, especially their emphasis on technical\vocational training and mathematical skills formation.[4] The overall quality of general education has also improved over the years. Introduction of computers in the classroom has been widespread, and new modes of educational delivery such as home-based videotext systems (through Teleview) and multimedia educational softwares are being actively promoted. A third polytechnic has been started and a fourth is being planned, while an existing technological institute had been upgraded into a university. A third university, modeled after the United Kingdom's Open University, has also been launched to make university education accessible to working adults.

Supporting Infrastructure Development

The Singapore government recognized quite early on that its competitive advantage in the region lies in superior supporting infrastructures, especially in telecommunications, sea/air transport, and public utilities. Indeed, public investments in these areas over the last three decades have more than kept pace with the needs of private industries, with the government often planning ahead and introducing cost-reducing or capability-enhancing technological improvements in advance of competing countries. In particular, continuous government investments in upgrading airport and seaport facilities have made these among the most efficient in the world.

By the early 1980s, the government had explicitly identified certain key clusters of generic enabling technologies that should be actively promoted in an integrated way through proactive public investment. These include information technology (IT), telecommunications, industrial automation, and biotechnology. A National Computer Board (NCB) was set up in the early 1980s to spearhead the diffusion of IT exploitation, and a National IT Plan was formulated in 1985 to coordinate this big push toward an IT society. Three years later, a National Automation Plan was also launched to promote the adoption of automation in all sectors of the economy, particularly the manufacturing sector.

In addition to the massive manpower development efforts mentioned earlier, the launching of the National IT Plan has resulted in a corresponding big expansion of public investment in IT infrastructures. These include a rapid program of digitalization of the public-switched telecommunications network, aggressive investments in optical fibers network, early introduction of ISDN, provision of EDI-network services such as TRADENET, PORTNET, LAWNET, and soon, introduction of a high-resolution videotext system (Teleview), and development of expert systems to improve port management and airline services. For the research community, the National University of Singapore (NUS) was one of the first universities in Asia to have a campus-wide computer network. More recently, a nationwide TECHNET was established among all major research institutes in the country, with connection to INTERNET. The acquisition of a supercomputer by a government agency several year ago also represents another strategic investment in supporting infrastructures.

Strong support has also been given to infrastructural development for promoting factory automation as part of the national automation plan. Besides providing subsidized automation equipment leasing, an Automation Applications Centre (AAC) was set up to provide consultancy and training in automation, especially among the SMEs, at highly subsidized rates. Automation cultures and awareness programs are also organized to popularize automation and to encourage worker acceptance.

Since the mid-1980s, efforts were also intensified to provide technological development assistance to local firms, especially the SMEs. Financial assistance in the forms of small industry technical assistance schemes (SITAS), product development assistance schemes (PDAS), and computerization grants was implemented. Other direct technical assistance programs were introduced through various government-funded centers such as the Design Services Centres, Technology Diagnostics Center, Software Quality Assurance Centre, and the industrial services arms of the universities and polytechnics.

Finally, to encourage the growth of "high-tech" industries, a Science Park was established in 1981. Although the initial take-up was slow, by the second half of the 1980s the park had attracted quite a number of high-tech firms especially in software, IT product development, and biotechnology. By the end of 1990, the first phase of the park was almost completely occupied, and a second phase was being developed. Although no systematic study has been carried out since to assess the economic impact of the park, impressionistic reports suggest that the park has achieved a critical mass of R&D-intensive activities.[5] Other specialized industrial facilities, such as business parks for the medical and media industries and a chemical island complex to support chemical process industries, are being planned or implemented.

Rapid Deployment of Technology in the Government Sector

As part of the strategy to improve the efficiency of supporting infrastructures for economic development, the Singapore government itself has invested heavily in adopting and deploying technology. Being a lead user of technology also provides the desirable demonstration effects to the private sector, especially the SMEs. For example, as part of the National IT Plan, the government embarked on an ambitious program of civil service computerization. Between 1985 and 1990, the number of mainframe\minicomputers installed in government departments jumped from 35 to 107, the number of systems developed increased from 72 to 293, while annual computer spending increased from S$14 million to S$200 million.

This rapid computerization in the government services made possible the provision of the various EDI network services to the business community (e.g., TRADENET for export–import customs declaration and related document processing). Other examples of government initiatives in technology adoption include a computerized land register and mapping system, an expert system for port management, and MediNet system for the national healthcare system, as well as a proposed smartcard system for implementing and electronic area road pricing system (the current system is manual). The Ministry of Defense has also invested heavily in technology as part of its national defense strategy.

In addition to technology absorption in the government sector, various government-owned enterprises have also been established to spearhead commercially oriented investments in various technology-intensive business areas. A good example is the Singapore Technologies Group, which has diverse investments in aerospace, electronics, testing services, and semiconductors. In addition to "green-field" investments, these companies have also increasingly engaged in joint-ventures and strategic alliances with selected overseas technology-based companies.

Promotion of R&D

Because of the stress on improving capacity to absorb and exploit existing technologies, Singapore's public sector investment in R&D, either directly through funded institutions or indirectly through grants to private sector, had been relatively low until very recently (see the next section). As for the private sector, the amount of investment in formal R&D activities had also been relatively low, although there has been a significant increase in recent years. Indeed, as several rounds of surveys of R&D expenditure and manpower over the period 1978–90 show (see appendix B), Singapore's gross expenditure in R&D as a share of GNP (GERD/GNP), although steadily increasing, had consistently trailed behind not only the major OECD countries, but behind Taiwan and Korea as well (see appendix C). As late as 1990, Singapore's GERD/GNP ratio of 1 percent and the ratio of research scientists and engineers (RSE) per 10,000 labor force of 28 percent are still somewhat lower than Taiwan's and Korea's, and significantly below those of Japan, the United States, and Germany.

Of the total estimated R&D expenditures, the private sector accounted for 67 percent in 1978. This dropped to less than half by the mid-1980s, but increased again to over 60 percent toward the end of 1980. The bulk of recorded private sector R&D occurs in the electronics industry, with MNCs predominating. The share of the services sector (including IT) in private sector R&D, although still small, has increased steadily (10 percent in 1981/82 versus 20 percent in 1990).

Until the second half of the 1980s, the Singapore government did not make significant investment in R&D institutions. Besides the higher educational institutions (which typically account for two-thirds of public sector R&D), the only other major industrial research institute is the Singapore Institute for Standards and Industrial Research (SISIR). It is only in the last few years that several new research institutes have been set up. These include the Information Technology Institute (ITI) set up under the NCB to pursue R&D in IT; the Institute for Molecular and Cell Biology (IMCB) set up as an autonomous unit within the National University to pursue R&D in biotechnology; and the Institute for Manufacturing Technologies (IMT), set up within the upgraded Nanyang Technological University to pursue R&D in advanced manufacturing technologies. In addition, several existing training institutions were expanded to cover R&D

work as well, including the Institute of Systems Science (ISS), GINTIC, and the Japan Singapore Institute for Software Technology (JSIST). The new Information Communications Institute of Singapore (ICIS), set up as a joint venture between Bell Labs and NCB to provide postgraduate training in advanced communications, is also expected to engage in R&D work.

Public funding to encourage R&D by private enterprises and private industry–university joint ventures was initiated only in 1980. This was pricipally channeled through two schemes, the R&D Assistance Scheme (RDAS) and Product Development Assistance Scheme (PDAS). The RDAS is intended to promote medium-to long-term mission-oriented research projects for the advancement of specific objectives, while PDAS provides grants to encourage locally owned firms to acquire new product\process design and development capabilities. The total amount of disbursement over the last ten years, although increasing, remained modest (S$75 million and S$10.5 million respectively, at the end of 1990). Moreover, the bulk of the RDAS grants had gone to the bigger companies and university research projects.

In more recent years, the effort to promote private sector R&D has expanded to cover a wider range of services. An R&D incubator scheme and a design and development support service were introduced by SISIR to speed up the process of commercialization of R&D outputs, while a new R&D grant scheme called INTECH was introduced to encourage new initiatives in technology development that do not fall within the existing guidelines for RDAS eligibility. The government also actively promoted the development of a venture capital industry.[6]

Technology Development Performance

The relatively poor performance of Singapore compared with the OECD countries and Taiwan and Korea, as measured by the various formal S&T indicators (see appendix C), seems to imply that Singapore's technology development performance has lagged behind these economies considerably. Other formal S&T indicators such as the number of patents granted and net flows of technology payments through royalties are not readily available for Singapore, but one would suspect that they too would indicate low performance.[3]

Despite this poor performance record on the technology-creation front, the relatively good economic performance and productivity growth achieved by Singapore suggests that Singapore has actually performed very well on the technology-absorption front. Indeed, Singapore now has among the highest ratios of robots, CNC machines, and computers per worker in the world. This points out the problem of traditional measures of S&T performance, which tend to emphasize indicators of "formal" S&T inputs and activities, principally R&D indicators and commercial technology transactions. The experience of Singapore strongly suggests that such indicators may be misleading for newly industrializing countries where technology-absorption-capability development has been more critical for their economic success than technology creation. A large part of the technology-absorption processes in these countries (e.g., technology transfer and inducement through DFI and learning by doing, process improvements, testing and maintenance know-how, quality assurance know-how, and the like) are often "informal" and hence not captured in statistics on R&D, technology licensing, or technical assistance agreement.[8] Moreover, the number of experienced managers, skilled workers, and technicians productively employed in technology absorption may be as important as the number of research scientists and engineers.[9]

Finally, there is an inherent bias toward manufacturing technologies and "hard" sciences in many of the traditional indicators of S&T. In contrast, technological competence in many business services sectors are often not well defined and hence tend to be underestimated. With Singapore being an extremely open economy and home to most world-class MNCs, Singapore-based firms were very market-driven and consequently focused a lot of their resources on investing in technology to improve service quality and productivity. Although many of these technology applications efforts in the services area are not classified as R&D, they do in fact involve a considerable amount of learning, adaptation, creation, and accumulation of new know-how that adds to Singapore's competitiveness. This is particularly true of a great deal of investment in information systems, software development, and operations management. Given that close to two-thirds of Singapore's economy now lie in services-related sectors, conventional S&T indicators that stress only the manufacturing sector will underestimate the technological strengths of Singapore's economic base.

The relatively high performance in technology absorption achieved by Singapore in the past thirty years suggests that the government intervention role has been generally effective. A major contributor to this relative absence of government failures is that the system for recruitment into the government technocracy has been relatively meritocratic, and that the technocrats have been able to act relatively autonomously due to the political leadership's ability to insulate the technocracy from interest-group pressures (Ng and Suedo, 1991).

Emerging Issues and Policies for the 1990s

The Need to Invest in Innovation

While the above account described the main thrusts of government technology development strategy over the past thirty years, a set of new priorities is beginning to emerge as Singapore enters the 1990s. While the past development phases have largely emphasized technology absorption, this new phase of economic development envisions a much greater need to invest in the capacity to create new technology. This calls for:

- increasing government funding for R&D;
- promotion of R&D by private enterprises;
- expanding the supply of S&T manpower;
- promotion of a more innovative and creative culture among the population.

The intensified focus on innovation and knowledge-intensive activities is motivated by competitive pressures from three directions. First, increasing competitiveness by the next-rung NIEs (Malaysia, Thailand, Mexico, etc.) is making Singapore less attractive for a wide range of existing economic activities. Singapore therefore needs to find new, higher-value-added niches to establish its comparative advantages as an offshore DFI platform despite its rising costs and labor-shortage constraints. This repositioning requires the country to increase the supply of knowledge-intensive and innovative talents, much of which can only be produced through learning by doing—by actually engaging in R&D-related work and creative design activities.

Second, Singapore is coming into increasing competition with other Asian NIEs in the race to penetrate into high-tech sectors. Both the Taiwan and Korean governments have embarked upon ambitious ten-year plans to accelerate R&D and to enhance the technological capabilities of their indigenous firms (Arensman, 1991). Over the last few years, Taiwan and Korean technology-based exports have expanded significantly and come increasingly into direct competition with exports from Singapore. Korean and Taiwan overseas investments in Southeast Asia have also soared.

Third, Singapore's attempt to move up the technological ladder is increasingly pitching her against previously more advanced countries, including many in the OECD league that have been source countries in terms of technology transfer in the past. As in other Asian NIEs, there is a growing concern that Singapore may face increasing reluctance on the part of firms from these countries to share their technological know-how with Singaporean firms, which are increasingly being perceived as rivals in the marketplace.

The New National Technology Plan (NTP)

It is largely in response to the above perceived needs to increase the nation's innovative capacity that the Singapore government (mid-September 1991) announced a new National Technology Plan (NTP) to promote R&D over the next five years. A new National Science and Technology Board (NSTB), formed at the beginning of the year to take over the functions of the Singapore Science Council, was entrusted with the responsibility for coordinating the implementation of the plan.

The NTP is formulated through a special ministerial committee on S&T chaired by the Minister for Trade and Industry (MTI). Nine expert committees comprising representatives from private, public, and academic sectors were established and their deliberations were reported to this ministerial committee. Each of these expert committees covers one of the nine key technology areas identified by the NTP. These include biotechnology, medical sciences, food and agrotechnology, microelectronics, electronics systems, information technology, manufacturing technology, materials technology, and energy, water, environment, and resources.

As part of the NTP, a S$2 billion government funding allocation for R&D over the period 1991–95 was announced. The allocations for specific programs is as indicated in appendix D. This dramatically increased public sector funding and its allocation is designed with the following objectives:

- to help develop broad-based technological and manpower capabilities in the nine key technological areas identified above;
- to help develop more specialized capabilities in a few selected key technologies in each area;
- to set up new, publicly funded R&D centers and institutes to undertake precompetitive R&D;
- to expand assistance and support to the private sector in their developmental and commercialization effort;
- to develop physical and other technology infrastructure to support R&D efforts

The NTP is targeted to help Singapore to raise its GERD/GNP ratio from the current 1 percent to 2 percent by 1995, and the corresponding RSE per 10,000 labor force figure of 28 to 40. While somewhat ambitious, it should be noted that, even if these targets are achieved, Singapore would still be somewhat behind current Taiwan RSE figures and projected Korean figures.

Under the NTP, NSTB will be the main coordinating body for the various programs funded. In addition to being the administrative and approving authority on the various research grant schemes, one of NSTB's responsibilities is to take over the coordination of the various research institutes and centers that have already been set up by the government. These include the autonomous research and technology institutes located within NUS, such as the Institute of Molecular and Cellular Biology (IMCB), Institute of Systems Science (ISS), Institute of Microelectronics (IME), and Clinical Research Centre; SISIR; the Information Technology Institute (ITI), the research arm of the National Computer Board; and research institutes and centers affiliated with NTU, such as the GINTIC Institute of CIM. In addition, NSTB is also expected to be involved in the planning and coordination of the setting up of new research cetners funded by the NTP budget. These are likely to include a new magnetics research center to support the disk-drive industry, and the new Institute of Manufacturing Technology (IMT) to be established in NTU to support research in advanced manufacturing and factory automation technologies.

The announcement of the NTP and its associated new funding allocation signals a more proactive approach to R&D promotion by the government. This proactive approach will definitely have an impact on Singapore's technological trajectory. It is expected that the NSTB will use the Economic Development Board (EDB) model of investment promotion with emphasis on flexibility and discretionary power to adapt to market opportunities, use of eminent foreign experts for external environment scanning, quick response in developing infrastructural supports, and close consultation with key foreign MNCs. Indeed, close collaboration with the EDB in synergizing and developing an overseas network of contacts and investment promotion is expected.

To improve the physical supporting infrastructures for R&D, a total of S$335 million out of the S$2 billion NTP budget, or nearly 17 percent, has been allocated to the development and expansion of the Science Park over the period 1991–95. As currently envisaged, the Science Park will eventually comprise four phases with a total area of 110 ha. (versus 30 ha. in the existing phase I area). In addition, new business parks and entertainment/commercial outlets are being planned to complement the science parks. This physical expansion will eventually link the science parks and the two existing universities into a "technology corridor" that integrates R&D facilities, supporting business parks, housing, recreation, and cultural and social amenities and fosters close interaction and pleasant living environment for the research community.

Other New Strategic Directions

Besides the new emphasis on R&D promotion, several strategic directions that have emerged in very recent years are also envisaged to take on much greater quantitative significance over the next few years. These include:

Promotion of Creative and Design Skills

As part of the move toward higher-value-added, innovative activities, the government recognizes the need to promote greater creativity and design skills, both in the industrial sectors (e.g., new product ideas, product design, and packaging) as well as in the services sectors (advertising, marketing entertainment, etc.). Many of these skills are also regarded as crucial supporting infrastructures for the successful commercialization of new products and services. Toward this end, the government established in early 1991 a high-level National Design Council (chaired by a senior minister of state) to spearhead design promotion and development. Under the council, a Design Centre has been set up to promote design awareness, provide design assistance to industry, and sell Singapore to the world as a design-conscious nation. A Design Institute has also been set up to conduct design education, training, and research. A Young Designers Award was also introduced to complement the existing Young Scientist and Engineer Awards.

International Acquisition of Technology-Based Companies

Over the last few years there has been a notable increase in the number of local firms investing abroad to acquire or buy into selected technology-based companies in Australia, the United States, and Europe. This trend is expected to accelerate over the next few years. While the various government-owned companies are likely to continue to play an important role in this regard, we can expect to see more local corporations entering the scene. More strategic alliances between Singapore firms and overseas technology-based companies are also expected. This increase in overseas technology acquisition activities is expected to form part of a larger strategy to internationalize Singapore's indigenous firms.[10]

Strategic Partnership with Key MNCs and Overseas Research Institutes

While the government has for some time emphasized the importance of strategic, long-term partnerships with the leading global MNCs that have invested in Singapore, the new emphasis over the next few years is likely to be on technology partnerships, whereby the MNCs are encouraged to set up more R&D facilities in Singapore and to initiate more joint R&D projects with local firms or government institutions. In strategic areas, the government will also enter into joint venture with foreign MNCs to share risk as well as to gain access to the technology. An example of this is the joint venture between EDB, Texas Instruments, Hewlett Packard, and Canon to set up a new US$330 million advanced semiconductor factory in Singapore initially to fabricate 16MB DRAM chips designed by TI. MNCs are also encouraged to use Singapore as their regional technology business center in the ASEAN and wider Asia-Pacific region. An example is Sony Precision Engineering Corporation (SPEC), which was initially established in Singapore to provide in-house automation system development services for Sony's various production plants in the ASEAN region, but is now positioned to provide such services to other companies in the region as well.

Besides partnership with MNCs, various government research institutes and public enterprises are also actively forging technology alliances with overseas research institutes. SISIR, for example, has recently established a collaborative relationship with selected research institutes in the People's Republic of China.

Attracting S&T Talents from Overseas

In addition to investment in local manpower development, the NTP explicitly recognizes that Singapore will be unable to produce the number of highly qualified and experienced technical professionals that will be needed to support the higher R&D intensity envisioned. Consequently, the budget allocation for manpower development (S$158 million) is likely to include significant provisions to attract foreign talents to come to work in Singapore.

To implement this strategy, the Economic Development Board (EDB) has established a new International Manpower Development Division specifically to attract overseas talents. While Malaysia, the People's Republic of China (PRC), and Hong Kong are expected to be major sources of such talent, the new division is likely to reach much wider to the more advanced industrial countries to cover strategic areas of skills and expertise. The emphasis is likely to be on quality at the very top level as well as quantity at the lower levels.[11]

In addition to these new strategic directions, the various existing technology absorption programs, such as the National IT Plan and the National Automation Masterplan, are being adapted and extended to take into consideration the new emphasis on promoting higher-value-added innovative applications. For example, a new National IT Plan (called IT2000) has recently been formulated to guide IT development for the next decade.

Conclusion

Singapore's technology strategy has always been an integral part of its overall economic development strategy. As the national economic development strategy has continuously evolved over the years in response to the constantly changing external environment, so too has its policies toward technology development. Being a small and very open economy, Singapore has relied heavily on attracting foreign investments and talents as a means to acquire technological competence, and it is only in very recent years that a more concerted attempt has been made to promote indigenous R&D and innovative capacity. Even then, the main thrust is not so much to reduce dependence on foreign technologies and talents but to strengthen Singapore's attractiveness as a regional hub for high-tech, knowledge-intensive, innovative activities for corporations and talents from all over the world. At the same time, local corporations are encouraged to upgrade into higher-value-added activities domestically as well as to internationalize their operations and acquire overseas firms that provide greater access to technologies. In summary, Singapore's technological trajectory in the 1990s can be described as one involving two parallel prongs: increasing *strategic partnership and networking* with high-tech MNCs and other international innovation sources on the one hand, and increasing *competition* with other NIEs and a significant number of OECD countries for technology-based product markets, technology-intensive investments, and talents on the other hand.

The challenge that Singapore will face in making this new strategic thrust is likely to be greater than before. First, Singaporean firms will come into increasing direct competition with firms in other NIEs. In this competition, Singapore is disadvantaged by its much smaller domestic market base as well as by human-resources supply constraint. For example, both Taiwan and Korea have been able to draw upon a large flow of highly trained returnees, who have studied in the

United States and subsequently acquired leading-edge technical expertise through working in various high-tech industries there. Moreover, the high dependence on MNCs as the source of technology in Singapore has resulted in a relatively underdeveloped base of indigenous high-tech firms, in strong contrast to Korea and Taiwan. With increasing competition for MNC investments from the next-rung NIEs, Singapore is more vulnerable than Korea or Taiwan.

Second, Singapore will also come into increasing competition with firms in the advanced OECD countries. As a result, some of these firms will become more reluctant to license technologies to Singaporean firms that they perceive as potential competitors. Moreover, in competing for market penetration in the OECD countries, Singapore is particularly disadvantaged by its relative lack of marketing expertise and international brand name reputation. Because of the high past dependence on MNCs, most of the indigenous technology-based firms that have emerged in Singapore are still OEM producers or contract manufacturers to MNCs rather than makers of own brand-name products. Thus, the attempt to become end-user product innovators involves more than developing R&D capability, but may require significant investment in building up international marketing management skills, brand names, and other complementary assets.

Third, as Singapore seeks to move into more technologically intensive activities such as product design and R&D, it will become increasingly difficult to attract foreign direct investment in such activities through investment incentives alone. Taking equity stakes in such ventures may be necessary, as illustrated by the recent joint venture between EDB and Texas Instruments. The risks involved in such equity investments, as well as the heightened public sector investment in R&D, will inherently be greater compared with past investments in infrastructure and manpower developments, and hence will test the technocratic as well as political leadership's ability to manage public risks.

Fourth, and more important, the new thrust will face an immediate bottleneck of highly trained and experienced R&D technical and creative talents. In tackling this problem, the political leadership will need to pay greater attention to the factors that are conducive to attract, keep, and motivate these scarce talents. While financial rewards will be important, other "quality of life" factors such as the social, cultural, and political environment will also matter. Yet, in trying to address the needs of this elite group, a sizable proportion of which will be noncitizens, the political leadership must ensure that it does not alienate the general population of citizens on whose votes its continued rule depends.

Last is the larger issue of how a society that has developed an extremely efficient system and educational culture for absorbing existing technological know-how can best move toward one that encourages creativity, nonconformist thinking, tolerance of failure, and new forms of risk taking. This issue, in fact, may be the most important, and yet most difficult one to confront and overcome.

Appendix A

Table A.1

Singapore GDP Distribution by Sectors

	1960	1970	1980	1990p
Agriculture & Mining	3.9	2.7	1.5	0.4
Manufacturing	11.7	20.2	28.1	26.4
Utilities	2.4	2.6	2.1	1.8
Construction	3.5	6.8	6.2	5.1
Commerce	33.0	27.4	20.9	15.7
Transport & Communication	13.6	10.7	13.5	11.8
Financial & Business Services	14.4	16.7	18.9	29.7
Other Services	17.6	12.9	8.7	9.2
Total	100%	100%	100%	100%

Source: Calculated from MTI (1990).
Notes: Figures may not add up to 100 due to rounding.

Table A.2

Aggregate Economic Growth Performance, 1960–90

	% real growth p.a.		
	1960–70	1970–80	1980–90
GDP	8.7	9.4	7.1
Productivity	n.a.	4.3	4.8
	1960	1970	1980
GNP per capita (S$) (at current prices)	1,330	2,825	9,941

Source: Calculated from MTI (1990).

Appendix B:
Estimated R&D Expenditure
and Manpower Trends, 1978–90

The tables in this appendix are based on data from the Science Council of Singapore (1989a, 1989b).

Table B.1

Gross R&D Expenditure (GERD) in Singapore, 1978–90

Year	GERD ($m)	GNP ($m)	GERD/GNP
1978	37.8	17,462	0.2
1981/82	81.0	26,389	0.3
1984/85	214.3	38,515	0.6
1987/88	374.7	43,272	0.9
1990	638	63,905	1.0

Table B.2

Gross R&D Expenditure by Sector, 1978–90 (in $m)

Year	Private Sector	Higher Education Sector	Government Sector	Total
1978	25.5	8.2	4.1	37.8
1981/82	44.2	24.3	12.5	81.0
1984/85	106.7	69.6	38.0	214.3
1987/88	225.6	95.4	53.7	374.7
1990	376.0	121.0	140.0	638.0
1978	67%	22%	11%	100%
1984/85	50%	32%	18%	100%
1990	59%	19%	22%	100%

Table B.3

R&D Expenditure per Researcher, 1978–90

Year	GERD ($m)	RSE*	R&D Expenditure (thousand) per Researcher
1978	37.8	818	46
1981/82	81.0	1193	68
1984/85	214.3	2403	89
1987/88	374.7	3361	111
1990	638.0	4276	149

*Research scientists and engineers

Table A.4

RSE* per 10,000 Labor Force, 1978–90

Year	RSE (in '00s)	Labor Force (in '000s)	RSE per 10,000 labor force
1978	0.8	975	8
1981/82	1.2	1128	10
1984/85	2.4	1188	20
1987/88	3.4	1252	27
1990	4.3	1536	28

*Research scientists and engineers.

Table B.5

R&D Manpower by Sector, 1978–88

Year	Private Sector	Higher Education Sector	Government Sector	Total
1978	739	*	*	1672
1981–82	1115	886	740	2741
1984–85	1736	1981	1169	4886
1987–88	2583	2285	1008	5876

*Total combined for Higher Education and Government sector is 933.

Table B.6

R&D Manpower by Occupation, 1978–90

Year	RSE	Technicians	Other Supporting Staff	Total
1978	818	505	349	1672
1981–82	1193	807	741	2741
1984–85	2401	1359	1126	4886
1987–88	3361	1526	989	5876
1990	4276	1658	1026	6960
1978	49%	30%	21%	100%
1984–85	49%	28%	23%	100%
1990	61%	24%	15%	100%

Table B.7

RSE* by Qualifications and Sector, 1990 (in percent)

Sector	Bachelor's	Master's	Ph.D.
Private	78	17	5
Government	63	25	12
Higher Education	34	27	39

*Research scientists and engineers.

Table B.8

RSE* by Qualification and Field of Training (1978–88)

Field of Training	Qualifications			
	Ph.D	Master's	Bachelor's	Total
Natural Science	199	50	130	379
Engineering	344	409	1254	2007
Computer and Related Science	52	122	310	484
Medical Science	142	151	43	436
Agricultural Science	7	11	37	55
Total	744	743	1874	3361

*Research scientists and engineers.

Table B.9

Number of Organizations Performing R&D, 1978–90

Year	Private Sector	Higher Education Sector	Government Sector	Total
1978	63	4	23	90
1981–82	135	4	38*	177
1984–85	143	4	20	167
1987–88	191	4	20	215
1990	264	4	20	288

*Some of the government departments were regrouped and considered as a single reply in the 1984–85 and 1987–88 surveys.

Table B.10

R&D Expenditure by Industry Group and Year

Industry Group	1981–82 ($m)	%	1984–85 ($m)	%	1987–88 ($m)	%	1990 ($m)	%
Agriculture	0.8	2	2.3	2	2.4	1	—	—
Manufacturing								
Electrical/ Electronic	27.5	62	53.4	50	147.1	65	229	61
Chemicals/ Petrochemicals	2.1	5	5.7	5	11.9	5	45	12
Chemical-linked	3.8	8	17.6	16	19.6	9		
Transport Equipment	2.2	5	3.3	3	1.2	1	N.A.	
Basic/Fabricated metals	1.8	4	9.3	9	2.0	1	4	1
Machinery/ Instrumentation Equipment	1.1	3	0.7	1	5.0	2	N.A.	
Others	0.4	1	1.1	1	2.2	1	23	6
Information Technology	N.A.		N.A.		N.A.		34	9
Construction	—	—	—	—	0.6		—	—
Services	4.5	10	13.3	13	33.6	15	42	11
All Industry Groups	44.2	100	106.7	100	225.6	100	376	100

Notes: Information Technology was grouped with services before 1990. Transport equipment, machinery/instrumentation equipment are grouped into "others" in 1990.

Table B.11

R&D Manpower by Industry Group and Year

Industry Group	1981–82	%	1984–85	%	1987–88	%
Agriculture	15	1	62	4	62	2
Manufacturing						
Electrical/Electronic	561	50	781	45	1,298	50
Chemicals/Petrochemicals	65	6	116	6	88	3
Chemical-linked	204	18	222	12	256	10
Transport Equipment	63	6	61	4	44	2
Basic/Fabricated metals	82	7	252	15	148	6
Machinery/Instrumentation Equipment						
Others	28	3	42	2	51	2
Construction	—	—	—	—	22	1
Services	78	10	168	10	552	21
All Industry Groups	1,115	100	1,736	100	2,583	100

Appendix C:
Comparative R&D Indicators, Singapore and Selected OECD/Asian NIEs

	(R&D/GNP)%	RSE per 10,000 LF
Japan (1988)	2.9	87
Germany (1988)	2.9	56
Switzerland (1986)	2.9	44
USA (1989)	2.8	77
U.K. (1988)	2.2	n.a.
Korea (1989)	1.8	33
Taiwan (1988)	1.3	43
Singapore (1990)	1.0	28
Australia (1989)	1.2	23
Sweden (1989)	2.8	51

Source: IMD (1991).

Appendix D:
Singapore Government's R&D Allocation for 1991–95 under the New National Technology Plan

Program	FY91–95	%
Technology Programs	$806 m	40.3
Key strategic thrusts in technology; Ad-hoc projects in the other areas	$556 m	27.8
Research and Development Assistance Scheme	$80 m	4.0
Manpower Development	$158 m	7.9
Technology Infrastructure	$45 m	2.3
Science Park Development	$335 m	16.8
Total	$2,000 m	100

Source: National Science and Technology Board (NSTB), Singapore 1991.

Notes

1. For more detailed accounts of Singapore's economic development over the last three decades, see, e.g., Lim et al. 91988, Toh and Low 91990, MTI (1986) and Chng et al. (1986).
2. See Ng and Wong (1991) for more details on the growth triangle development concept.
3. For example, when Conner Peripherals, a disk-drive maker, decided to set up a manufacturing plant in Scotland, they modeled it entirely on the Singaporean operation, and Singaporean engineers were centrally involved in the transplanting process.
4. For a more detailed discussion of Singapore's educational policies and how they have evolved over the years, see Soon (1991).
5. By mid-1991, the number of tenant organizations in the park had reached eighty-four, with a staff population exceeding 3000. Close to 50 percent of the staff are engaged in R&D, and nearly three-quarters have at least a diploma qualification or above (bachelor's, 38 percent; master's and Ph.D.s, 11 percent). For a more detailed analysis of Singapore's science park development, see Toh, Low, and Wong (1991) and NSTB (1991).
6. For more details on the growth of the venture capital industry in Singapore, see Chia and Wong (1989).
7. The National Technology Plan reported a ratio of 0.2 patents granted to residents per 100,000 inhabitants in Singapore, compared with 43.7 in Japan, 42 in Switzerland, 31.3 in Taiwan, and 18 in the United States in the 1986–89 period.
8. The IMD/WEF *World Competitiveness Report* (1991) recognizes the need to incorporate a larger number of indicators than the conventional S&T indicators as a measure of a country's competitiveness. Although not all these additional indicators are suitable measures of the level of technological competence per se, taken as a whole, they do provide a more comprehensive picture of the overall technological development of a country. Based on the indicators of this report, Singapore's technology development performance ranking is consistently higher than that of many OECD countries.
9. For a fuller discussion of the importance of organizational context and capacity in enhancing technology absorption, see Nelson (1990) and Park (1991).
10. For a more detailed discussion of Singapore's internationalization strategy in the 1990s, see Wong and Ng (1991). For statistics on Singapore's recent overseas investment trend, see Department of Statistics, Singapore (1991).
11. Besides attracting foreign talents, the Singapore government is also adopting a more pragmatic policy to network with, and possibly attract back, Singaporean nationals who have migrated overseas, rather than to adopt an adversarial attitude toward them. A "Singapore International Foundation" has recently been established partly for this purpose.

References

Arensman, R., et al. "Asia Turns on to R&D." *Electronic Business Asia* (December 1991), pp. 42–52.
Chia, K. G., and Wong, K. C. *Venture Capital in the Asia Pacific Region, with special reference to Singapore.* Toppan, 1989.
Chng Meng Kng, et al. *Technology and Skills in Singapore.* Singapore: ISEAS, 1986.
Department of Statistics, Singapore. *Singapore's Investment Abroad 1976–1989.* 1991.
Economic Development Board (EDB). *Census of Industrial Production.* Singapore: EDB, various years.
———. *Yearbook,* Singapore: EDB, various years.
———. *SME Master Plan.* Singapore: National Printers, 1989.
Evenson, R. E., and Ranis, G. *Science and Technology: Lessons for Development Policy,* Boulder, Colo.: Westview Press, 1990.

Fransman, M. "Promoting Technological Capability in the Capital Good Sector: The Case of Singapore." *Research Policy 13* (1984), pp. 13–54.

Government of Singapore. *Singapore: The Next Lap.* Singapore: Times Editions, 1991.

Hill, H., and Pang, E. F. "Technology Exports from a Small, Very Open NICs: The Case of Singapore." *World Development 19*, 5 (1991), pp. 553–568.

IMD. *The World Competitive Report 1991.* Switzerland: 1991.

Lim, C. Y., et al. *Policy Options for the Singapore Economy.* Singapore: McGraw-Hill, 1988.

Ministry of Trade and Industry (MTI), Singapore. *The Singapore Economy: New Directions (Report of the Economic Committee).* Singapore: National Printers, 1986.

———. *Economic Survey of Singapore 1990.* Singapore: National Printers, 1990.

———. *Towards a Developed Nation: The Strategic Economic Plan.* Singapore: National Printers, 1991.

National Computer Board (NCB), Singapore. *Annual Report.* Singapore: NCB, various years.

National Science and Technology Board (NSTB), Singapore. *National Technology Plan 1991.* Singapore: National Printers, 1991.

Nelson, R. R. "Acquiring Technology." In H. Soestro and M. Pangestu (eds.), *Technological Challenge in the Asia-Pacific Economy.* London: Allen and Unwin, 1990, pp. 38–47.

Ng, C. Y., and Suedo, S. *Development Trends in the Asia-Pacific.* Singapore: Institute of South East Asian Studies, 1991.

Ng, C. Y., and Wong, P. K. "The Growth Triangle: A Market-driven Response?" *Asia Club Papers 2.* Tokyo: Tokyo Club Foundation for Global Studies, 1991, pp. 123–52.

Park, E. Y. "Social Capability and Long-Term Economic Growth: The Case of Korea." Seoul: Korean Development Institute, 1991.

Porter, M. *Competitive Advantage of Nations.* London: Macmillan, 1990.

Science Council of Singapore. *Science Park Update.* July/August 1989.

———. *National Survey of R&D Expenditure and Manpower, 1984/85.* Singapore: 1989a.

———. *National Survey of R&D Expenditure and Manpower, 1987/88.* Singapore: 1989b.

Soon, T. W. "Development of Human Resources and Technological Capability in Singapore." paper presented at World Bank/EDI Seminar on the Development of Physical and Supporting Infrastructure for Industrial Adjustment and Restructuring, Kuala Lumpur, Malaysia, March 4–9, 1991.

Ting, W. *Business and Technological Dynamics in Newly Industrializing Asia.* Quorum Books, 1985.

Toh, M. H., and Low, L. *Singapore's Economy: A Framework.* Singapore: 1990.

Toh, M. H., Low, L., and Wong, P. K. "The Role of Science Park in S&T Development: The Case of Singapore's Science Park." Paper presented at the *PECC S&T Task-Force Symposium on Science and Technology Park*, Shanghai, PRC, October 10–23, 1991.

Wade, R. *Governing the Market.* Princeton, N.J.: Princeton University Press, 1991.

Wong, P. K. *Technological Development through Subcontracting Linkages.* Tokyo: Asian Productivity Organization, 1991a.

———. "Technology Acquisition Mechanisms and Strategies: Lessons from Successful Small and Medium Enterprises in Singapore." *Proceedings of the National Science and Technology Conference.* Singapore: NSTB, September 10–11, pp. 75–83.

Wong, P. K., and Ng, C. Y. "Singapore's Internationalization Strategy for the 1990s." *Southeast Asian Affairs 1991.* Singapore: ISEAS, 1991, pp. 267–76.

Part III
The Southeast Asian Nations

6

Science and Technology Collaboration at the Regional Level: Lessons from ASEAN

Anuwar Ali

1. Introduction

Given that all the ASEAN economies (with the exception of Singapore) are still preoccupied with efforts to expand their industrial base, their science and technological base is still relatively small, and to a large extent, dependent on many inputs, including investments and expertise from the industrial countries. Like most developing countries, all the ASEAN countries have depended heavily on imported or transferred technologies because these technologies are not only relatively cheap and easy to acquire, but they have been tested and standardized. While the development of indigenous technologies is perceived to be costly and risky, the experience of many countries has shown that the enhancement of such capability requires a mixture of indigenous and imported technologies. As such, S&T development within each of the ASEAN countries is seen in the context of each country's interest, following the main thrust of its own industrial program.

Cooperation among the ASEAN countries in terms of science and technology is therefore in its formative stage. In recent years, a lot of efforts have been directed toward the strengthening of S&T organizational structure within ASEAN, rather than actual S&T programs. It is in this respect that the lack of funding for S&T collaboration within ASEAN is also a critical issue. It was only in 1971 that the ASEAN Ministerial Meeting established the ASEAN Permanent Committee on Science and Technology. As a result of the restructuring of the ASEAN coordinating machinery, the Permanent Committee was renamed the

ASEAN Committee on Science and Technology (COST) in 1978. In 1983, a meeting of the ASEAN ministers for science and technology formulated guidelines for ASEAN cooperation in S&T, including defining the objectives of such cooperation; the principles, areas, and mode of cooperation; and the financing of ASEAN programs in science and technology.

With the above background, this paper will look first at the future of ASEAN science and technology collaboration and highlight the ASEAN S&T plan, including a brief analysis of its objectives and strategies. This is followed by a review of the major ASEAN S&T programs as well as the priority areas that have been agreed among the ASEAN countries. An important area in S&T planning at the regional level involves the institutional framework to monitor and implement those programs or projects that have been planned. This is discussed in the following section. This is followed by a discussion on the funding mechanism, another area of critical importance. Finally, we will assess the future directions of S&T cooperation among the ASEAN countries, identifying thrusts to be adopted.

ASEAN S&T Plan: Objectives and Strategies

The preparation of an ASEAN Plan of Action on Science and Technology was first initiated by the ASEAN secretariat at the first meeting of COST. The plan was considered at various meetings of COST and was finally approved in January 1989 by the ASEAN ministers of science and technology. Recognizing the need to achieve economic development to serve the general basic needs of ASEAN, the plan set the following principal objective, namely to strengthen and enhance the capability of ASEAN in science and technology so that it can promote economic development and help achieve a high quality of life for the peoples of ASEAN. This is also important in the context of a changing economic structure within each of the ASEAN countries, where the role of the manufacturing sector is increasingly apparent.

To achieve the above-mentioned principal objective, the following policy guidelines have been formulated for the implementation of the plan:

a. Cooperation among its member countries in the field of science and technology shall be promoted, with emphasis on the following priority areas: food, biotechnology, microelectronics and computers, materials science and technology, nonconventional energy, marine sciences, meteorology and geophysics, remote sensing, and the development of science and technology infrastructure and resources.

b. Technology transfer and the commercialization of research results shall be encouraged with a view to promoting investments in ASEAN.

c. Human resource development shall be emphasized in order to have an intelligent and productive work force capable of responding to rapid global scientific and technological advancement and consistent with the development of ASEAN's creativity in S&T.

d. Scientific and technical information dissemination and exchange shall be intensified, as well as cooperation in the development of software and hardware components of information technology.

The following strategic plan and actions will be pursued:

a. To intensify cooperation in S&T, strong and well-coordinated regional research and development projects will be implemented in the priority areas identified in the policy guidelines, especially in biotechnology, materials science, microelectronics, and new energy sources.

b. To widen involvement and increase participation and cooperation among the scientists and researchers of member countries, three regional research networks in biotechnology, materials science, and microelectronics, one regional institutional network in meteorology and geophysics, and two network-like linkages on food data and technological information will be established.

c. To maintain a high level of scientific and technological expertise and, in the process, develop an intelligent work force in a rapidly changing and highly competitive world, ASEAN centers of excellence as well as science parks will be identified and established in respective member countries.

d. To promote technology transfer and the commercialization of research results, pilot plants, demonstration plants, and the like will be constructed and operated.

e. To ensure human resources development for promoting scientific, technological, and economic development, regional conferences, workshops, seminars, training programs, and the ASEAN Science and Technology Week will be conducted.

f. To provide an overall awareness in ASEAN on the strategic role that science and technology plays in economic development, dissemination and exchange of information, as well as scientific visits, and exchange of researchers will be intensified.

The fact that ASEAN has managed, through years of consultation and consensus building, to identify areas of mutual benefit in S&T collaboration is in itself an achievement that could be translated into concrete endeavors in the future. Past experience in S&T collaboration among the ASEAN countries, which was less focused, can now be prioritized in a more meaningful way, although it must also be emphasized that there exist numerous constraints on effective S&T cooperation among the ASEAN economies. However, collaborative interaction is expected to bring about a number of positive effects.

First, the exercise itself should broaden the areas of networking or interaction among S&T policymakers and personnel within ASEAN through the various institutional mechanisms and projects identified. Second, the priority areas that have been agreed upon by ASEAN, as reflected in the action plan, are mutually beneficial to all ASEAN countries. For example, these would include areas such as biotechnology, marine science, research on sea tides, and the like. Third, it is through S&T collaborative programs that each of the ASEAN countries is able to build up or enhance its S&T infrastructure and expertise. For instance, the procurement of new equipment for research institutes within each country under the ASEAN science and technology collaboration (including with its dialogue partners) can generate or be utilized for further research domestically. This, of course, assumes that local research institutes as well as the universities in the ASEAN countries have already developed a certain level of capability to utilize them.

Program Areas for Collaboration

ASEAN cooperation in science and technology has been grouped into eight program areas: biotechnology; microelectronics and computers; materials science and technology; food science and technology; nonconventional energy; meteorology and geophysics; marine sciences; and information, infrastructure, and human resources development. Almost all of these program areas are relatively new to the ASEAN countries in view of the technological gap that exists between these countries and the industrial countries. There is so much to be learned and acquired from the latter. While this section mainly highlights the priority areas of ASEAN S&T cooperation, some of the projects that have been initiated and completed under these respective areas will also be mentioned.

Biotechnology

ASEAN cooperation in biotechnology emphasizes the following areas: development of drugs, diagnostics, and vaccines; improvement and production of selected biomaterials for agriculture and industry; application of biotechnology for improving quality and production of plants/animals and their products; pilot plant design and computer control of biological reactors; and ligno-cellulose conversion.

In the area of biotechnology, emphasis is also being given to ASEAN cooperation with its main trading partners; and in these cases, the question of funding, as indicated earlier, is an important aspect. An ASEAN-Australia cooperative program in biotechnology emphasizes three areas: the development of therapeutically and biologically active substances from plants; production and utilization of cells and enzymes for improved carbohydrate conversion; and other areas linked to existing activities in food and food waste utilization technologies in the realm of biotechnology. ASEAN-EC cooperation focuses on the development of an ASEAN-EC research network on nitrogen fixation while ASEAN-Japan cooperation in biotechnology emphasizes the area of enzyme technology. In future, a regional research network on biotechnology will be established.

Microelectronics and Computers

Regional cooperation in microelectronics covers the following activities: computer-aided design of integrated circuits; multiproject chip (MPC) fabrication; and electronic communication networks. In the future, funding will be secured from within ASEAN and from its dialogue partners to support the establishment of a regional research network on microelectronics. In addition to those areas already identified, regional cooperative activities will be expanded to cover applications of microelectronics in communications, process control, and instrumentation.

Materials Science and Technology

Regional activities in materials science include four broad areas of cooperation: building materials, minerals and metals, materials for chemicals and medicines, and materials standardization and performance. With Japan, joint cooperation projects are being pursued in the fields of atmospheric corrosion of structures and building materials, fine ceramics and inorganic materials, and polymeric materials. Long-term and short-term experts from Japan have facilitated technology transfer in research methodology, analysis of experimental data, and the maintenance of sophisticated scientific instruments.

The cooperation of other ASEAN dialogue partners is being sought and regional programs will cover research and development work on metals and corrosion, polymers and plastics, ceramics and building materials. An ASEAN regional research network on materials science and technology will also be established.

Food Science and Technology

Regional cooperation in food science and technology includes three broad areas: food habits research and development, including the development of the ASEAN food data network; food technology research and development, including food standards; and management and utilization of food waste materials. According to the annual report of the ASEAN Standing Committee 1989–90, cooperative efforts on food habits research and development and the management and utilization of food waste materials have been successfully completed under the ASEAN-Australian Economic Cooperation Program (AAECP). The food technology research and development project is in the final stage of completion.

The objectives of regional cooperation in food science and technology include: the development of technologies using resources endogenous to the

ASEAN region and transferring these technologies to industry for commercialization; upgrading of the quality and value of food products in ASEAN and, consequently, generate trade, investment, and employment; and improvement of the nutrition in the ASEAN region.

Cooperation with ASEAN dialogue partners, particularly Australia, is being intensified in the areas of food standards, resource recovery, and food flavors. In addition, comprehensive projects, from the R&D stage to the technology transfer stage, will be developed and implemented. Projects will include the upgrading of research facilities, development of human resources, and increased interaction between relevant dialogue countries and ASEAN institutions and scientists.

Nonconventional Energy

Under the ASEAN Committee on Science and Technology, regional cooperation in the field of energy is limited to energy conservation and to nonconventional energy technologies in the research and development stage. ASEAN-Australia cooperation projects have been tailored to R&D activities in three areas: biomass for heat and power, energy conservation technologies, and coal technologies. Cooperation with the United States has focused on research and development in energy conservation in buildings and manpower development in coal technology and energy management and conservation. ASEAN-Canada cooperation in energy involves human resource development projects on energy management and conservation; industrial biogas reactors; and industrial-scale demonstration of solar drying technology.

Up to the mid-1990s ASEAN cooperation in nonconventional energy R&D is expected to be focused on bioenergy conversion relating to industrial scale applications and cogeneration; coal technologies; energy conservation in industry, buildings and transportation; and advanced industrial solar energy technology. Environmental issues relating to energy resources development and energy utilization are being covered. Intra-ASEAN technology transfer and commercialization of energy technology and products developed is being actively promoted. Joint projects and funding assistance from the EC, Japan, and New Zealand will be pursued to attain the desired objectives of these program areas.

Meteorology and Geophysics

ASEAN cooperation in the field of meteorology and geophysics aims to develop climatological applications to address, among other areas, drought-related problems, water resources management, solar and wind energy resources, coastal and offshore installation, and urban and building climatology, and to improve forecasting services for the mitigation of natural disasters caused by adverse meteorological and geophysical phenomena. An ASEAN *Climatic Atlas and*

Compendium of Climatic Statistics has in fact been completed, comprising a two-volume analysis of the climatic data of the ASEAN region, with technical assistance from the United Nations Development Programme (UNDP) and the World Meteorological Organisation (WMO). New projects on monsoon climatology and the CLICOM system are in progress. While the former has the objective of conducting a biannual review on the monsoon, the latter aims to adopt a common data base format for ASEAN meteorological services in order to provide a platform for the exchange of expertise in the use of the CLICOM system.

   In the future, an ASEAN network on meteorology and geophysics and an ASEAN regional specialized meteorological center will be established (subject to the availability of funding from dialogue partners and UNDP) to further enhance cooperation in this area. Funding from dialogue partners will be obtained to support studies on the assessment of solar and daylight resources in the ASEAN region, satellite crop monitoring and marine assessment system, research on very short range forecasting, standardization of meteorological measurements, and others.

Marine Sciences

The ASEAN-Australia Cooperative Programme on Marine Science has two components: Regional Ocean Dynamics (ROD) scheduled for three years and Coastal Living Resources (CLR) for five years, to be implemented under the AAECP Phase II. The ASEAN-U.S. Cooperative Programme also has two components: living resource assessment, planning, and research; and training and information dissemination. The ASEAN-Canada Cooperative Programme has two components: resource management and development, and pollution monitoring.

   In the future, ASEAN regional projects in marine sciences will focus on coastal resources management and marine pollution monitoring and control. The protection and proper management of mangrove and coral reef ecosystems will be given particular emphasis, as these are resources common to all ASEAN countries. In addition, the protection of ASEAN's common seas from both land and ocean pollution sources will be given attention.

Information Infrastructure and Human Resource Development

Under this category, activities include S&T policy studies, management of S&T, information dissemination, remote sensing, and the publication of an S&T journal. As an important source of information dissemination, the *ASEAN Journal on Science and Technology for Development* will continue to be published. One of the important objectives of this journal is to become a conduit for making known the work of ASEAN researchers and scientists as well as the policy makers in science and technology. At the same time, it aims to become an internationally recognized publication and the most authoritative source of information on S&T in ASEAN.

The management of science and technology continues to be a concern of COST. With funding support from Australia, training programs have been conducted in two areas: science and technology policy development and program management, and R&D management. In the future, suitable funding will be obtained for regional and national training programs. To promote S&T awareness, to provide a venue for showing ASEAN capabilities in science and technology, and to encourage interaction between scientists and technologists from both within and outside of ASEAN, the ASEAN Science and Technology Week will be a continuing project.

So far, the ASEAN Science and Technology Week has been held three times; the first was in Malaysia in 1986 with the theme of the development of science and technology for advancement in ASEAN. This was followed by a second in the Philippines in 1989, with the theme of new and emerging technologies in ASEAN. A third was organized by COST, and was held in Singapore in September 1992, with the new theme of socioeconomic growth in ASEAN through science and technology.

Institutional Framework

The overall organizational structure for ASEAN science and technology regional cooperation is composed of four components: policy making; program formulation, management, coordination, evaluation, and monitoring; project management, coordination, and implementation; and coordination and support services. The policies for ASEAN science and technology cooperation are decided at the meeting of ASEAN ministers for science and technology that is held every three years, preferably during the ASEAN Science and Technology Week.

The ASEAN Committee on Science and Technology (COST) is responsible for program formulation, management, coordination, evaluation, and monitoring. COST will meet twice a year to review the overall regional programs and to provide directives for implementation by its subsidiary bodies. The actual management, coordination, and implementation of regional projects under the purview of COST is discharged by the following eight subcommittees:

- Subcommittee on Food Science and Technology;
- Subcommittee on Meteorology and Geophysics;
- Subcommittee on Microelectronics and Computers;
- Subcommittee On Materials Science and Technology;
- Subcommittee on Biotechnology;
- Subcommittee on Nonconventional Energy Research;
- Subcommittee on Marine Sciences; and
- Subcommittee on Science and Technology Infrastructure and Resources Development.

In addition, an advisory body on the ASEAN Science Fund will be established to assist COST in the management of the fund. The various projects under each subcommittee will be managed, coordinated, and implemented by the subcommittee itself or, if the projects are large enough, project management committees (PMCs) are to be established for their management and implementation.

The chairmanship of the subcommittees will be rotated every three years following the ASEAN system of rotation and in line with the rotation of the COST chairmanship. However, in order to ensure continuity, the chairmanship of the PMCs will be for the duration of the respective projects.

Through the various S&T programs, it is certainly important that greater cooperation and interaction among related institutions and/or organizations within ASEAN will be nurtured. In this respect, regional research networks and/or networklike linkages in specific fields of regional cooperation will be established. Initially, these may include the following: ASEAN Network on Meteorology and Geophysics; ASEAN Food Data Network; ASEAN Research Network on Biotechnology; ASEAN Research Network on Material Science; ASEAN Research Network on Microelectronics; and ASEAN Technological Information Network.

ASEAN centers of excellence in various fields may also be established in respective member countries. At the initial stage, these will include the ASEAN Regional Specialized Meteorological Center (RSMC) and the ASEAN Materials Technology Information Center (AMTIC). The Bureau of Science and Technology of the ASEAN secretariat will continue to provide coordinative and support services and will be strengthened to enable it to respond to the needs of an expanded and intensified ASEAN S&T cooperation.

Project Funding for ASEAN Collaboration

Funding from Dialogue Partners and UNDP

Given the nature of the ASEAN science and technological base, regional projects that are promoted by ASEAN COST have been largely dependent on financial contributions from ASEAN dialogue partners (including Australia, Canada, New Zealand, Japan, the United States, the EC, and lately the Republic of Korea and UNDP) for their implementation. This is done chiefly because of the availability of expertise and technologies within the dialogue partners and the fact that ASEAN has maintained strong economic and trading relationships with these countries.

While this is so, there is also a need to enhance the development of mutual interests between ASEAN and its dialogue partners through the promotion of S&T projects. Currently, Australia appears to be the most active dialogue partner in terms of funding. In fact, projects on science and technology account for 75 percent of the AAECP Phase II funds.

In view of the fact that scientific investigations generally have a long gestation period, the sourcing of funding from dialogue partners may create problems of implementation and continuity, as well as dependence. As such, there is a need to provide a more secure source of funding, especially in the long-term interests of ASEAN. This means that such funding is independent of the vagaries of the economies of ASEAN's dialogue partners and the changes in their priorities.

In terms of the latter, for example, funding by dialogue partners could be substantially influenced by their economic interests such that the projects initiated under their funding program would be geared mainly to their industrial needs. An example is Japan's interest in materials science. In this sense, funding by dialogue partners could have the consequence of emphasizing only the commercial orientation of science and technology collaboration. On the other hand, UNDP funding, although limited in its coverage, has the element of neutrality. However, the latter kind of funding is rather limited, since UNDP funding is mostly channeled through it to country programs.

Establishing the ASEAN Science Fund

While ASEAN cooperation in S&T will continue to draw upon the support of ASEAN's dialogue partners for the implementation of its projects and activities, the ASEAN Science Fund has been established to provide, first, a more secure source of funding for priority projects which the dialogue partners may be unable to support directly. Second, within the ASEAN science and technology framework, the fund is expected to establish an ASEAN internal capability to generate mutually beneficial projects within the region.

The ASEAN Science Fund will also be supported by contributions from dialogue partners, international and regional organizations, and other third countries. However, to initiate the Science Fund, ASEAN member countries made an initial voluntary contribution amounting to US$50,000 per member country, although the total fund is targeted to reach US$6.0 million.

The ASEAN Science Fund will be a common regional fund that will be managed and administered by ASEAN COST, assisted by the advisory body on the ASEAN Science Fund. To ensure the smooth operation of the ASEAN Science Fund, COST is currently preparing the guidelines for the formulation and selection of project proposals for financing from the Science Fund. At the same time it has been agreed that the utilization of the fund will cover projects that promote human resource development, have immediate commercial application, and require seed money for the preproject funding stage, or for prefeasibility studies in new technological areas.

Future Directions for ASEAN S&T Cooperation

There is a general consensus among the ASEAN countries that collaborative science and technology programs are useful and beneficial to all the countries concerned. The benefits of such programs are derived from various factors such as complementarity of skills, resource advantages, even simply the cross exchange of ideas and approaches through either formal or informal information exchange between individuals or organizations within ASEAN. It is also within this context that the ASEAN region as a whole will be able to enhance its economic and trade relations with its dialogue partners. At the same time, it should also be recognized that ASEAN economic integration must evolve at the outset before effective S&T cooperation can be established. The experience of the EEC countries testifies to this critical factor.

In view of the disparity in the region in terms of S&T capabilities and infrastructure, a collective approach is crucial in the development and implementation of regional science and technology programs. The latter must be set at a level that makes them relevant and accessible to all member countries and that allows shared responsibility in their delivery. In this sense, it is vital that there is a strong political and intellectual commitment to ensure the implementation of programs. Such a commitment is indeed critical to maintain focus and access to resources, and to sustain interest. It must also be emphasized that stated goals and expected results should be realistic. Priorities should be given to areas of science and technology in which ASEAN has comparative advantage. In order to achieve these objectives, it is also critical that the current structure for decision making within ASEAN be made more effective.

In line with the above, the future thrust of enhancing ASEAN science and technology collaboration will certainly be based on the priority areas that have been established within the framework of the ASEAN Plan of Action on Science and Technology. In the long run, it is indeed critical that ASEAN countries will together generate their own funding to sustain their S&T needs. It is only through this means that they can truly influence the technological trajectory of ASEAN. In this context the ASEAN Science Fund could provide the base from which internal funding could be generated. If such internal funding could be generated at a sufficiently high level, this could strengthen ASEAN's case vis-à-vis its dialogue partners.

It is certainly possible for ASEAN to pursue joint funding of projects with dialogue partners, rather depend too heavily on them for funding of science and technology projects. Currently, in comparison with the dialogue partners, most of the ASEAN countries do not have large R&D allocations, so they are dependent for funding from the dialogue partners. It is also in this sense that ASEAN as a regional economic bloc would need strong support from its dialogue partners. At the same time, research activities in their research institutes and universities are still lagging behind those of the industrial countries. It is also in this sense that ASEAN as a regional economic bloc would need strong support from its dialogue partners.

An important area that could be emphasized for future ASEAN science and technology collaboration is the commercialization of research projects. As indicated in the policy guidelines and strategic actions discussed above, the ASEAN Science and Technology Plan calls for greater technology transfer and the commercialization of research results to promote investments in the region. To do this, the plan also recognizes the need for infrastructure facilities such as pilot plants and demonstration plants. However, these activities are yet to be established.

While such commercialization is an important aspect of domestic technological development, it has not been fully developed in most of the ASEAN countries. The objective is to encourage project implementors (including research institutes and universities) within ASEAN to develop linkages not only among themselves, but more important, with industry or the users of such research results. This could perhaps be supplemented by programs to enhance awareness in the private sector or industry that they too could benefit from such networking. An important prerequisite in this respect is the need to enhance the information exchange system within ASEAN. Such a system has not been fully developed within the ASEAN context, as it has been in the industrialized countries.

Finally, it is equally important to emphasize the need for an active role for ASEAN governments in S&T development, in terms of both policy direction and direct involvement in activities related to science and technology, including the development of R&D infrastructure and human resources. Without the full support of the government, the amount of R&D activities in society, for example, would become less than optimum. At the same time, doing research is an extremely risky enterprise, and as such the role of the government becomes crucial. It is in the area of human resource development, as aptly emphasized by the ASEAN Science and Technology Plan, that highly skilled manpower can be enhanced so that the region's industrial labor is better able to respond to the rapid and complex technological advances worldwide. This would necessitate a reassessment of the current educational systems within most of the ASEAN countries as well as in-house training programs that are available at the industry level.

Note

The author is indebted to Mr. Danil Taridi Ghazali (of the Ministry of Science, Technology and the Environment of Malaysia) for his invaluable assistance in providing the appropriate information and insight into ASEAN S & T mechanisms and cooperation.

References

ASEAN Secretariat. *Annual Report of the ASEAN Standing Committee, 1989–90*. Jakarta, Indonesia: ASEAN, 1990a.
———. *ASEAN Plan of Action on Science and Technology*. Prepared by the ASEAN Committee on Science & Technology. Jakarta, Indonesia: ASEAN, 1990b.
ASEAN Committee on Science and Technology. *ASEAN Journal on Science & Technology for Development, 7*, 2 (1990).

7

Technology Upgrading in Thailand: A Strategic Perspective

Chatri Sripaipan

Recent Development of the Thai Economy and Its Policies

The Thai Economy and Its Structure

Thailand has experienced spectacular economic growth over the past few years. From 1987 to 1990, the growth rate of GDP averaged 11.2 percent in real terms, making Thailand one of the fastest growing economies in the world. Despite the Gulf War, a military coup, and the economic slow-down in major industrialized countries, the growth rate for 1991 is estimated at 8.0 percent. The National Economic and Social Development Board (NESDB) expects the economy to grow at an average rate of 8.2 percent throughout its Seventh Plan (1992–96).

However, a double-digit growth rate for a few years is not as significant as the fact that the economy of Thailand has been expanding at an average rate of 7 percent per annum throughout the past three decades. Such development has caused two important structural changes in the productive sectors. The first occurred in 1979, when the output of the manufacturing sector exceeded that of the agricultural sector for the first time. The manufacturing sector had 22.1 percent of GDP, followed by the agricultural sector and the trade sector at 21.2 and 16.4 percent, respectively. The second change was in 1988, when the agricultural sector was overtaken by the trade sector. The GDP percentages of the manufacturing, trade, and agricultural sectors were 23.3, 17.1, and 16.9, respectively. This was because the industrial sector had been expanding at a rapid average rate of 9.2 percent during the period from 1970 to 1989, while the

Table 7.1

The Top Ten Export Items of Thailand (in million baht)

Item	1989 Value	Rank	1990 Value	Rank	1991 Value	Rank
Garments	57,892.4	(1)	65,804.2	(1)	76,000	(1)
Gems and jewelry	28,421.9	(3)	34,891.8	(3)	42,000	(2)
Computers and peripherals	26,835.1	(4)	38,694.5	(2)	40,000	(3)
Rice	45,462.3	(2)	27,769.4	(4)	27,000	(4)
Tapioca	25,052.3	(6)	24,465.2	(5)	27,000	(4)
Integrated circuits	18,426.2	(8)	21,580.5	(8)	27,000	(4)
Foot wear and parts	13,524.4	(10)	20,219.5	(10)	25,000	(7)
Rubber	26,431.7	(5)	23,557.3	(6)	24,600	(8)
Canned sea food	19,767.9	(7)	21,623.4	(7)	23,600	(9)
Frozen shrimp	16,058.6	(9)	20,453.7	(9)	22,000	(10)

Source: Ministry of Commerce. Export target in 1991 (as of June 1991).

agricultural sector grew at an average rate of only 3.9 percent during the same period. Consequently, Thailand is becoming industrialized despite the fact that the majority of the work force (over 60 percent) is still in the agricultural sector.

Within the manufacturing sector, the shift of the production structure from resource-intensive to labor-intensive industries has been significant (Dahlman and Brimble, 1990). Between 1970 and 1987, the marked decrease in the share of resource-intensive industries, from 54.3 percent to 39.7 percent, was offset by an increase in labor-intensive industries, from 23.3 to 38.7 percent, while there has been little change in the shares of scale-intensive, differentiated, or science-based industries.[1] As for exports, their structure over the same period has undergone a more profound change. There has been a large fall in the share of resource-intensive industries, from 86.8 percent in 1970 to 37.4 percent in 1987, while all four others made substantial increases. In particular, labor-intensive industries increased from 10.7 to 39.0 percent. Compared with the production structure, this shows that the shares of resource-intensive, labor-intensive, and science-based industries are similar to those in production. However, the share of differentiated goods exports is more than twice as large. This suggests that Thailand is beginning to develop some comparative advantage in this area. Nevertheless, differentiated goods exports were a mere 12.9 percent. The bulk of exports (over 75 percent) belonged to the resource-intensive and labor-intensive industries.

Table 7.1 illustrates the points made in the previous paragraph while showing more recent trends. Although the majority of industries are still resource-intensive, labor-intensive industries, which have been rapidly developed over the past decade, took over the top two places as well as the seventh. The differentiated goods—integrated circuits—and the science-based industries—computer and peripherals—are not doing too badly, but both belong largely to multinational subsidiaries, which shifted the more labor-intensive portions of their operation into Thailand primarily to seek a lower-cost manufacturing base.

Recent Changes in Policies

The Thai government's monetary policy of international liberalization was initiated toward the end of the Prem government (1980–88). This policy picked up its pace in the Chatchai government (August 1988–February 1991), and in spite of the military coup on February 23, 1991, it continues and has even accelerated under the interim government. Under the Anand administration, liberalization and laissez-faire have become the fundamental philosophy propelling tax reform and the dismantling of government regulatory controls. Some developments are listed below.

Monetary Policy

After complying with Article 8 of the International Monetary Fund in May 1990, the second phase, liberalization of foreign exchange, came into effect in April 1991, as planned. The Bank of Thailand is considering the right timing to announce the third phase of liberalization, in which foreign exchange controls will be abolished entirely.

Tariff Policy

Thailand has made an offer to GATT to reduce import duties on 1,700 additional items. As of October 1990, the tariff rate for production machinery was reduced from 20–40 percent to 5 percent. In July 1991, import duties on completely built-up (CBU) cars and completely knocked-down (CKD) parts were sharply reduced, resulting in reduced protection for the domestic car industry. At about the same time, computer taxes were also sharply reduced to promote the usage of computers in businesses and industries. In this effort, less attention was paid to the infant domestic computer industry, which would certainly be affected.

The Ministry of Finance has a plan to reduce the ceiling tariff rate from 60 to 30 percent, to decrease the number of tariff rates to only six, and to correct tariff anomalies between finished goods, intermediate products, and raw materials.

Tax Policy

Perhaps the development that has had the most far-reaching effect is the value added tax (VAT) which is currently in the process of being enacted into law. When implemented, it should bring in a broader tax base and eliminate the present problem of cascading business taxes, at each stage of transaction between different companies, which has long been plaguing the development of subcontracting industries. Other important tax and related changes that have been or are in the process of being implemented by the Ministry of Finance are a leasing tax, corporate merger tax, bad debt reserve, depreciation rules, gold bullion importing, corporate income tax, savings interest tax, and holding company dividend tax.

Energy Pricing Policy

The gasoline price has been floated. The electricity rate will follow suit soon.

Industry Policy

The Ministry of Industry has lifted bans and restrictions on the establishment and expansion of twenty-one types of industries, including rice milling, machinery adaptation for mining, ice making, matches, electric cable, asphalt, polyester policol, alum, large plastic bags, sulphuric acid, steel reinforced concrete, plastic mats, cotton spinning, the export of radiated minerals, textiles and garments, tapioca products, bottles, ethyl alcohol, fishing nets, soda ash, and cement. The power to license factories has been delegated to provincial authorities. At the same time, the ministry has stepped up its efforts to control industrial pollution. It has taken action against 301 factories out of the 717 complaints it had received on environment.

Status of Science and Technology in Thailand

A Brief Historical Account

The importance of scientific research has been recognized since the announcement of the Constitution of the Royal Thai Kingdom B.E. 2492 (1949), which states in Article 65 that "The government should support research in the fields of liberal arts and sciences." Later in 1956, the government passed the National Research Council Act, with the view that the progress of the country had to be based on scientific research to sustain long-term development. The establishment of the National Research Council can be seen as the starting point to encourage research and development (R&D) to systematically increase the scientific and technological capability of the country. In 1963, the National Applied Science Research Institute was established to take charge of implementing research in applied sciences to promote and utilize natural resources to develop industry and the country. In 1979, the Ministry of Science, Technology and Energy (MOSTE) was established with the aim of playing the central role for setting national policy and for planning in science, technology, and energy. A number of organizations concerning science and technology were brought under its wing from the Ministry of Industry and the Office of the Prime Minister. They are the Department of Science Services, the National Research Council of Thailand, the Office of the National Environmental Board, the Office of Atomic Energy for Peace, the National Energy Administration, and the Thailand Institute of Scientific and Technological Research (TISTR) (previously called the National Applied Science Research Institute) (Boonyubol et al., 1991b). However, a number of science and technology (S&T) activities remain with other ministries. Research in agriculture is mainly conducted in the Ministry of Agriculture and Cooperatives, which consumes over 40 percent of the government research budget. The Ministries of Education and University Affairs are two large R&D performers which spent about another half of the country's R&D budget. Furthermore, the Ministry of Industry is responsible for industrial standards and has been providing technical assistance to small and medium-sized industries.

After the establishment of MOSTE, the next Five-Year National Economic and Social Development Plan, the Fifth Plan (1982–86) (NESDB, 1982), was the first five-year development plan in which science and technology issues were explicitly addressed in a separate chapter. The two issues addressed in the plan were: first, the use of science and technology to increase production efficiency was still rather limited; and second, modification or improvement of imported technology and technological development was slow. The proposed measures were:

1. To promote the survey of basic data essential to technological development.
2. To promote appropriate foreign technology transfer.
3. To increase the country's scientific and technological research and development capability.
4. To mobilize manpower for scientific and technological development.

The achievement in that period was rather limited. More visible results were a number of signed agreements for science and technology cooperation with foreign countries. The most significant of these was the Science and Technology for Development Project, with a total fund of U.S.$49 million over a period of seven years with assistance from the United States. Another achievement is the establishment of the National Center for Genetic Engineering and Biotechnology (NCGEB) at MOSTE as a funding agency for a network of research laboratories in universities and TISTR in the same discipline.

The Sixth Plan (1987–91) (NESDB, 1987), also contained a chapter on the Science and Technology Development Plan. It recognized the significance of developing S&T capability and identified two key issues: that cooperation between S&T units of all government agencies and the private sector was the key to success, and that effective linkage between developers and users of S&T was needed to have an impact on the problems and the needs of the private sector. The S&T Development Plan has four main implementation plans:

1. S&T management system and infrastructure development;
2. increase in efficiency of S&T activities;
3. S&T manpower development; and
4. increase in efficiency of production.

Table 7.2

R&D Expenditures (in million baht)

	1983	1984	1985	1986	1987
R&D expenditures	1,411	2,824	2,452	2,010	2,664.5
CNP	903,353	961,961	996,802	1,072,242	1,211,431
% of GNP	0.16	0.29	0.24	0.18	0.22

Source: NESDB, National Research Council of Thailand.

Under this plan, the Office of Science and Technology Development Board (STDB) was established to operate the Science and Technology for Development Project. MOSTE also established two more national centers: the National Center for Metals and Materials Technology (NCMMT) and the National Electronics and Computer Technology Center (NECTEC). This makes a total of three national centers at MOSTE, corresponding to the three areas of emphasis by STDB, namely: biotechnology, materials, and electronics. These three priority areas have been targeted by MOSTE since the beginning of the Sixth Plan.

One of the most important milestones in promoting science and technology is the Law for Development of Science and Technology. This law establishes STDB as a juristic entity to administer a "Science and Technology Development Fund" to be obtained from the government and other sources, including international agencies. The law also establishes the three national centers as specialized research institutes with the role of carrying out research and development, both in-house and under contract from industries (Yuthavong, 1991).

Research and Development

R&D Expenditure

Both the Fifth and the Sixth National Economic and Social Development Plans set a target R&D budget of 0.5 percent of GNP, or roughly about 2 percent of the government budget. However, as shown in Table 7.2, the actual R&D expenditure between 1983 and 1987 averaged only 2,272 million baht a year, or 0.22 percent of GNP. The R&D expenditure figure of 1987 was the first to be derived from actual surveys, whereas those of previous years were budget allocations. In any case, it is very low. It is much lower than the R&D expenditures of developed countries, which range between 2.5 percent and 3 percent of GNP, and than those of newly industrialized countries, which range between 1.0 percent and 2.0 percent of GNP. Other distinct features from Table 7.3 are that R&D expenditures of state enterprises and private firms were both very low: only 277.24 and

Table 7.3

National R&D Expenditure in 1987 (in million baht)

Implementing Agency	Natural Science	Engineering	Agriculture	Medical Science	Social Science and Humanities	Other[a]	Total
Government	11.30 (12.44%)	55.70 (12.13%)	567.90 (77.41%)	53.70 (24.61%)	574.60 (76.06%)	117.80 (28.94%)	1,381.00 (51.83%)
University	79.50 (87.56%)	234.50 (51.06%)	165.30 (22.53%)	164.50 (75.39%)	165.50 (21.91%)	—	809.30 (30.37%)
Private sector and State enterprise[b]	—	169.10 (36.82%)	0.40 (0.05%)	—	—	289.30 (71.06%)	458.80 (17.22%)
Nonprofit private	—	—	—	—	15.40	0	15.40
Total	90.80 (100.00%)	459.30 (100.00%)	733.60 (100.00%)	218.20 (100.00%)	755.50 (100.00%)	407.10 (100.00%)	2,664.50 (100.00%)
Share of each area	3.41%	17.24%	27.53%	8.19%	28.35%	15.28%	100%

[a]Such as services and public utilities.
[b]Private firms spent 181.56 million baht, accounting for 6.81 percent.
Source: National Research Council of Thailand.

181.56 million baht or 10.41 and 6.81 percent respectively. To make matters worse, the state enterprise category included TISTR, which is the only major research institute in the country, with an annual budget of about 200 million baht. Therefore, the R&D expenditures of all other state enterprises were actually very low indeed.

R&D Funding

For individual researchers, there are a number of research funding sources. A university lecturer may start to apply for research grants from his or her own university on the order of tens of thousands of baht per project. For bigger projects, that lecturer should seek outside funding. The National Research Council of Thailand (NRCT) is a possible source, but the amount of each grant is very limited and the coverage is very wide. In 1990, NRCT funded 120 projects with a budget of 21.75 million baht. The three national centers can accommodate research projects of about one million baht, while STDB sets a limit of 6 million baht per project. Apart from domestic sources, there are a number of foreign funds. Table 7.4 shows that foreign sources accounted for 14.55 percent of R&D funding or 387.60 million baht in 1987.

Research funding in the three priority areas of biotechnology, materials, and electronics are shown in Tables 7.5, 7.6, and 7.7, respectively. It is quite clear that the area of biotechnology, by virtue of the strength of researchers and the interest of foreign funding sources, has been able to attract a much larger level of support compared with the other two areas. The total research fund in the past five years for biotechnology was 709 million baht, compared with 272 million baht and 187 million baht, respectively, for materials and electronics.

R&D Outputs

Research and development outputs are usually in the form of research reports and articles published in journals or presented at academic conferences. The research community of Thailand has been able to publish about 300 articles a year in international journals covered by the Science Citation Index (see Table 7.8). Of these, health science contributed about 130 articles a year, followed by biological science and physical science at about fifty articles each. The other three areas of natural resources and environmental science, agriculture, and engineering and technology produced about twenty to forty articles each. Although the number of articles published internationally by field may roughly reflect the field's scientific strength, it should also be noted that about one-third of these articles were contributed by foreign scientists in joint research efforts. This could be interpreted as suggestive that foreign interest and funding would also affect the number of published articles in a particular field. Furthermore, the number of research articles published in international journals does not represent the re-

155

Table 7.4

Sources and Distribution of R&D Funds (in million baht)

			Funds User				
Source of Funds	Government	University	State Enterprise	Private Firms	Nonprofit Private	Total	%
Government	1,143.60	676.20*	6.00	—	—	1,825.80	68.52
State enterprise	0.20	5.50	253.80	—	—	259.50	9.74
Private firm	0.00	2.90	—	181.60	—	184.50	6.92
Nonprofit private organization	0.50	2.20	—	—	4.40	7.10	0.27
Foreign source	236.70	122.60	17.30	—	11.00	387.60	14.55
Total	1,381.00	809.40	277.10	181.60	15.40	2,664.50	100.00
%	51.83	30.38	10.40	6.82	0.58	100.00	

*Includes university funds.
Source: National Research Council of Thailand.

Table 7.5

Funding of Biotechnology Projects from Five Sources

Areas of Biotechnology	STDB 1987–91	NCGEB 1984–90	ATT 1985–90	CDR 1985–90	PSTC 1984–90	Total (No. of projects)
1. Agriculture	40	50	34	8	26	158
—plant	18	22	16	4	18	78
—animal	13	7	16	1	2	39
—food	5	14	2	3	3	27
—fertilizer	4	7	—	—	3	17
2. Public health	4	9	—	6	20	39
3. Environment	3	7	2	4	1	17
4. Energy	—	2	—	—	1	3
5. Others	—	12	2	1	—	15
Total (No. of Projects)	47	80	38	19	48	232
Budget (million baht)	198,634	10,892	200.59	37.53	163.61	709.28

Key:
STDB = Science and Technology Development Board;
NCGEB = National Center for Genetic Engineering and Biotechnology;
ATT = Agricultural Technology Transfer Project, U.S.A.;
CDR = U.S.–Israel Cooperative Research Development Program, U.S.A.;
PSTC = Program in Science and Technology Cooperation, U.S.A.
Source: Proceedings of the 1991 Annual Conference on Thai Science and Technology in the Year 2000, Office of the Science and Technology Development Board, September 1991.

Table 7.6

Funding of Material Technology Projects from STDB and NCMMT

	1987	1988	1989	1990	1991
1. STDB					
—No. of projects	7	6	4	2	NA
—Amount[a]	20.01	33.39	17.67	10.48	NA
2. NCMMT					
—No. of projects	2	31	43	40	40[b]
—Amount[a]	1.10	12.20	30.40	64.20	82.50[b]
Total no. of projects	9	37	47	42	40
Total amount[a]	21.11	45.59	48.07	74.68	82.50

[a]In million baht.
[b]Budget only.
Source: Office of Science and Technology Development Board (STDB), National Center for Metal and Material Technology (NCMMT).

Table 7.7

Funding of Electronics and Computer Projects from STDB and NECTEC

	1988	1989	1990	1991
1. STDB				
—No. of projects	6	0	3	1
—Amount*	13.74	0	10.62	3.91
2. NECTEC				
—No. of projects	55	60	65	66
—Amount*	23.29	24.81	54.16	56.22
Total no. of projects	61	60	68	67
Total amount*	37.03	24.81	64.78	60.13

Source: Office of Science and Technology Development Board (STDB), National Electronics and Computer Technology Center (NECTEC).
   *In million baht.

Table 7.8

Number of Articles by Thai Scientists Published in International Periodicals

Year	Number of Articles	Share of Participating Foreign Scientists (%)
1986	305	27.2
1987	324	27.7
1988	316	38.0
1989	267	37.8

Source: Compiled from Science Citation Index by Joe Anderson, Chatri Sripaipan, and Suchata Jinachitra.

search strength of the whole country due to the small number of researchers involved (Boonyubol et al., 1991b). A more comprehensive evaluation should include other local journals and conferences.

In developed countries, the number of patents registered can be used as a measure of technological capability in a particular field. However, in a developing country like Thailand with very few commercializable research results, this number is meaningless as an indicator. Since the enactment of the Patent Act in 1979, 1,827 patents were issued up to June 1990. Out of these issued patents, 1,304 were of industrial designs, some of which were of rather simple nature. Up to August 1990, 526 patents on engineering and chemical inventions were issued: 456 belonged to foreign nationals, 63 belonged to Thais, and 7 were not specified (see Table 7.9). Therefore, it is clear that the Thai patent system is being used by foreigners more than by Thai nationals. An effort to track down

Table 7.9

Patents Classified by Nationality of Inventors

Inventor	Nature of invention	No. of patents*	Percentage
Foreigners		456	100.00
	Invented alone	193	42.32
	Jointly invented	263	57.68
Thai nationals		63	100.00
	Invented alone	60	95.24
	Jointly invented	3	4.76
Not specified	—	5	—
Jointly invented			
(Thai and foreign)	—	2	—
Total		526	—

*From July 1982 to August 1990.
Source: Department of Trade Registration.

the 63 inventors resulted in 13 respondents, of which 4 had commercialized their inventions. Most of the inventors worked on their own and relied on their own income for funding, and few of the inventions required a large amount of money for investment (Kaosa-ard, 1991).

It should be noted that some of the research funded by STDB and the three national centers has so far been commercialized. We can certainly expect more to come in the next five years. It should be very interesting to evaluate the impact (both direct and indirect) of these research projects on Thailand's technological capability.

R&D in the Private Sector

Research in the private sector is much less than that of the public sector. All the companies in Thailand spent only 181.6 million baht (US$7 million) or 6.8 percent of total R&D expenditure in 1987. A previous survey suggested that Thai companies only invest 0.1 percent of their sales on R&D which is well below the Asian NIEs (Sutabutr et al., 1983).

This low level of expenditure explains the reported weakness of innovative capacity in Thai companies. A major study revealed that Thai industries were quite good in "operating" technology as well as "adapting" technology, but were remarkably incapable of "innovating" and creating new technology (Kritayakirana et al., 1989).

A study of the R&D of the private sector (Sripaipan et al., 1990) found that the majority of Thai companies concentrate on "operating" or utilizing existing technology. This does not mean that they run outdated or primitive operations. Actually, some have acquired state-of-the-art technology and operate ultramodern plants. Some are quite large. Some are subsidiaries of world-class multi-nationals. They have not, however, felt the need to undertake development work locally. A smaller group of companies have undertaken their own "ad-aptation" and development of existing technology, usually driven to do so by the nature of the local operating environment or by market needs. For exam-ple, in adapting to the local operating environment, a foreign joint venture in aquaculture modified Taiwan hatchery equipment and aimed to produce least-cost feed formulations using locally available raw materials. Other com-panies were led to technology development by market needs. Two consumer goods multinationals have continuing programs to modify products such as soap, detergents, and foods to suit local customs and habits. Predictably, cases of R&D to create new technology are extremely rare and are affordable only to a few large companies. Recent results from such companies' research are, for example, the production of special high-grade refractories and the for-mulation of shrimp feed, which has a better growth efficiency ratio than equiva-lent products manufactured in Taiwan and Indonesia.

Private companies are not conducting more R&D because of the constraints of economic and policy factors and S&T infrastructure, including the following factors:

1. Due to a high-growth economy, firms are rapidly scaling up production capacity to meet excess demand. Therefore, they do not feel the pressure for innovation or differentiation of products.
2. Government policies limit the number of companies entering individual sectors and therefore lessen the competitive pressure needed to stimulate R&D activity.
3. Import taxes on R&D equipment and precision instruments remain high, limiting the ability of small and medium-sized companies to acquire them.
4. Taxes on royalties and license fees for foreign technology further increase its cost.
5. There is a need for improved availability of technical consultancy services and information on S&T activities in the public sector.
6. There is a clear shortage of technical manpower to satisfy present levels of demand for production engineers and technicians necessary for operating and absorbing the imported technology. Although there is no obvious shortage of manpower for technology development or generation, this is more due to underactivity in R&D on the part of Thai companies than to an oversupply of R&D personnel.
7. Existing companies finance technology acquisition using internal re-sources or raise loans from commercial banks as part of an overall busi-ness development plan. Some financial assistance to small and medium-sized companies does exist, but its impact has yet to be felt.

Table 7.10

Performance of the Public Sector Funds for R&D (up to September 1991)

Funding Source	Total Fund (million baht)	No. of Projects approved	Value approved (million baht)
1. MOSTE soft loan	105	10	75.3
2. Bank of Thailand soft loan	100	1	10.0
3. STDB			
—loan	110	7	35.0
—grant	38	4	9.8
	353	22	130.1

Assistance to the Private Sector

The Board of Investment (BOI) is providing incentives to R&D projects by exempting import taxes on machinery and corporate tax irrespective of the location of the project. So far there are fifteen projects approved with a total investment of 996 million baht (Auansakul, 1991).

There are currently three sources of soft loans at low interest for private sector R&D activities: MOSTE, STDB, and the Bank of Thailand (BOT). In addition, STDB also operates a grant fund that requires a matching allocation from the granted company.

The performance of these funds is summarized in Table 7.10. It should be noted that MOSTE's loan fund has the longest history—three years—and has been the most heavily utilized, with ten projects approved totaling 75.3 million baht. STDB's activities have improved markedly since March 1990, from only two loan projects to seven loan projects and four grant projects. The Bank of Thailand's fund is least utilized since it is restricted to R&D projects promoted by BOI.

S&T Manpower

It was estimated that in 1990 there were 36,700 scientists, 49,934 engineers, and 33,847 agriculturists with a bachelor's degree or higher level of education. Below the bachelor's degree there were 1,494, 706,317, and 115,256 persons with science, engineering, and agriculture education respectively. This makes a total of 120,481 persons or 12.8 percent with a bachelor's degree or higher qualification, and 823,067 persons or 87.2 percent with less than a bachelor's degree. Thus, the total number of S&T personnel is 943,548 persons, which is 2.9 percent of the country's labor force; Thailand has 15 scientists and engineers per 10,000 population (Boonyubol et al., 1990). This is very low compared with, say, Korea, which has 122 scientists and engineers per 10,000 population (Boonyubol et al., 1991a).

In the past few years, because of the economic boom, Thailand has been experiencing a severe S&T manpower shortage due to excess demand. In 1990, 1,250 scientists and 2,531 engineers were graduated but the demand forecasts for scientists and engineers in 1992 estimated a need for 2,532 and 5,136 persons, respectively (Boonyubol et al., 1990). Despite the recent effort of the Ministry of University Affairs to accelerate the production of engineers in fields of severe shortage—that is, mechanical, electrical, industrial and chemical engineers—the shortage is expected to persist throughout the Seventh Plan (1992–96). This shortage has already resulted in an alarming rate of brain drain from the public sector to the private sector for a much higher salary. In the private sector, there are complaints about the difficulty of recruitment, high salary demand, and high turnover rate.

R&D manpower in 1987 is shown in Table 7.11, which indicates that Thailand has a total of 8,493 researchers and a full-time equivalent (FTE) of 5,539 persons. The university has the higher number of researchers, 4,898, but the FTE is lowered considerably to 2,518, which is only slightly higher than FTE of government, 2,416.75. State enterprises, private firms, and non-profit private organizations have far fewer researchers: 527, 145, and 21, respectively. As for the number of researchers in each academic discipline, Table 7.12 shows that medical science has the highest number, 8,261. Ninety percent of them are physicians, who are classified as having master's degrees. Social science and humanities come second at 2,229, and engineering is last at 1,176.

To make an international comparison, the number of research scientists and engineers (RSE) in Thailand totals 2,846 persons or 1 person per 10,000 workers. This is much lower than those of other countries; for example, there are 32 RSE per 10,000 workers in Taiwan, 44 in Sweden, and 79 in Japan.

Scientific and Technological Services

Scientific and technological services are support services enabling the smooth and efficient operation of S&T activities. They encompass metrology (industrial standards), calibration services, testing service, information service, technical consultancy service, and other supportive infrastructural services.

The Ministry of Commerce is empowered by the Weight and Measurements Act 1923 to maintain primary standards; i.e., the licensing and certifying authority for weighing machines and linear and volumetric measuring instruments. In 1985, the cabinet assigned the Department of Scientific Services to maintain mechanical primary standards and the Thailand Institute of Scientific and Technological Research (TISTR) to maintain electrical primary standards. The Thai Industrial Standards Institute is responsible for the preparation and publication of Thai industrial documentation standards. Most of Thai calibration services are operated by the public sector except the Technological Promotion Association (Thai-Japan), which is a private organization. Product testing services are carried out by about thirty authorized laboratories in the public sector. To take care of

Table 7.11

R&D Manpower in 1987 (in persons)

	Researcher		Researcher Assistant		Other Supporting Staff		Total	
	Actual No.	FTE*	Actual No.	FTE	Actual No.	FTE	Actual No.	FTE
Government	2,902	2,416.75	1,952	1,835.00	1,160	913.50	6,014	5,165.25
University	4,898	2,518.00	969	613.75	1,465	983.00	7,332	4,114.75
State enterprise	527	446.50	278	259.50	331	307.75	1,136	1,013.75
Private firm	145	138.25	66	62.50	50	45.50	261	246.25
Nonprofit private	21	19.50	19	14.00	158	47.25	198	80.75
Total	8,493	5,539.00	3,284	2,784.75	3,164	2,297.00	14,941	10,620.75

*FTE = full time equivalent.
Source: National Research Council of Thailand.

Table 7.12

Educational Qualifications of Researchers Classified by Area (in persons)

Area	Ph.D.	Master's	Bachelor's	Diploma	Total
Natural science	295	899	463	13	1,670
Engineering	234	493	429	20	1,176
Medical science	291	7,434	531	5	8,261
Agricultural science	189	591	871	198	1,849
Social science					2,229
and humanities	356	1,363	493	17	
Total	1,365	10,780	2,787	253	15,185

Source: National Research Council of Thailand.

the ever-increasing work load, about seven testing laboratories in the private sector have been certified.

Apart from major libraries in universities, a number of organizations provide specialized information services. For example, the Scientific and Technological Information Division, Department of Science Services, offers patents and industrial standards services; the Technology Information Center, Technological Promotion Association (Thai-Japan) provides practical technical information such as trade catalogues; and Technical Information Access Center (TIAC) of STDB supplies an on-line information search service from a number of foreign databases.

However, there are a lot of expressed needs for information not only from foreign sources, but also about domestic science and technology activities. Another complaint from manufacturers who want to export is the lack of internationally certified testing facilities to eliminate the need for testing products abroad.

Technology Strategy of Thailand: The Seventh Plan

The Seventh National Economic and Social Development Plan (1992–96) will have a chapter on Science and Technology Development (NESDB, 1991). Its essence is described briefly below.

There are three main achievements in the development of science and technology to date. First is the creation of awareness in the role of science and technology among the populace. The top administrators in the government are becoming more supportive in the promotion of science and technology. Second, there is more R&D in the public and private sectors. The government has established STDB and the three national centers to fund R&D. For the private sector, it provides low-interest soft loans and a grant for R&D through a number of agencies, and fiscal incentives for R&D projects promoted by BOI.

Third, about 1,200 scholarships for advanced degrees in science and technology in industrialized countries are being granted for future researchers and university teachers.

The targets set by the Seventh Plan are:

1. To expand the use of technology in industry and agriculture to increase productivity at a rate of 2.6 and 1.8 percent per annum to support their expansion at a rate of 9.5 and 3.4 percent a year, respectively.
2. To increase the production of S&T manpower in the following categories: engineers from 9.8 to 14.9 persons per 10,000 population; scientists from 7.2 to 10.2; agriculturists from 6.7 to 10.5 and technicians from 141.5 to 221.5; and researchers (full-time equivalent research scientists and engineers) from 1.4 to 2.5.
3. To increase the R&D expenditure to 0.75 percent of GNP in 1996. It is to comprise 0.5 percent of GNP from the government and another 0.25 from the private sector.

The strategies to achieve the above targets are:

1. Stimulate the private sector to utilize more technology by creating a competitive atmosphere, by providing fiscal incentives, by disseminating technologies to industries, by improving governmental regulations, and by supporting the development of specific technologies for the targeted industries. It is interesting to note that this is the first time that a Five-Year Development Plan has targeted industries at sector levels. They are metalworking and machinery, electronics, textiles, food, plastic, gems and jewelry, and iron and steel.
2. Promote the utilization of modern technologies and management techniques to increase productivity and reduce cost by stabilizing the price of farm produce, promoting organizations of farmers, improving extension services, and increasing the role of the private sector in technology transfer. Specific measures are designed for each sector of agriculture, livestock, and fisheries.
3. Increase the efficiency of technology acquisition and transfer by building up bargaining power, by promoting the diffusion of imported technology, by upgrading the technological capability of state enterprises, and by monitoring the technology transfer program of large projects.
4. Develop S&T manpower by accelerating the production of scientists, engineers, mathematicians, technicians, and skilled labor in areas of high demand, building up the stock of university teachers and researchers, stressing the urgency for training, and improving the working environment of academic staff.
5. Organize the R&D system to support industrial development by concen-

trating R&D on the selection, adaptation, and improvement of imported technology, reorienting public R&D institutes to solve technical problems of industry, supporting research in education institutions to serve as S&T knowledge centers, and increasing the role of private sector R&D through fiscal and financial incentives, domestic markets development, and intellectual property protection, and developing R&D as a career for researchers.

6. Improve the S&T infrastructure by developing metrology, industrial standards, and product-testing systems, organizing the S&T information system, increasing the capability of engineering consultancy services, and creating the atmosphere and awareness of science and technology.

Such a brief summary probably does not do justice to the Science and Technology Development Plan. Some of its features are discussed in more detail in the following section.

Sectoral Technology Strategies

Because the Science and Technology Development Plan has to satisfy a number of committees with representatives from all concerned government departments as well as the private sector, it needs to cover all aspects of S&T development. However, there has been a clear shift toward more private sector participation in practically all strategies. For R&D, the plan set a clear target of 0.25 percent of GNP in the private sector by the year 1996. But only one of the six strategies mentions R&D. Most of them address the utilization, acquisition, transfer, and diffusion of technology as well as developing S&T manpower. Even then, R&D were to concentrate on selecting, adapting, and improving the imported technologies rather than on inventing new ones. Public sector R&D institutions are to be reoriented to solve industrial problems. These are signs that the plan takes a more pragmatic approach to the current S&T situation.

Another significant feature of the plan is that it has for the first time targeted industries at sectoral levels. These industries are those crucial to the development of Thailand during the Seventh Plan or in a future time frame of only five years. Therefore, they tend to be those that already exist, rather than futuristic ones. The selection process involves economic analysis, technology assessment, and expert group prioritization. The main criteria used for economic analysis include industry growth potential, the competitiveness of international markets, and a linkage effect to select ten industrial groups out of seventeen from the I-O classification. Technology assessment based on the four factors of dynamism, versatility, viability and accessibility further narrows down the industrial groups to get a clearer picture. For instance, the electrical and electronic product group is limited to electronic products that have been growing dramatically. The "other industries" group is restricted to the gems and jewelry industry which generates very high employment and export earnings. Finally, six industries were selected using a group of experts to consider technological and market suitability as well as social and environmental impact. A technique called Analytical Hierarchy Process, or AHP, was used to get prioritized ratings for the selection (Chintayarangsarn et al., 1991). It happened that the six targeted industries here almost coincided with the six selected by another study group on strategic industries. The exception is that they picked iron and steel instead of gems and jewelry. Key technologies and technology strategies for all seven industries have been worked out and are described in sequence below.

Electronics Industry

The key technologies identified include: computer-aided technologies; software engineering; circuit design; process technology; production management; and mechanical technology. Strategies for development include: promotion for investments in higher technology products manufacturing; promotion of needed supporting industries; promotion of product design; and development of target products such as personal computers, small PABX, mobile telephone, facsimile, and application-specific integrated circuits (ASIC).

Metal-Working and Machinery Industries

The key technologies include: computer-aided technologies; production management; and metal-working technologies such as casting, forging, machining, heat treatment, electroplating, and stamping. Development strategies include: promotion of investment in machine tools industry; promotion of metal-working industries; promotion of mold and die industry development; and development of automotive parts such as engines, transmissions, steering systems, and suspension systems.

Petrochemical and Plastics Industry

Emphasis in key technologies is aimed at the downstream plastic products industry. Key technologies identified include: compounding; molds for plastic products; and production management technologies. Development strategies include: improving plastics properties from commodity plastics to intermediate and engineering plastics; and establishing a design center to provide products and mold and die design.

Textile Industry

The key technologies include: the efficient use of modern machinery; production management; and textile chemical technology. Development strategies include: subcontracting of world-famous, brand-name garment manufacturing; promotion of investments for dyeing industry; and promotion for switching to modern machinery.

Food Industry

The key technologies include: sterilization; production management; packaging; and waste management. Development strategies include: planting of fruits and vegetables to industry standard; the use of modern machinery and incentives for waste utilization technologies.

Gems and Jewelry Industry

The key technologies include: a set of color standards for gems; computer-aided technologies; and precious metal metallurgy. Development strategies include: establishing gem standards; R&D in precious metal alloying; and tariff rate reduction for R&D equipment.

Iron and Steel Industry

The key technologies include: ladle technology; steel alloying. Development strategies include: increasing the efficiency of furnaces; acquiring alloy steel casting technology.

Nearly all of the six selected industries have targeted computer-aided technologies[2] and production management[3] as important key technologies. They are therefore referred to as generic technology. Although metal-working technology has not been explicitly identified as a key technology in some of the industries, it is nevertheless a common fact that all industries to a varying degree possess production machinery and make products involving metal parts as constituents. Consequently, metal-working technology is included as another generic technology.

In addition, there is another group of technologies that do not bear directly on manufacturing processes or product quality, but only on production cost and environment. These are referred to as auxiliary technologies and include energy conservation technology, which significantly affects the motor vehicle, metal-working and machining industries, the textiles industry, and the food industry, as well as waste management technology, which is vital in the food and textile industries.

Strategy for Technology Acquisition

The two most popular modes of technology acquisition are capital goods imports and foreign investment. In 1990, they totaled 362,008 and 74,818 million baht respectively. Foreign investments bring in product management technology and process technology but not design technology or product-specific technology. Machinery is sometimes imported with minimal instructions from suppliers on operational procedure, resulting in inefficient operation and insufficient maintenance of machines.

Compared with the above import figures, technology payments through contractual arrangements on royalties, trademark, technical fees, and management fees totaling 5,334 baht in 1989 were simply inadequate. They equaled a mere expenditure of 1.1 percent and 0.73 percent of the capital goods imported in 1989 on technology purchase and technical assistance, respectively. This means that Thai manufacturers have not been using licensing or consultancy as main modes of technology acquisition.

Although it is certain that R&D activities will increase, judging from the performance of public R&D institutions on technology commercialization and levels of R&D activities in the private sector (Sripaipan et al., 1990), it is unlikely that R&D will become the main mode of technology acquisition for Thai industry in the next few years. Mergers and acquisitions of foreign companies for technology are unlikely to be prevalent, despite some cases of acquisition for access to market.

We therefore suggest here that subcontracting be used as a strategy for technology acquisition in the Seventh Plan. The high level of foreign investment presents a favored condition for mutual benefits. This strategy fits in well with those for the development of the electronics, metal-working, and plastic industries described above. We must not be content, however, with only producing parts and components to order. After mastering product management and process technology, we should attempt to learn the product-specific technology and the design technology. This will enable us not only to attain high quality at low price but also to adopt products according to market demands or new raw materials, and to build a more complex product that is close to the consumer, for higher value added. These are technological activities that lead from technology utilization and technology development ultimately to technology creation through R&D. A number of government policies are needed to facilitate the formation of a competitive subcontracting network, but further discussion of this is beyond the scope of this paper (see, for example, Chintayarangsarn et al., 1991; Kaosa-ard et al., 1991).

Another strategy that has been employed by some governments of the NIEs is the purchase of technology by government agencies. Such technology is then transferred to domestic private manufacturers. This method is mainly used in cases of advanced technology that require large investment beyond the means of the private sector or constitutes major technology critical to the development of a large number of related industries. The Thai government may like to support the development of certain sectors through this method if it wants to be more proactive in technology acquisition.

Conclusion

This chapter has reviewed recent developments of the Thai economy and its policies. Although the economy is growing at a rapid pace, some weaknesses persist in technological capability and human-resource development that will make such growth unsustainable in the long run. The present policy trend toward liberalization is good for industries and businesses, but there is a danger that the market economy will be pushed to an extreme. The two weaknesses mentioned above take a long time to develop and therefore cannot be expected to respond instantly to market forces. A senior government official's remark that the government is changing its role from controller to supervisor hopefully does not mean that government ought to know less. In fact, there is a great need for information in many fields in order to make decisions less fallible and planning more effective.

Science and technology have yet to assert their influence on the economy of Thailand. Despite a number of programs to boost R&D in both the public and the private sectors, time is still needed for these efforts to bear significant fruits. If proper technology strategy is pursued, the technological capability of the country can be substantially improved by the end of the Seventh Plan. However, the ultimate limitation could be due to S&T manpower. This present shortage, if allowed to persist, will certainly have detrimental effects on investment and industry and can affect the development of the country as a whole. In the short term there is no choice but to import needed personnel and launch massive training programs. In the medium term, the ability of educational institutions to expand enrollment will be limited by the availability of teachers. In the long term there are more options and fewer excuses for not working out a good solution.

Needless to say, effective implementation is more important than an immaculate strategic plan. A good NESDB plan can only serve as a guideline for ministries to draw up their yearly implementation plans. It is up to the ministries to make the plans work. However, NESDB should closely monitor these plans to ensure conformity. On the other hand, long-term sectoral plans (beyond ten years) will need to be developed to guide Thailand into the type of society in which the people of Thailand want to live.

Notes

1. This classification of the manufacturing sector is taken from the Organization for Economic Cooperation and Development Report of 1988. Resource-intensive industries are ISIC categories 31 food and beverages, 32.3 leather, 331 wood products, 341 pulp and paper, 354 petroleum and coal products, 364 nonmetallic mineral products, and 372 nonferrous metal industries. Labor-intensive industries are 321–2 and 324 textile, wearing apparel and footwear industries, 332 furniture, 380–1 fabricated metal products, and 39 other manufacturing industries. Scale-intensive industries are 34 paper products, printing and publishing, 351 industrial chemical, 355 rubber products, 356 plastic products, 361–2 pottery and glass products, 371 iron and steel basic industries, 384 transport equipment. Differentiated goods are 3821 engines and turbines, 3822 agricultural machinery, 3823 metal and woodworking machinery, 3824 special industrial machinery, 3829 nonelectrical machinery, 383 electrical machinery, and 3842–3 photographic and optical goods, watches, and clocks. Science-based industries are 352 other products, 3825 office and computing machinery, 3851 professional and scientific equipment, and 3845 aircraft.

2. Computer-aided technologies in production include (1) computer-aided design (CAD), (2) computer-aided drafting (CAD), (3) computer-aided engineering (CAE), (4) computer-aided testing (CAT), (5) computer-aided software engineering (CASE), (6) computer-aided manufacturing (CAM), and (7) computer-integrated manufacturing (CIM).

3. Product management technologies include TQC, to control production quality from start to finish; JIT, for time- and cost-saving inventory management; MRP II, for planning efficient production and control of raw material utilization; and SQC and SPC, which employ statistical means of control over the production process and output quality.

References

Auansakul, A. "From Research to Market: Success in RD&E Investment in the Thai Private Sector." Chonburi, Thailand: Office of the Science and Technology Development Board, September 1991.
Boonyubol, C., et al. "The Demand Forecast and Direction of S&T Manpower Development." Chula Unisearch, Chulalongkorn University, 1990.
————. "The Management of the R&D System to Support Industrial Development." Bangkok: Thailand Development Research Institute, 1991b.
————. "Human Resources Development in the Era of Rapid Technological Change." Chonburi, Thailand: Office of the Science and Technology Development Board, September 1991a.
Chintayarangsarn, R., et al. "The Identification of Key Technologies for Industrial Development. Bangkok: Thailand Development Research Institute, 1991.
Dahlman, C. J., and Brimble, P. "Technology Strategy and Policy for Industrial Competitiveness: A Case Study of Thailand." World Bank, Industrial Series, paper no. 24, April 1990.
Kaosa-ard, M., et al. "The Barriers to and Strategies for Technology Acquisition." Bangkok: Thailand Development Research Institute, 1991.
Kritayakirana, K., et al. "The Development of Thailand's Technological Capability in Industry." 6 vols. Bangkok: Thailand Development Research Institute, 1989.
NESDB. "The Fifth National Economic and Social Development Plan (1982–1986)." Bangkok: National Economic and Social Development Board, Bangkok, 1982.
————. "The Sixth National Economic and Social Development Plan (1987–1991)." Bangkok: National Economic and Social Development Board, 1987.
————. "Science and Technology Development Plan in the Seventh Development Plan (1992–1996)" (draft). Bangkok: Subcommittee on Science and Technology Planning, National Economic and Social Development Board, June 1991.
Satyarakwit, W., and Pongsaksri, T. "Scientific and Technological Services in Thailand." Annual Conference on Thai Science and Technology in the Year 2000, Office of the Science and Technology Development Board, Chonburi, Thailand, September 1991.
Sopon, B., et al. *National Study of Research and Development (R&D) Expenditure and Manpower in 1987.* Office of the National Research Council, July 1990, Table 2.4, p. 23.
Sripaipan, C., et al. "Enhancing Private Sector Research and Development in Thailand." Bangkok: Thailand Development Research Institute, 1990.
Sutabutr, H., et al. "Survey of Science and Technology Manpower and Research and Development R&D in the Private Sector in Thailand." Bangkok: Ministry of Science, Technology and Energy and the Science Committee of the Thailand National Commission for UNESCO, 1983.
Yuthavong, Y. "Legal and Organizational Structure for Development of Science and Technology in Thailand." Annual Conference on Thai Science and Technology in the Year 2000, Office of the Science and Technology Development Board, September 13–15, 1991, Chonburi, Thailand.

8

Building a Workable S&T Infrastructure in Malaysia

Hamzah Kassim

For many industrializing countries like Malaysia, the issues associated with technological development are beginning to assume an important dimension. These countries are attempting to industrialize without the benefits of the long, more or less evolutionary process of technological change characteristic of mature industrial nations. The industrial world has had three centuries of experience in S&T following the seventeenth-century scientific revolution and the eighteenth-century industrial revolution. For Malaysia, the process of industrialization depends critically on the process of acquiring technological competencies. The process of national industrial development can be identified with the process by which the nation keeps on accumulating technological capabilities. The direction and speed of such development are influenced by the direction and speed of a nation's endeavor to develop its S&T capabilities. Unless there is a concurrent development of strong S&T capabilities, the country runs the risk of being in a permanent state of dependence without acquiring its own know-how and skill to manage its industrial development.

If there are common factors in the success stories of industrialization, most certainly one of them is the attainment of confidence and competence in technology. Technology provides the means to achieve the transformation of available inputs into desired outputs. It allows value enhancement through the process of transformation of primary products to semifinished consumer and capital goods. Technology has demonstrated an extraordinary capacity to generate wealth and power.

The *Industrial Development Report of Malaysia* reiterated the vital role of industrial progress to sustain future economic growth of the country.[1] It represents a watershed in the structural shift of the country's economy from one dependent largely upon agriculture and primary products to one in which the manufacturing sector plays a much greater role. It also signaled a change from a largely laissez-faire approach to a distinctly target-oriented approach to industrialization, within a free-enterprise economy. These changes are now becoming apparent; a comfortable, protected industrial sector, oriented toward import substitution, is gradually but inexorably being replaced by one whose sights are firmly set on exports, taking an aggressive and competitive position in the world market. The manufacturing sector became the largest contributor to GDP for the first time in 1984, marginally superseding agriculture, which had hitherto been the leading sector. Today, its contribution to GDP is on the order of 25 percent, and the sector also accounted for an estimated 34 percent of new jobs in 1989. The stage has been set. Manufacturing is a critical sector of the Malaysian economy, and its importance is growing. Malaysia needs the most vigorous development of its industrial technology because we must industrialize rapidly.

The Changing Economic Structure

Malaysia's GDP is targeted to grow at 7 percent in real terms during the next ten years, based on the projected trends in the world's economy, the rich resource endowment of the nation, the reorientation of economic management toward the private sector, and marketplace dominance.

As a result, greater emphasis has been given to technological innovation and human resource development. Some of these measures initiated during the last four years have produced good results that Malaysia is enjoying—a high economic growth of 8.7 percent in 1989, 10 percent in 1990, and 8.5 percent in 1991.

The share of GDP of the secondary sector comprising manufacturing and construction will expand from 30.2 percent in 1990 to reach 38.7 percent by the year 2000 (Second Outline Perspective Plan, 1991). The tertiary sector is also anticipated to improve further and account for 43 percent of GDP in the year 2000. The secondary sector will grow by more than three times the rate of the primary sector, thus significantly changing each sector's share of GDP by the year 2000. It is anticipated that agriculture and mining will continue to be important to the economy, even though their share is projected to decline further, from 28.1 percent in GDP in 1990 to 18.3 percent in the year 2000.

Industrial Performance

The main strategy in the next few years is to broaden the base of manufacturing activities. The structure of the industrial base remains potentially weak and is heavily concentrated on two subsectors, the electrical and electronic, and the textile and apparel subsectors (see Sixth Malaysia Plan, 1991). These industries constituted some one-quarter of the sectors' output and grew by 26.8 percent per annum and 11 percent per annum, respectively, from 1986 to 1990. The export performance of the manufacturing sector increased by 31 percent per annum, from $12.471 million in 1985 to $48,047 million in 1990. As a result, its shares in total merchandise exports almost doubled, from 32.8 percent in 1985 to 60.4 percent in 1990. It is anticipated that by the year 2000, the manufacturing sector would contribute 80 percent of the total merchandise exported. Although these two subsectors continue to be the major contributors to output growth and export earnings, major issues will have to be resolved, particularly the development of linkages with small- and medium-scale industries.

The manufacturing sector's contribution to GDP rose from 19.7 percent in 1985 to 27 percent in 1990, surpassing that of the agricultural sector since 1987. Foreign investment in (approved cases) amounted to $34.908 million during the last five years. The main sources of foreign investment in these approved projects were Japan, Taiwan, Singapore, the United Kingdom, the United States, Indonesia, and Hong Kong which, together, constituted 70.79 percent of the total proposed foreign investment. About one-third of the proposed total foreign investment came from Taiwan and a quarter from Japan.

The manufacturing sector has been given the leading role in achieving the GDP growth target of 7 percent. Policy reforms in manufacturing focused on removing the constraints and will aim at widening and deepening the industrial base, leading to high-value-added products and increased linkages with small- and medium-scale industries. The major industrial strategy in this decade is to transform Malaysian manufacturing industries to more high-value-added and high-technology industries. Hence, Malaysia is now entering into a new phase in industrial development with greater emphasis on the development of export-oriented high-value-added, high-technology industries with strong support from domestic R&D.

The government will emphasize measures to accelerate industrial restructuring, technological upgrading, human resource development, and industrial linkages that would ensure a greater and higher level of domestic value added contribution to growth. Hence, to complement the industrial restructuring, the government is accelerating the technological transformation in Malaysian industries through the development of comprehensive technology strategies. The action plan for industrial technology provides a comprehensive guideline to accelerate the technological transformation process (Ministry of Science, Technology and the Environment, 1990).

Technology and Industrial Development

The status of industrial technology is intimately linked with the science and technology (S&T) policy framework as a whole. First, in the larger context, the priority assigned to S&T in relation to overall national goals and aspirations is of crucial importance, as it impinges both directly and indirectly on the development of industrial technological capabilities. Both the national Science and Technology Government Policy and the Fifth Malaysia Plan (1986–1990) have emphasized the development of self-reliance in S&T in support of economic growth. However, statements of intent have not always been matched by tangible achievements; effective results can only be generated with sustained commitment of resources and continuity of purpose in S&T, facilitated by a coherent organisational structure. For long-term success it is crucial to increase national awareness, and to create an S&T-oriented society.

The Shifting of R&D Resources

The relative emphasis accorded to industrial technology within S&T policy has a direct bearing on the resources that can be assembled and deployed, and the effectiveness of actions to develop national industrial capabilities. While a structure of research institutes, public agencies, and institutions of higher learning exists with functions in various fields of science and technology, the greater successes have been achieved in agriculture and the primary product areas, rather than in manufacturing and other secondary sectors of the economy.

There is also little emphasis on applications-directed research. The level of industrial R&D expenditure, an indicator of industrial technology development, sector accounting for 90 percent of this. It is relevant to note the experience of the industrialized countries, where the "research" component of industrial R&D represents, on the average, only about 10 percent of the total cost, while subsequent activities such as design engineering, prototype building, production, diffusion, and so on account for the bulk of the R&D effort. As in most developing countries, it is the development stage that forms the weakest link in the chain, and this is where a body of expertise must be built up. Industrial development cannot take place in a technological vacuum. A major reorientation is called for: industry must recognize the need for R&D, and in turn research bodies must emphasize practical industry-aligned applications[2].

To an extent, therefore, existing policy instruments and institutional mechanisms to foster industrial technology development have been less than adequate, with little attention given to the generation of a minimum level of indigenous technology through product enhancements and innovation. There is a growing realization that market forces alone may not be sufficient to generate technological development, and that there is a role for governments to shape and promote technological development. Similarly, while it is recognized that market mechanisms are indispensable, it is also realized that there is a role for the process of rational planning in achieving development objectives. The challenge is in seeking the judicious mix, the golden mean.

The Need for Collective Action

It is therefore timely to adopt a course that reflects the growing awareness that technology development is a shared responsibility of the government, academia, and the business community. A statement that sets down clearly the broad technology development objectives and strategies of the nation and priority areas—a technology plan—would be a means of guiding all parties in a collective national effort toward industrial technology development.

Malaysia must be prepared to adopt a strategic long-term approach to technology policy. It must develop a greater sense of vision regarding its desired technological trajectory. This will be based on an assessment of the current technological status of the nation, our capabilities and endowments, and future trends and associated commercial opportunities. It will also consider the global environment, and national economic and social needs and aspirations. It will take into account other policy imperatives as defined on the overall national policy framework. It will tackle in a comprehensive fashion the building up of the technology infrastructure in human resources and policy instruments, and represent a positive consensus between government, industry, and society.

Public Policy in Promoting Technology Development

The process of structural adjustment is essential in order to increase the technological capacity of Malaysian enterprises. Technology development can be the engine of this transformation process and the foundation of Malaysia's enhanced international competitiveness. Malaysia needs to deepen its technological base and to draw more heavily on its greatest asset, the skills of its people. The significance for firm-level competitiveness, the national S&T infrastructure, the structure of the domestic industrial sector, and the size of the local market demand have been perennial issues in policy-oriented innovation studies. As Chesnais (1986) pointed out, "It is probably quite erroneous and misleading for policy-makers to equate R&D with innovative capacity as it is to equate competitiveness of most industries in advanced industrial countries with wage costs. The finding that the technology competitiveness of firms and industries . . . [is] dependent on the structural attributes of firms and environment" implies that measures aimed at promoting innovation are unlikely to have a significant lasting effect in isolation. Identifying the major points in the firms' environment that impede or promote their capacity and readiness to innovate is the key step in formulating national technology policies.

Justifications for Intervention

The focus on adjustment to improve the transformation of Malaysian industries is leading to an emphasis on the growing issues of technological innovation such as the importance of learning strategies, the diffusion of technologies and practices, the role of domestic enterprise firms and the challenges of integrating technology policies with industrial management. The need for the transformation has arisen from recognition of the limited role of market forces in generating or signaling clearly the requirement for major structural changes.

The role of government in technology development is a particularly delicate one in Malaysia. Technology development displays many of the features and characteristics of a public good, and the market often cannot be relied upon to send appropriate signals to stimulate change. Riskiness, uncertain gestation periods, and high attrition rates for frontier technologies are among the factors that make it difficult to rely purely upon market mechanisms to govern the process of development effectively. Policy formulation must pay particular attention to the need to encourage adaptive and innovative technological improvements, and to inculcate a spirit of entrepreneurship in technology-inclined activities. This is particularly important for key areas in new and emerging technologies that will play a critical role in the industrial society of tomorrow, for Malaysia must stay close to the leading edge if it is to succeed.

Thus, while much of industrial technology development can be expected to be demand-driven, areas still remain where only government is in a position to influence the course of technology development in the national interest. Risks and uncertainties provide grounds for Malaysian government intervention for scientific and technological development. Individuals and companies can be too short-sighted on actions to be adopted for developing new technologies even when they can expect substantial long-term gains from adapting or developing new technologies. Therefore there is a need for the Malaysian government to intervene to counteract this kind of myopia. There is a case for government assisting with the development and dissemination of scientific knowledge, in particular, with relevance to small firms. Small firms have restricted access to funds and this can retard their capital performance (see Lim, 1987, p. 80).

Imperfect capital markets also form a basis for government's intervention in technological efforts. This implies that the government needs to coordinate and encourage the development of selected industrial fields and back its industrial strategy by giving support to science and industrial research, and development appropriate to the selected fields of industries.

Strengthening Technological Capability of Enterprises

Malaysia has begun to formulate technology development programs in an attempt to tackle comprehensively the building up of technology infrastructure in human resources and institutions, the optimum use of technological capabilities, and the increase in efficiency of technological activities. This has required that priorities be specified in accordance with the development of style and national needs and the program defined and carried out to attain them. Much effort has

THE S&T INFRASTRUCTURE IN MALAYSIA 177

been made to formulate this detailed industrial strategy covering the period from 1986 to 1995.

The Importance of Indigenous Efforts

The dependency syndrome that afflicts today's developing world, Malaysia included, is reflected in and exacerbated by technological dependence. Manifestations of this are all too familiar. There is a vicious circle: weak technology increases dependence, and as a result technological capabilities cannot be enhanced. A conscious effort must be made to break free. This requires a clear appreciation of the problem, and a sustained effort to remedy technological shortcomings. In turn, we must understand the nature of technology and its characteristics.

While many countries are proud of occasional centers of technological sophistication in their industrial sectors, often based around foreign or multinational enterprises, these very centers often form enclaves, providing only the barest contribution to the robustness of the national economy[3]. Their isolation and lack of interaction mean that the benefits of technological sophistication are not passed on to local activities. Technology builds upon itself, and to develop indigenous capabilities, technology must permeate through local industrial activity, to generate a self-sustaining and progressive critical mass.

In recent years there has been some increase in the technological capacity of Malaysian firms. As might be expected, the increase has been spread unevenly among firms. This is indicated by rising expenditure on research and development and by some evidence of incipient exports of technology. While these developments are potentially significant, particularly in relation to policy, they are relatively insignificant in the general picture. Technological innovation among Malaysian small- and medium-scale industries is at a low level in many respects. R&D activities are generally weak and those in small-scale firms are almost nonexistent.

For a number of growing economies, the ability to make independent technological choices, to adapt and improve upon chosen techniques and products, and eventually to generate new technology endogenously is an essential aspect of the process of development. The ability to acquire technological capability is developed cumulatively over time via the acquisition of skills obtained through production experience, investment in R&D, and learning and imitation. As noted by Nelson and Winter (1982), the knowledge is, in part, tacit, which means that one may know or learn how to do something and yet at the same time be unable to explain satisfactorily how it is done. All of this is a way of saying that an important part of technology is firm-specific; it cannot be simply transplanted but must be learned by experience, or more precisely, by interaction between experienced technology transfer and R&D.

But in its search to master new technologies and turn out products, including those that involve radical jumps from the past, the enterprise will be constrained by its existing technology base and experience. Hence absorption of imported technology is important because it is a process by which imported technology spreads and grows. Without it, technology will remain localized in the hands of the initial suppliers of technology. Technology transfer in Malaysia appears to be associated with production management capability but the acquisition of production capability will not ensure the viability and independence of local firms to develop and expand their technological base. Initially, the basic production function provides the foundation for its initial stage.

Fiscal and Financial Support

Incentives are aimed at inducing firms to enhance technical performance. These instruments are particularly critical in developing countries, since technology imports from multinationals usually dominate the industrial infrastructure, and indigenous firms at an early stage of development are particularly risk-averse in modifying technology and usually engage in no research activities beyond quality control and maintenance. More recently, Malaysia has become more aware of the necessity to make its industrial structure more technology-intensive. One of the immediate measures taken by the government is the provision of financial and fiscal support to Malaysian industries. The financial assistance is made available through the Industrial Technical Assistance Fund (ITAF), which was set up by the government in early 1990 with an initial allocation. Small and medium industries (SMIs) represent an important sector in this country. The introduction of this assistance is therefore expected to enhance the development of the SMIs into a progressive, high-quality, and modern industry capable of providing support facilities to the large industries in this country.

This fund was set up with the purpose of providing grants to SMIs that undertake the following activities:-

• Feasibility studies;
• Product development and design;
• Quality and productivity improvement; and
• Marketing.

Assistance is given in the form of a matching grant whereby 50 percent of the project costs is borne by the government and the remaining 50 percent is borne by the applicant company. Priority will be given to SMIs that manufacture or intend to manufacture product(s) promoted under the Promotion of Investment Act of 1986.

Fiscal measures to support technology development have been incorporated in the 1991 budget. These are:

1. A tax exemption of five years is to be given to approved companies or institutions that are established companies or institutions that are established for the purpose of carrying out research for a particular industry. Furthermore, dividends distributed by these companies will also be tax-exempted in the hands of shareholders.
2. Accumulated losses incurred by the approved companies or institutions may be carried forward after the tax-exempt period.
3. A double deduction is to be given to persons who contribute cash to approved research institutions.
4. A double deduction is to be given to companies that undertake to use the facilities and services of approved research companies or institutions.
5. A tax exemption of five years is to be given to new technology-based firms.

The above incentives are additions to those already in operation, which include:

1. A double tax deduction on moneys spent on approved training or on infrastructure and equipment for approved training to upgrade the technology skills of the workforce, and
2. A double tax deduction on moneys spent on infrastructure and/or conduct of in-house R&D.

Strengthening the R&D System

Clearly, the importation of technology from abroad and the building up of an internally strong S&T capability must be complementary. An economy that lacks indigenuous research and technology capability is most unlikely to make successful use of innovation developed far away and in response to a very different set of circumstances. R&D plays a crucial role in acquiring knowledge in S&T competence. A growing concern in Malaysia is the lack of private sector R&D. Nevertheless, this should be seen within the context of the current industrial structure. Most domestic firms in Malaysia grew out of the import-substitution industry. Within the last few years, a small number of domestic firms have moved into new industries, such as telecommunications.

The prevailing industrial structure plays a major role in determining the amount of R&D the country will perform. Companies operating in industries associated with the early stages of the innovation cycle will invest heavily in R&D, typically 5 to 10 percent of their turnover. Here, R&D is a major factor in the competitiveness of the industry. Conversely, companies that operate in traditional industries will invest less in R&D, often less than one percent of their turnover. It is therefore crucial that Malaysian firms aim to develop industries in the emerging technology areas related to biotechnology, microelectronics, telecommunications, and pharmaceuticals, where the potential for export is enormous. This structural adjustment will require vigorous effort toward technology application. The result will be substantial growth in industries that produce goods with high-value-added contents.

Commercialization of Technology

As Malaysia moves to a higher plane of industrialization, the S&T component will become crucial and play a major role in industrial development. The shifting of the manufacturing sector to more high-value and high-technology content is aimed at making the manufacturing process more technology-intensive. This will accelerate public and private investment in R&D with the objective of at least doubling its share as a percentage of GNP by the year 2000 from the current level of 0.8 percent per annum.

The development of a strong private R&D system will increase our capability to exploit research from the public sector. Commercial exploitation of R&D requires both a strong public and private R&D system. The Malaysian government has increased its investment in the public R&D system. This must, however, be matched by stronger private sector participation. Strategic partnerships must be developed between firms and R&D institutions to promote exploitation of R&D results. Partnerships between R&D centers can play a catalytic role in promoting innovation in Malaysian industries. One must consider the framework of promoting a research consortium, particularly in new technologies that can be directly applied to the market. A national system of innovation is essential to ensure the exploitation of research. Currently, the Malaysian scientific and technology infrastructure is still in the development stage and the linkages between the production system and scientific institutions need to be strengthened.

One of the major weaknesses of developing countries is their inability to address issues that involve the entire innovation process. R&D is only an element of the innovation process to ensure commercial exploitation. One must look at the whole innovation process carefully, and this will involve other elements such as human resources, financing, innovation culture, technological entrepreneurships, market-driven R&D, and other institutional frameworks essential to promote the innovation process.

Reshaping the R&D System

On the management of industrial R&D, the national technology strategies have explicitly articulated various issues and made the following recommendations:

1. Increase private and public sector investment in R&D. This would help strengthen manpower and facilities for applications-oriented, market-driven research. R&D expenditure levels should be at least 1.5 percent of

GDP by 1995, and 2 percent by 2000, with 60 percent of this coming from the private sector.

2. Accord high priority to R&D in industrial technology in order to develop a dynamic and self-sustaining industrial sector. The allocation of R&D funding would have to reflect the critical importance of the industrial sector.

3. Focus public sector R&D to draw up five-year budget plans detailing research programs and priorities. The budgets should be reviewed annually. This will help create greater awareness in key public and private sector organizations, about research programs underway or being planned.

4. Implement a system of contract research as a first step toward corporatization of all public industrial research institutes. The objective is to encourage market-driven and user-oriented research through a clear understanding of priority areas, such as the monitoring of R&D performance.

5. Aim for a greater degree of financial autonomy for public R&D institution. The decision-making process could thus be accelerated, manpower and skills would be better utilized, and R&D programs would be more clearly geared to performance.

The Vital Role of Indigenous Enterprises

Although foreign investment has contributed to the rapid development of Malaysia's manufacturing base, it has also raised concerns over the impact on domestic industries. Widespread foreign investment is not healthy because domestic firms may be excluded from venturing into new areas. It is critical to enhance the capability of domestic enterprises since they can contribute more to the development of technology. The success of a small number of Malaysian firms in the high-tech sectors has prompted the country to upgrade its technological capability. Domestic firms tend to create specialized assets and they can graduate to multinational companies. Dependence on foreign investment should be viewed as one of the component industrial strategies and it is timely now to focus on the development of high-tech indigenous companies. Efforts to promote the location of multinational R&D in order to enhance our technological capability are influenced by their business strategy. Nevertheless, concerted efforts must be made to increase the location of multinational firms in high-value-added activities, including R&D. The growing shortages of highly qualified professional personnel could be a major limiting factor in attracting foreign firms to locate their R&D in Malaysia.

The Need for a Venture Fund

Malaysia is not an easy place to launch a fast-growth firm based on new technologies, especially compared with economies like Taiwan. Experience in financing product development indicates that Malaysian firms have difficulty getting access to venture capital. Most of these problems are associated with the relative immaturity of the venture capital market in Malaysia and its lack of experience in funding companies. There are very few examples of personnel leaving multinationals to set up their own firms. There is a great potential to tap the experiences of personnel in multinational corporations that have developed very strong international networks, management, and technical expertise. However, funding has become a major problem for many of these multinational personnel who aspire to set up their own new, technology-based firms.

Creating Strong Exporting Firms

Successful industrial economies always include strong firms that export a large part of their output to the world at large. Japan has Toyota, Matsushita, and many others. But Malaysia, apart from its resource sector, is very deficient in such strong exporting firms that are locally based. Strong exporting firms are usually strategic exporters rather than opportunistic ones. They view exports as central to their business over the long term. This means developing strong marketing offices and distribution networks throughout the world. Some of the functions include gathering information on customers' needs and engaging in product development. They tend to make more strategic decisions in their home base and frequently undertake new product development and initial launches in their home environment. Malaysia is very deficient in strong export manufacturing firms of its own except in the resource-processing sector. Currently, no statistics are available on the high-tech exports, although it has been assumed that 90 percent of the electrical/electronic components are derived from subsidiaries of multinational corporations. Almost all of these firms are foreign-owned. Because of the small size of Malaysia's domestic market, it is imperative that local firms export in the very early stages of production. One of the major constraints faced by small firms is the high cost of human resources and management as well as distribution and service networks abroad, which is particularly hard for fledgling companies. This is why most small firms, particularly those in Taiwan, prefer to act as original equipment manufacturers (OEM).

The OEM Path

One important strategy to increase demand for technology is to encourage Malaysian firms to be OEM suppliers to foreign firms. Taiwan firms, for example, have played a major role as OEM suppliers. It is important to promote domestic firms as OEM suppliers. Greater emphasis should be given to upgrading domestic enterprises to be OEM suppliers in the next five years. The increasing cost of production in Taiwan and the other NIEs would provide opportunities for Malaysia to be a player in the OEM market.

The next phase of industrial development hinges on the rapid growth of domestic enterprises and their capacity to invest aggressively to acquire more complex foreign product and process technology through licenses, joint ventures, and other means, which will allow competition in more sophisticated industries and industry segments. The presence of firm strategies that support investments in technology and capital assets is an important condition. It is essential that the government consider taking the lead in making investments in high-quality industrial infrastructure, including human resource development.

S&T Human Resource Development

Human resource development policies form an important aspect of the strategic approach to technology, particularly at a time when accelerated pace of technological innovation calls for increasingly sophisticated skills. The development of human development resource bases at various levels is necessary to perform a wide range of technological and economic functions and requires a fairly comprehensive policy framework at the macro level.

The full spectrum of technically proficient manpower in Malaysia needs to be addressed, from semiskilled craftsmen and artisans through to postgraduate technology professionals; the full gamut of activities, from design through to maintenance, needs to be considered. The balance between these strata of manpower requirements, both in level of skill and in function, must be carefully maintained.

The need for manpower to support industrial development in Malaysia requires little justification; the best-laid plans come to nothing unless supported by people to implement, operate, and maintain industrial activities. Manpower planning is not just a question of numbers. The education system must aim for the highest standards of excellence, so that their products are of the highest quality to support Malaysia's needs. Currently the breadth, depth, and technology orientation of the skills base is relatively weak; this implies that the labor force is likely to face difficulties in absorbing and adjusting to newer technologies in manufacturing processes.

There are many issues relating to the type, level and appropriateness of technical manpower for industry's needs that warrant additional consideration. Given the lead times involved in developing human resources, it is essential to promote a sense of urgency in manpower development programs; a lack of trained and skilled personnel cannot be remedied overnight, no matter how pressing the need for resolution. Malaysia's expenditure on manpower development was a laudable 15.4 percent of the public development allocation for 1991 to 1995, and the scope of the current infrastructure for technical-related education and training is wide. This emphasis must be sustained, for it is critical that attention be focused on technical manpower planning for the industrial sector.

A number of incentives are in place to encourage industry-based training, but it appears that, for a variety of reasons, a large number of manufacturing enterprises are unable or unwilling to avail themselves of these benefits. These incentives are not performing the important task of encouraging a training-oriented outlook in Malaysian industry. The importance of this cannot be understated. A skilled worker takes pride in the quality of his work, and is often a source of innovation of incremental improvements in work practice.

Malaysian technology strategies have addressed these issues and it is essential that cooperation be established with industrialized countries, particularly to support our human resource development plan. Cooperation at the international level will remain an important factor in developing our technology dimension. The intensification of technological cooperation with the industrial countries should be more widespread, in the form of concerted efforts in the realm of joint R&D, training, exchange of personnel, and advisory services.

Conclusion

The need to develop a sound S&T infrastructure is based on the following premise: *Malaysia needs technology to consolidate the process of industrialization; indeed, its areas of natural advantage will be of limited value in setting its future technological trajectory if they are not matched by technological competence that will grant it a competitive advantage.*

A two-pronged attack must be mounted: on the one hand, technology must be acquired through technology transfer mechanisms that recognize the essential commercial nature of such transactions; and on the other hand, the country must develop indigenous capabilities to analyze and apply incremental improvements.

Technological transformation is a necessity if Malaysia wishes to take its place as a competitor in the international marketplace. This can be achieved, but it must be selective, based upon a clear realization of the potential and limitations of the options that will present themselves, and a sustained effort built up around a core of technological expertise that needs to be developed.

The R&D system is a key component of the supporting infrastructure for technology development, and Malaysia must take positive steps to upgrade its abilities in R&D, not only through government institutes but also through the mobilization of private sector R&D.

Finally, urgent and serious attention must be paid to developing human resources in technology, both through the formal education system and through industrial training programs.

Notes

1. The *Industrial Master Plan* (1991) was prepared with assistance from UNDP. The Plan was completed in 1985 and maps out the path for the country's industrial development up to the year 1995.

2. See Industrial Master Plan, MIDA/UNDP (1991) on issues of low technological capability in Malaysian industries.

3. See *Industrial Master Plan* MIDA/UNDP (1991) on weak linkages between the export processing zone and domestic firms.

References

Chesnais, F. "Science, Technology and Competitiveness." *STI Review*, 1 (Autumn 1986): 124.

Cooper, Charles. *Policy Intervention for Technological Innovation in Developing Countries.* Washington, D C: World Bank, 1982.

Lim, Chee Peng. *Industrial Development—An Introduction to the Malaysian Industrial Master Plan.* Kuala Lumpur Pelanduk Publication, 1987.

Dahlman, C. J., and Westphal, L. E. *The Meaning of Technological Mastery in Relation to Transfer of Technology.* Washington, DC: World Bank, July 1981.

Industrial Master Plan, MIDA/UNDP 1984. *Sixth Malaysia Plan 1991–1995.* Kuala Lumpur National Printing Department, 1991.

Ministry of Science, Technology and the Environment. *Industrial Technology Development —A National Plan of Action.* 1990.

Nelson, R. R., and Winter, S. G. *An Evolutionary Theory of Economic Change.* Cambridge, MA: Harvard University Press, 1982.

Second Outline Perspective Plan—1991–2000. Kuala Lumpur: National Printing Department, 1991.

Sixth Malaysia Plan, 1991–1995. Kuala Lumpur: National Printing Department, 1991.

9

Building a Strong S&T System in Indonesia: Policies in a Transitional Economy

Dipo Alam

An indication that a developing country has a strong S&T system is its ability to assimilate and develop manufacturing and high technology from outside its boundaries, and that it can eventually become competitive in manufactured and high-tech products. An S&T system, related to industrial and economic development, might include four elements: (1) national commitment to technology-based development, (2) technological infrastructure, (3) socioeconomic infrastructure, and (4) productive capacity.[1]

Manufacturing and high technology (high-tech) are characterized by leading-edge technologies, whose application in industry may have wide economic effects and affect national economic strength and competitiveness. The character of manufacturing and high-tech is also reflected by "strategic" potency, whereby national security, militarily and economically, depends upon their progress. Given these characteristics, governments need to provide policies that promote manufacturing and high-tech development.

Manufacturing and high-tech development demands large R&D expenditures, in the form of direct government assistance to support basic and generic research, as well as science and technology (S&T) education and training. Such funding is usually part of the government's S&T policy, which reflects support for strengthening the first two elements of the S&T system: that is, national commitment to technology-based development and technological infrastructure.

To assist manufacturing and high-tech development, especially for a developing country, the government can also employ economic or industrial policies that promote and encourage domestic and foreign direct investments in high-tech industries. This may allow firms to acquire high-tech capability through the technology transfer process and to learn by "adopted" industrial practice. These policies suggest support for strengthening the last two elements of an S&T system: socioeconomic infrastructure and productive capacity.

Although Indonesia still lacks comparable industrial and S&T infrastructure, it has implemented policies to develop manufacturing and high-tech industries. The first policy attempts through specific S&T policy to support the development of government-owned high-tech "strategic" industries. These industries were initially launched when Indonesian economic development was fueled by the high oil prices of the 1970s. Oil export was the main revenue for the government, causing rapid economic growth and enabling the government to support the development of strategic industries.

However, with Indonesia's current transitional economy—characterized by a shift from a high dependency on revenues from oil exports to revenues from manufactured exports, from high government interventions to deregulation and privatization, and from inward-oriented industrialization to export-oriented industrialization—the direct intervention policy seems to be challenged by the indirect policy.

The indirect policy is implemented through economic reform policies, which have been increasingly influential in Indonesia's current state of transition. These policies have been encouraging firms to invest in manufacturing and high-tech industries. This trend of investment has also been made possible by the rapid economic growth in the Pacific Rim, which has been characterized by a substantial increase of intraregional capital flow (Table 9.1) and interregional trade of the region (Table 9.2). Therefore, the transitional economy of Indonesia is also mirrored by the growing economies of countries in the Pacific Rim.

Some mature manufacturing and high-tech capabilities possessed by Japan and four of Asia's newly industrialized economies (NIEs) (Korea, Taiwan, Hong Kong, and Singapore) have been shifted or diffused to ASEAN. Japan and the Asian NIEs are striving to adjust their strategies to give them competitive advantage in high-tech industries such as aerospace and industrial automation. Accordingly, given the present trend of economic and technological capabilities of the countries in the Pacific Rim, Indonesia may also have an opportunity to engage in sustained efforts to move into manufacturing and high-tech industries.

The purpose here is to explore the two different policies over time that may promote manufacturing and high-tech industries in Indonesia, in an effort to discover the effective combination of both policies in the current transitional economy, rather than to suggest mutually exclusive choices between them.

Reasons to Support Manufacturing and High-Tech Industries

Every country has "strategic" reasons or "critical" criteria for supporting manufacturing high-tech industries. For example, the United States recently determined the

Table 9.1

Asia Pacific Investment in ASEAN (in US$ millions)

From	Malaysia[1] 1989	Change from 1988	Indonesia[2] 1989	Change from 1988	Thailand[3] 1989	Change from 1988	Philippines[4] 1989	Change from 1988
Japan	996	13%	760	240%	3,251	15%	157	65%
South Korea	70	367%	466	123%	171	57%	18	800%
Taiwan	800	161%	158	–83%	867	2%	148	36%
Singapore	338	118%	166	–35%	407	48%	24	1,100%
Hong Kong	130	17%	407	75%	561	26%	132	388%
World total	3,205	78%	4,719	7%	7,979	28%	800	77%

[1]Foreign investment flow (foreign equity and loan attributed to foreign interest) in manufacturing projects approved by the Malaysian Industrial Development Authority.

[2]Total foreign capital in projects approved by BKPM—the National Investment Coordinating Board.

[3]Applications for foreign investment approved by the country's Board of Investment.

[4]Inward investment approved by the country's Board of Investment.

Source: Merrill Lynch, cited in *IEEE Spectrum* (1991).

criteria of critical technologies, and these reveal that country's interests in maintaining economic competitiveness, national security, and quality of life. Based upon these criteria, twenty-two critical technologies[2] have been selected from six broad areas, such as in advanced materials, manufacturing, information and communications, biotechnology and life sciences, aeronautics and surface transportation, and energy and environment (National Critical Technologies Panel, 1991).

Similarly, South Korea has established five technical priorities—information technology, robotics, new materials, chemicals, and biotechnology—in order to achieve international competitiveness. Taiwan's six-year National Construction Plan (1990–96) identifies eight key technologies that Taiwan needs to develop for competitiveness. The key technologies are: optoelectronics, computer software, application of materials, industrial automation, advanced sensors, energy conservation, resource development, and biotechnology (*IEEE Spectrum*, 1991). These technologies are similar to those that the United States is pursuing.

Indonesia, although not on the same level of technology, has its own reasons for developing manufacturing and high-tech industries. The first has to do with supporting Indonesia's political and economic aims in the unity concept of *"Wawasan Nusantara."*[3] This concept expresses the unity of the Indonesian archipelago, with a political, social and cultural, and economic unity, as well as unity for defense and security.

The basic rationale of *Wawasan Nusantara* applied to the development of high-tech industries has to do with the unique transportation and communication

Table 9.2

World Trade by Region (in percent*)

	1979	1989
Asia–North America	6.4	11.9
Within Asia	6.3	10.0
Asia–West Europe	5.0	7.6
North America–West Europe	6.6	7.3
North America–Latin America	4.0	3.6
Within North America	4.6	5.3
Within West Europe	28	31.1
Other	39.1	23.2

*Total trade in 1979 was US$2.2 trillion; in 1989, US$3.1 trillion.
Source: GATT, cited in *IEEE Spectrum* (1991).

problems that characterize Indonesia's dispersed islands. When one appreciates the rich potential of Indonesia's natural resources, one can see how relatively unexplored the richness of the country is. Indonesia's wealth is dispersed over more than 13,000 islands, and the country comprises more than 200 tribes that speak different languages. Even though Indonesia has a formal language, *Bahasa Indonesia*, this diversity threatens the unity of the republic.

To fulfill the concept of *Wawasan Nusantara*, Indonesia needs most to develop its telecommunications and air and water transportation. It needs to develop its own strategic industry free from dependency on other countries. Efforts to buy or license high-tech from advanced countries, and to develop it domestically, were considered justified by the Indonesian government.

The country's telecommunication system was developed by buying the *Palapa* satellite from the United States and by contracts with the Hughes Aircraft Co. Preparation for the Palapa satellite was begun in the early 1970s. The first generation of Indonesian satellites, Palapa A–1 and A–2, were launched in 1976. Indonesia was the first developing country that utilized such a satellite. The second-generation satellites, Palapa B–1 and B–2, were launched in 1983 and 1987; the next generation of the satellites is scheduled for 1992.

The impact of the satellites was substantial. They increased Indonesia's ability to provide nationwide telephone, telex, television, facsimile, and data transmission services. The satellites also provide television programs for public education. Ground stations have been established involving Indonesian research institutes and private Indonesian companies, which have provided services and products produced locally. The Palapa satellite was an important opportunity for Indonesian companies and research institutes to enter the new era of electronics and telecommunications technology.

The second reason for supporting high-tech industries has to do with ideas for promoting the "take-off" stage of Indonesian development in 1997. There is no clear definition or exact measurement of what is meant by "Indonesia's take-off." In political terms, however, the National State Guideline (GBHN, 1983) states that Indonesian take-off should be achieved after the completion of five consecutive five-year development plans (twenty-five years, 1972–97). This "take-off" would be characterized by strong industry supported by a solid base of agricultural development. In other words, the government's first through fourth five-year development plans (PELITAs: 1972–88) emphasized the development of agriculture, especially self-sufficiency in rice production.[4] PELITA V (1988–93), as the State Guideline declares, was committed to a strong performance in agriculture and also emphasized industrial development. This objective is being emphasized further in PELITA VI (1993–98), which is the period for development "take-off" in Indonesia.

The early 1970s, when the idea of high-tech industries was introduced, were also the years when developing countries began through the United Nations to demand a new international economic order. Issues concerning self-reliance for development were popular among developing countries, including self-reliance for science and technology development.

In the effort to create self-reliance in technology, the Indonesian government initiated its programs to achieve "indigenous" high-tech. These initiatives were also a reaction to and rejection of the idea of "appropriate technology" for developing countries, which too often was characterized by simple technologies for rural areas.

In addition to "appropriate" and "intermediate" technologies through the government's agricultural and industrial development programs, Indonesia also desires advanced technology as part of its strategy to support future economic and national security objectives. As a big nation with more than 170 million people, the fifth most populous in the world, and rich in natural resources, the country cannot depend perpetually on foreign countries for its technological capability.

To justify the development of aircraft and ship building, as parts of the high-tech industries, B. J. Habibie (1873, p. 3), the Minister for Research and Technology, contends: "The only criterion for the appropriateness of technologies for any particular country including technologically less-developed countries, is their utility in solving actual problems in that particular country. . . . To develop its technology, no country can continue to be a net technological importer indefinitely. At some point it must be able to develop its own technologies."

In addition, by pursuing the development of high-tech industry, Indonesia has an opportunity to transfer high technology. Habibie believes that once Indonesia has established an aircraft industry, other high technologies can be more easily obtained and adopted. Aircraft technology, according to Habibie, is the most advanced and complex technology. The knowledge that is acquired through practical experience in the development of an aircraft industry can be applied and adjusted to other areas of high technology (*Tempo*, 1986). It is also believed that Indonesian private companies are not prepared to develop and produce aircraft, and therefore the government needs to initiate such development.

Eight Vehicles for Industrial Transformation

Under Habibie's leadership, the idea of developing high-tech industries has been introduced into Eight Vehicles for Industrial Transformation (EVIT). EVIT refers to eight state-owned "high-tech" industries in: (1) aeronautics and aerospace; (2) maritime and ship building; (3) land transportation; (4) electronics and telecommunications; (5) the energy industry; (6) the engineering industry; (7) agricultural equipment; and (8) the defense industry.[5] These eight Indonesian high-tech industries are linked to government research institutes, mainly the Agency for the Assessment and Application of Technology (BPPT) and the Center for the Development of Research, Science, and Technology (PUSPIPTEK).

The strategy of government intervention for supporting S&T, through EVIT, was set in five basic principles and four phases of transformation. The five basic principles, as stated by Habibie are: (1) commitment to education and training in the various sciences and technologies that relate to the needs of development and nation building; (2) a realistic and consistent concept of the nature of the society that would be developed and of the technologies needed to realize that society's future needs, and directing these technologies to solve the actual problems of the country; (3) conducting the process of technology transfer, technology adaptation, and technology development in a concrete manner, with awareness that technologies cannot be learned, let alone be developed, in an abstract way; (4) belief that a country cannot perpetually be a technology importer, but that it must at some point be able to develop its own technologies; and (5) belief that a country should be able to achieve international competitiveness as soon as possible.

Habibie's five principles suggest that science and engineering education should be attached directly to the process of industrialization. The industries that should be available for the practice of young scientists and engineers, in order to have an opportunity for "hands-on" experience and application of their theoretical knowledge, are industries that have strategic value for the future of Indonesian development. At present, few, if any, Indonesian private companies are interested in or capable of developing such an enterprise. This is parallel with President Suharto's strategy for Indonesia's long-range development plan, which is directed at maintaining *Wawasan Nusantara*. This long-term, and possibly expensive, approach to technological and industrial development may be out of the reach of most private companies in Indonesia, which must show profits and a reasonable rate of return in the short run.

The plan to implement these five basic principles, according to Habibie, includes four phases of industrialization. The first phase is the use of existing technologies for value-added processes in the assembly and manufacture of products for both domestic and international markets. In this phase, existing technology can be used to process raw materials and intermediate goods into higher-value-added products.

The second phase is to integrate the existing technologies that have been acquired through licensing into the adaptation process to design and manufacture new products. In this phase, creativity is added to the technological level of the first phase.[6] The third phase is to improve upon the borrowed technology. In this stage applied research and experimentation may be needed to achieve improvement. Finally, in the fourth phase, basic research is needed to maintain the improvement of technology development achieved in the first three phases. For a developing country like Indonesia, Habibie suggests (1983, p. 8) the following:

> While some developing countries do make investments in basic research, many find that their scarce financial, material and human resources are better spent in more urgent tasks. The great bulk of basic research is therefore undertaken in developed countries, [and developing countries should] maintain access to this research and its results through cooperative agreements in science and technology. While not completely irrelevant to less-developed countries, this fourth phase of development is not as central to their transformation as are the first three phases.

In the aircraft industry, IPTN, the first phase of industrialization was conducted by assembling several types of planes and helicopters, such as the Hercules-like NC–212 and MBB's NBO–105. Over 100 units have been sold since production was initiated in 1976. With manufacturing experience in the first phase, the second phase, integration of existing technology to make a new product, began in 1979 when IPTN cooperated with CASA (Spain's aircraft company) to design a new plane, the CN–235 (a two-engine plane with thirty-five seats). The plane was produced in 1984 and was certified by the U.S. Federal Aviation Authority in May 1989. Since 1987, IPTN has been preparing to produce the N–250 (a two-engine plane with fifty seats), which reflects how IPTN has been entering the third phase of the industrialization strategy. At this time IPTN has adequate technological capability—the N–250 is being fully designed by Indonesian engineers at the IPTN and is scheduled to be produced in 1995. IPTN's fourth phase is to produce a 100-seat regional jetliner by the end of the 1990s (see some achievements of IPTN in Tables 9.3, 9.4, and 9.5).

Other industries included in EVIT, apparently, are not as critical as the aircraft industry. However, their development stages are expected to follow the pattern of the four phases of S&T development achieved by IPTN.

Policies in the Transitional Economy

Despite political backing by the president, EVIT has not been unchallenged. These challenges come from economists,[7] who criticize EVIT for several reasons: (1) the high-technology character of EVIT is not consistent with

Table 9.3

Types of Aircraft Produced by IPTN

Since	Name	Type	Number of Seats
1976	NC–212	Fixed-wing aircraft produced under license from USA	19–26
1976	NBO–105	Helicopter produced under license of MBB	5
1981	NAS–330 Puma	Helicopter from Aerospatiale (now replaced with NAS–332)	
1981	NBK–117	Helicopter produced in cooperation with MBB/Kawasaki	20
1983	NAS–332 Super Puma	Helicopter under license of Aerospatiale	15
1984	NBELL–412	Helicopter produced with the Bell Helicopter Textron Co.	35
1984	CN–235	Fixed-wing aircraft joint production with CASA (Airtech),FAA certified	
1987	N–250	Fixed-wing IPTN-designed aircraft preparation	50
1989	N–250	N–20 certified by FAA in the U.S.	

Source: IPTN.

Indonesia's limited skilled manpower and financial resources; (2) EVIT encompasses a set of capital-intensive industries with little interrelatedness (small multiplier effects) to other economic activities, and will offer relatively few job opportunities (this is an especially serious problem in light of Indonesia's severe unemployment problem); (3) EVIT needs a high level of investment and involvement from government, which has a potential tendency to misallocate development resources; (4) the experimental results of EVIT, technologically or economically, cannot instantaneously and significantly help the current unfortunate situation of the economy; and (5) EVIT needs government protection for domestic markets, which in turn may distort the economic system. These criticisms have been especially loud when austerity measures have been pursued by the government because of the drop of government revenue from oil exports.

Several external factors influenced the low growth of the Indonesian economy during the final two years of PELITA III (1982–83) and PELITA IV (1983–88). The most significant factor was the weak demand for oil in the international market, which caused a decline in oil prices. In 1980, the price of oil reached $35

Table 9.4

Delivery Status of IPTN-Produced Aircraft up to 1989

Type of Aircraft and Helicopters	Domestic Customers	Foreign Customers	Total
NC–212	79	8	87
NBO–105	94		94
NAS–330 Puma	11		11
NAS–332 Super Puma	8	1	9
NBK–117	4		4
CN–235	10	19	29
NBELL–412	12		12
Total	218	28	246

Source: IPTN.

per barrel and fell to $29 in early 1983. The oil price again declined to $25 per barrel in January 1986, $14.50 in March 1986, and $9.80 in August 1986. The government's gross earnings from oil exports and liquified natural gas (LNG) fell sharply and caused the fall of government revenues from the oil tax.

In addition, the prices of some of Indonesia's primary commodity exports were also down in the world market. World demand for primary commodities had weakened, as indicated by the World Bank's index of prices for thirty-three commodities in the mid-1980s, which was 20 percent below its 1978–81 level.

Another external economic factor was the depreciation of the dollar against the yen and other foreign currencies in 1985. This increased the burden of Indonesia's external debt, especially that amount borrowed in yen. In addition, in the early 1980s, high interest rates in the world financial market discouraged investment in Indonesia.

Besides the external factors that influenced the Indonesian economy in the 1980s, two internal factors contributed to economic circumstances that significantly inhibited the development of manufacturing goods for export. First, government revenues from oil exports, which tended to pay for imports, permitted the government in the oil boom era to expand expenditures on nontrade goods (for example, highways, schools, etc.), and to neglect policies and programs to encourage production for export. In addition, the government's reliance on oil revenues permitted the government to neglect the mobilization of domestic financial resources by other means, such as taxes. It failed to encourage the private sector to create business that would grow and expand, and provide the basis for tax revenues to finance development programs.

The second internal factor that inhibited development of manufacturing and export was the government's extensive industrial protection and regulations that distorted the market mechanism. The combination of the "oil boom" that enlarged government expenditures and the increasing political power of the government's bureaucracy were elements that stimulated government intervention. This includes government's leadership in S&T development.

For Indonesia, with more than 170 million people in the early 1980s, the low rate of economic growth of that decade caused a serious problem in terms of employment opportunities. The labor-absorptive capacity declined from 1980 through 1985, especially in the construction sector and government services, because of government austerity measures that rephased many government projects.

Faced by severe external economic shocks, and internal factors as well, the government needed to reform its economic policy. This included adjustment of fiscal, monetary, financial, and trade policies, as well as regulatory reforms (see the summary of reform measures in Table 9.6 on page 199).

In fiscal policy, the government employed austerity measures by curtailing government expenditures to a reduced level of resource availability. This was carried out by restraining public investments. Several large-scale government projects were postponed or canceled, and import-intensive public investments were curtailed. The government also reduced subsidies financed from the budget and froze government employees' salaries. The austerity measures were directed at saving foreign exchange and reducing the balance-of-payments deficit on current accounts from $6.3 billion (9.2 percent of GNP) in 1983 to about $1.3 billion (less than 1.9 percent of GNP) in 1988.

An extensive tax reform was implemented over 1984–86; this reform increased nonoil tax revenues and enhanced the efficiency of the tax system. As a result of these fiscal measures, total nonoil taxes as a percentage of nonoil GDP grew from 8.3 percent in 1983 to 11.5 percent in 1988. Since revenues from taxes have been considered an effective domestic resource, and in the long term must replace the government's reliance on revenue from oil, then trade regulations should be eased in order to stimulate private businesses, production, and the generation of a tax base.

In exchange rate policy, the government carried out several devaluations. On September 30, 1983, the government devalued Indonesia's currency, the Rupiah, by 38 percent and again on September 12, 1986, by 45 percent. These devaluations were used to help restore the nation's balance of payments, in an effort to restrain imports and stimulate nonoil exports. Also, the exchange rate was made more flexible after March 1983 through management of the date.

To boost business activities in the private sector, the government carried out banking reforms. It employed policies to offset inflationary pressures, to hinder capital flight, and to mobilize financial resources and enhance the efficient use of financial resources. It eliminated most of the system of credit ceilings and selective credit policies with subsidies, liquidity credits, and interest rates, which had been in operation for a decade since 1974. The banking reform has improved competition in the financial system.

Some of the above macroeconomic adjustment policies reflect government efforts to stimulate the role of the market and to encourage the private sector to

Table 9.5

Summary of Reform Measures

Reform	Main Contents	Effects
Financial: 1983 June 1 Banking Deregulation	—Remove interest rate control for state banks —Reduce liquidity credit —Remove credit ceilings	—Rise in deposit rates —Some fall in intermediation costs —But liquidity credits in fact increased
1986, October	—Removal of ceiling on central bank swap	
1988, October 27 (PAKTO)	—Open up licenses for new banks, including joint ventures —Lending limits regulation —Reserve requirement lowered	—Opening up of many banks and joint ventures —Intense competition between banks —Rising interest rates and failing spreads initially
1987, December (PAKDES)	—Deregulation of capital markets —Reduce government role in stock exchange —Foreigners can buy stock	
1988, December (PAKDES)	—Further capital markets deregulation	—Sharp increase in capital markets activity and index
	—Deregulation in insurance industry —Rationalization of financial services sector	—Many major companies going public —Many major companies going public
Fiscal: 1984, April Tax Reform	—Remove withholding tax and introduce VAT —Rationalization of income and sales tax	—Increased government revenues
Trade and Shipping: 1985, March Tariff Rationalization	—Range reduction from 0–225% to 0–60% —Number of tariff levels reduced from 25 to 11	—Some reduction in protection

Date	Actions	Effects
1985, April Customs Reform (INPRES NO. 4)	—Removal of customs department in goods clearance —Appointment of private surveyor SGS —Removal of restrictions on choice of international carrier	—Reduced substantially average time of imports and exports clearance —Important psychological effect
1986, May (PAKEM)	—Duty drawback and bypass monopoly —Armslength transactions and computerized processing	—Improve duty drawback process —Important factor to increase exports
1986, October	—Some change from import licensing to general imports —Phasing down of NTB with some increase in tariff to offset —Reduction in tariff needed in production	—Improved investment climate —Increased investments
1987, January	—Some change from import licensing to general imports	
1987, July Simplification of Textile Quota	—Transparency of allocation —Some allocation to newcomers	—Some improvements although now some complaints
1988, November (PAKNOP)	—Removal of import monopolies: plastic and steel —Interisland shipping deregulation	
1990, May	—Further removal of NTB to tariff —Deregulation pharmaceutical and animal husbandry —Some adjustment in tariffs and increased number of surcharges	—Improve investment climate

(continued)

Table 9.5 *continued*

Investment:		
1986, May (PAKEM)	—95% foreign ownership possible for export-oriented foreign investments —export-oriented firms allowed to distribute domestically —Joint ventures can participate in government export credit scheme	—Improve investment climate and encourage export-oriented investments
1987, July	—Deregulation of investment and capacity licensing —Broad banding —Closed sector open to export-oriented firms	—Improve investment climate
1988, November	—Joint ventures allowed to distribute own products domestically	
1989, May	—Removal of priority scale list for investment through board of investment —Introduction of negative list	—Improve investment climate and ease investment application
Privatization:		
1989, June	—Categorization of state enterprises by soundness —Alternatives in privatization: go public, joint venture and management, merger, etc.	—Improved efficiency and industrial productivity on overall basis.

Source: Pangestu (1991).

Table 9.6

Indonesia's Exports in 1984–1990, in US$ billion

Type of Exports	1984	1985	1986	1987	1988	1989	1990
Oil and gas	16.02	12.72	8.28	8.56	7.68	9.37	12.75
Nonoil and gas	5.87	5.87	6.53	8.58	11.54	14.50	15.40
Total	21.89	18.59	14.81	17.14	19.22	23.87	28.15

Source: Department of Trade, *Monthly Report,* March 1989, and speech of the president, August 16, 1991.

improve business activities. Deregulations have been introduced by the governments through several "economy policy packages" in May 1986, October 1986, January and December 1987, November 1988, May 1990, and June 1991. These packages have been directed at reducing the investment and capacity licensing requirements, reducing the import licensing restrictions, reducing the anti-export bias of trade policy through the reduction of regulatory restrictions for exporters, relaxing foreign investment regulations, and reducing the role of the local content program. Meanwhile, proposals for selling and dissolving some of the government-owned companies, under the idea of "privatization," have been considered (Pangetsu, 1991).

The drive for deregulation, "debureaucratization," and "privatization" has been increasingly popular among influential scholars and government policy makers. As a result, government investment in some EVIT programs has been a controversial issue. The proponents of deregulation now prevail in Indonesia. In fact, economic reform policy has shown an improvement in the business sector in which Indonesia's nonoil exports have increased significantly since 1987, and have passed oil and gas exports in value. Oil and gas previously dominated Indonesia's exports (see Table 9.6).

**Impact of the Economic Reform Policies
on S&T Development**

There are two major indirect impacts of economic reform policies on S&T development. The first is the tremendous increase in manufacturing and high-tech investments by the private sector (see Tables 9.7 and 9.8). These industries, most of which employ high-tech, might open opportunity for Indonesian companies and their workers to experience, adopt, and develop high-tech in the near future.

According to Henderson (1989), the investments of U.S. semiconductor companies in some East Asia countries, notably Hong Kong and Taiwan, increased the technological and managerial capabilities of locally owned companies. The contribution of these companies to economic growth is now much more important than is foreign-owned production.

Table 9.7

Approved Domestic Investment Projects by Economic Sector, 1987–1990, in Rp. Million, excluding oil, insurance and banking

Sector	1987		1988		1989		Jan.–Feb. 1990	
	Project	Capital	Project	Capital	Project	Capital	Project	Capital
1. Agriculture	159	3,554	200	4,744	178	4,369	20	807
Agriculture	83	2,389	98	3,369	128	3,607	17	597
Forestry	12	650	8	658	−1	282	1	50
Fishery	64	515	94	717	51	480	2	160
2. Mining and quarrying	20	299	19	156	9	109	1	24
3. Manufacturing	268	6,328	486	8,922	481	14,336	137	7,604
4. Electricity, gas, and water	0	0	0	0	0	0	0	0
5. Construction	3	49	3	31	5	135	0	13
6. Trade, restaurants and hotels	15	344	28	517	32	1,333	11	461
7. Tranport, storage and communications	12	433	25	166	26	299	7	206
8. Finance, real estate and business services	12	183	15	784	17	1,068	4	166
9. Community and personal services	21	214	30	360	29	257	11	119
Total	11,404	806	15,681	777	21,907	191	9,400	5,992

Source: Investment Coordinating Board, cited in Nasution (1991).

Investment in high-tech industries demands more scientific and technical manpower, which will be employed in both operational and laboratory jobs. R & D is especially needed by these types of industries to maintain competitiveness. Demand for skilled S&T manpower to support these industries is expected to move S&T education into a more industrial technical orientation, and in turn such demands also drive the improvement of S&T infrastructure.

The second impact of the economic reform can be identified by the increase of companies, especially in the electronics industry, that conduct applied research activities for the promotion of technological capabilities. This is especially true in designing capability that enables firms to improve their electronic products (see some examples in the appendix). The development of applied research and development activities has stimulated cooperation between producers, R&D agencies, and universities. In addition, many small innovative electronics companies involving young technicians and engineering students now have been creatively assembled and have produced some computers and peripherals that could compete with those produced by large companies.

As a result of the May 1990 deregulation policy, which allows domestic industry to have low import duty facilities for component parts, the electronics industry has increased exports 111 percent, from $38.5 million in the second semester of 1989, to $81.3 million in the same period in 1990. The increase of domestic and foreign investments in the electronics industry, from Rp 63.8 billion and US$2.2 million in the second semester of 1989, to Rp 167 billion and US$20.8 million in the same period of 1990, has absorbed 742 workers in the period 1989 and 4,449 in 1990. In the first quarter of 1991, the government has licensed twelve electronics companies and permitted the expansion of investment to total Rp 14.37 billion and US$153 million. This additional investment absorbed 6,052 workers. In the same quarter, the government approved five foreign electronics companies that have invested US$21.40 million with employment of an additional 2,092 workers.

Conclusion

This analysis of the government's economic reform policies has shown positive impacts on S&T development. This is not to suggest, however, that direct government intervention to promote S&T development through S&T policy is meaningless.

In the case of EVIT, the intention of the government of Indonesia is clearly not to replace the role of the private sector, or to monopolize an industry. The rationale for EVIT is to push the development of S&T infrastructure in Indonesia, to address the interests of national security, and to provide young scientists and engineers with experience in the government's "giant laboratories." In addition, few, if any, private companies are interested

Table 9.8

Approved Foreign Investment Projects by Countries of Origin, 1967–1990, in US$ million

Country of Origin	1987		1988		1989		Jan.–Feb. 1990		1967 to Feb. 1990	
	No. of Projects	Capital	No. of Projects	Capital	No. of Projects	Capital	No. of Projects	Capital	No. of Projects	Capital
America	12	−28	1	604	12	215	0	1	139	2,404
United States	8	−62	2	534	12	167	0	1	108	2,029
Canada	2	7	−1	−5	0	2	0	0	6	16
Other America	2	27	0	75	0	45	0	0	25	360
Europe	14	531	24	1,357	37	747	3	14	284	5,767
Belgium	1	6	0	0	3	43	0	0	15	133
Denmark	2	4	0	0	1	9	0	1	6	57
France	1	76	3	9	5	19	0	0	23	215
Italy	1	15	0	0	2	2	0	0	3	17
The Netherlands	4	123	8	271	9	284	2	12	75	1,436
Norway	0	0	1	14	2	183	0	0	5	211
West Germany	5	322	5	956	4	16	1	0	45	1,840
United Kingdom	2	16	4	89	8	162	0	0	83	670
Switzerland	−1	−1	2	17	1	11	0	0	17	198
Other Europe	−1	−30	1	1	2	18	0	0	12	992

Asia	24	661	94	1,845	222	2,249	57	840	807	14,131
Japan	15	512	23	225	65	920	5	401	320	7,633
South Korea	4	16	26	209	65	481	20	152	132	1,103
Hong Kong	1	122	12	232	14	377	8	75	149	2,817
Taiwan	3	8	15	923	52	190	16	126	91	1,396
Singapore	1	13	18	255	20	183	8	87	79	875
India	−1	−11	0	0	2	59	0	0	12	187
Other Asia	1	1	0	2	4	39	0	0	24	121
Australia	−1	21	7	357	13	157	4	147	105	763
Other Oceania	0	0	0	5	1	1	0	0	4	13
All Other Regions	2	55	3	257	10	2,553	0	75	87	6,444
Total	51	1,240	129	4,426	295	5,920	64	1,077	1,426	29,521

Source: Investment Coordinating Board, cited in Nasution (1991).

in industries built by EVIT (especially aircraft, shipbuilding, and rolling stock industries). The government allows private companies to build similar industries as long as they cooperate with EVIT's government companies. The latter requirement, since it relates to defense matters, is required by all countries in the world.

The government's support for science and technology through the development of defense technology has occurred also in the United States, South Korea, and now in Japan. Without a threat from foreign countries or the challenge of an arms race, however, Indonesia's strategic industry is not especially developed for military purposes. It is developed only to overcome its own interisland transportation problems.

The EVIT program has resulted in increased technological capability, in which Indonesian engineers can design and produce some "high-tech" products such as aircraft, ships, electronics, and other products related to transportation and defense equipment.[8] In addition, as a consequence of the development of industries in EVIT, the government has increased fellowships for S&T manpower development (see Tables 9.9 and 9.10).

The government's S&T policy is represented not only by EVIT, but also by S&T institutions that may promote the development of S&T infrastructure such as research, educational and training institutions, laboratories, standardization, and libraries. Figure 9.1 presents a chart of such agencies. It is the responsibility of the government to develop such an infrastructure, especially when the development of S&T infrastructure is still in the early stage and in poor condition.

Our analysis suggests that government intervention to promote technological innovation in Indonesia, through science and technology policy and economic reform policies, have been carried out on a "right" track. However, the cooperation and the synergism of the two policies need further attention.

The government's direct intervention through science and technology development policy should be maintained, especially for programs that support science and engineering education to prepare technically skilled manpower. This is considered a serious problem, when the private sector still faces a very limited availability of skilled technical manpower.

Science and technology development through the Eight Vehicles for Industrial Transformation program should be maintained as well, especially that part focused on overcoming the interisland transportation problem and those related to defense.

However, direct intervention through government-owned companies related to science and technology development should be reduced in the future. This is all the more true as the private sector becomes interested and able economically and technologically to develop some of the industries both in and beyond the EVIT programs as well as those that are not expected to create a risk for Indonesia's national security.

Table 9.9

Program of Study and Degree to Be Obtained Abroad

OFP Subprograms	Nominal Period Allowed by the GOI	Type of Degree to Be Obtained	Equivalent Degree Level in Indonesia	Number of Available Fellowships	Percentage of Total
Program 1	3 years	Ph.D., Dr., Dr. Ing., Dr. Ir.	S3	250	17%
Program 2A	2.5 years	MSc., MS equivalent	S2		
				650	43%
Program 2B	5 years	Ir.,Dipl. Ing.,DEA,DESS	S2		
Program 3	5 years	BSc.	S1	300	20%
Program 4A	1.5 years	Industrial Training Certificate	—		
Program 4B	1.5 years	Academic Training Certificate		300	20%

Source: Djojonegoro (1990).

Table 9.10

Distributions of OFP Fellows Abroad, by Country and Program, as of May 31, 1990

	Program						
Countries	1	2A	2B	3	4A	4B	Total
USA	26	70	—	49	—	5	150
UK	31	39	—	26	—	1	97
Canada	1	22	—	—	—	—	23
Australia	2	5	—	10	—	—	17
Germany	33	9	59	—	—	2	103
Holland	1	3	158	—	11	—	173
France	27	2	56	—	—	—	85
Japan	20	50	—	162	1	4	237
Thailand	—	—	—	—	—	—	0
Belgium	1	—	—	—	—	—	1
Austria	—	—	10	—	—	—	10
Philippines	—	3	—	—	—	—	3
Norway	1	—	—	—	—	—	1
New Zealand	1	—	—	—	—	—	1
Total	144	203	283	247	12	12	901
Returned	19	182	20	3	169	17	410
Total active fellows to date:							1,311

Source: Djojonegoro (1990).

206

Figure 9.1. Government R&D Agencies

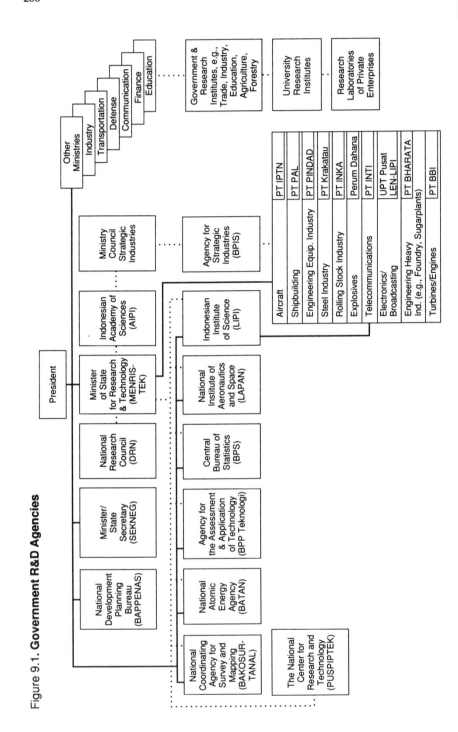

Appendix

The following are some examples of technological capabilities of electronics companies in Indonesia, from *Business News* (1991).

The Consumer Electronics Industry

1. PT Panggung Electronics Industries, a successful domestic company that has relied on the know-how and trademarks of foreign companies, has set up a development division equipped with facilities for applied research and development activities. This division has developed designing and engineering research so that at present the company produces the trademarks of its principals, as well as its own mark. For its own trademark, the company is free to conduct development and to purchase components from various sources, thereby ensuring fairly high value added and competitiveness. This method can speed up the reduction of the company's dependence on principals. The company produces TVs, radio receivers, radio cassette recorders, and audio systems.

2. PT Hartono Istana Electronics is a domestic company that has from the start conducted applied research and development activities in design and engineering, and so is not bound by foreign principals. Components are produced from various sources both at home and abroad, thus increasing value added. The company's products have penetrated the European market, as proof that goods developed domestically can already be internationally recognized. Products include TV sets, radio cassette recorders, and VCRs.

3. PT Asia Permai Electronics benefits from applied research and development available at higher educational institutes and training, and fosters informal workers to become production personnel while carrying out technology transfer. This policy can enhance competitiveness so that the company's products are capable of penetrating the export market to Europe, in the form of finished goods and modules.

4. PT National Gobel, a joint venture with Japanese multinational businessmen, has developed applied research and development, so that in its production activities the company can strive for maximum use of domestic components, produced in-house, such as loudspeakers, variable resistors, transformers, TV tuners, etc. The exports of the company keep increasing from year to year.

The Professional Electronics Industry

1. PT Inti has developed STDIK (small digital telephone exchange of Indonesia) based on the experience in producing STDI (digital telephone exchange of Indonesia) under license from Siemens. STDIK is designed according to the conditions of Indonesia, for remote areas with a capacity of up to 1,600 connection units. This product is independent of the central exchange, and has the same technical capacity as STDI.

2. PT Electrindo Nusantara is developing STKE (small Electrindo telephone exchange) based on experience in handling satellite communications equipment and systems. The product is designed for a capacity of up to 1,000 connection units and can be integrated with the existing system, STDI.

3. PT Multi Kontrol Nusantara (PT MKN) develops and designs automatic message switching for telex with a capacity of twenty-four connections units. The company also develops and designs computer-telex adaptors and card readers in the form of a time recorder capable of storing attendance data for 200 people.

The Components and Subassembly Industry

1. PT Sukma Beta Sampurna develops and produces printed circuit boards (PCB), double-sided through holes and multilayers, of international quality.

2. PT Compact Microwave Indonesia develops and designs voltage control oscillators as one of the modules in communications satellite instruments. The oscillators have been widely used by communication satellite industries and are exported to the United States for Hughes Aircraft.

3. PT Electrindo Nusantara develops echo cancelers to reduce echoes during long distance transmission in satellite communication. The company also develops and produces up-down converters to raise and lower frequencies to the frequency of transmitters and receivers through satellites.

Notes

1. See Roessner, Porter, and Fouts (1987), whose study defines the first element, *national commitment to technology-based development*, as a condition of "a nation undertaking directed action to achieve technological competitiveness, which is manifested at the business, government, or cultural levels." The second element, *technological infrastructure*, illustrates "institutions and resources that contribute directly to a nation's capacity to develop, produce and market new technology." The third element, *socioeconomic infrastructure*, depicts "the social and economic institutions that support and maintain physical, human, organizational, and economic resources essential to the functioning of a modern, technology-based industrial nation." The fourth element, *productive capacity*, illustrates the physical and human resources devoted to manufacturing products, and the efficiency with which those resources are used. Values added in manufacturing are indicators of productive capacity.

2. In the area of *advanced materials:* materials synthesis and processing; electronics and photonic materials; ceramics; composites; and high-performance metals and alloys. In the area of *manufacturing:* flexible computer-integrated manufacturing; intelligent processing equipment; micro- and nanofabrication; and systems management technologies. In the area of *information and communications:* software; microelectronics and optoelectronics; high-performance computing and networking; high-definition imaging and displays; sensors and signal processing; data storage and peripherals; and computer simulation and modeling. In the area of *biotechnology and life sciences:* applied molecular biology and medical technology. In the area of *aeronautics and surface transportation:* aeronautics and surface transportation technologies. In the area of *energy and environment:* energy technologies and pollution minimization, remediation, and waste management.

3. The first formal statement of *Wawasan Nusantara* was delivered by President Suharto in a speech in 1971.

4. For the first time in its history Indonesia did not import rice in 1984, the second year of PELITA IV.

5. Right now EVIT comprises a total of ten companies, which are managed by the Agency for Strategic Industries Management (BPIS). The BPIS is coordinated under the Ministerial Council on Strategic Industries (DPIS). The DPIS is chaired by the president, the minister for research and technology as vice-chairman, and ministers of industry, defense, communication, tourism and telecommunication, the State Secretary, the State Minister for Planning, and the commander in chief of the armed forces. The ten high-tech companies of EVIT are : (1) PT IPTN: aircraft and weapons; (2) PTPAL: shipbuilding and engineering; (3) PT Krakatau Steel: integrated iron and steel products; (4) PT PINDAD: small arms and heavy equipment; (5) Public Corporation PERUM Dahana: explosives; (6) PT INTI: telecommunications; (7) PT INKA: rolling stock; (8) PT BBI: machine tools, construction equipment; (9) PT Barata: machinery and engineering services; and (10) LEN: electronics and communications.

6. This phase is exactly the same as what Freeman (1987, p. 16) observes about the Japanese and some new industrializing countries (NICs) that devised technology transfer process. Freeman refers to such a phase as activities in *reverse engineering* that were carried out by Japan and NICs: "newly industrializing countries can make rapid progress by imports of technical know-how and reverse engineering combined with relatively small-scale research and development. As they become industrialized they will experience a growing need for more research and development activities, if only to make effective use of imported technology."

7. I use the term "economists" here particularly to refer to some academic economists who work in universities or research institutes, and include a few former ministers. They may have influence over the opinions of some government officials who primarily work at the Development Planning Agency (BAPPENAS) and offices of economic and finance ministries (EKUIN). Criticisms of EVIT can be found in the *Far Eastern Economic Review* (1987). Some criticisms of EVIT were also obtained by the author from interviews with fifteen prominent Indonesian economists in Jakarta during April 1987. Most of the criticisms are especially directed at EVIT's aircraft and shipbuilding industries.

8. The assessment of EVIT's results is based only on its output without considering the costs of "inputs" that were utilized to produce the output. The problem, in the opinion of most economists who criticized EVIT, is that no "clear" data or figures are available to investigate the cost-benefit analysis of the investments of EVIT. This is the most difficult aspect of assessing the cost-effectiveness of many "big science" or "political defense" projects. In the United States, for example, it is difficult to assess the cost-effectiveness of the Apollo or SDI projects. The same situation was also experienced in the United Kingdom in terms of government support to the aircraft industry.

References

Business News. "Electronic Industry Keeps Developing." *184* (1991).

Djojonegoro, Wardiman. "Comprehensive 'Catch-Up' S&T Development Strategies, An Indonesian Perspective." Paper presented at the S&T Policy Asian Network (STEPAN) Meeting, Bangkok, August 20–22, 1990.

Far Eastern Economic Review (1987): 111–16.

Habibie, B. J. "Some Thoughts Concerning a Strategy for the Industrial Transformation of a Developing Country." Address delivered to the Deutsche Gessellschaft furund Raumhart, June 14, 1983.

Henderson, Jeffrey. *The Globalization of High Technology Production.* London: Routledge, 1989.

IEEE Spectrum. "Poised for Technological Leadership" (June 1991): 30–48.

National Critical Technologies Panel. *Report of the National Critical Technologies Panel.* Washington, DC: 1991.

Nasution, Anwar. "Recent Economic Reform in Indonesia." *Indonesian Quarterly, 19,* 1 (1991): 12–26.

Pangestu, Mari. "The Role of the Private Sector in Indonesia: Deregulation and Privatization." *Indonesia Quarterly, 19,* 1 (1991): 27–51.

Roessner, David J.; Porter, Alan L.; and Fouts, Susan. "Technology Absorption, Institutionalization, and International Competitiveness in High Technology Industries." Paper for presentation at the International Conference on Technology Management, University of Miami, February 17–19, 1988.

Tempo. June 28, 1986.

Part IV
The East Asian Nations

10

Reform and Restructuring of China's Science and Technology System

Zhou Yuan

Over the past ten years or so, great changes have taken place in China's science and technology system. These changes have become an important part of the emerging technological trajectory of the Pacific Rim. However, what is more important is the fact that the restructuring and development trend of China's S&T system will influence the region's future technological trajectory to an even greater degree in the future. For this reason it is important to study the process and future structure of China's S&T system reform.

This chapter therefore focuses on the premise and process of China's S&T system reform, and on China's future model of S&T reform and restructuring. The first section below reviews the situation and drawbacks of China's former S&T system. The second section considers the main content and process of reform. The third section covers the status quo, future policy, and objectives of China's S&T system reform.

Prereform Conditions

The reform of China's S&T system has not been determined arbitrarily. Rather, it has been deeply affected by recent development trends of S&T abroad and the current large-scale economic construction at home. It has also been influenced by the urgent need to overcome defects in the original system.

Since the beginning of the 1960s, many foreign countries have realized the relevance of S&T to achieve national goals and have taken concrete measures to strengthen the links between S&T and the development of their economy and society. Relieved from the ten-year turmoil of the "Cultural Revolution," and strongly desiring to advance its economy, China began to study the scientific and technological achievements of other countries. What interested China most was Japan's postwar introduction and utilization of foreign technologies, which were mastered and developed domestically to produce high-tech products for the international market. The widespread dissemination descriptions of these kinds of experiences in China gradually led to important changes in the state's policies concerning S&T. Among the major changes instituted were the following:

- Emphasis was placed on the coordinated development of S&T with the advancement of the nation's economy and society.
- Efforts were stepped up in the research and development of applied science and technology.
- Horizontal links were established between scientific research institutes and industries, enterprises, and local governments.
- The commercialization of scientific research achievements was accelerated.
- The funding system was restructured to give research institutes more stimulus to orient their work toward economic construction.

Domestically, China has entered a new historical phase during which the nation's primary task was to develop its economy. The specific goal is to quadruple the value of the nation's gross annual industrial and agricultural production by the turn of the century, and to approach the level of developed countries in another thirty to fifty years. To attain such a goal, it is clearly necessary to develop China's S&T. (See chapter Appendix for tables on national expenditures.)

In China, however, S&T has long been separated from economic construction. A research institute was only answerable to its superior unit and lacked any ties with factories. The result of this has been that, on the one hand, a great number of technical problems arising from production were not solved, while on the other, the majority of research findings were not be widely utilized in production due to drawbacks in both the economic structure and the S&T system.

Drawbacks in China's S&T system can be divided into three areas: the first area is operating mechanism. Government control and management of S&T has been too rigid and all-embracing. Planned management has been favored over economic levers and market regulation. Scientific research institutes and production units have not been bound by common interest through such economic incentives as technology contracts. As a result, research institutes have lacked any capability for self-development and the initiative to serve economic construction. The prevailing appropriation system, for example, before reform, was a "supply system" whereby the funds for independent research institutes and development institutions at and above the prefectural and municipal levels were supplied by the government. Such a "supply" style of funding inevitably had defects:

- The research institutes were assigned their tasks by the higher authorities, who allocated funds, according to unit and staff size; the institutes' actual work performance and level of achievement were not subject to the checks and tests of economic and social needs. Since it was difficult for the state to assign tasks entirely in keeping with production needs, S&T and production became disjointed. Moreover, under the "supply system," funds were allocated according to units and staff size regardless of actual performance and achievement so that research institutes were responsible only to the higher authorities who gave them the money and were not oriented to serving the needs of society and production units.
- When state expenditure was insufficient to meet all research needs, the method of funding scientific research chiefly through state appropriations only reduced the investment intensity. Consequently, projects that should have been completed in one or two years dragged on for three to five years or even longer. Thus many research institutes functioned under capacity with insufficient tasks, and large numbers of scientific and technological personnel were unable to develop their potential while many small and medium-sized enterprises were confronted with numerous technical problems. The result, in effect, was tremendous waste.
- Since each research institute had its own separate share of funds, it was not obligated to arrange its topics according to the needs of the national economy. Research projects were inevitably repeated at low levels, which obviously was an inefficient use of S&T investment.
- The lack of a management system that could classify research institutes according to characteristics of research activities gave scientific and technological personnel little incentive to work hard within their fields of specialization to win reasonable financial support. This too contributed nothing to the improvement of research quality and work efficiency.
- The "supply" style of funding was oriented to the research unit, rather than to specific topics and projects, thus creating a situation where "everyone shared from the same big pot" within each institute. Individual competence and achievement received no special notice, and so talented people remained undiscovered and their talent remained undeveloped. In short, under the old funding system, which was unfavorable to the integration of S&T with production, research achievements were not easily or readily transformed into productive forces.

The second arena of drawbacks in China's pre-1978 S&T system was personnel management. Technicians and researchers were severely restricted in their work and the reasonable flow of talent was stymied. Intellectual work was not properly valued or respected. The distribution of scientists and technicians in China did not fit the development of the national economy. Most scientists and technicians were concentrated in the institutions of higher learning and research units, whereas the scientific and technical strength of enterprises was quite weak. As official Chinese statistics show, the number of scientists and technicians in the industrial and agricultural forefront was below that in the administrative units and public services. The average number employed per enterprise was less than five, which hindered enterprises' capacity for technical exploitation.

At such a juncture, China needed urgently to develop energy sources, communication and transport, building materials, textiles, and other such industries. There was an acute shortage of talented scientists and technicians in these fields, which could boast less than one-tenth the number of such personnel employed in the heavy industries.

In the past few years, the agricultural structure of China underwent significant changes, with the township enterprises springing up vigorously. However, these enterprises were deficient in technical strength. For one thing, there were only nine S&T personnel for every 10,000 employees, less than one-thousandth. This deficiency constituted a serious barrier to the development of township enterprises in China.

In terms of geographical distribution, the remote regions, which occupy two-thirds of the nation's total acreage and enjoy rich resources, had a scientific and technical force of no more than one-tenth of the nation's total. Among them, only 13 percent of the S&T personnel were involved in endeavors that took advantage of local resources to develop the local economy.

The third drawback was one of organizational structure. Because research institutes were unduly cut off from commercial enterprises, research, design, education, and production lacked coordination or connection. The military and civilian sectors, and the various government departments and administrative regions of the country were also isolated. Under such circumstances the research and development capabilities of production enterprises were weak, as was the link for transforming research findings into production. All these prevailing conditions necessitated the reform of the S&T system, which was launched in March 1985, immediately after the central government decided its national economic reform policy in October 1984.

The Process of S&T Reform

The reform of the S&T system's operating mechanism entailed reforming the fund appropriation system, developing the technology market, and addressing the rigidity of the government's managerial control over S&T. While it was decided that research projects of national priority should remain under the control of the state plans, other research activities were to be subjected to economic levers and market regulations to ensure that the research institutes develop indigenous capability and become invigorated to serve economic development on their own initiative.

In the area of organizational structure, efforts would be made to establish stronger linkages between research institutes and industrial enterprises, among research, design, education, and production, between the military and the civilian sector, and among different regions. The objective is to strengthen the technology absorption and development capabilities of industrial enterprises as well as the intermediate link in the process of transferring research achievements to production; to promote cooperation and association among research institutes, design institutes, institutions of higher learning, and industrial enterprises; and to help achieve a rational distribution of China's S&T. The personnel management system would be reformed through efforts to overcome the "left" mistaken ideas and to ease restrictions imposed on scientists and technicians, as well as to allow rational mobility of S&T personnel and to end a climate in which intellectual work was belittled, creating a more favorable climate for the emergence of large numbers of talented people who could feel free and willing to perform their best.

The reform of the S&T system has actually undergone three major phases. The first phase, the embryonic phase, lasted from 1978 to 1980. At the National Science Conference of 1978 the modernization of S&T was affirmed as the key to the realization of the four modernizations: agriculture, industry, science and technology, and national defense. With this stage came technology trade activities aimed at diffusing technological achievements through the domestic technology market, as a part of the S&T system's operating mechanism reform, was just beginning to grow. The technology market at this stage became characterized by voluntary cooperation between research institutes and production units in tackling key problems. Research institutes began the compensated transfer of technological achievements to production units, engaged in technical consulting, and assisted enterprises in solving technical production problems.

Meanwhile, the government adopted a series of measures to implement the new policy regarding intellectuals, including redressing grievances, wrong and misjudged cases, restoring technical posts and rank evaluation system, adjusting the practice of choosing people whose skills were not appropriate to the research topic under study, recruiting unemployed people, and improving the working and living conditions of scientific and technical personnel. In order to maximize the role of scientists and technicians, the Chinese government made it a priority to increase their representation in the leading bodies of the government and in the administration and establishment of public services. Since 1981, government at various levels has ensured that a group of competent scientists and technicians be selected and absorbed into the leading bodies. Today scientists and technicians comprised about one-third of members of the leading bodies at and above the county level. This measure undoubtedly has helped to heighten the innovative spirit of China's scientific and technical community.

In the meantime, most of the organs of state set up various forms of advisory bodies and brain trusts to organize experts and scholars in different fields for discussing major strategic and political problems in relation to science and to put forward proposals. In so doing, policy decisions were made much more scientific and the status and role of scientists and technicians in the macro decision making of the state were greatly enhanced.

The second phase covered the years from 1981 to 1984. At the National S&T Awards Conference held in 1982, the Chinese government suggested the strategic principle that "our economic construction must rely on S&T and technological work must be oriented to economic construction." This principle promised the coordinated development of S&T, economy, and society, and to speed up the formation of the technology market. Activities of the technology market grew in this stage with leadership and in an organized way. As a result, various modes and channels of management appeared, the size and scope of the technology market were being constantly expanded, and the technology market was initially formed.

Meanwhile personnel management continued to be reformed; in fact, at this stage, the development of this area of reform was remarkable. Since 1981, a series of documents had been issued by the State Council to encourage the proper flow of talent. The "pool of stagnant water" where inflow of new talent was virtually impossible was beginning to stir and momentum was gained in a favorable direction, which was of significance to the effective use of talent resources. In promoting the flow of talent, the central government adopted the following important measures:

- Implementation of a system of bringing scientists in from research and design entities, and from universities. In the latter half of 1984, China experimented with this system in selected cities and departments. The purpose of this new system was to bestow equal rights on the units and on the scientists and technicians to make mutual choices in order to develop a system of talent management that would be full of vitality and offer interaction and incentive. Where free association used to be practiced only within units or with supporting personnel or those immediately involved in a unit, this practice allowed the organized transfer of information and access of personnel to other units. This reform successfully stimulated the innovative spirit of scientific and technical workers, optimizing the composition of scientific research groups, promoting the proper flow of talent, and accelerating the improvement of nonproductive personnel.
- Reform of the post and rank system. Scientists and technicians were invited to assume professional duties. Since July 1984 the system of inviting scientists and technicians to assume professional duties had been tried out in seventy-one units under seven departments in the fields of education, scientific research, agriculture, and others. This reform has brought about fundamental changes for scientific and technical workers. They now work in a more rational organizational structure, with clear lines of authority and accountability. Reform abolished the system of lifelong tenure of office and established a relationship between responsibility and pay. Starting in 1984,

China pursued this system in stages and in groups, according to a plan formulated on the basis of efficiencies produced in workplace simulations. The implementation of this reform had a significant impact on the whole system of scientist and technician management, gave great impetus to the flow of talent, and optimized the talent pool and skill level of this area, with personnel's work performance improving and their role in the S&T system maximized.

• The adoption of special policies to encourage scientists and technicians to work in medium-sized and small enterprises, as well as in border areas and regions where ethnic minorities tend to live in compact communities. Since 1983, the Chinese government has followed a special policy toward scientists and technicians working in remote districts and at the agricultural forefront; this policy permits these districts to adopt their own incentive policies for employment issues including time limits of service, remuneration, retirement of scientific and technical workers, and job assignments for college graduates. Trial implementation of this policy had achieved positive results in stabilizing the contingent of scientific and technical workers in these districts, encouraging economically developed districts to support the remote ones. Lately, Guizhou, Gansu, Inner Mongolia, and Tibet have begun to reverse the tendency of brain drain and have started to realize the prospect of more inflow than drain. Many scientists and technicians have actually demanded assignment to a border area, countryside, or mountainous area to contribute to the development of such regions.

In order to maximize the role of scientists and technicians, the Chinese government has established rules and regulations for awarding high prizes to individuals for major contributions. In 1984, the state selected 420 scientists and technicians who had made outstanding contributions and gave them favorable treatment in housing, provision of support staff, health care, and other "perks," as well as raising their pay. Meanwhile, some districts, such as Shanghai, Jiling, Ningxia, and Guangxi, have each singled out a group of local exemplary people for praise. This approach has greatly stimulated the enterprising spirit of the scientists and technicians.

Veteran experts constitute one of China's most valuable assets and the Chinese government has always attached great importance to giving them a chance to participate fully. Measures to support this policy have included providing assistants, postponing retirement, and giving consideration to such matters as using cars, medical treatment, and health care. Lately, specific protective measures had been arranged to provide for medical treatment and health care for veteran experts while abroad.

In the first and second stages of China's S&T system reform, reform was limited to developing the technology market (as a part of the reform of the operating mechanism) and to the personnel management system.

The third stage, the stage of development, has been underway since 1985. After March 1985, the reform of S&T system was accorded top priority. The major steps are described in the following paragraphs.

The funding system—an important part of the operating mechanism—has been changed to a multifaceted fund management system for research institutes. Funds for important research and local development projects planned by the central government and construction projects of key laboratories and experimental centers are supported by the central and local financial departments respectively. A public bidding system and a contract system have been gradually instituted for the management of most projects. A contract system has also been gradually introduced for technological development programs and research projects that have the potential to yield quick profits. Institutes engaged in such research earned their incomes by contracting the state's projects and accepting research programs entrusted to them by the state. The research funds previously granted by the state have been gradually reduced, but are not canceled until the institute shows it is able to support itself.

Science foundations were established in February 1986, on a trial basis, for research programs in the basic sciences and in some applied sciences. Priority support was given to the best research subjects advanced by scientists and technicians and selected through appraisal by specialists, in order to concentrate the limited pool of funds in major S&T projects. According to the plan, in a few years all institutes in charge of such programs will operate on money granted by these foundations. However, the state might still grant a fixed amount to those institutions engaged in public welfare activities and technical services. To support high-technology development programs, the state established a special "start-up" fund.

The government hopes to speed up the commercialization of research results by sponsoring technical information fairs, by opening up channels for the smooth flow of research findings into areas of production, and by changing the practice of free transfer of technology achievements. As this stage began, the position and role of the technology market were fully confirmed. Since then a significant breakthrough has been made in some matters of principle in the commercialization of technological achievements; China's technology market has been swiftly developing with the rise of reform. The state further encourages the development of the technical trade market, protects the ownership of intellectual property, and provides favorable tax exemption or reduction treatment for technical transfers and the manufacture of new products.

To reform the organizational structure in the S&T system, the government is attempting to foster enterprises' ability to incorporate advanced technology and to develop new products (see chapter 11). All technological development research institutes run by the Chinese Academy of Sciences, colleges, ministries, and commissions under the State Council, as well as those institutes under local governments, are encouraged to cooperate with enterprises and institutions to establish a variety of interunit associations with the goal of gradually merging them into unified economic entities. Research institutes can be developed into research-production type enterprises or into a technological development institution serving a joint entity involving a number of medium-sized and small enterprises. Moreover, enterprises should actively seek to enhance their own technological development capability while making good use of the technical potential of society.

Further reform of the management system for technical personnel will include a gradual introduction of the system of recruiting research workers and technicians from research institutes, design offices, and colleges. Scientists and technicians are also permitted to take on extra jobs concurrent with their own jobs.

In view of the phenomenon of irrational talent distribution and hoarding, the PRC government has since 1985 allowed scientists and technicians to hold additional posts during their spare time. This policy has already played a positive part in accelerating the intellectual exchange and mutual permeation between disciplines and has allowed fuller use of the abilities of scientists and technicians. The state is currently implementing legislation so that a clear distinction is made between one's own job and a concurrent job, between the technical rights and interests of a department and the legal rights of its scientific and technical personnel, and between rightful income and illegal income. The main goal is to assist in linking up the scientific and technical talent and the units, making use of them so that both sides have mutual understanding and make mutual choices, and to promote the flow of talent.

Restructuring China's S&T System

Status Quo

Since 1985 China's science and technology system reform has made important progress and remarkable changes in operational mechanisms, organizational structures, management of scientific and technical personnel, and their environment.

The far-reaching reform of the fund appropriation system further changed the main structure of science and technology investment, thus promoting the transfer of S&T achievements to production and the establishment of China's new S&T investment system. One of the important features of the appropriation system reform is the reduction of the operational expenses allocated for the development-oriented research institutes. According to the 1991 annual report of S&T statistics, among the state-owned research and development (R&D) institutes above the county level in the field of natural S&T throughout China, 42 percent had, as of the end of 1989, reduced their R&D operational expenses—including 1,187 units that became financially independent, accounting for 24 percent of the total number of the institutions. The R&D units under the ministries of the central government reduced their operational funds by 53 percent on the average, while those under provincial or municipal government reduced the fund by 65 percent on the average.[1]

This item of reform has changed the unitary R&D investment structure of just depending on top-down support from government, thus resulting in a fairly rapid increase in income in a horizontal direction by the R&D institutes. In 1989 national R&D operational expenses accounted for 16 percent of total income, compared with 25 percent in 1986, while R&D horizontal income increased from 25 percent to 44 percent, an increase of 19 percentage points (Table 10.1). China's new approach to S&T is part of a scientific and cultural/organizational trend. A number of new financial organizations and social fund-raising groups for S&T have emerged, such as the "venture investment company" and the "Bank of S&T." With the emergence of these kinds of financial organizations, a new system is gradually taking shape.

Research and development institutes, through internal reform and strengthening ties with other similar organizations, are growing vigorously in the new economy. As of the end of 1989, 70 percent of the nationwide R&D institutes had implemented the "director responsibility system" and the "project contract system," especially those under the Chinese Academy of Sciences and under the State Council (Table 10.2). Some R&D units have introduced the mechanism of competition, and conducted the separation between management and ownership by applying leases and contracts. This has brought about changes in orientation, mergers of R&D units, and other similar modifications in behavior.

With the increase in connections between the R&D institutes and enterprises, the role of S&T is gradually growing into the economy. By the end of 1989, 54 percent of the R&D institutions throughout the country had kept close contact with enterprises or economic entities, including 361 institutions incorporated into large or medium-sized enterprises or groups of enterprises, and 333 institutions undertaking projects of and contracting projects to medium-sized or small enterprises (Table 10.3). Furthermore, nearly 15 percent of staff members and workers of the R&D institutions throughout the country had participated in the above-mentioned transverse economic associations. The following are the primary modes of association for the R&D institutes: (1) those that enter large and medium-sized enterprises or groups of enterprises; (2) those that undertake projects of or contracting projects to medium-sized or small enterprises; (3) those that participate in, or become, professional technical development centers; (4) those that join the design institutes or enterprises to establish a fully integrated "concept-to-product" engineering or technical corporation; (5) those that develop techniques jointly with enterprises, and (6) others.

The reform of the management system and the development of intimate associations have invigorated the R&D institutes. According to a sampling survey of directors of institutes in seven industries (metallurgy, machinery, chemistry, electronics, light industry, textiles, and building materials), the average period of a research project in their respective institutes has been shortened, as reported by

Table 10.1

1986–89 R&D Fund Income in the Field of Natural Science and Technology in China (in billion yuan)

Item of Statistics

Year	1 Number of Organizations	2 Number of Financially Independent Organizations	2/1	3 Total Fund Income	4 Government Appropriation	4/3	Including				Including	
							5 Operating Fund	5/3	6 Horizontal Income	6/3	7 Technical Income	7/6
1986	5,136	533	10%	10.938	6.787	62%	2.751	25%	2.747	25%	1.646	60%
1987	5,222	676	13%	11.386	6.724	59%	2.533	22%	3.611	32%	2.389	66%
1989	5,011	1,087	21%	16.146	7.359	46%	2.549	16%	7.065	44%	4.455	63%

Source: Annual Report of S&T Statistics (1987, 1990).

Table 10.2

Reforms of Internal Management in R&D Institutions above the County Level

	Total Number of Institutions	Applying Director Responsibility System (or System of Fixed Objective during Term of Office)	Applying Project Contract System or Research Responsibility System*	Applying Project Economic Accounting*
Total	5,011	3,485 (70)	3,770 (75)	3,400 (68)
Subordinate to government departments above the county level	4,001	2,715 (68)	2,869 (72)	2,558 (64)
Subordinate to ministries under the State Council	1,010	770 (76)	901 (89)	842 (83)
Subordinate to the Chinese Academy of Sciences	123	70 (57)	123 (100)	122 (99)

*Percentage of total in parentheses.
Source: Annual Report of S&T Statistics (1990).

Table 10.3

Relations between R&D Institutes above County Level and Enterprises or Economic Entities throughout China

Modes of Association with Enterprises and Economic Entities

	Total Number of Institutes	(1) Entering Large or Medium-sized Enterprises or Groups of Enterprises	(2) Undertaking Projects of or Contracting Projects to Medium-sized or Small Enterprises	(3) Participating in or Becoming Professional and Technical Development Centers	(4) Joining Design Institutes or Enterprises to Establish the Wholeset Type Engineering or Technical Corporations	(5) Developing Techniques Jointly with Enterprises	(6) Others
Total	2,683	361	333	320	160	968	541
Subordinate to government departments above county level	1,837	247	237	198	78	692	385
Subordinate to ministries under the State Council	846	114	96	122	82	276	156
Subordinate to the Chinese Academy of Sciences	94	6	13	13	9	32	21

Source: Annual Report of S&T Statistics (1989).

54 percent of respondents, and the research level of their institutes as a whole has been raised, as reported by 59 percent. The increase in income of the R&D institutes has enhanced their developing strength. This is conducive to the improvement of working conditions and welfare benefits.

The reform of the S&T personnel management system and the encouragement for S&T personnel to go into the field of economic construction have further increased the vigor of those personnel. As of the end of 1989, there were over 100,000 staff members and workers in the R&D institutes throughout China plunging into the forefront of industrial and agricultural production, and being engaged in paid technical services and technical-economic contracts (Table 10.4). Some provinces or cities have selected and sent S&T experts to take concurrent jobs in township and county governments to strengthen the leadership of local economic development with S&T as the mainstay. These efforts have borne fruit: quite a few regions have been able to absorb a great number of agricultural scientific research personnel to contribute to the development of the agricultural economy in the countryside.

With the promulgation of relevant regulations by the State Council and by some local authorities, there has been a growing tendency of talented personnel movement since 1987. According to a survey on the S&T personnel flow among the R&D institutes, higher educational institutions, and large and medium-sized enterprises in twenty-eight provinces, autonomous regions, and the municipalities directly under the central government (excluding Tibet) made by the Scientific-Technical Cadres Bureau of the State S&T Commission in June 1987 (Table 10.5), there has been a freer flow of scientific and technical personnel. While great effort has been devoted to promoting the flow of S&T personnel to wherever they can be fully integrated and used, the S&T personnel of some research institutes, design institutes, universities, and enterprises were engaged in concurrent jobs or spare-time work of various forms, offering technical services on condition that they complete the tasks assigned according to the contracts with, or the responsibility system of, their own respective units, and that they could not violate the technical or economic rights of their own relevant units. According to a random-sample questionnaire of 34,000 professional S&T personnel of different levels made by the State S&T Commission in November 1987, there were 1.39 million persons engaged in concurrent jobs, accounting for 14 percent of the total S&T personnel.

In the reform of the S&T personnel management system, some provinces and municipalities are actively exploring a new system whereby S&T personnel offer social services. For example, a double residence registration system and service agency have been proposed to help solve problems such as the personal file and wages (salary); another proposal is the establishment of an office to urge employer units to employ S&T personnel reasonably and to carry out supervision and arbitration work in this respect. Some provinces and municipalities have introduced a competition mechanism to select the operations manager and project director. For example, the agent of state-owned assets invited applications for the

Table 10.4

Personnel Input in the Associations between R&D Institutes above County Level and Enterprises or Economic Entities

Modes of Associations	Total Personnel Input	Professional Technical Cadres
	107,418	68,693
1	59,048	34,072
2	3,572	2,345
3	15,524	10,365
4	2,886	2,255
5	15,996	12,676
6	10,392	6,980

Modes of associations 1–6 are the same as in Table 3.
Source: Annual Report of S&T Statistics (1989).

manager or director position and any individual, collective or legal person was free to make a bid. After a qualification check and appraisal, a qualified person was chosen.

The reform and development of industry and agriculture have managed to improve the objective economic environment and to strengthen the capacity and consciousness for technical progress. The reform of industrial enterprises was one of the focal points of China's economic system restructuring in 1987. Through the practice of various forms of the contracted responsibility system, as well as the enrichment and perfection of the market, the decision-making power of the enterprise as a production operator was further enlarged, thus gradually intensifying competition. With the deepening of the reform, the dependence of the industrial enterprise on governmental administration has gradually diminished, while its dependence on market forces has become stronger and stronger. According to a 1987 survey by NRCSTD of 200 enterprises of seven trades, their dependence on market forces for revenue has reached, respectively, 69 percent, 70 percent, 51 percent, and 80 percent in the following areas: information needed for production planning, sales of products, supply of materials and raw materials, and investment needed for enlarged reproduction. The strengthening of the independence of the enterprises and the formation of the external competition environment make it possible for them to seek technical progress.

In the countryside, quite a few regions have been actively seeking ways to set up a new system suitable for the development of the local commodity economy. In order to develop the rural commodity economy with S&T as a mainstay, some provinces and municipalities have appointed a county vice-magistrate in charge of S&T. Some county S&T commissions have begun to establish technical-agri-cultural trade entities to serve the peasants. The system for demonstration, popu-

Table 10.5

Tendency of S&T Personnel Flow (in 10,000 persons)

	1984		1985		1986		1987	
	Outflow	% of Total	Outflow	% of Total	Outflow	% of Total	Outflow	% of Total
Total	9.87	2.70	10.52	2.76	7.64	1.90	3.43	0.84
R&D Institutes	1.70	3.27	2.23	4.14	1.54	2.73	0.70	1.24
Colleges and Universities	1.14	2.43	1.23	2.46	0.97	1.83	0.36	0.67
Large and Medium-sized Enterprises	7.02	2.63	7.05	2.54	5.11	1.76	2.36	0.80

Source: The S&T Cadres Bureau of the State Science and Technology Commission.

larization, and service of agricultural S&T is being gradually perfected and developed as it provides systematic service for pre-, in- and postproduction of agriculture. The implementation of the "Sparks Program" sponsored by the State S&T Commission and the "Bumper Harvest Program" sponsored by the Ministry of Agriculture, Animal Husbandry and Fishery has scored some success in training agriculture professional personnel and in developing local economy. In the course of reform, the countryside in China has already voiced a higher demand for S&T, thus providing a new opportunity to reform the agricultural S&T system.

As for the reform of the scientific research system in national defense, new steps have been made along the path from a solely "military-oriented" to a simultaneously "civilian-oriented" system. The year 1987 saw the establishment of the nationwide "military-to-civil," multilevel, technical information exchange networks and the national defense S&T achievements-boosting networks as well as a number of research production complexes. At the end of 1987, the first batch of confidential national defense scientific research achievements, totaling 210 items, was lifted to public status, thus accelerating the shift of military techniques to civil-use techniques.

With the deepening of reform, an in-depth deployment of S&T was strengthened, the basic research was emphasized, and the development plan of high technology research came into effect, thus speeding up the development of high-tech industries. In 1987, the state continued to invest funds in natural science, key facilities for basic research, and the establishment of key laboratories. In the same year the National Natural Science Foundation gave financial aid, totaling 77.59 million yuan, to 2,647 projects of basic research, accounting for 24 percent of total applied projects.

The high-tech development plan (863 Plan) formulated by the State Council came into effect in 1987. By the end of 1987, 764 subjects of the 15 key projects and 142 special topics had been analytically proved by the expert committees in the seven relevant key fields, and 361 contracts or agreements had been signed. In order to speed up the commercialization of high- and new-tech research achievements and to boost the formation and development of high- and new-tech industries, the State S&T Commission formulated and implemented the "Torch program" in 1988.

Problems

Among the major problems involving the mechanism of operation, a close interdependent relationship between R&D and economic development has not yet completely formed due to a lack of pressure and vigor. The state-run large and medium-sized industries enterprises are lacking pressure and ability to absorb new technology and develop new products. The R&D institutes also lack systematic design and development capacities. The combination of the S&T investment system and the financial system is not so adequate that there is no room for some rather mature technical achievements with certain market value to be applied in a timely way in production to bring about economical results.

In the structure of the present organization, vestiges of the old, isolated, closed system remain, somewhat impeding the connection and communication among S&T, production, and education. More than 1,000 research institutes subordinate to the Chinese Academy of Sciences and to the ministries of the State Council possess 50 percent of the country's research personnel and around 80 percent of the country's scientific research equipment and facilities. This high-level S&T force has considerable S&T superiority. But viewed from the perspective of economic development, this superiority is far from being transformed into commodity and market superiority.

The distribution of S&T personnel is irrational; the departmental monopoly of S&T personnel has not basically changed so that the flow of S&T personnel is still difficult. The distribution of the 8.68 million S&T personnel is yet to be readjusted. The ability of systematic development of engineering and technology is yet to be strengthened. The proportion of technical personnel engaged in production and operations in industry and agriculture is yet to be increased. A great number of S&T personnel are still overly concentrated in some large institutes, higher educational institutions, and government organizations, and have yet to become actively involved in this reform process. At present, the social environment does not exist to allow this personnel congestion to flow out to areas where they may be able to contribute more productively to economic construction and social development (Table 10.6).

Generally speaking, the reform of the S&T system not only is affected by the progress of economic reform and economic development but is also restricted by such factors as the political system, the social culture, personnel quality, and the pattern of S&T development.

Measures

Based on an objective assessment of the present S&T system reform, the central government hopes successively to deepen the reform by adopting the policies and measures described below.

The research institutes are being encouraged to introduce and to respond to the competition mechanism, to practice actively various forms of a contracted operation responsibility system, and to separate the operations wing from the ownership wing in research institutions. It is necessary gradually to adopt a public bidding system within the research institutes or in society as a whole, and to select managers by means of competition. It is necessary to reorient, incorporate, and even close down some poorly operated and ineffective research institutes. At present, the big academies or big institutes have particularly to adopt the way of "one institute, two systems" in order to release the vigor of this S&T main force.

The research institutes are encouraged to grow in various ways into the economy and to develop into a new type of scientific research and production entity.

Table 10.6

Changes of S&T Personnel in the Reform

Item	Volume of Work			Efficiency of Work			Research Achievements			Role Played			Actual Living Standard			Sense of Stability of Personal Prospect		
Change % Rank	+	0	–	+	0	–	+	0	–	+	0	–	+	0	–	+	0	–
Senior	82.3	13.3	4.4	61.6	29.4	9	55.6	36	8.4	59.9	32.2	7.9	58	32	10	32.2	37.2	30.6
Middle	74.8	20.1	5	66.6	27.8	5.6	54.8	33.2	12	58	34.1	7.9	53.7	31	15.3	30.2	41.2	28.6
Junior	73.1	21.2	5.7	59.4	36.7	3.6	46.9	44.4	8.7	51.5	42.6	5.9	35.6	40.6	23.8	27.4	40	32.6

Source: Survey of 3,000 S&T personnel conducted in China in 1987 by the National Research Center for Science and Technology for Development.

+ = increased; 0 = no change; – = declined

The research institutes and enterprises can cooperate with each other via such mechanisms as mutual contract, lease, participation through public ownership, amalgamation, joint operation, participation in an enterprise, or by forming a group of enterprises or developing into a research-oriented enterprise. Full use must be made of the superiority of the center cities, the coastal open areas, and the intelligence-intensive areas to be oriented to both the domestic and the world markets in order to run or jointly run various forms of branch institute, corporation, enterprise, or enterprise group—thus actively developing and organizing the production of new products and high-technology products, facilitating the absorption and innovation of imported technology, and promoting the development of the export-oriented economy and the formation of the new-technology enterprises. It is also possible to directly arrange agencies abroad by setting up various forms of monocapital or joint-venture businesses. In the intelligence-intensive municipalities, necessary conditions must be created for performing trial runs of new technology industrial development zones and to formulate corresponding supporting policies. Decision-making power must be extended in foreign affairs and ratification procedures must be simplified in the foreign affairs of research institutes. Financial institutions at various levels must further open and dredge the S&T credit channel and increase the credit quotas for S&T.

The research institutes and S&T personnel are to be encouraged to improve their own working conditions and material welfare by creating wealth for society and making contributions to the S&T progress. The research-prize taxing point may be raised and different prize policies defined according to the actual conditions of different types of research institutes. Every institute should carry out overall economic accounting, and basically reduce the appropriations for research operation expenses to targeted levels by the end of 1990.

To ensure the long-range development of S&T and the economy, the steady and continuous development of basic science research must be guaranteed. State funding to the basic sciences should be successively increased along with increases in the state's revenue. The scientific research foundation system must be perfected, the competition mechanism furthered, new forms of management explored, and a body of keen-witted and capable personnel developed for basic research.

In the reform of the administration system, the governmental departments at different levels should simplify administration and give more decision-making power to the lower-level unit, to enable the research institutes to develop independently in the direction of an "open door," "coalition," and "competition." The research institutes should strengthen the transverse association and develop business entities.

While deepening the system reform of the state-owned research institutes, it is important for nongovernmental research institutes to create a cooperative environment in which the state, collectives, and individuals work together to develop S&T.

Government must itself play an active role at different levels to train and include current S&T personnel fully. S&T personnel shall be encouraged in a planned way and in the form of transferring, resigning, stopping pay but keeping the position, and taking a concurrent job to run, lead, contract, or lease the small or medium-sized enterprises and rural enterprises, or to conduct paid services and techno-economic contracted businesses in rural areas.

Every region has to formulate suitable policies according to its own conditions to promote the rational flow of talented personnel. Those cities with adequate conditions must actively engage in the comprehensive reform of the S&T personnel management system. The following measures shall be adopted in a step-by-step way: the employer units have the right to engage or dismiss S&T personnel, and the S&T personnel have the right to accept the appointment or to resign—that is, there is a two-way employment choice mechanism.

Training and selection of S&T personnel and of different talented professionals from among the workers, peasants, other laborers, are crucial. The technology market and the labor-service market must be developed to create opportunities for competition among different categories of ability.

The reform of enterprises' operating mechanisms must enable the enterprise to rely on technical progress. Such technical progress indicators as technical reconstruction, renewal of products, improvement of product quality, and reduction of consumption should be brought into the orbit of the enterprise's contracted responsibility system, the manager's objective responsibility system during his or her tenure of office, and the enterprise's grading indication system. Large and medium-sized enterprises and enterprise groups in particular should establish or improve the system of technical development and management during the reform process, and should strengthen the capacity of technical development and absorption by means of various forms of association and coordination. The enterprises should take powerful measures to arouse the initiatives and enthusiasm of the S&T personnel, thereby including them in the acceleration of technical progress.

The present mechanism for spreading information and service organizations must be reformed in order to form a network for the development of a commodity economy in rural areas.

The input for S&T should be increased at a faster than normal rate of increase of financial revenue.

Objectives

Based on analysis of the reform trend, some ideas of the objective model of restructuring China's S&T system for several years to come can be distilled, all aimed at setting up a framework capable of efficiently expanding the national economy by relying on S&T progress:

• Management of the national economy and S&T should be standardized and legislated by the state.

- A market system of materials, finance, technology, labor service, etc., should be established.
- The S&T investment system must be financed and given credit.
- The management of S&T personnel should be socialized.
- The R&D system must be made adaptable to the development of China's commodity economy and to the worldwide S&T revolution: China must maintain a select high-level scientific research force to ensure the long-range development of its S&T and economic construction and national defense. The country must establish a new industrial R&D system centered around enterprise-run and nongovernmental research institutes. China must set up an agrotechnical data base and service system dependent on the integrated entity of technology, agriculture, and trade, and must establish a new type of S&T industry that can compete in the international market.

In view of the theoretical consideration of the present reform process and the review of past reform practices, China's reform cannot pin its hope entirely on the self-perfection of the structure, but should emphasize the growth and development of new system factors by successively using such factors to replace the old system, thereby steadily consolidating the new system's leading position. With this in mind, the basic principles that will underlie the S&T system reform for several years to come are:

- Government functions must be transformed to improve macromanagement, take effective measures, form an equal opportunity environment, and release the dependency of R&D units and S&T personnel on governmental administration to enable them to be independent commodity producers and operators.
- Attention must be focused on ways to produce and to strengthen the core of the new system, to develop various kinds of scientific production and business entities that can raise their own capital, can operate independently, and can assume sole responsibility for profit and losses. These entities should be helped to become the new vital force of China's new R&D system and S&T industry.
- Emphasis must also be placed on cultivating the market system of material, finance, technology and service, on establishing a supporting system of S&T information, technical operation, and social protection of personnel, and on establishing a policy and regulation system to protect S&T progress.
- Along with the deepening of the political and economic system reforms, the state-run research institutes have to be re-focused and reorganized to ensure the long-range development of the economy and of S&T, as well as the rational allocation of S&T and economic productive capacity, in order to realize progressively the general integration of S&T into the economy, thereby forming a new type of organization and structure for the S&T system oriented to the market, relying on society, and characterized by its S&T industry.

Appendix

Table A.1

National expenditures for R&D in aggregate, by source, for selected countries

Country	Total (100 million)	Source (%) Government	Industry	Other
China (1987)	Y56.7	60.9	39.1	1/N
Japan (1985)	$545.5	21.0	68.9	10.1
Four Asian NICs & Rs (1985)	$24.80	33.4	65.4	1.2
India (1986)	$21.15	88.1	11.9	1/N
Thailand (1985)	$1.19	48.3	3.3	48.4

Source: Guide to China's S&T Policy, 1989.

Table A.2

National expenditures for R&D by performer for selected countries (%)

Country	Government	University	Industry
China (1987)	54.4	15.9	29.7
Japan (1986)	9.1	19.9	66.6
Four Asian NICs & Rs (1985)	26.3	11.4	62.3
India (1984)	73.8	0.1	26.0
Thailand (1985)	54.9	30.0	15.1

Source: Same as Table A.1.

Table A.3

National expenditures for R&D by sector for selected countries (%)

Country	Basic	Applied	Development
China (1987)	7.7	31.9	60.4
Japan (1986)	13.3	24.4	62.3
Four Asian NICs & Rs (1985)	14.6	29.7	55.7
India (1984)	9.15	20.95	70.9
Thailand (1985)	43.7	26.1	30.2

Source: Same as Table A.1.

236 PART IV: THE EAST ASIAN NATIONS

Table A.4

Employment status of S&T personnel by field in China, for selected years (in 10 thousands)

	1985	1987	1988	1989
Total S&T personnel	823.8	936.6	1,015.9	1,097.3
Natural sciences	33.6	31.5	31.4	30.2
Engineering and technology	354.5	425.3	455.5	506.8
Medical sciences	241.7	248.5	271.1	291.5
Agricultural sciences	47.5	51.3	52.8	56.7
Higher learning teachers	146.4	180.0	205.1	212.1

Source: Statistical Yearbook of China, 1990.

Table A.5

Degree and training level employed of R&D institutes of Chinese government, by sector, 1989 (number of persons)

	Total	State Government	Local Government
Doctor	1,841	1,644	187
Master	22,076	17,221	4,855
Bachelor	105,523	63,341	42,182
University graduate	267,924	168,873	99,051
Graduate of special course of university	123,000	67,644	55,356
Technical secondary school graduate	123,766	67,455	56,311
Others	462,721	257,844	204,877

Source: Same as Table A.4.

Table A.6

Patents granted and foreign patents, 1986-89

	1986	1987	1988	1989
Total	3,024	6,811	11,947	17,129
Foreign patents	353	410	654	1,649

Source: Same as Table A.4.

Table A.7

Technology trade for selected countries ($100 million)

Country	Income	Payment	Balance
China (1987)	1.61	22.16	−20.55
Japan (1986)	9.82	12.29	−2.47

Source: Same as Table A.4.

Table A.8

S&T priorities and target areas and defense expenditure by R&D expenditure for selected countries (%)

	China (1985)	Japan (1986)	Thailand (1985)	India (1984)
Development and evaluation of biosphere	2.10	6.36	3.08	4.55
Application of civil space technology	1.50	10.91	0.35	9.35
Development of agriculture husbandry and fishery	10.40	14.55	11.31	17.90
Development of industry	32.30	10.91	9.33	17.99
Production conservation and distribution of energy	7.90	10.91	11.78	16.77
Development of transport and communication	6.20	6.36	10.46	5.23
Development of education	1.70	1.18	8.69	0.05
Development of health care	4.60	5.45	13.32	3.83
Development of urban and rural residential housing	1/N	3.64	0.74	1/N
Social development and relative targets	3.70	1.81	11.44	0.53
Environment protection	2.30	6.36	3.73	1.30
Progress of general knowledge	5.20	3.64	7.41	4.30
National defense	17.90	9.10	8.44	15.40
Miscellaneous	4.20	8.19	0.40	0.30

Source: Same as Table A.4.

Table A.9

S&T priorities and target areas, defense expenditure by R&D projects input in fund and personnel in China, 1989

	Fund (in thousand RMB yuan)	Personnel
Total	2,140,604	172,431
Development and evaluation on biosphere	56,020	5,134
Application of civil space technology	49,306	2,593
Development of agriculture husbandry and fishery	220,875	28,058
Development of industry	443,036	41,967
Production, conservation and distribution of energy	100,079	7,235
Development of transport and communication	101,886	6,310
Development of education	1,548	180
Development of health care	110,860	16,675
Social development and relative targets	48,932	4,924
Environment protection	33,720	4,096
Progress of general knowledge	169,941	14,437
National defense	729,743	34,768
Miscellaneous	74,658	6,054

Source: Guide to China's S&T Policy of 1989.

Notes:

1. R&D comprises basic research, applied research and experimental development.

2. S&T personnel refer to kinds of R&D project team personnel, S&T service personnel (persons dealing with books, information and consultation work), S&T managerial personnel, personnel working in laboratories, workers in pilot factories (workshops) and agricultural farms; not including car drivers, janitors, personnel working in mess halls, medical houses, kindergartens, nurseries and labor service companies, and sanitation workers.

3. Scientists and engineers refer to those who are of university or higher educational level or conferred with senior or intermediate academic titles.

Note

1. *Annual Report of Science and Technology Statistics* (Beijing: State Science and Technology Commission, 1990).

11

Technical Transformation and Renovation in PRC Industry

Jingping Ding

Technical transformation in China means improving production technology, processes, and equipment to modernize existing enterprises. This concept does not usually include capital construction, which involves building new factories with advanced technology and equipment. Because the pace of technical change is rapid, technical transformation actually should be an ongoing task within enterprises so that they can keep pace with the worldwide trend of technological development. Most Chinese enterprises, however, still lack the authority and the money to do the job. Therefore, it remains a task to which the Chinese government should pay attention.

The large-scale technical transformation in China's industrial field started in the early 1980s. Now, ten years later, China has to start another large-scale technical transformation. At present, the Chinese State Planning Commission and the State Economic Trade Commission of the central government have been making plans to carry out this new technical transformation. The plan of technical transformation is different from that of ten years ago in terms of not only the background in which it has emerged, but also in terms of its targets and measures. It also reflects some of the problems that constrain the technical progress of Chinese industries.

This chapter is divided into four parts. The first reviews the background of the present technical transformation program in China. The second discusses further reasons for the backwardness of Chinese industrial technology. The third part examines the tasks and measures of Chinese technical transformation and renovation, and the final part evaluates the government's technical transformation plan.

The Background of Technical Transformation in China

In the early 1980s, the Chinese government voiced this guiding principle: "Economic construction must depend on science and technology, and science and technology must serve economic construction." The government then decided to implement a technology transformation program in existing enterprises. After ten years of such transformation, the results may be summarized as follows:

- Investment in technical transformation has been a large portion of total fixed capital investment. From 1981 to 1990, there were more than 450,000 total projects of transformation and renovation, and total investment for them was 546.9 billion Chinese yuan. The proportion of transformation and renovation in fixed capital investment has been raised from 18.4 percent in 1980 to 28.3 percent. The average proportion during this ten-year period was 30.8 percent in 1990. In some industrial sectors the investment scale for technological transformation was even larger than the investment scale for new firms such as machine-building, the electronics, automobiles, light industry, textiles, iron and steel, chemicals, construction materials, and medicine. During these ten years of technical transformation, the technical level of Chinese industries has improved rapidly, as evidenced not only by an improved ability to create new products, but also by improved quality of the enterprises themselves.
- Technological imports also have increased dramatically. In the last ten years, the central government has spent about US$29.85 billion for imported technologies. There were 7,063 major projects; 72 percent were for imported hardware such as equipment and product lines, and the rest were for software such as design and process technology. Middle-sized and small firms, which belong to each local government, also initiated more than 10,000 technical import projects and spent more than US$12 billion.
- Absorbing large-scale foreign capital also brought advanced technologies into China. Foreign investment in China not only makes up the shortage of Chinese capital but also brings in some advanced technology, equipment, and management experience. All of this has benefited China. By late 1990, China had, in total, utilized US$102.29 billion in contracts and $67.9 billion in arrived direct foreign investment. Among these figures, direct foreign investment was $40.3 billion in contracts and $19 billion in arrived direct foreign investment. Also during this period, more than 29,000 foreign-invested firms have been approved, including 16,000 joint ventures, 9,300 cooperative projects, and 3,300 fully foreign investments.

Research and development (R&D) has improved in many fields. Eighty per-cent of new R&D results created by Chinese research institutions, universities, and enterprises have been utilized in real production and have created profits of 30 billion Chinese yuan.

The above developments show that China has made great progress. Why, then, does it need to launch another large-scale technical transformation move-ment? There are several seasons, the most important of which have to do with pressure from domestic problems and from world competition.

Pressure from Domestic Problems

Although the technical level of Chinese industries has improved rapidly during the last ten years, Chinese industry still faces problems due to such factors as shortages of capital, advanced technologies, and knowledgeable people. These shortages are being felt increasingly in Chinese industry. Examples of the prob-lems are:

Poor Quality of Processing Equipment

Among the processing equipment in enterprises all over the country, at least one-third was made within China during the 1960s and 1970s. The quality of this equipment is now terribly backward. Advanced equipment at a technological level similar to the level of developed countries in the 1970s and 1980s accounts for only about 20 percent of the total.

According to a survey in 941 large-middle-size enterprises in Liaoning Prov-ince, only 38 have so far been completely transformed. Among the existing equipment, the technical level of the 1950s characterizes over 30 percent of the total, of the 1960s and 1970s, about 50 percent of the total, and the rest is at the level of the 1980s. Only about 7 percent of total equipment has reached an advanced level (1990) by world standards.

Poor-Quality Functioning of Industrial Products

The quality of many machine parts and components still cannot satisfy the cur-rent requirements and therefore affects the quality of the whole machine. For example, the sampling inspection certification rate of manufacturing products is about 75 percent, compared with about 98 percent in advanced countries. Chi-nese products still have a way to go to achieve the levels of the advanced world.

High Material Consumption

Compared with developed countries, many Chinese indexes of raw material consumption are relatively high. For example, energy consumption per unit of

GNP in China is twice that of developed countries, steel consumption is two to three times higher, and even pig iron consumption is two to nine times higher. So far, the efficiency utilization rate in advanced enterprises in China is about 60 percent, but in Japan and the United States it is over 80 percent. The utilization rate of wood in China is less than 60 percent, but more than 70 percent in Japan, Sweden, and the nations of the former USSR.

Low Education of Workers and Staff

The education level of workers and staff in Chinese enterprises, compared with ten years ago, has increased, but still cannot meet the needs of the enterprises in general. In 1987, the State Statistic Bureau investigated 1.7 million workers in 960 state-owned industrial enterprises in 48 cities. The composition, by education level, of workers and staff is: 7.1 percent graduated from college or higher degree; 6.6 percent were from mechanic school; 26 percent graduated from senior high school; 45.3 percent had a junior high school education; and 14.8 percent were educated at the elementary school level or lower.

Lack of Skillful Persons and R&D Institutions

At present, engineers account for only about 4.4 percent of personnel in most state-owned enterprises in China, and for many reasons, the abilities of those engineers are not yet being given full play.

Many enterprises also lack complete R&D institutions. Among the large and middle-size enterprises, two-thirds have no R&D department. Two-fifths have neither an R&D department nor persons for R&D. Most small enterprises in general have no capacity for R&D.

All of the above problems contribute to an overall problem of low efficiency. In other words: high input, but low output. According to Shi Qinqi's calculation, from 1952 to 1982, the rate of gross output value of state-owned enterprises was 10.6 percent, of which 72.2 percent was dependent on the increased input of capital and labor; the technological contribution rate to GNP was only 27.8 percent (Qingqi, 1985, p. 8). However, even from the 1950s to the 1970s, the technological contribution rate to GNP was 50 to 70 percent in advanced countries. If we look at some particular industrial sectors, the inefficiency problem is even more serious. For example, productivity calculated with all workers and staff in the Chinese machine-building industry is only one-twentieth of the rate in the United States. Clearly, such serious shortfalls compel China to start another large-scale technical transformation.

Pressure from World Competition

Since China implemented the open-door policy, it has benefited from world trade and other forms of international exchanges. However, it has also started to feel the pressures of world competition, which have grown heavier and heavier in recent years. The pressures are mainly from three places: advanced countries; newly industrialized countries and areas; and foreign competition within China.

Although Chinese industry is well ahead of the very poor base on which it began forty years ago, it still suffers from a large gap in technology compared with the advanced countries. In some industries, the gap is still growing and China cannot help but feel this gap as a crisis of technology.

Since World War II, many countries and areas have been developing into new industrialized economies; this is especially the case in the Pacific region, of which China is now an active member. The success of the Pacific Rim countries and areas, no doubt, can serve as a good example for China, and can also stimulate China to accelerate its technological and economic progress. If China had excuses in the past forty years for its slower technological development, such excuses are no longer valid in the face of the progress of the Asian NIEs. Furthermore, the fast growth of some Southeast Asian countries such as Thailand, Malaysia, and Indonesia adds to the pressure on China to speed up its technology development.

There are basically three types of foreign investment in China at present: joint venture, cooperative production, and wholly foreign-owned firms. Since such enterprises came into China, it has not mattered whether they were fully export firms or part export, part domestic sales firms: either way, they represent competition for Chinese enterprises with their technologies, management experience, new products, and efficiency. Chinese enterprises are starting to learn that they will be lost one day if they don't improve themselves now.

In addition to these factors, it should be mentioned that the Gulf War also acted as a spur to the Chinese government's technological transformation and renovation. The success of American "smart weapons" in the war against Iraq helped to heighten the awareness of Chinese leaders to the importance of the microelectronics revolution and its consequences for modern warfare.

Further Reasons for the Backwardness of Chinese Industrial Technology

There are many reasons why Chinese industrial technologies still need to be improved, including a low original technological level, a lack of capital resources and talented people, and a lack of investment for education. But in addition to these we must also examine China's economic development strategy and its problems in economic reform.

Economic Development Strategy

Since 1978, the Chinese government has turned its attention away from political struggle and toward economic development. No doubt, this change of focus is good for national economic development. The problem, however, is that the economic strategy was not implemented completely and was changed too often during the last ten years. For instance, China has declared that the gross value of the country's industrial and agricultural output should be increased four times by the year 2000. To reach this goal, all areas and all industrial sectors have to increase their productivity and reach their targets as soon as possible. Therefore, many factories have to work very hard and end up with no time to maintain their machines. They also often have no time to improve their products and equipment with advanced technology.

China had also made a strategic plan to develop energy and transportation industries as the main body of economic development after the "Cultural Revolution," but lately the country has tried to change direction to follow the high-technology waves of the "World Revolution of New Technology" in 1984. Then, a strategy of coastal-area development was implemented in 1987 and the theory of "joining to the international cycle" expanded throughout the country. Finally, the policy turned its attention to the development of township and village enterprises (TVEs), resulting in a growth explosion among TVEs in 1988. The uncertainty of the development strategy that was implemented led to insufficient attention to technological development in existing industries. Enterprises consequently found it difficult to decide on targets of technological development, and distorted the distribution of financial resources and human capital to realize the original strategy.

Slowness of Economic Reform

Another basic factor affecting the improvement of industrial technology is the slowness of economic reform. In a sense, this is an even more serious problem than the uncertainty of the economic development strategy. The key problem of economic reform is still to change the relationships among government, market, and enterprises. A simple description of the major problems involving those elements follows.

First, the financial contract system between the central government and local governments is a significant hindrance to industrial technological progress. The central government still faces problems, such as its own inherent inability to guide the economy on a macro level and a lack of clarity concerning who is responsible for the daily functioning of state-owned enterprises owned jointly by the central and the local governments. The most serious problem, however, is the implementation of the financial contract system between the central government and local governments. Because of this system, local governments are beginning to have their own interest and are likely to be concerned only with their own business and benefits, with little regard for the national economy. The confusion over development of the technology for color TVs, washing machines, and refrigerators in China was clear evidence of the weakness of the central government's guidance as it stands. Evidence also can be found in the textiles and cigarette industries. Because local governments want to keep more benefits for their own jurisdiction, they do not sell the raw materials such as wool or cotton to textile factories in other regions. Because of limited investment, the factories that belong to the local government are usually small and new, and use old equipment with backward technology that has been eliminated by the big factories. This is clearly a waste of raw materials and causes a split in the domestic market into a duchy-style economy. It also hinders technology transfer among industries.

Second, an incomplete market system is a hindrance to industrial technical transformation. China has been trying to develop a market for more than ten years, but for many reasons the market mechanism has not yet been fully implemented. The incomplete market mechanism provides no encouragement to technical transformation in enterprises. Weakness of competition has not really force firms to speed up technology improvement; a no-firing labor system has not stimulated enterprises to use more efficient technology; fixed prices protect low-quality products and enable the persistence of low technology. Thus, clearly, the role of the market mechanism should be completed and strengthened. Without this piece of the reform process, technical transformation is impossible.

A third problem is the lack of a dynamic mechanism of technical progress in China's business enterprises. The internal dynamic mechanism of technical progress in enterprises involves the motivation, consciousness, requirements, and ability of enterprises to achieve technological improvement. In the present situation, although both macroeconomic conditions and the microeconomic mechanism of enterprises have been changing a lot under ten years of reform, the differences in the dynamic mechanism among Chinese enterprises are still very big. These differences fall roughly into four groups: (1) Ownership is deficient; therefore, the dynamic mechanism of technical improvement is deficient. Large and middle-sized state-owned enterprises are firmly controlled by state plans and have less of a dynamic mechanism to facilitate technological improvement. In contrast with large and middle-sized state-owned enterprises, this aspect of TVEs is stronger. (2) Among enterprises under the same ownership, the dynamic of enterprises is also different due to the behavior of managers or to some other elements such as different government policies. Therefore, some state-owned enterprises run well, some do not. The same is true of the TVEs. (3) Enterprises in coastal areas have a stronger dynamic mechanism, while inland enterprises are weaker.

Fourth, different industries have different levels of dynamism. High-tech industries are stronger, while relatively traditional industries are weaker. The reasons for such differences are manifold. From a macroeconomic perspective, the dynamic mechanism is affected by government policies, market competition, conditions of regional economy, and other factors. From a microeconomic perspective, it is affected by factors such as the rights of autonomy of enterprises, the experience of managers, and the completion of internal management systems in enterprises. In general, the dynamic mechanism of the state-owned enterprises, especially large and middle-sized ones, is limited and also supported by state plans, the guaranteed supply of capital, material, and skilled labor, the limitations on operational rights (the talent of a manager as a person does not have a very strong influence on the development of an enterprise), and the general rigidity of management systems. Finally, the causal link between workers' contributions and the distribution of benefits is not close enough.

Compared with large and middle-scale state-owned enterprises, the environment and capacity for technical transformation of TVEs is completely different. They have a strong sense of the crisis of competition and so they are more highly motivated to improve their technology. Their problems, however, are that their production planning is primarily driven by market forces, which makes them more vulnerable to fluctuations in demand than state-owned enterprises. Despite their desires to improve their technology, they lack capital resources, advanced technology, management experience, and a good deal of necessary information. Hence, they lack the capability to be innovative. Many TVEs can only produce copies of products or, at best, introduce minor modifications to products already in the market. Also, because of the high level of risk associated with TVEs, it may be too soon for them to seek high-profit, short-term investment returns, or short-term benefits. And this too plays a part in their desire to implement technological improvement and renovation.

China does not have many private manufacturing enterprises, but those that do exist are very complex operationally. Because of the high risk they face, the small amount of capital investment available, and the limited experience of their managers, they tend often to seek shorter-run returns and to pay less attention to improving technology.

The key reason for the lack of a dynamic mechanism of technical progress within China's state-owned enterprises lies in their operational mechanism. Most state-owned enterprises are still controlled directly by the government at one level or another. According to Chinese "enterprise law," enterprises have some rights regarding hiring or firing of employees; some enterprises were actually able to implement those rights through the contract system established between them and the government during the past ten years. Since 1989, however, the government has rescinded some of those rights in the name of economic readjustment. For purposes of benefit distribution between the government and enterprises, government control is as strong as it was in several domains before reform. For example, state-owned enterprises now must hand over 90 percent of their profit to the government, by means of twenty kinds of taxes and more than sixty kinds of other charges imposed in 1989; there were only two kinds of taxes in 1978. Out of the remaining 10 percent of their profits, enterprises have to pay for medical care and other employee benefits. They obviously have no money left for updating equipment or modernizing technology. As long as Chinese enterprises are controlled directly by the government, they cannot be fully responsible for management or for their own profits or losses. Such clearly is not an environment in which to talk about self-development or creating an internal dynamic system for technological transformation.

Tasks and Measures

The tasks and measures of Chinese technical transformation and renovation are spelled out in the "Ten-Year Economic and Society Development Program" and "The Eighth Five-Year Plan," both of which describe the task of technical transformation in the next ten years as meeting the need to readjust the economic structure and to raise economic efficiency. China plans to transform existing enterprises with advanced technology, equipment, and processes, and to modernize technology and equipment, organize R&D, and solve key technical problems (Simon and Ding, in press). The tasks China faces in particular are: (a) decreasing consumption of energy and material; (b) raising product quality, developing fine, new products that are in short supply, and increasing effective supply; and (c) increasing exports.

To realize these tasks, the Chinese State Planning Commission (SPC), State Economic and Trade Commission (SETC), and other ministries are formulating plans. The SPC and SETC are in charge of the technical transformation plan for the whole country, and has decided on the following measures:

1. Arrange key transformation projects at the state level that are urgently needed in important industries; some of these involve saving energy, some involve raising product quality, and some aim at increasing exports or for implementing substitution.
2. Manage the use of advanced technologies in key large or middle-sized state-owned enterprises, on both the state and the province level.
3. Oversee technical transformation in certain old industrial cities during the Eighth Five-Year Plan—the six cities of Shanghai, Tianjing, Shenyang, Harbin, Wuhan, and Chongqing will be transformed by means of key projects to allow them to play a more important role in the national economy, to transform them into centers of integrated technological manufacturing industries, intellectual resources, and commerce.
4. Concentrate technological imports on projects that are within the technical transformation plan: in the near future, the ratio of imported technology to total imports should be increased, and the direction of currency expense should be concentrated on technical transformation for existing enterprises. The means of technology import should be made more flexible, and could include such methods as combining technology imports with trade, cooperative design, coproduction, and compensation trade.
5. Assign high priority within the national economy to the development of the electronics industry, with particular emphasis on transforming more traditional industries by using electronics; this represents a long-term strat-

egy for Chinese industries. In the Eighth Five-Year Plan, China will mainly use electronic technology to increase automatic control, to increase the value added of products, to improve the enterprises' capacity for design and R&D, and to increase the management efficiency of large enterprises.

China's State Science and Technology Commission (SSTC) is also involved in this program. The SSTC's plan includes the following measures: (1) paying close attention to the application of new technology to traditional industries, and organizing important large-scale projects in new materials development, energy production, biological engineering, and computer software design; (2) setting up an engineering testing center for multiuse technologies in industrial sectors through coordination of key scientific and technology projects; (3) enhancing R&D for new products for increasing exports and competitive ability; and (4) implementing key technologies for state technological integrated projects. The SSTC will implement the plan as follows:

1. Government will gradually increase investment to basic research in the Eighth Five-Year Plan. Seventy-nine subjects in fifteen fields will be chosen and strongly supported by the SSTC. Some national laboratories and laboratories in industrial sectors also will be chosen and given some favorable support.
2. The "Spark Plan" will focus on rural economic development, and on supporting key industries and comprehensive regional development. During the five years of the plan, 300 key industrial products will be targeted for investment and 100 comprehensive development areas will be set up. Two million people will be trained and 100 projects established and assigned throughout the areas selected.
3. By the end of 1995, China should reach the target of 50 billion yuan gross output value of high-tech industries. To reach this target, the SSTC will have to expand the scale of the "Torch Plan," which will bring more universities and military enterprises into the arena of high-tech development. This plan will establish high-tech development areas, especially in Shuzhou, Wuxi, Changzhou, and the Zhujiang river delta areas. It aims also to encourage the transfer of high-tech into traditional industries, to attract foreign capital into high-tech developing zones, and to strengthen the technical exchange between inland and coastal areas.
4. R&D efforts will be expanded from research institutes to industries, and enterprises will be encouraged to exploit military technology transfer for commercial products by government pushing military enterprises to produce commercial goods.

Based on the SPC/SETC plan, every ministry has also made its own plan for transforming technology. For example, the Ministry of Machinery and Electronics Industry in conjunction with the Ministry of Machine-Building Industry have formulated the following plan to transform traditional industries with electronic technology:

1. Key technology systems
   a. Spread CAD to the enterprises whose products need rapid change.
   b. Spread CAT to enterprises that need high quality.
   c. Spread CAM to the enterprises that make diversified products.
   d. Spread office automation to large-scale enterprises.
   e. Spread digital control, digital display technologies for renovated machine tools.
   f. Spread engineering control systems for the renovation of industrial kilns or furnaces.
   g. Spread separate industrial control systems for individual product lines.
   h. Spread AC speed controller technology for air blowers and water pumps.
   i. Use an electric load control system for electric networks and electric supply systems.
   j. Use a computer-assisted transportation control system for airports, seaports, railways, and highway systems.
2. Tasks in detail
   a. Enterprises within MEI and MMBI:
      i. Machine tools: Renew 20,000 old machines; produce 25,000 digital control systems; produce 15,000 sets of digital display equipment; renew 1,000 sets of punching machines and shearing machines.
      ii. Industrial boilers: renew 3,000 old boilers; produce 1,000 boilers with an engineering control system.
      iii. Renew 3,000 sets of other types of kilns and caves.
      iv. Renew 20,000 air blowers and water pumps.
      v. Apply 500 sets of a CAD/CAM system.
      vi. Set up 20 automatic stereoscopic warehouses.
      vii. Set up a CAM system in 500 factories.
      viii. Set up or renew 500 product lines.
   b. Enterprises outside the purview of MEI/MMBI: the main focus is on processing control, textile machine control, automatic tobacco processing, power station inspection, transportation control, office automation, and CAD/CAM systems. MEI/MMBI will provide services such as:
      i. Renew 50,000 old machine tools.
      ii. Renew 10,000 kilns.
      iii. Renew 100,000 air blowers and water pumps.
      iv. Renew 2,000 punching machines.
      v. Provide 3,000 CAD/CAM systems.
      vi. Provide 300 sets of automatic stereoscopic warehouse systems.
      vii. Provide 200 industrial robots.

viii. Provide 1,000 transportation control systems.
iv. Provide electronic-load control systems for 36 big cities.
x. Provide half a million office automation systems.
xi. Provide textile machine control systems for half a million spindles.

Evaluating the Government's Plan for Technical Transformation

In the past ten years, despite persistent problems, technical transformation in China has had many successes. New industries have been established, enabling China to produce a large number of new products, and Chinese industries in general are making strides. The results of the plan overall war positive. Compared with the previous plan, the Eighth Five-Year Plan is different in response to both macroeconomic and microeconomic factors. The current plan focuses on more crucial areas such as main industrial bases, main projects, main technologies, and main enterprises; it also more strongly emphasizes the importance of the electronics industry and pays greater attention to domestic adaptation of imported technologies rather than simply importing more equipment. The current plan aims to speed up transfer of new technologies from laboratories to commercial production. Even this plan, however, is plagued by some serious persistent problems, reviewed in the following paragraphs.

A Government-Driven Plan

In general, under this plan the government is still the driving force and most enterprises are still in a passive position, where they lack any internal motivation or dynamic to improve their technology. China has more than 100,000 state-owned enterprises and more than 1.7 million collective enterprises, including TVEs. If the enterprises themselves are not motivated to renovate their technologies as part of their daily functioning, and rely on a push from the government, China can have little hope of reaching the advanced technology level of the rest of the world. For this reason, how to make further reform and to give enterprises enough authority and responsibility, as well as how to create the internal dynamic mechanism enterprises will need to constitute the government's first important task. Without resolving these issues, transformation will remain government-driven, with little hope for the success an enterprise-driven effort could produce.

A Lack of Measures for Implementing Industrial Policy

While the central government has been decentralizing authority to local governments and to some enterprises, it has neglected to provide them with industrial policies to guide industrial development. This created inefficient competition among local governments and enterprises, as well as a waste of resources. Good examples can be found in the transformation of the color TV, washing machine, and refrigerator industries. Because of the lack of a central policy guide, almost every province that produces them has been trying to transform old factories or to set up new factories. As a result, these industries depend heavily on imported parts and components. The lack of guidance also led to too much market demand in too short a time.

In March 1989 China issued industrial policies, but the policies were too unrefined for the local government and industries to follow and provided no detailed measures for enterprises to follow. The key problem now is to complete and to revise the industrial policies, and to strengthen the statements of specific measures. China's State Planning Commission has specifically been charged with the task of solving this problem.

Decentralized Power without Local Government Responsibility

Because of the decentralization of power, capital resources are more diverse: where once investment capital came only from the central government, now resources are available from local governments, domestic bank loans, foreign capital, and capital collected by enterprises themselves. The ratio of central government investment to total investment was 17.6 percent in 1980 and only 4.4 percent in 1985, and it is getting smaller and smaller. Bank loans, on the other hand, are getting bigger and bigger, from 24.5 percent in 1980 to 41.6 percent in 1985 (Table 11.1). With this alteration in financial capacity, the investment ability of collectives and private business is getting stronger compared with state-owned enterprises. The investment capacity of local governments, banks, and enterprises is likewise getting stronger compared with the central government. The central government, however, is still responsible for almost everything, although its power has been split among local governments and some enterprises. This remains a big burden for the central government and leads to a lack of order in the division of investment among the central government, local governments, and enterprises.

Irrational Input Ratio between Imported Technological Equipment and Domestic R&D

In the past ten years, China has paid considerable attention to importing technology. The total expenditure over this period for imported technology and equipment was about US$50 billion. Expenditures for domestic R&D, on the other hand, constituted less than 1 percent of GNP: the highest year (1986) was 9.59 billion yuan. At the exchange rate between the U.S. dollar and the Chinese yuan at that time (US$1:RMB¥3.45), 9.59 billion yuan comes to about US$2.78 billion. Expenditure for domestic R&D was just over half of a percent of expenditures on

Table 11.1

Capital Resources of State-owned Enterprises for Technical Transformation (%)

Resources	1980	1981	1982	1983	1984	1985	1981- 85
Financial allocations from state	17.6	17.9	13.1	12.5	14.8	16.0	11.3
Domestic loans	24.5	20.5	25.6	25.6	29.7	41.6	30.6
Foreign investment	—	0.6	1.1	0.9	0.9	1.2	1.0
Funds collected by localities and enterprises themselves	57.9	57.9	57.1	59.1	53.0	50.8	54.8
Others	—	3.1	3.1	1.9	1.6	2.3	2.3

Source: *China's Fixed Assets Investment Statistical Data (1950-85)*, p. 218. Beijing: State Statistical Bureau.

imported technology and equipment. This low figure for domestic R&D makes sense in the early days of economic reform, with its open-door policy toward new technology that can vastly improve the productivity of Chinese industry. In the meantime, however, it has an impact on domestic R&D ability, a well as on China's domestic enterprises' ability to absorb and utilize imported technology. This is one important reason why China has imported so much foreign technology, but this latter ability is still weak and affects the process of technical transformation.

Irrational Ratio between Investment for Technical Transformation and Investment for New Factories.

During the 1950s, 1960s and the 1970s, investment in the transformation of existing enterprises increased rapidly. In the last ten years, however, investment in existing enterprises has remained almost level at 33 percent (Table 11.2). At present, China has 1,178.7 billion yuan fixed assets calculated in the original value (only state-owned assets), but had only 823.8 billion yuan fixed assets calculated in net value at the end of 1988. If China does not close this gap by increasing investment for existing assets, the effects could threaten the country's economy. It is therefore better for China to increase investment for technological transformation, instead of increasing investment for setting up new factories. As of 1993, there is evidence that this is indeed what has started to happen in China.

Low Depreciation Rate for Fixed Assets

China's depreciation rate for fixed assets is too low to meet the needs of technical change. To enhance enterprises' capacity for technical transformation, the

Table 11.2

Structure of Fixed Assets Investment for State-owned Enterprises (%)

	Capital Construction Investment	Technical Transformation Investment
1958–62	92.28	7.72
1963–65	84.47	15.53
1966–70	81.72	18.28
1971–75	77.49	22.51
1976–80	73.51	26.49
1981–85	63.97	28.03
1986–89	58.76	33.03
1986	59.48	31.30
1987	58.45	33.01
1988	56.98	35.49
1989	61.20	31.11

Source: *Planning Economy Study* (1991), p. 76. Beijing: State Statistical Bureau.

depreciation system for enterprises' fixed assets must be improved so that it can be a source of funds for enterprises to renovate their technology and equipment in a timely way. During the last ten years the depreciation rate has been raised from 4.1–4.2 percent to 5 percent as a result of economic reform. This ratio is still too low. At such a rate, the depreciation period of fixed assets would be about twenty years, compared with only five years for machine-tool equipment in the United States and only seven years in Japan.

Another problem is that depreciation funds cannot be guaranteed to enable enterprises to renovate equipment. Every so often the fund would be needed for other purposes, such as floating capital or welfare, or part might be taken away by the leading department of the government.

Remedies

To overcome the problems discussed above, and ultimately to improve the technical transformation process in China, the following measures are recommended:

First, further reform should focus on increasing the vitality of state-owned enterprises, with particular emphasis on their operational system so that they can become independent economic entities with full management authority and full responsibility for their own profits and losses. Autonomous operational systems can be a rational system for Chinese state-owned enterprises, as opposed to privatization. In other words, if the rights and responsibilities of the owners are separated from those of the operators of the enterprise, and the latter are allowed to function by themselves, they will benefit from their own output and will be more motivated to improve their technology.

In the meantime, the creation of market functions to produce a competitive environment for enterprises should also force them to improve their technology. Measures that can help this process include loosening price controls and allowing high-tech products to have higher prices and yield higher profits, charging lower or no taxes for higher-technology items and subsidizing banks to provide lower interest rates to high-tech industries.

Second, China must define and complete its industrial development strategy and tasks for a certain period and then formulate practical, achievable industrial and technology policies to guide local governments and enterprises. The key issue here is the convergence of the two kinds of policies—especially of high-tech and traditional industry. Only in this way can China establish a well-defined technological trajectory for itself.

Third, the central government must clearly define its own responsibilities, as well as those of local governments and enterprises in economic development. The central government should be responsible for nationwide projects such as infrastructure, basic industries, and new industries. Enterprises should be responsible for their own technological progress, including technical transformation and renovation. Local governments could do something in between, such as developing industries that use local resources. After power is decentralized to local government, the central government will no longer need or be able to take care of everything.

Fourth, investment for technical transformation must be increased, especially when requested by local governments and enterprises. Under the present contract system between the central and local governments, and between government and enterprises, short-run behavior is all too common. Local governments generally pay attention only to the number of new factories in terms of added job opportunities, tax income, and so on, and are less interested in taking care of existing enterprises. Enterprises are generally interested in ways to increase their profits and are less interested in maintenance of old equipment. The government must therefore enact measures to force local governments and enterprises to increase their input to technical improvement.

Finally, China must raise its depreciation rate for fixed assets from an average of 5 percent to 12–15 percent—with a minimum of 10 percent. This would allow Chinese industries to depreciate their equipment within seven to ten years which would in turn allow them sufficient funds to allocate to timely technological improvement.

In conclusion, technical transformation in China will be an important task in the 1990s. The targets and measures of this program are more clear and more practical than they were in the previous decade. The fundamental style of technical transformation, however, has not changed—it is still government-driven. This must change to an enterprise-driven style if China is to keep pace with the worldwide trend of technical change. Such a change of orientation will no doubt bring a series of reforms in China's existing economic structure—no small task, and something still, apparently, far off. Nonetheless, this is the only way China can go; it cannot stop following the global trend of technology development. China's present economy is much closer to the world market than it was ten years ago. It has felt increasing pressure and greater challenges from the world market that compel it to hasten the development of its own technology. This also compels China to accelerate its economic reform. Thus, economic reform will be the only choice for China to develop its economy, including changes affecting its system of technical transformation.

References

China's Fixed Assets Investment Statistical Data, 1950–85. Beijing's State Statistical Bureau.

Planning Economy Study, 1991. Beijing: State Statistical Bureau.

Qing-Qi, Shi. *Technological Progress and Economic Growth*. Science and Technology Data Press, 1985.

Simon, Denis, and Jingping Ding. *China's Acquisition and Assimilation of Foreign Technology: A Forty-Year Assessment*. In press.

12

Upgrading Hong Kong's Technology Base

Winston W. Liang and W. Michael Denny

Hong Kong: Past and Present

Since its founding as a British settlement in 1841, hard work, entrepreneurial energy, and a government policy of "positive nonintervention" have made Hong Kong one of the most prosperous and most productive societies in the world. Per capita income (adjusted for purchasing power) is nearly US$14,000, a figure higher than both Britain and Japan. Life expectancy in fast-paced Hong Kong averages 77.5 years, one of the highest among industrialized countries. Hong Kong is also the world's eleventh largest trading entity. With a population of 5.8 million, the city's per capita exports are almost $15,000—over ten times that of the average American per capita export and six times that of Japan. The total land area is only 1,075 square kilometers, making Hong Kong one of the most densely populated places in the world. Indeed, the density in the metropolitan areas exceeds 20,000 people per square kilometer. Carrying over 2.1 million passengers daily, the mass transit railway is, relative to the length of the system, the busiest underground railway in the world (Roberts, 1991, p. 244).

Hong Kong's traditional role has been as a trade link between China and the rest of the world, and as a regional light manufacturing and financial center. Today, Hong Kong is in transition. At the end of the 1970s, it remained a low-cost manufacturing center whose economy could be considered independently from that of China. Today, due to China's open-door policies, the Hong Kong and Chinese economies are increasingly integrated. Thus, if we consider Hong Kong as an independent economic entity, the relative contributions of the manu-

Figure 12.1. **Relative Contributions of Industrial Sectors to Employment in Hong Kong**

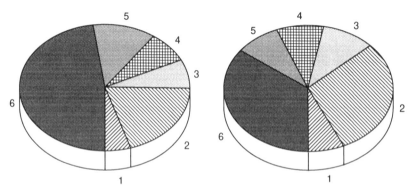

1: Transportation
2: Trade
3: Finance, Insurance, Real Estate
4: Service
5: Others
6: Manufacturing

Source: Stanford Research Institute, 1989, (p. 10).

facturing and services sectors have changed dramatically during the past two decades (see Figure 12.1).

Accompanying the decline of manufacturing and the ascent of the services industry, the most significant change has been the replacement of the textile industry by electronics manufacturing. The contribution of textiles to GDP declined from 27 percent in 1973 to 16 percent in 1988 and has been almost entirely offset by the increase (from 10 percent to 19 percent) of electrical appliances, electronics, watches, and clocks during the same period (Roberts, 1991, p. 56).

This shift from manufacturing to services and, within manufacturing, from textiles to electronics is true enough; but it reflects an obsolete view of an isolated Hong Kong economy. Taken as an economy integrated with Southern China, the statistics tell a different story.

Although manufacturing accounts for some 700,000 employees within Hong Kong, another 2 million by official estimate (4 million unofficially) are employed in Guangdong and managed from Hong Kong—up from essentially none in the late 1970s. An estimated 50,000 Hong Kong managers commute regularly to and from Guangdong to supervise employees in some 16,000 Hong Kong-owned factories—primarily in the textiles, electronics, and plastics industries (*Economist*, 1991, p. 15). Travel is now so frequent between Guangdong and Hong Kong that the average Hong Kong resident makes three trips per year to China.

The shift to services is much more dramatic than an isolated view of Hong Kong's economy would anticipate. Hong Kong is now servicing a major increase in the manufacturing and export sector of Southern China. In addition, Hong Kong has become the regional headquarters for Western business in Asia. As of 1991, some 600 multinational companies use Hong Kong as their regional head-quarters in Asia and an increasing number of other Asian countries are setting up subsidiaries in Hong Kong to access China.

The success of Hong Kong's changing economy thus depends on its ability to quickly absorb and incorporate emerging technologies into its growing electronics and global service industries. Its increasing integration with China requires that it use technology to support growing design, marketing, and management of existing manufacturing industries (e.g., electronics, textiles, plastics, toys, watches, electrical appliances, etc.), and to develop new knowledge-based industries, software applications, and biotechnology industries such as pharmaceuticals and food.

Hong Kong's Governmental Environment

Hong Kong has flourished with a strong and well-publicized governmental policy of nonintervention. Historically, government expenditure accounts for only about 16 percent of GDP and all other levels of funding in this report must be seen in this light (Roberts, 1991, p. 412). This does not mean that the government is unconcerned with economic development. However, rather than positively guide the development of science and technology, the government has seen its role as removing obstacles and providing a supportive infrastructure in which business can flourish. Through an extensive network of committees and councils, the government enjoys a wide consultation with senior business executives. In fact, specific business sectors are explicitly represented in the legislative council along with representatives from townships and geographical regions.

Hong Kong's Strengths and Limitations

Entrepreneurial Business Climate

Praised by Nobel laureate Milton Friedman as the world's best example of free enterprise, Hong Kong businesses are generally constrained only by "the bottom line." Regulatory agencies impose few constraints, taxes are low, and starting one's own company is an almost universal aspiration. This entrepreneurial culture has fostered a very business-oriented culture in Hong Kong. "Where are you making your fortune?" (*Hai bin do fai choi?*) is a common greeting during the day, and if science and technology is to be valued, it, like any other business skill, must contribute to the bottom line.

Entrepot to China

Widespread use of English, familiarity with both Western and Asian trade practices, and geographical location have long made Hong Kong the trade entrepot
with China and much of Asia. Its deep-seaport is now the world's busiest, handling over 7 million tones of cargo per month. Hong Kong's position as a Special
Administrative Region (SAR) of China in 1997 will give it unique access to both
low-cost labor and the immense Chinese market. Already some 80 percent of
Hong Kong's re-exports either originate in or are destined for China (Roberts,
1991, p. 58).

In addition to trade, Hong Kong is also increasingly China's business skills
entrepot. As manufacturing relocates from Hong Kong to Guangdong Province,
Hong Kong manufacturing and management skills are taught "on the job" in
South China. Given the success of the emerging Hong Kong and Southern Chinese economy, China is likely to increase its reliance on Hong Kong's international marketing and business expertise.

Telecommunications Infrastructure

The sophistication and extent of Hong Kong's telecommunications infrastructure
have grown to support its growing trade and service sectors. This communications network is a major reason companies give for locating in Hong Kong
(second only to geographical location, according to the 1991 *American Chamber
of Commerce Annual Business Survey*) (ACCHK, 1991, p. 13).

With 1.8 persons per telephone, pagers used by 12 percent of the population,
the largest urban optical fiber network, and the highest penetration of hand-held
cellular telephones in the world (2.3 percent, with an annual growth rate of 47
percent), Hong Kong businesses are exceptionally well connected (Kao and
Young, 1991, pp. 39, 40). Food critics often cite the number of pagers per table
as a measure of the relative tranquility customers can expect at Hong Kong
restaurants. FAX and computer telecommunications are so prevalent that data
traffic is growing at 80 percent per year (Bell, 1991, p. 37).

International telecommunications service is exceptionally strong in Hong
Kong. Almost one-third of Hong Kong's 210 million outgoing IDD calls are data
calls, and FAX communications now exceed voice communications between the
United States and Hong Kong. This intensive data-related business traffic requires a very reliable, high-bandwidth service. Since 1985 Hong Kong
Telecomms International has not had any disruptions of international service to
more than 50 percent of its subscribers (while countries such as Japan, the
United States, and Singapore have had two, four, and six such disruptions respectively).

Businesses in Hong Kong are also supported by several specialized services
such as video conferencing, FAX store and forward, and a variety of interna-

tional data services. As another example, an international "800" service allows callers in the United States to dial Hong Kong companies toll-free. A similar service allows Hong Kong customers to call U.S. companies at no charge to the caller.

Hong Kong is served by several long distance service providers (among them, AT&T, MCI, and SPRINT), and its international telecommunications rates are the second lowest in the world. Communication with China, North America, Europe, Taiwan, Japan, and Korea is via optical fiber. Within a few years Hong Kong will become the center of the Asia Pacific Cable System (APC) linking Singapore (with its first fiber-optics submarine cable) to Hong Kong, Malaysia, Taiwan, and Japan. In addition, six satellite stations and two more under construction link Hong Kong to the Pacific and Indian Ocean Intel/Sat satellites.

Telecommunications service to China is growing rapidly and currently consists of some 800 satellite, 3,000 fiber-optic, and 1,200 microwave circuits.

Hong Kong International

All of the above factors have begun to propel Hong Kong into the global marketplace. A few representative examples: Semitech HK has purchased U.S.-based Singer, internationalized its market, broadened its product line, and announced joint consumer electronics ventures with Emerson Electric; Hutchison Telecoms has become a global telecommunications company through purchases of similar operations in England and Australia. AsiaSat 1, Asia's first domestic communications satellite, is jointly owned by Hutchison (HK), Cable and Wireless System Ltd., and CITIC of China. Its catchment area includes some 2.7 billion people in the most economically active region in the world. While the financial outcome of this massive investment may not be known for another three to five years, it has given Hong Kong substantial experience in integrating the technical, sociopolitical, and financial issues of pan-Asian telecommunications.

Impediments to Growth of Science and Technology

Shortage of Professionals

The labor market in Hong Kong has been tight since the mid-1970s, with seasonally adjusted unemployment and underemployment during 1989 and 1990 of approximately 1.4 percent and 0.8 percent, respectively (Roberts, 1991, p. 54). Against this background, it is not surprising that a shortage of trained technical and technical management professionals is the largest single issue restraining Hong Kong's technological progress.

Hong Kong's rapid growth as a regional financial center has, paradoxically, contributed to this labor power shortage. Finance, management, and trading draw their share of talented students away from engineering. And within the science and technology professions, graduates prefer "fast track" careers in marketing and management to those in product design and development.

Predominance of Small Companies and "Small Company Perceptions"

Some 95 percent of Hong Kong businesses have fewer than fifty employees and 45 percent of Hong Kong employees are employed in companies with fewer than one hundred. Because of their small size, companies are reluctant to take the risks of a technology-driven approach to business. They have instead evolved the business attitude of responding to markets and orders rather than attempting to "lead the market" with technological innovation. These attitudes, in addition to the capital required, make it difficult to develop new high-technology-driven products.

Small companies have added difficulties in incorporating emerging technologies that they themselves have not invented. Besides often being unaware of recent developments, they are often not equipped to evaluate the risks, trade-offs, and potential rewards of using them. They are usually unfamiliar with high-tech decisions, contracting, and licensing procedures.

Small owner-managed companies in Hong Kong also have a tradition of carrying little external debt and a very short-term investment horizon. Financing is usually from within the family rather than from banks or venture capital firms. Correspondingly, banks and other sources of capital are inexperienced in venture capital issues, and are reluctant to provide funds to small companies without objective evaluations of the risk/reward of the investment.

Technologies Essential to Hong Kong's Prosperity

Which technologies are most crucial to Hong Kong's future? Technical management and information technology are crucial enabling technologies that underpin both the service sector and manufacturing.

In the shift of labor-intensive manufacturing to China, Hong Kong firms have generally retained the skilled activities such as testing, quality control, marketing, and management in Hong Kong. Also, an increasing number of firms recognize the benefits of doing their own design work and developing their own products.

Technology Management and Technical Project Management

Upgrading management skills has thus become increasingly important. Not only must traditional face-to-face techniques of owner-managers give way to increased telecommunications and management information systems (MIS), but management itself must be increasingly aware of the impact of technology on company financing, product design, and manufacture. This will require management training with an increased differentiation to increase sector focus, seniority of trainees, and participation of the private sector.

The new Hong Kong University of Science and Technology, through cooperative programs with UCLA's Anderson School of Business and the American Chamber of Commerce in Hong Kong, has recently begun to address this issue. Short one- to two-week executive management courses have been targeted specifically on technology management and complement other courses offered by the Hong Kong Management Association.

In addition to management skills, Hong Kong has recently begun to identify key technologies for emphasis. The fields of information, manufacturing, advanced materials, and biotechnology provide the multidisciplinary support Hong Kong's economy needs.

Information Technology

Information technology has become a major tool by which service companies secure a competitive advantage. The combination of data processing, telecommunications, and other emerging technologies has changed the face of finance, tourism, and business offices in the last decade. Most of these changes have allowed smaller work forces to accomplish more with higher quality—exactly the sort of improvement needed in Hong Kong's tight labor market.

Moreover, information technologies are exceptionally well suited to Hong Kong businesses. First, microprocessors, software, and telecommunications support cost reductions all along the value-added chain from production inputs to market distribution and post-sales service. Second, and even more important, information technologies can cost-effectively support very heterogeneous markets. This move away from mass markets to tailored products with a short development cycle is especially suitable for Hong Kong's small businesses and market-driven business culture, and is already emerging in Hong Kong's apparel industry.

Computer-aided and integrated design and manufacturing have become tools that are not simply used to reduce labor costs. Now CAD/CAM/CIM is widely used to improve the quality of manufacture, shorten the time between concept and delivery of finished products, and replace mass manufacturing with more varied "targeted" products. As more design and product prototyping is done in Hong Kong in support of global marketing, these technologies will become critical to all existing industries: apparel, plastics, electronics, toys, watches, and so on.

Hong Kong's future ability to create wealth will thus depend on its flexible response to changing markets and technologies. Speed to market with the best appropriate technology will be vital for success. All this will depend on both an advanced informatics infrastructure and its connection to global networks of markets, banks, production centers, and laboratories. Only this constant exchange of knowledge on markets, technologies, designs, specifications, drawings, and the like will allow production to be altered rapidly to meet changing market requirements.

Thus, sophisticated telecommunications, combined with market-driven telecommunications policies and state-of-the-art value-added services built on this informatics infrastructure will assume even greater importance. For example, new techniques for "paperless" handling of business information have made electronic data interchange (EDI) increasingly important. Many vendors, offering EDI products and service, are active in Hong Kong, and there are already a number of private sector projects using this technique. The Hong Kong government is keen to adopt EDI and has indicated that it will use international standards wherever they are available. Because of the liberal environment in this area, Hong Kong will continue to enjoy the services provided by a multiplicity of international vendors.

Advanced Manufacturing Technology

Recent advances in automated garment production allow rapid inclusion of design changes in finished products, short customized production runs, and high uniform quality, and operate at approximately 30 percent reduction in floor space. All of these advantages support Hong Kong's strategic shift to an apparel design and marketing center.

In plastics, the approximately fifteen precision mold makers will require multiaxis computer numeric controlled machine tools of increased accuracy. Plastics producers themselves will require an increased variety of new molding techniques including reaction-injection molding and reinforced reaction-injection molding.

A key element of increased local electronics design is the ability to produce application-specific integrated circuits (ASICs) as a part of locally designed products. In order to be responsive to customer and product needs, ASICs should be designed locally and with close interaction between the designer and the end users.

Materials Technology

Material technologies are important to Hong Kong because the factories in Guangdong use so many materials. Understanding the behavior of new materials, especially "designer materials," is crucial for effective designs that use them and for implementing effective manufacturing techniques.

Understanding materials is also important to Hong Kong, not because Hong Kong intends to compete with industrialized countries to develop new materials, but because the proper use of advanced materials in the plastics, textile, and electronic components industries will allow Hong Kong to combine the low-cost labor of Southern China with state-of-the-art materials technology.

In the apparel and textile industries, new dyes and new thermal (heat), moisture, elasticity, and wear properties of woven and knitted cloth would increase Hong Kong's competitiveness in world markets. The plastics industries would benefit from developments in polymeric resins and fiber-reinforced composites (e.g., sporting goods, automobile parts, or bicycles).

Biotechnology

Biotechnology has several attractions for Hong Kong. Waste treatment by membrane separation and microbial treatment would reduce the environmental impact of both the plastics and the textile industries. Moreover, biotechnology cuts across the related areas of medicine, agriculture, food processing, and the production of organic chemicals. It also has large potential markets in both developing countries such as China and the industrialized world. Finally, it requires relatively modest capitalization and seems well suited to university laboratories and small start-up companies.

Mechanisms for Upgrading Science and Technology in Hong Kong

Effective upgrading of science and technology in Hong Kong embraces a number of activities: applied research and development, consulting services, degree granting and professional postgraduate education, technology transfer, and "incubator" facilities for start-up high technology companies. All of these activities ultimately apply and adapt technologies developed in Hong Kong and abroad to Hong Kong business—either through their products or services, or by improving the effectiveness of the business itself. Both uses of technology contribute to "the bottom line" of corporate success.

An oft-repeated strategy for implementing technology transfer and upgrading throughout Asia combines (a) strong government support, (b) precise national technical objectives, (c) dynamic science and technology centers and (d) robust educational institutions. Hong Kong has pursued this strategy "from the bottom up." Rather than decide technology policy from the top down and then provide funding and financial incentives consistent with the government's policy, Hong Kong has instead identified constraints to its economic growth and then established institutions and removed obstacles to local industry to alleviate these restrictions.

Higher Education Institutions

Hong Kong's traditional contacts with Britain and, more recently, with the United States have helped it build a strong tertiary educational system. Extensive use is made of Western-educated professors and expatriates. Moreover, an extensive peer review system has been developed whereby course syllabi, final examinations, and students' papers are constantly reviewed and validated by external examiners from other industrialized countries.

The seven institutions of tertiary education produce some 10,000 graduates annually with another 140,000 enrolled in technician-level courses. With the new Hong Kong University of Science and Technology and increased enrollments, this number is expected to increase by about 50 percent by 1995. Postgraduate research positions will increase from about 900 in 1990–91 to over 2,000 by 1994–95 (Roberts, 1991, p. 128).

Joint research projects with partners outside Hong Kong are an important part of higher education in Hong Kong: in 1990–91 264 such projects were underway in Hong Kong universities. An additional 21,000 students furthered their tertiary education by studying in Europe, Australia, and North America in 1991.

Academic contributions to industrial applied research in Hong Kong have, in the past, been limited. However, the Polytechnics and Universities have recently adopted new policies and institutions to change this. Through financial incentives and sabbaticals from teaching, faculty have been encouraged to seek independent joint projects with local and overseas industries. Also, to support long-term projects and relationships with industry, the tertiary institutions have recently formed several applied research institutes. They are listed (along with date of establishment) as examples and represent all such institutes (see Appendix, Figure A.1, page 272).

City Polytechnic of Hong Kong:
• UNISYS and City Polytechnic Joint R&D Facility (1990);
• Centre for Environmental Technology for Industry (1990).

Hong Kong Polytechnic:
• China Business Development Centre (1991);
• Business and Technology Centre (1990) (incorporating the Quality and Reliability Centre and the Precision Engineering Centre)
• Hong Kong Plastics Technology Centre (1988);
• Centre for Maritime Studies (1991);
• Rehabilitation Engineering Centre (1987).

University of Hong Kong:
• Swire Marine Laboratory (1990);
• Institute for Molecular Biology (1989);
• The Centre for Urban Studies and Urban Planning (1980);
• Kadoorie Agriculture Research Centre (1986);
• Dental Materials Science Unit (1980);
• Centre for Asian Studies (1967) (Macroeconomic and Geopolitical Issues).

Chinese University of Hong Kong:
- Asia-Pacific Institute of Business (1990);
- Biotechnology Laboratory (1986);
- Marine Science Laboratory (1970);
- Centre for Environmental Studies (1990);
- Chinese Medicinal Materials Research Centre (1979);
- Research Laboratory for Food Protein Production (1977);
- Hong Kong Institute of Biotechnology (1988).

Hong Kong University of Science and Technology:
- Biotechnology Research Institute (1990);
- Technology Transfer Centre (1991);
- Information Technology Research Institute (1990).

Science and Technology Centers

In addition to the on-campus industrial centers, a broadly based group of independent technical centers has been established to improve the use of technology in Hong Kong's business context. The approach has been to establish a series of separate institutions, each of which is partially or wholly self-supporting and each of which plays a unique role in technology development and its integration with business.

Broadly coordinated through a network of cross-board memberships, these institutions address the issues of:

1. Incubation and technology transfer for high-tech start-up companies, particularly in information and materials technology (Hong Kong Industrial Technology Centre);
2. Providing multidisciplinary consultation and professional postgraduate and technical education to companies in Hong Kong (Hong Kong Productivity Council and Hong Kong Industrial Technology Centre);
3. Providing industry-specific technical centers for applied research (several design centers under the auspices of the Vocational Training Council):
   a. Management Development Centre (research and training, especially of small, owner-managed companies);
   b. Application-specific Integrated Circuit (ASIC) Design Centre;
   c. Electronic Data Processing Centre;
   d. Precision Sheet Metal Processing Centre.

Technology Roadmaps for Hong Kong

The Hong Kong government has generally refrained from naming specific technologies, or products, for fear of directing local businesses into specific technologies. Hong Kong's prosperity has largely resulted from little government intervention. (Indeed, the 1991 *Annual Business Survey* by the American Chamber of Commerce [p. 21] found that only one-third of responding companies favored increased government control over economic development). A major issue for Hong Kong government is how to provide support for science and technology development while remaining true to its highly publicized, popular, and successful policy of "positive nonintervention" in Hong Kong business.

In mid-1991, six tertiary educational institutions with the support of the Hong Kong Industrial Development Board collaborated on a report on "Technology Roadmaps for Hong Kong," an in-depth study of four technology areas that hold special promise for Hong Kong business. The report was published in book form (Kao and Young, 1991), has enjoyed wide circulation in Hong Kong, and was the subject of a major follow-up conference in November, 1991. The conference brought together academic researchers, entrepreneurs, and professionals from the public and private sectors to extend the report by further identifying emerging high-tech business opportunities. Several specific products and R&D projects in these technological fields formed the basis of discussions and emerging business plans (see Figure 12.2).

Technology and R&D Linkage with China

Just as technology follows business directives in Hong Kong, so technology linkage with China is based on business motivations. Since the adoption of China's open door policies in 1978, China and Hong Kong have become each other's largest trading partners. In addition, Hong Kong is increasingly important as a center for entrepot, transshipment, and other supporting activities involving China. More than 80 percent of the goods re-exported through Hong Kong are destined for or originate in China. This makes Hong Kong a vital services center for China in general and Southern China in particular.

Technical linkage with China falls into three categories: The first includes academic exchange programs supported by the University and Polytechnic Grants Committee (UPGC) (See Figure 12.3).

The second category comprises the transfer of business, manufacturing, and marketing skills, which accompanies the relocation of Hong Kong's manufacturing to China and development of Chinese interfaces with Hong Kong's technologically sophisticated services. Although more difficult to quantify, the economic impact of this restructuring has been described earlier. Finally, in the third category are joint ventures between Chinese and Hong Kong companies that combine Chinese-developed technologies with Hong Kong's marketing and product development expertise. Through annual "technology trade fairs" held in Hong Kong by the Trade Development Council and through programs such as TORCH, Chinese technology is increasingly accessible to Hong Kong companies and universities. Institutions such as the Technology Transfer Center of The

Figure 12.2. **Technology Roadmaps for Hong Kong Proposed Technologies and Products**

Information Technology
- Medical imaging system for hospital groups via broadband telecommunications networks

Biotechnology
- Medical electronics devices and instruments, e.g., portable multiparameter patient monitors
- Diagnositc reagents, e.g., diagnostics for regional diseases
- Food products, e.g., cost reduction through the use of microorganisms in fermentation

Materials
- Metals and plastics, e.g., use of conform extrusion equipment for very flexible processes
- Electronic materials, e.g., studies of insulating thin films and electrically active dopants
- Building materials, e.g., establishment of permanent facilities for fire rating period testing

Large-scale Environmental Technology
- Multidisciplinary survey, assessment, evaluation, planning (may require access to super computing facilities)
- Waste treatment technologies adapted to Hong Kong's stringent space requirements

---

Hong Kong University of Science and Technology (HKUST), Hong Kong Institute of Biotechnology, Hong Kong Productivity Council, and the Hong Kong Industrial Technology Centre are expected to accelerate this integration.

Future Trend of Hong Kong Science and Technology

Closer Links with China

Hong Kong's improved access to the growing Chinese market will be coupled with access to China's very large pool of scientists. Although small as a percentage of the total population, the number of highly trained scientists in China is numerically quite large, and this sector of the work force is not yet fully utilized in the Chinese economy. Increased cooperation between Hong Kong and Chinese scientists and technologists should go a long way toward remedying the chronic shortage of scientists in Hong Kong (see Appendix, Figure A.2, page 273).

Figure 12.3. **Recurrent Funding for Academic Linkages with China**
(Exchanges and Joint Projects)

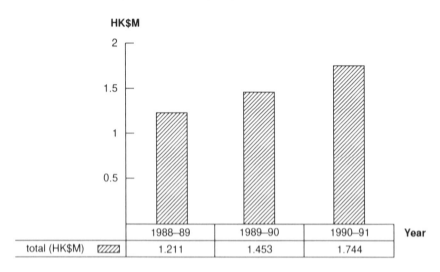

	1988–89	1989–90	1990–91	Year
total (HK$M)	1.211	1.453	1.744	

Closer Cooperation among Government, Industry, and Higher Education

The Hong Kong Government has recognized the need to provide more incentives to encourage cooperation among government, industry, and academic sectors. A new fund, now in the planning stage, will provide additional applied R&D funds for selected projects on a cost-sharing basis with industries. This new fund will bring together scientists and engineers from institutes of higher education and from industry to develop new products for the world market.

Strengthen the Necessary Infrastructure

Present trends indicate that by the year 2000 Hong Kong may become a "servopolis" linking Asia and especially China to Europe and North America and focusing primarily on service and high technology production. In order to support this trend, the Hong Kong government continues to strengthen the intellectual infrastructure of the territory. First among these is a major effort to increase the number of science, technology, and management professionals in Hong Kong with bachelor's degrees and above.

HKUST is Hong Kong's newest publicly funded university. Founded to emphasize science, engineering, technology, business, and management studies, HKUST has occupied its new sixty-hectare campus since the Fall of 1991 with an initial enrollment of 700. Senior academics from the Anderson Graduate

School of Management of UCLA and other centers of excellence are being seconded to help set up the various departments. Phase II was completed in 1993, and 1996 enrollment is planned to be 7,000. The Polytechnic Industrial Center, a project that began in 1989, is scheduled for completion in early 1992. It will house expanded industrial training facilities for students of the Hong Kong Polytechnic and the City Polytechnic of Hong Kong. It will also house the Plastics Technology Centre and coordinate with expansions of both polytechnic campuses.

Science Park

The Hong Kong Industrial Technology Centre occupied its initial premises in Fall 1991 and moved to its purpose-built facilities in 1993. Modeled after similar institutions in Japan, Europe, and the United States, HKITC acts as an "incubator" for high-technology start-up companies and a technology transfer agent between academia, industry, and sources of overseas technology (see Appendix, Figure A.3, page 274). Past experience has shown that with the support of an incubator the success rate of start-ups jumps to around 80 percent. The HKITC also acts as an independent third party in assisting resident start-up companies to obtain financing. Because of its in-depth knowledge of each company, HKITC is able to objectively evaluate the financial risk/reward for banks and venture capital firms, and assist the bank and the start-up company to reach a common understanding. This service is vital in introducing Hong Kong financial institutions to the emerging world of high-technology financing.

In addition to the HKITC, the Industrial Development Board (the principle advisory body to the Hong Kong government on industrial development issues) has endorsed a recommendation that a site be earmarked for a science park in Hong Kong. Such a park would be a logical addition to the technology infrastructure of Hong Kong, and should be finally approved when the HKITC has provided evidence of a substantial demand from suitable resident companies.

Strategic Alliances between Hong Kong and Overseas Technology Companies

Another aspect of Hong Kong's emerging high tech service sector has been an increasing trend to form strategic alliances between Hong Kong, regional manufacturing, and overseas technology companies. As with the present alliances with Chinese manufacturing, we can expect future affiliations to be based principally on clear business reasons rather than on temporary (and often market-distorting) government initiatives.

Several such business motivations are emerging. Technology companies in Europe and North America need increasing access to low-cost labor, Asian markets, and capital. Hong Kong's multilingual business community is itself increasingly technologically sophisticated and able to deal with the various business cultures in the region. This should increasingly make Hong Kong a business, marketing, and design entrepot for high-technology industries from industrialized countries.

Hong Kong companies themselves often need access to overseas technologies to upgrade their own services and products. They also need overseas partners to gain access to European Community and North American markets, and they need and use the low-cost manufacturing available in the region. Because of this, we can expect Hong Kong companies increasingly to seek joint ventures with both overseas companies and regional manufacturing facilities.

Summary and Conclusions

Hong Kong's prosperity is largely the result of its enterprise, geopolitical position, familiarity with multiple business cultures, excellent telecommunications, the positive nonintervention policy of its government, and, more recently, China's open-door policy. As it evolves into a service-oriented economy, Hong Kong's infrastructure will be both strengthened and modified, and government policies may well be adapted to suit these changes. In particular, Hong Kong's science and technology policy is being reviewed to determine if "key" technology areas should receive preferential treatment in the allocation of proposed matching and applied research grants. Should "critical technologies" be identified to stimulate debate, research, and investment, or should the government go even further at the risk of distorting the very market it is trying to serve?

Hong Kong's approach has been cautiously to develop a science and technology policy with a keen ear to market forces. Such a market-driven strategy will probably involve technical reviews by local and outside experts to identify key technologies and determine approximate "technology roadmaps." Such maps could then be used to coordinate some matching and applied research grants.

Coupling such an approach with an improved intellectual infrastructure should allow Hong Kong's natural business instincts to propel it onto a unique technological trajectory in the coming decade. Just as the move to services has been within the last ten years, we can envision the new high-tech Hong Kong emerging by the turn of the century. When they hear the familiar greeting "And where are you making your fortune?" (*Hai bin do fat choi?*), the Hong Kong SAR businesspeople of the twenty-first century may well reply "*Everywhere.*" Hong Kong will be integrating Asian, European, and American joint ventures, markets, and technologies, and combining low-cost manufacturing from the region with Hong Kong's own design, marketing, and value-added and targeted manufacturing. Science and technology, valued not as ends in themselves, but as an integrated component of successful business enterprise, will give Hong Kong a unique place in the global economy.

Appendix

Figure A.1. **Government Funding for University and Polytechnic Research**

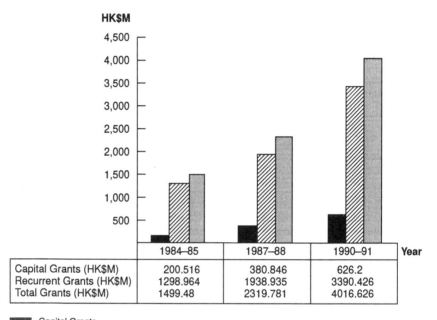

	1984–85	1987–88	1990–91
Capital Grants (HK$M)	200.516	380.846	626.2
Recurrent Grants (HK$M)	1298.964	1938.935	3390.426
Total Grants (HK$M)	1499.48	2319.781	4016.626

▇ Capital Grants

▨ Recurrent Grants

▨ Total Grants

Figure A.2. **Projected Employment by Occupational Category**

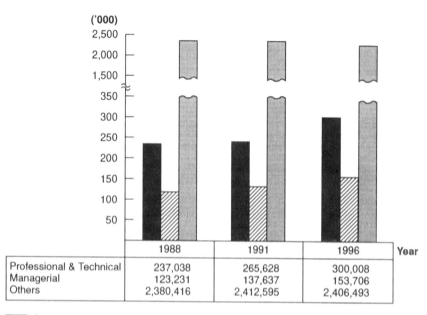

	1988	1991	1996	Year
Professional & Technical	237,038	265,628	300,008	
Managerial	123,231	137,637	153,706	
Others	2,380,416	2,412,595	2,406,493	

■ Professional & Technical
▨ Managerial
▢ Others

(*Source:* "A Statistical Projection of Manpower Requirement and Supply for HK," Education and Manpower Branch, Government Secretariat, March 1990).

Figure A.3. **Students Granted Visas for Study in United Kingdom, Australia, and North America**

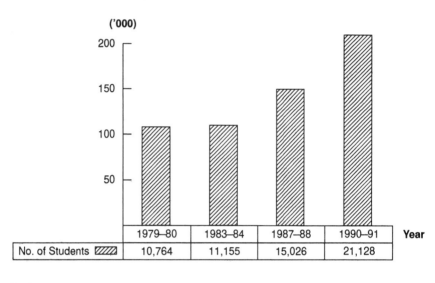

	1979–80	1983–84	1987–88	1990–91	Year
No. of Students	10,764	11,155	15,026	21,128	

References

American Chamber of Commerce in Hong Kong (ACCHK). *1991 Annual Business Survey. Summary of Results.* Hong Kong: American Chamber of Commerce in Hong Kong, May, 1991.

Bell, Trudy E. "Poised for Technological Leadership." *IEEE Spectrum* (June, 1991)

The Economist. "As Close as Teeth and Lips." August 10–16, 1991, pp. 15, 16.

Kao, Charles K., and Young, Kenneth, eds. *Technology Roadmaps for Hong Kong: An In-depth Study of Four Technology Areas.* Hong Kong: Chinese University Press, 1991.

Roberts, David. *Hong Kong 1991, A Review of 1990.* Hong Kong: Hong Kong Government Information Services, Hong Kong, 1991.

Stanford Research Institute. *Building Prosperity: A Five Part Economic Strategy for Hong Kong's Future.* Stanford Research Institute report to Hong Kong Economic Survey Limited, September 1989.

13

Japan's Evolving Strategies for Science and Technology: Toward the 21st Century

Yasunori Baba and Tokio Suzuki

After the Second World War, Japan was totally demilitarized and a new institutional alliance was formed by the government, industry, and academia to foster economic growth by catching up with Europe and the United States. The government was successful in formulating ideal policies; industry was successful in strategies, and academia was successful in capabilities. Their collaboration resulted in a very effective, nationwide catch-up science and technology (S&T) system. Within this framework, a number of private firms imported and improved foreign advanced technologies; this was accompanied by government-guided resource allocation and by capability building in academia. The result was strong international competitiveness, especially in manufacturing industries including automobiles and electronic appliances.

This success was obviously a major driving force for Japan's rapid economic expansion, but the excessive efficiency of the S&T system also raised several issues. Triggered by U.S.-Japan trade friction, Japanese industry, now operating globally, faces the problem of being a "free rider" in the area of science and technology. Most Japanese universities are underinvested and organizationally rigid. It is unclear whether they will be able to provide competent human resources in key areas such as computers and biotechnology. Furthermore, new graduates from science and engineering departments seem to be more interested in nonmanufacturing firms, and the birth rate may decline monotonically.

In order to cope with these emergent issues, the government began to look for a different industrial policy in the early 1980s, while industry sought a post-catch-up strategy in the mid-1980s, although there has been certain path-dependency, particularly in the institutional sectors. The purpose of this chapter is to identify how the collaborative framework of government, industry, and academia will develop evolving strategies for the next century, through the observation of current movements.

The next section reviews the catch-up process up to the 1980s. The third section deals with the inherent problems and other S&T issues. We then examine new movements and emerging post-catch-up strategies, using data and information mainly from reports published at the National Institute of Science and Technology Policy (NISTEP) (especially Niwa et al., 1991).

Systematic Reevaluation of Japan's Catch-up Performance

Japan's Science and Technology Infrastructure

R&D Expenditures

In the United States and Europe, R&D activity is measured by use of the concept of full-time equivalent (FTE) as a calculation method, and OECD data dealing with R&D activities are based on the FTE. However, R&D manpower in Japan is simply represented by the number of researchers. The data obviously overestimate R&D activity in Japan, but we rely first on officially published data for our discussion.

First, it is appropriate to make an international comparison of R&D expenditures.[1] In 1989, the amount spent in the United States was 26,500 billion yen, much higher than other countries. This was followed by Japan, with 11,800 billion yen; then came West Germany, France, and the United Kingdom. West Germany spent 5,500 billion, only half of Japan's expenditure. For the past twenty years, from 1970 to 1990, R&D expenditures in Japan have increased faster than in any other country, except for a small period of stagnation in 1985–86. The ratio of R&D expenditure to GNP was 1.8 percent in 1970, and grew almost every year, exceeding 2.5 percent in 1983, and 2.9 percent in 1989 and 1990.

To generate more precision, Niwa (1991) and National Institute of Science and Technology Policy (NISTEP) attempted to adjust the number of R&D personnel in Japan on an FTE base. As an FTE coefficient, 0.7 was taken for researchers in industry, 0.5 for those in national, public, and private universities, and 1.0 for those at national research institutes. These figures should be regarded as first approximations because they were derived from sampling data. Nevertheless, in view of the fact that R&D manpower in Japan had previously been expressed simply by number of researchers, the following FTE-based results should be considered much more realistic. After adjustment, the amount of R&D personnel expenditure in the industry was 3,247,500 million yen, and adjusted personnel expenditure in the universities was 711,200 million yen in 1989. The FTE-adjusted total R&D expenditure in the same year became about 10,100 billion yen, or 85.7 percent of the gross amount, and 38.2 percent of the FTE-adjusted total R&D expenditure in the United States. Concerning the ratio of the R&D expenditure to the GNP, the gross ratio has appeared higher than that in the United States since 1984, and almost the same as West Germany. After FTE adjustment, however, the ratio in Japan was about 2.5 percent in 1990, almost the same as that in the United States.

It is notable that a very small portion of Japan's R&D expenditure was spent for national defense. In 1989, the R&D budget for defense, classified as the science and technology budget in the Defense Agency, was only 4 percent of the total S&T budget—100 billion yen—and only 0.85 percent of the total R&D expenditure in 1989.

This means that the ratio of R&D expenditure for civil purposes to the GNP is higher than in other countries. For the past twenty years, the ratio in the United States has been less than 2 percent, but that in Japan has been continuously increasing, and approached 3 percent in 1989. To appreciate the actual situation, however, two points should also be noted. First, in absolute terms, the United States has spent much more for nonmilitary R&D activities than Japan. Second, after FTE adjustment, R&D activities for civil purposes were estimated at 10 trillion yen. Then the ratio of this amount to the GNP becomes approximately 2.5 percent, lower than in West Germany.

S&T Budgets

According to the *White Paper on Science and Technology* (Science and Technology Agency, 1990), the ratio of Japan's science and technology (S&T) budgets (consisting of subsidies, expenses for national universities and research institutes, etc.) to the general account was the lowest among the advanced nations, namely, 3.0 percent in the fiscal year 1989. In that same year, France allocated 6.3 percent, the United States 5.3 percent, West Germany 4.9 percent, and the United Kingdom 3.1 percent, although the definition of S&T budget is slightly different in these countries, and total national budget is used instead of the general account. Concerning the ratio of the S&T budget to the GNP, we should note that in the 1980s, it was approximately 0.5 percent (0.58 percent in 1985), about half of that in the above-mentioned countries. The rate of budget increase from 1985 to 1989 was 29 percent in the United States, 21 percent in France, 18 percent in Japan, 12 percent in the United Kingdom, and 11 percent in West Germany.

S&T Personnel

According to the official R&D manpower data, using the number of researchers only, Japan had 535,000 researchers in 1989 and 560,300 in 1990, while the

United States had 949,000 in 1988, West Germany 166,000 in 1987, and France 115,000 in 1988. If the FTE is applied, the total number of Japanese researchers in 1990 becomes about 360,000, or 65 percent of the gross number. This means that although Japan's ratio of researchers to total work force and population appears higher than that of the United States, the FTE-adjusted ratios become 0.5 percent of the total work force, and less than 0.3 percent of the total population. Both are lower than in the United States.

The number of researchers in the manufacturing sector has been continually increasing, except during the periods of the oil crisis in the 1970s and 1980s. The number was about 40,000 in 1960, exceeded 100,000 in 1971, and reached 300,000 in 1990. The increase reflects how important R&D activities have become in the manufacturing sector. Regarding academic background, in 1990 about 61 percent of researchers had a background in engineering, and 27 percent in science. Of those who majored in the natural sciences, only 3 percent were specialists in agriculture and medical science each.

In 1990, the Japanese universities, junior colleges, and affiliated institutes had 205,509 full-time members for research and educational activities. Of these, 146,456 (71.2 percent) were classified as teaching staff, 28,203 (13.7 percent) were Ph.D. students, and 30,850 (15.0 percent) were engaged in medical research. The total number is increasing each year, although the rate of increase is relatively slow—about 3.7 percent per year since 1973. In 1990, the total number of researchers in the natural sciences was 134,133 (65.5 percent of all researchers). The breakdown by major field was 80,547 (39.2 percent of all researchers) in medical science, 33,279 (16.2 percent) in engineering, 12,528 (6.1 percent) in physical science, and 7,779 (3.8 percent) in agricultural science. There were 71,376 (34.78 percent of all researchers) researchers in the humanities and social sciences. In the same year, the Japanese national, public, and independent private research institutes had 40,819 researchers, or 8 percent of the total number of researchers. The number of researchers at those institutes has remained essentially constant.

Industrial S&T Infrastructures

In 1988, Japanese industries financed 76.3 percent, the government 18.4 percent, and the universities 4.5 percent of R&D activities. On the other hand, 76.3 percent of the total national R&D expenditure was made by industry, 12.6 percent by national, public, and private universities, 9.3 percent by national research institutes, and 4.3 percent by private research institutes. This means that industry is dominant and almost self-sufficient in the financial flow, whereas the U.S. government transfers almost 50 percent of it S&T budget to industries, and a similar situation exists in the European countries. In Japan, only 4 percent of the S&T budget was transferred to industry, which amounted to 1.5 percent of the R&D expenditures in that sector.

The NISTEP survey (Niwa et al., 1991) clarified the R&D expenditures in Japanese industries by product classification.[2] In 1989, the largest amount— 2,258 billion yen or 20 percent of the total—was spent for telecommunications, electronic products, and electric measuring appliances. This was followed by the expenditure for automobiles—1,194,200 million yen or 10 percent of the total— and then the expenditure for electric machinery—840,400 million yen. These were followed by the expenditures for general tools and machines, pharmaceutical products, and inorganic and organic chemical products.

The largest amount of R&D expenditure by new entrants by product class (as opposed to incumbent firms), 892,100 million yen, spent in 1989 was for telecommunications, electronic products, and electric measuring appliances. This was approximately 40 percent of the total R&D expenditure in that classification. 387,800 million yen were spent by manufacturers of electric machinery, and the rest was spent by transportation, telecommunication, and public enterprises (45,700 million yen), steel producers (35,100 million yen), ceramic producers (35,800 million yen), and chemicals (34,300 million yen). A high entrant ratio was also shown in electric machinery (22 percent), followed by general machinery, general chemical products, pharmaceutical products, and automobiles. The expenditure for telecommunications, electronic products, and electric measuring appliances was consistently the largest portion of R&D expenditure throughout the period 1969–89. For that product class, new entrants are spending less each year; the rapid increase of expenditure for those products can therefore be attributed to incumbent firms. Expenditure for automobiles is also increasing.

Science and Technology Performance

Papers and Patents

Throughout the 1980s, almost 36 percent of articles published in the major scientific journals were from the United States; the rest are from the United Kingdom, Japan, Russia, Germany, and France. The proportion of articles from Japan was almost the same as from Germany in the early 1980s, exceeded 7 percent in the late 1980s, and became the third after the United States and the United Kingdom. Most of the published articles from Japan were in chemistry and engineering. The share of cited papers was 50 percent from the United States; the rest were from the United Kingdom, Japan, Germany, and France. Japan's share exceeded 7 percent in the late 1980s.

Japan's performance in terms of patents is also gaining ground. In 1988, more than 20 percent of patents acknowledged in the United States were from Japan. The share of non-American patent holders was 47.1 percent in total. Japan's share outstripped Germany's in 1975, and was 19.3 percent in 1987. In 1988, the top ten non-American patent holders included Hitachi, Toshiba, Canon, Fuji Film, and Mitsubishi Electric.

Japan received 329,300 million yen in 1989 for the provision of technologies exported overseas, and paid 329,900 million yen for foreign technologies. According to data compiled by the Management and Coordination Agency, which cover all items of the technology trade including patents and guidances, Japanese industries can be divided into three groups based on balance of technology trade. The first group consists of the steel and construction industry, where technology export has been greater than import throughout the past fifteen years. Next, technology export in the automobile industry exceeded imports in the early 1980s, and since then exports were increasing remarkably. In 1985, the rate of export was 2.3 times larger than that of import, but the ratio became 11.5 in 1989. This expansion of technology exporting can be attributed to technology transfer to overseas factories. The third group consists of industries producing pharmaceutical products, telecommunications, electronic appliances, and electric measuring appliances, where exports almost exceed imports. The export/import ratio of telecommunications, electronic and electric measuring appliances attained 0.5 in the mid-1980s, and became 0.64 in 1989.

However, when we confine our definition of technology trade to patents, the balance shifts completely. According to data compiled by the Bank of Japan, the export/import ratio was only 0.33 in 1988, while that in the United States was 5.24, in the United Kingdom it was 0.92 in 1987, in France 0.51, and in West Germany 0.49. Although it has increased for the past five years, the ratio in Japan is still lower than that in the major industrialized countries.

According to the Bank of Japan, payment for foreign computer-related technologies was 456,500 million yen more than the value of exports in 1989. A large amount was paid for Texas Instrument's DRAM patents, for IBM's basic software, and for computer-assisted design systems. According to the NISTEP survey, 1,306 contracts were completed in 1989 to import computer technologies, and 1,213—that is, 93 percent—were related to software. Concerning exports, NEC and other computer manufacturers admit that they are mostly transferring know-how, and the like, to their overseas companies.

S&T Priorities and the Target Areas in the 1970s and 1980s

The award system of the Science and Technology Agency (STA) is an indicator of science and technology priorities (Nishimoto and Nagahama, 1990). From 1959 to 1989, 637 new technologies won the STA award. In the 1970s, the total number was 154, 14 of which were in the area of electronic and communications, 12 in organic chemicals, 11 in chemical plants, 10 in steel, and 10 in construction. In addition, 17 were classified as high technologies, 5 in computers, 5 in semiconductors, 2 in pharmaceuticals, and 2 in biotechnology. It can be inferred that priority was given to electronic technologies in the 1970s.

On the other hand, 290 technologies won the award in the 1980s, namely 24 in transport machinery, 21 in precision machinery, 21 in electronics and communications, 19 in organic chemicals, 17 in steel, 17 in ceramics. Furthermore, 83 technologies were classified as high technologies, 15 in computers, 12 in semiconductors, 11 in pharmaceuticals, 11 in fine ceramics, 8 in biotechnology, and 8 in atomic energy. It should be noted that the number of high technologies had increased almost four times since the 1970s. Another remarkable feature in the 1980s was a technological fusion, with microelectronics as a core, and future technologies such as biotechnology, new materials, and utilization of space and ocean showed advances.

Emerging Challenge to Japan's Science and Technology

S&T Environment: Aggravating Trade Friction

The demise of Japan's catch-up process has brought about a series of serious trade frictions in the high-tech industries. Faced with the aggravating situation (particularly with the United States), Japan seems to have set a new target—that is, to promote S&T not only to enhance the domestic standard of living, but also to contribute to the advancement of other countries. A good example of Japan's changing S&T policies are the Ministry of International Trade and Industry's (MITI) R&D projects.

An R&D promotion scheme was established in 1981 with the purpose of developing future-generation generic technologies. The scheme covers innovative technologies with large diffusion effects, such as new materials for superconductivity. For risk-aversion and research integration, each program is to be conducted cooperatively by private firms, universities, and national research institutes. Furthermore, the programs are, in principle, open to foreign participation. For instance, BASF, Germany, joined the development program of new materials for optical data processing. SRI International, USA, is a member of the research team to develop software with new learning and responding functions. In the promotion of large-scale technologies, the development of a supersonic jet propulsion system for transporters is being jointly conducted by Rolls Royce, UK and GE, USA. This international cooperation is now promoted through legal support for the favorable treatment of technological achievements, such as in patents.

Many additional international projects are underway. The development of the fifth-generation computer is being organized with the participation of foreign research associates. A future-generation production system called the intelligent manufacturing system (IMS) is also under development. The IMS project is intended to systematize the present production technologies through information exchange, joint development of new technologies, and construction of subsystems that are to become fundamental components for the industrialization of developing countries, because each country can combine them and establish a system appropriate to its own S&T environment. The IMS project can be viewed as a part of MITI's "technoglobalism," a policy aimed at global technology development motivated by the disclosure of Japanese advanced technologies.

S&T Infrastructure: Current Issues and the Future

As shown above, Japanese industry spends a large amount for R&D (9,031,800 million yen in 1989). The R&D expenditure by the government for the same year, however, was only 1,867,900 million yen. This skewed structure gives rise to underinvestment in domestic universities. A general consensus has emerged that R&D expenditures for the universities and national research institutes are not enough to allow them to accomplish their tasks, such as the promotion of basic research. It also seems generally understood that although applied R&D by industry can be carried out extensively as long as the government provides reasonable S&T infrastructure, basic research and other risky but socially important R&D will have to be conducted by the government organizations.

The Labor Shortage as a Trend

The excess demand for labor seems to have become chronic in Japan, irrespective of industry. While the ratio of job openings to job seekers had remained less than 1.0 since 1974, in 1988 it reached 1.01, and the job situation has remained tight. This is obviously due to the present economic boom, but the mismatch of labor is also becoming a serious problem. Many positions that require special knowledge and skills, such as computer science and biotechnology, remain vacant, while a large number of experienced but ordinary engineers, for instance, cannot satisfy the job requirements. This mismatch may be negatively affected by changes in demographic structure—namely, a shift to an aging society—as well as in industrial and occupational structure.

What, then, are the middle- and long-term trends in Japan's labor market? According to an estimation by the Ministry of Labor in 1990,[3] manpower in 1995 will be 520,000 less than needed, and the shortage will reach 9,100,000 in 2010. Even if women and the elderly are utilized to the maximum, Japan's industries will need 1,860,000 more workers in 2010.

Leaving Manufacturing

According to a NISTEP survey (Nishigata and Hirano, 1989) based on data collected by the Ministry of Education, 40 percent of the university graduates with majors in the natural sciences and engineering, among other S&T fields, entered nonmanufacturing businesses in 1986. This percentage increased rapidly, to 42 percent in 1987 and 47 percent in 1988. Focusing on the engineering departments of eight sample universities, the NISTEP survey clarified that this percentage tended to be higher among certain universities located in Tokyo and other large cities, where 7.8 percent of the students joined banking and insurance-related companies in 1988.

These data suggest that Japanese industry is experiencing a structural change, with a shift toward a service and information-oriented economy. Because of the very rapid spread of computers, the supply of computer software tends to be too small to meet demand. According to a recent MITI estimate, 2,150,000 software engineers will be needed in Japan in 2000. At present, however, there are only 400,000 software engineers with professional qualifications, and the supply is expected to be only 1,180,000 by that time. This gap of about 970,000 is large enough to trigger a software crisis.

S&T Priorities and Target Areas toward the Twenty-First Century

For setting national priorities, a subcommittee of the Council for Science and Technology designates fields such as new materials, information processing, life science, and the so-called science of frontier spaces—the ocean and outside the Earth. On the other hand, a questionnaire distributed to private firms in 1990 (*Nikkan Kogyo Shinbun*, July 27, 1990), identified the following R&D fields as target areas in the first half of the 1990s: about 26 percent of respondents gave priority to information processing and communications, including artificial intelligence (AI), fuzzy technology, ISDN, and the CIM; another 20 percent named new materials; and 12 percent placed priority on the utilization of biotechnology (new medicines, biosensors, etc.). We should note, however, that an increasing number of firms are aware of the importance of improving and preserving natural environments.

Post-Catch-up Corporate Strategies

Japanese firms appear to have been searching for post-catch-up strategies since the mid-1980s. With no forerunners to serve as models, the firms are deploying some rather experimental strategies.

R&D for Market Creation

Intensification of Basic Research

It was around 1985 when Japanese firms began to establish an affiliated institute for basic research. In particular, industries such as telecommunications, electronic appliances, electric measuring appliances, chemical products, and ceramics are actively conducting research. For example, Hitachi established an institute for basic research in 1985, IBM Japan in 1986, Asahi Chemicals in 1986, and NGK Insulators in 1988. Research cooperation between industry and universities has gained importance. In 1983, the Ministry of Education permitted the national universities to work with private firms. That is, researchers from industry are allowed to conduct research in a national university, and promising joint projects can qualify for financial support from the government. Since then, the number of joint projects has increased rapidly—from 56 in 1983 to almost 600 in 1988. In 1990 more than 60 percent of the national universities conducted joint projects, mainly in the area of new materials, precision equipment, and software. The total number of projects was 869; 1,031 researchers from the industry worked in the universities, and the budget was 3,750 million yen (*Nikkei*, August 15, 1991).

Dynamic Diversification with Core Technologies

The next question is why Japanese firms are changing their R&D strategy. According to an NISTEP survey of the top fifty manufacturing firms in Japan (in terms of sales) (Kagita and Kodama, 1991), firms actually increased R&D expenditure by 10.6 percent on average each year from 1984 to 1988. The survey also revealed that 40 percent of the respondents plan to invest more in R&D than in facilities and equipment, and 30 percent plan more or less equal investments. Seventy percent of the respondents pointed out as a reason the need to conduct basic research and comprehensive R&D for product diversification. The shift to basics should thus be considered as the basis for a wide range of new technologies. The severe competition in the market leads firms to conduct comprehensive R&D in order to increase their competitiveness in the incumbent position, and to enter different markets.

Emerging Global Strategies for S&T

New Patterns of Technology Transfer

The changing pattern of technology transfer, through direct foreign investment (DFIs) in the present context, can be attributed to the current world economy, where almost any firm has to plunge into heightened competition in order to ensure its own demand share of a saturating market. In this economic climate, fear of displacement of labor is so strong that the appearance of protectionism has become quite inevitable. Obviously, accessibility to the market has become a crucial and intangible asset, and the new trade barriers have resulted in the DFIs by Japanese firms deployed all over the world. On the contrary, the role of production costs, and of differential wage rates in particular, seems to require further examination. Firms consider labor costs (as a proportion of total costs), rather than a low wage rate itself, to be the important index. A low wage rate, although an advantage, does not necessarily lead to low labor costs. In regard to the DFIs in the developing countries, Japanese firms all agree that cheap labor itself can be meaningfully advantageous only if they carry out strict production control and under painstaking labor management.

We should stress that firms' recent technological change has been tinged with a spirit of rationalization. Regarding the influence of the results on DFI, first, by having the option of introducing all the advantages stemming from advanced automation, firms have clearly reduced the advantage of cheap labor in the South. With a wider range of technical ability, such as various levels of automation technology, the wage rate no longer acts as a major determinant of the international location of industries. Firms can capitalize on their initiative in choosing which technology to apply at a particular location. In other words, a higher wage rate at one location may pay well once a firm introduces a high level of automation, and a lower wage may do so with the introduction of a lesser level of automation.

Overall, turning away from the traditional line of causal relationship—that is, considering internationalization at a given stage of technical ability—Japanese firms have now tried to benefit from the same coupling of strategies (Baba, 1989). If firms use original technology (e.g., the VCR), trade friction is unlikely to occur. As the former president of Matsushita noted, Matsushita is going to develop new products one after another, initially using the Japanese market as a test bench for new products (Yamaichi Research Institute, 1981). It could be inferred that technological changes can nowadays lay a foundation for corporate internationalization strategy.

Technology Transfer to the Pacific Rim Nations

As the above theoretical discussion suggests, Japanese firms have shown a characteristic DFI performance in the Pacific Rim nations (PRNs) (see chapters 14 and 16 in this volume). Triggered by the rapid appreciation of the yen, an increasing number of Japanese firms have been investing in the PRNs since 1986. We should also note that trade friction affected this trend. Because of intensified trade friction, purchasing more foreign industrial products became Japan's national target in the late 1980s. Proposed and led by MITI, the firms started a program to increase imports, keep exports at the same level or less, and then produce more overseas. Obviously, one effective solution to this problem was to shift the final production of ordinary products to the PRNs, and to produce advanced products in Japan. Since ongoing DFIs are mainly export-oriented, firms would also transfer high technologies to the PRNs. For example, Sony decided recently to produce its 8mm camcorders in Malaysia (*Nikkei*, February 21, 1991). The production of camcorders requires very accurate processing and delicate parts, but with the transfer of advanced automation, the Malaysian industrial base proved to be capable of this kind of production, and the parts will also be produced locally (Simon, 1995).

Toward the Global Utilization of Human Resources

An increasing number of non-Japanese researchers work for manufacturers of electric and electronic appliances. In 1989, 35 researchers, many with doctoral degrees, were employed by Hitachi, 30 by Toshiba, 26 by NEC, and 18 by Fujitsu. Most of them worked on one-year contracts. Apart from specialists for basic research, many engaged in computer software development. Furthermore, some firms are employing newly graduated non-Japanese S&T personnel on a lifelong basis. For example, a software house sent a selection team to Hong Kong in 1989, and hired eight students from Hong Kong University. In the same year, Sharp employed ten non-Japanese new graduates, and Honda hired ten as well on such a contractual basis. These new hires are expected not only to contribute to the companies' activities in Japan, but also to play a leading role in overseas companies.

Second, in parallel with the globalization of R&D activity, Japanese firms decided to utilize the S&T personnel in the host countries. Since the activities are no longer experimental, the firms are increasing the number of overseas R&D personnel rapidly. For example, Sony announced in 1991 that the number of personnel would reach 1,000, or 10 percent of their total R&D manpower, by the end of 1992. In addition, the projected numbers of overseas engineers working for automobile manufacturers illustrate this emerging trend: Toyota plans to employ 680 engineers and Honda 800 in 1995.

Since the above trend is rather mutual (for example, Motorola decided to establish an R&D center in Japan by 1994, and to employ 200 Japanese engineers), Japanese industries appear to have entered the "borderless age" in the utilization of S&T personnel. This can be observed in the record of S&T exchanges. NISTEP analyzed the flow of researchers and engineers between Japan and overseas (Nishimoto and Nagahama, 1991) and found that the exchange expanded gradually from 1970 to 1985, and then was very rapid. In 1989, 146,488 Japanese S&T personnel went overseas, and almost 80 percent of them did so in order to obtain technical knowledge and skills. Geographically, an increasing proportion of personnel have been sent to the United States (69,556 in 1989). In the same year, 84,295 non-Japanese S&T personnel entered Japan, mostly for training or study. About 90 percent of the students in and 75 percent of the trainees came from Asia (20,286 from Korea, or 25 percent of the total; 15,015 from Taiwan; and 11,763 from China).

In coping with the emerging software crisis described above, the Japanese software houses resorted to an active global strategy. As Simon describes in chapter 2 of this volume, more than 20 Japanese software houses were conducting joint projects in China in the late 1980s. Apart from such joint ventures, there have been joint research projects in software development by Japanese firms and Chinese universities. The purpose seems to be in the long run to enhance the technological capabilities of both parties. Similar trends are also seen in Korea. So far, Korean partners have acted as a subcontractor of Japanese software houses, which are suffering from a shortage of software engineers. Entering the 1990s, an increasing number of Japanese firms are going to establish centers for software development, mainly as joint ventures with local partners, in the PRNS such as Thailand, Indonesia, the Philippines, and India. Apart from the emerging political conflicts in China and wage increases in Korea, the decision by Japanese firms can be due to two undeniable facts: first, the PRNs are enjoying steady economic growth, and the demand for information processing is increasing accordingly; and second, economic conditions differ from country to country, and thus the development of software must fit the local requirements.

In spite of the positive side, we must note that the tendency toward globalization may cause some problems. At the government level, there is a policy against admitting foreign manual workers out of concern for the domestic labor market. Since the government does allow the hiring of foreign S&T personnel, this will be a new political issue. At the firm level, firms will have to bear certain coordination costs in order to maintain the active utilization of foreign human resources. And working manuals may have to be reformulated in English, and present practices of personnel management may have to change.

Emerging Strategic Options: The Case of HDTV

As the innovation process becomes increasingly systemic, the number of strategic alliances among firms in Japan, the United States, and Europe increases (Imai and Baba, 1991). Japanese firms have also established centers for R&D activities in the United States, Europe, and Asia. Before 1985 the centers were mostly in the United States, but the number in Europe and Asia is increasing. The case of the HDTV business is a handy illustration of how firms have taken their strategic options.

At the beginning of the 1990s, the HDTV business in Japan seems to have shifted to a commercial stage. In 1990, Japanese manufacturers—Sony, Matsushita, Hitachi, among others—released an HDTV receiver based on the Hivision format developed by NHK for the household market. HDTV programs are no longer considered experimental. Obviously, the HDTV market is expanding, and the market size, including the market for related equipment, is estimated to reach 3,400 billion yen in 2000. In spite of these achievements, there appears to be no movement toward a universal HDTV format. As a result, Europe, Japan, and the United States will each have a different format, which can represent an entry barrier for this industry to each market. The situation, however, appears to be changing because of the accumulation of HDTV technology in Japan. In order to fully utilize technological advantage in foreign markets, Japanese firms have taken definitive steps toward active globalization.

First, after failing to reach a universal format, Japanese firms established new R&D centers in the United States in 1990. Examples are Sony's Advanced Video Technology Center and Matsushita's Panasonic Advanced TV-Video Laboratories. The centers are specialized in the development of HDTV technology, in order to accommodate different formats. Sanyo and Sharp established an R&D center for HDTV in Spain at around the same time. As a localized project, the R&D of the HDTV on the HD-Mac, EC format, will start in the near future.

Second, as a target of the firms' strategic alliances, the joint development of special ICs for HDTV seems most promising. Motorola and Toshiba decided in 1990 jointly to develop the signal decoder, a central part of every HDTV receiver, in the Japanese Hivision format. This was followed by joint development projects by LSI Logic and Sanyo, and Fujitsu, Hitachi, Sony, and Texas Instruments. The American participants will first receive technological assistance from the Japanese; then the accumulated know-how will be applied to the development of different ICs for HDTV in European and American formats.

Third, Sony's purchase of Columbia and Matsushita's acquisition of MCA around 1990 should also be considered part of the strategic alliance for HDTV. The Japanese firms acquired the major American movie producers, and this is expected to provide a large volume of audiovisual software for HDTV. This will boost the whole HDTV business. In this context, Sony's Advanced Video Technology Center is conducting joint projects with American universities in order to apply the backlog of HDTV technology to movie production.

Notes

The authors are indebted to Fujio Niwa for his provision of data.

1. When comparing R&D activities among different countries, the OECD and the advanced nations rely on exchange rates derived from purchasing power differences. The present chapter also followed this method.

2. In the *Survey of S&T Activities in Japan*, the Management and Coordination Agency (1991) employed the following statistical method: each respondent was asked to report R&D expenditure on the basis of the product classification compiled by the agency, irrespective of financial source. The sum of the amounts is to be equal to the total R&D expenditure. An estimation procedure using the number of researchers, among other data, is available in case some expenditures cannot be classified. Although there are thirty-one product groups in the original classification, the number was reduced to twenty-nine, almost coinciding with the SIC classification.

3. The estimate is based on the assumption that the ratio of working population for each age group remains the same, the annual economic growth rate is 4.0 percent, and the annual population growth rate is 1.8 percent based on the 1985 census.

References

Baba, Y. "Characteristics of Innovating Japanese Firms—Reverse Product Cycles." In M. Dodgson (ed.), *Technology Strategy and the Firm*. London: Longman, 1989.

Hirano, C., and Nishigata, C. *"Basic Research" in Major Companies of Japan*. NISTEP Report no. 8. Tokyo: NISTEP, 1990.

Imai, K., and Baba, Y. "Systemic Innovation and Cross-Border Networks." In OECD (Ed.), *Technology and Productivity*. Paris: OECD, 1991.

Kagita, Y., and Kodama, F. *From Producing to Thinking Organizations*. NISTEP Report no. 15. Tokyo: NISTEP, 1991.

Kodama, F. *Analysing Japanese High Technologies*. London: Pinter, 1991.

Management and Coordination Agency. *Survey of S&T Activities in Japan*. Tokyo: MCA, 1991.

Nishigata, C., and Hirano, Y. *Employment Trends of Science and Engineering Graduates*. NISTEP Report no. 1. Tokyo: NISTEP, 1989.

Nishimoto, A., and Nagahama, H. *Hyosho Seido kara mita Wagakuni no Kagaku Gijutsu Doko*. [Japan's Science and Technology Trends from the Viewpoint of the Award System]. NISTEP Report no. 10. Tokyo: NISTEP, 1990.

———. *Wagakuni to Kaigi Shokokukan ni okeru Kenkyu Gijutsu Koryu* [Research and Technological Exchanges between Japan and Overseas]. NISTEP Report no. 17. Tokyo: NISTEP, 1991.

Niwa, F., Camargo, O., Hirahara, F., Kakizaki, F., and Tomizawa, H. *Taikei Kagaku Gijutsu Shihyo* [A System of Science and Technology Indicators]. NISTEP Report no. 19. Tokyo: NISTEP, 1991.

Science and Technology Agency. *White Paper on Science and Technology*. Tokyo: STA, 1990.

Simon, Denis Fred. *The Technology Strategy of Japanese Firms Toward the Pacific Rim*. Cambridge University Press, 1995, forthcoming.

Yamaichi Research Institute, ed. *Matsushita Denki no Kenkyu* [A Study on Matsushita Electrics]. Tokyo: Keizai Shimposha, 1981.

Part V
Regional Science and Technology Issues

14

Emerging Technology Transfer Patterns in Pacific Asia

Tran Van Tho and Shujiro Urata

Technology plays an important role in promoting economic growth and economic development. With better technology, production would be greater, even without any increases in the use of factors of production. Improvement in technology leads to reduction in cost. Furthermore, new technology may help produce a new product. The effect of technological improvement or creation of new technology, therefore, is to increase the competitiveness of a firm. This in turn influences the competitive position of the particular industry and of the country. These observations are not only derived from theoretical models but are also supported by empirical findings. A number of studies have shown that technological progress has contributed substantially to economic growth.[1]

International technology transfer (ITT) has increased its importance in recent decades in determining the course of economic development and economic growth of a country. This phenomenon may be seen from two different perspectives. One is the transfer of technology from developed countries to developing countries, and the other is between developed countries. ITT of the first type is not a new phenomenon, as almost all of the developing countries, past and present, have utilized technologies imported from developed countries. Indeed, there is ample evidence that imported technologies have been a critical factor behind the successful economic development of countries such as Japan, Korea, and Taiwan.[2] The importance of ITT in economic development appears to have increased in recent years, as technology has increased its role in determining the competitiveness of a firm, and thereby of a country. The same observation may be made regarding the importance of ITT among developed countries. In addition, one should note that the significance of interfirm, international collaboration in R&D has increased among developed countries because the amount of resources, both financial and human, necessary for technological breakthrough has increased dramatically in recent years in important high-technology sectors such as electronics and automobiles.

With these observations in mind, we attempt here to examine the pattern of ITT and to identify some important developments in Pacific Asia. Since our interest is in Pacific Asia, we examine mainly the pattern of the first type of ITT. The Pacific Asian countries have experienced rapid economic expansion compared with the rest of the world. An important factor contributing to favorable economic development in Pacific Asia appears to be successful transfer of foreign technologies. Before the mid-1980s, the United States and Japan were major technology suppliers, while the newly industrialized economies (NIEs) and ASEAN countries were major technology recipients.[3] After the mid-1980s, the NIEs have joined the United States and Japan as important technology suppliers to ASEAN. An important question at present is whether favorable economic expansion may be maintained in the future. Considering past patterns of development, it is reasonable to assume that the future economic development depends crucially on how successfully the Pacific Asian countries can upgrade their technological capability.

The structure of this chapter is as follows: in the next section some conceptual issues related to technology and technology transfer are discussed, as the evaluation of the effectiveness of technology transfer depends on how technology and technology transfer are understood. Then recent developments in ITT in Pacific Asia is explored through an examination of the pattern of ITT through three different channels: foreign direct investment (FDI), trade in technology, and trade in capital goods. In this context we examine the pattern of ITT mainly from the recipient perspective. We then look closely at the pattern of ITT in Pacific Asia by focusing on FDI as a channel of ITT, examining first the pattern of ITT by Japanese firms in East Asia and then the pattern of ITT by Korean and Taiwanese firms in ASEAN. We finish with some concluding comments.

Technology and International Technology Transfer (ITT): Some Conceptual Issues

The term "technology" has been used to mean different things to different parties. Some narrowly define it as information necessary to manufacture a product (manufacturing technology), while others use a broader definition that includes information necessary to develop a product (developmental technology). There are also analysts whose definition encompasses management know-how as a part of technology. Although discussion of the definition of technology may appear irrelevant to the issue of technology transfer, it is indeed very important; unless technology is clearly defined, one cannot know what it is that should be transferred through technology transfer. A commonly accepted definition of technology may be a broad one. Specifically, technology is often defined as systematic knowledge for the manufacturing of a product, for the application of a process, or for the rendering of a service, including any integrally associated managerial and marketing techniques. Although we do not specify types of technologies in the discussion of technology transfer here, we do have a broad definition in mind.

Our working definition of technology was derived by focusing on its use or its functional characteristics. There are, however, other definitions. For example, focusing basically on the factors necessary for the production of technology, one would categorize technologies as advanced or standard (matured). In our discussion of technology transfer, the concept of "appropriate technology" frequently arises. Transferred technology is considered "appropriate" if it suits the economic condition of the recipients. For example, labor-using technology is considered appropriate if the recipient country is abundant in labor. Often multinational corporations are criticized for transferring inappropriate technologies through FDI.

Let us turn now to some of the special characteristics of technology, which turn out to be an important factor in determining the channels of ITT. First, technology has a characteristic of public good. In other words, use of a technology by a firm does not affect the use of the same technology by a different firm. Moreover, as technology is knowledge, which is intangible, it is difficult to preclude others from using that knowledge (this is called the problem of "appropriability"). Because of the appropriability problem, private firms tend to be discouraged from investing in the creation of new technologies, unless they have some right to exclusive use. But if the technology is used exclusively by a firm or by a few firms, the benefits from the technology would be limited. In order to deal with the problem, a patent system was established. Even so, this issue suggests the possible difficulty inherent in allocating resources in the technology market through the market mechanism.

Somewhat related to this point, another characteristic of technology is that creation of a new technology generally requires a substantial amount of resources, including human and financial resources. Moreover, investment in technology creation, or research and development (R&D) investment, is risky since there is no assurance that these investments will materialize in the form of new technology. The large investment and high risk associated with R&D investment give an advantage to large firms over small firms in technology creation. Although creation of new technology requires large investment, use of technology does not incur much additional cost. Therefore, the problem of appropriability arises, leading to market failure.

Finally, we should mention that technology exists in various forms. It may be embodied in physical capital such as machinery or in human capital such as engineers and managers, or it may be disembodied as in product design. These differences in form lead to different channels for technology transfer.

We have argued that the term "technology" is used in a variety of ways. It follows that "technology transfer" is also used in a variety of ways. Some argue that technology transfer means transmission of technological knowledge that enables the recipient to manufacture a particular product, while others argue that technology transfer is not undertaken unless the recipient can assimilate the technology; that is, the recipients acquire the ability to detect and to correct problems. Some researchers go further, arguing that technology is not completely transferred unless the recipient masters the technology; that is, acquires the ability to develop the technology being transferred. Finally, in a somewhat different context, imported technology is said to be diffused when it is used extensively in economic activities in the technology importing country.

Since technology usually exists in three different forms, technology is transferred internationally mainly through three different channels. one is through trading capital goods such as machinery, in which technology is embodied. In this case the recipient acquires the technology by learning how to operate the machinery. "Reverse engineering" may be included in this category. Another channel of transferring technology is through technology trade such as the sale of patented production process. Technology transfer through arrangements such as production cooperation, technological cooperation, and OEM is classified under this category. This type of technology transfer usually entails a long-term business relationship between the two parties, as remuneration accrued to the supplier usually depends on the performance of the recipient. For example, royalty fees are often quoted at a certain percentage of the sales made by the use of transferred technologies. As such, this type of arrangement is often called a new form of investment (NFI).[4] One may also include technology transfer in the form of inviting foreign engineers under this category, as it means the purchase of technology embodied in engineers.

The other channel of technology transfer is through foreign direct investment (FDI). FDI involves international transmission not only of financial capital, but also of technology, including management know-how. At least one important element is found in technology transfer through FDI but not in technology transfer through either capital goods trade or technology trade. In the case of FDI technology transfer takes the form of intrafirm transfer, whereas in other cases it usually takes the form of interfirm transfer.

Issues involving the characteristics of ITT through different channels provide important implications for the choice of channels of ITT for the technology supplier as well as for the recipient. We examine the likely choice of the channels by looking at the factors associated with the technology supplier and with the technology recipient in turn. A firm with superior technology has at least four alternatives in serving a foreign market. The first three alternatives are those already discussed, namely, sale of capital goods, technology trade, and FDI. In addition, as a fourth option, the firm may export the products produced with the technology. Important factors affecting the decision are the types of technology to be transferred and the availability of resources endowed on the part of the technology supplier. If the technology is a standard one, then channels other than FDI may be preferred. On the other hand, if the technology is new, the supplier may choose FDI to avoid the problems associated with appropriability and asymmetric information. If the technology is new, the supplier may be interested in exclusive use and may therefore opt for FDI. The problem of asymmetric information arises when the technology supplier and recipient do not have the same information regarding the characteristics of the technology. More specifically, a lack of knowledge about the importance of technology precludes prospective technology recipients from appreciating the technology fully. Under such circumstances, transaction does not take place because the price quoted by the technology supplier is higher than the price the recipient is willing to pay. To deal with the problem, the supplier chooses FDI rather than an arms-length transaction.

Availability of resources also affects the channel of technology transfer. Although a firm may be interested in transferring technology through FDI, lack of financial and/or managerial resources makes it difficult for the firm to undertake FDI. In that case the firm may be forced to resort to other channels.

So far we have looked at the factors associated with the supplier of technologies, but the channel of technology transfer is also influenced by the recipient. In this regard, the technology policy of the government and the availability of the resources such as technological capability and managerial and financial resources of the recipient play an important role. If the government as well as its people are sensitive to foreign presence, then FDI may be difficult. On the other hand, FDI may be preferred if the recipient suffers from the shortage of resources necessary for assimilating foreign technologies.

Technology is transferred from one company to another locally within a country as well as internationally. It should be noted here that ITT faces more difficulties than local transfer. This is because ITT involves two different economies, where economic situations such as social infrastructure, including capability of engineers and workers, differ significantly.

The Pattern of Technology Transfer in Pacific Asia

We have identified three different channels of international technology transfer (ITT): foreign direct investment (FDI), trade in technology, and trade in capital goods. Among these three channels, FDI has been most extensively used for ITT in recent years, as the growth rate of FDI in the latter half of the 1980s was by far the greatest of the three. World FDI outflow in nominal terms more than tripled from $63.1 billion in 1985 to $197.9 billion in 1989. The rates of increase for trade in technology and for capital goods trade are respectively estimated to be much lower—around 15 percent a year during the same period.[5] These statistics on FDI, technology trade, and trade in capital goods are closely interrelated; for example, FDI may involve technology trade as well as capital goods trade. Because of the increased importance of FDI as a channel of ITT, we first examine the changes in the pattern of FDI in Pacific Asia, and then examine the pattern of trade in technology and in capital goods in the region.

A number of notable changes have been observed regarding the pattern of FDI in the world since the latter half of the 1980s. First, developed countries increased their importance as both a supplier and a recipient of FDI. There are differences in the FDI patterns among developed countries, however. As a supplier of FDI, Japan has gained a significant position as it became the world's largest FDI supplier in terms of annual outflow in 1989, recording $44 billion. As a recipient, the United States, the world's largest recipient, has increased its FDI inflow significantly: in 1989 the U.S. annual FDI inflow stood at $72 billion.

The second notable development is the importance of Asian countries as hosts to FDI. Although the share of developing countries in world FDI inflow declined in the second half of the 1980s, developing Asian countries maintained their attractiveness as FDI hosts. In particular, ASEAN countries have been successful in attracting FDI in recent years, as shown in Table 14.1. One word of caution is in order regarding the statistics in this table. These statistics are based on approval, and therefore they are likely to be greater than FDI values that are actually undertaken. The gap between the approved and actual figures appears in some cases to be substantial. Third, the Asian NIEs became active FDI suppliers in the latter half of the 1980s. Before the mid-1980s, the United States and Japan supplied a large part of FDI not only in the NIEs but also in the ASEAN countries, but after the mid-1980s, the NIEs joined the United States and Japan as major suppliers of FDI to ASEAN. Indeed, for every single ASEAN country and for China, the NIEs as a group were the largest investors in 1990.

Various factors have contributed to the rapid expansion of FDI in the second half of the 1980s. First, substantial realignment of the exchange rates changed the pattern of international competitiveness, leading to relocation of industries through FDI. Specifically, countries such as Japan whose currency appreciated found their products losing competitiveness in the world market. In order to deal with the problem, Japanese firms moved their production overseas. Similar developments were observed for the NIEs toward the end of the 1980s. Second, protectionist policies adopted in a number of developed countries have left foreign producers no alternative but local production to serve these markets. Third, FDI promotion policies have been pursued in both the host (FDI recipient) and the home (FDI supplier) countries. In the host countries, such as the ASEAN countries, inflow of FDI has been encouraged for the purpose of promoting economic activities since it creates jobs and introduces efficient technology, whereas in some home countries, such as Japan and Korea, outflow of FDI has been encouraged since it is considered necessary for industrial restructuring. Finally, advances in methods of communication and transportation in recent years have facilitated the international transfer not only of products such as

Table 14.1

Foreign Direct Investment in Asian Countries by Country of Origin

Recipients	U.S.		Japan		NIEs		Total	
			Investing Countries and Regions					
Malaysia								
1986	7	(3.3)	23	(11.1)	48	(23.7)	203	(100)
1988	96	(12.6)	214	(27.9)	271	(35.3)	768	(100)
1990	69	(3.0)	657	(28.5)	1,100	(47.8)	2,302	(100)
Thailand								
1986	41	(7.0)	251	(43.3)	91	(15.7)	579	(100)
1988	673	(10.8)	3,063	(49.0)	1,709	(17.4)	6,249	(100)
1990	1,091	(7.7)	2,706	(19.2)	8,794	(62.2)	14,128	(100)
Philippines								
1986	22	(28.7)	22	(28.5)	8	(10.2)	78	(100)
1988	153	(32.3)	96	(20.2)	140	(29.7)	473	(100)
1990	59	(6.2)	306	(31.8)	384	(39.9)	961	(100)
Indonesia								
1986	128	(16.0)	325	(40.6)	84	(10.5)	800	(100)
1988	731	(16.6)	256	(5.8)	1,530	(34.7)	4,409	(100)
1990	153	(1.7)	2,241	(25.6)	2,598	(29.7)	8,750	(100)
Korea								
1986	125	(35.4)	138	(38.9)	16	(4.5)	354	(100)
1988	284	(22.2)	696	(54.3)	15	(1.2)	1,283	(100)
1990	317	(39.5)	235	(29.3)	21	(2.6)	803	(100)
Taiwan								
1986	138	(19.5)	254	(36.0)	65	(9.2)	706	(100)
1988	135	(12.7)	432	(40.7)	129	(12.2)	1,061	(100)
1990	540	(25.9)	827	(39.7)	247	(11.9)	2,082	(100)
Singapore								
1986	204	(37.3)	226	(41.3)	n.a.		547	(100)
1988	291	(35.3)	344	(41.7)	n.a.		824	(100)
1990	582	(47.6)	391	(32.0)	n.a.		1,223	(100)
China								
1986	326	(14.5)	263	(11.7)	1,342	(59.8)	2,244	(100)
1988	236	(7.4)	515	(16.1)	2,123	(66.5)	3,194	(100)
1989	284	(8.4)	356	(10.5)	2,162	(63.7)	3,393	(100)

Sources: Official statistics of respective recipient countries.

All figures are on an approved basis. For both Korea and Taiwan, the NIEs include Hong Kong and Singapore. For China, the NIEs include Hong Kong, Macau, and Singapore.

Table 14.2

Technology Trade in Pacific Asia (in US$ million)

Exporters	Importing Countries and Regions			
	NIEs	ASEAN	China	World Total
U.S.				
1986	232	77	n.a.	7,531
1989	492	78	n.a.	12,288
Japan				
1985	135	86	110	981
1987	321	145	65	1,490

Source: For the U.S. statistics, *Survey of Current Business*, (September 1990). For the Japanese statistics, Statistics Bureau, Management and Coordination Agency, Japan.

Figures are based on statistics reported by exporting countries. ASEAN includes Indonesia, Malaysia, and the Phillipines.

machinery but also of services such as financial capital and technological information necessary for undertaking FDI.

Growth of trade in technology and in capital goods has been less spectacular in the 1980s. Table 14.2 presents the pattern of technology trade in Pacific Asia. Constrained by data availability, we cannot discern fully the sources of technology import for the Pacific Asian countries; technology supplier is limited only to the United States and Japan in the table. This may not cause much difficulty in depicting the pattern of technology imports for the Pacific Asian countries, however, since these two countries are two major technology suppliers in the region. The table shows that the United States is by far the dominant supplier of technology through trade in the world, unlike the case of FDI. In Asia, however, Japan is an equally important supplier of technology through trade. These observations indicate that Japan's exports of technology are relatively concentrated in Asia, whereas no such concentration is observed for the United States. As for the recipient of technology through trade, the NIEs absorbed a significantly larger amount of technology than did ASEAN. This is quite a contrast to the pattern observed for FDI. These differences in the pattern of technology imports through trade and that for FDI inflow between the NIEs and ASEAN appear to stem from the differences in the availability of resources (human, financial, and technological) and FDI policies pursued in the two groups of countries. The ASEAN countries, which are poorly endowed with such resources, tend to prefer FDI to importing technologies.

Finally, we look at the pattern of trade in capital goods in Pacific Asia (Table 14.3). The NIEs increased their import of capital goods from approximately $19

Table 14.3

Trade Flow Matrix of Capital Goods in the Pacific Rim (in US$ million and per-
centage shares)

Importers	U.S.	Japan	NIEs	ASEAN	World Total
		Exporting Countries and Regions			
NIEs					
1980	5,907 (30.7)	6,775 (35.1)	600 (3.1)	646 (3.4)	19,264 (100)
1985	7,088 (24.8)	9,810 (34.4)	1,464 (5.2)	1,333 (4.7)	28,531 (100)
1987	9,600 (21.6)	18,511 (41.6)	2,477 (5.6)	2,218 (5.0)	44,478 (100)
ASEAN					
1980	2,753 (29.2)	2,945 (31.2)	466 (4.9)	119 (1.3)	9,431 (100)
1985	2,903 (27.0)	3,201 (29.8)	1,195 (11.1)	305 (2.8)	10,732 (100)
1987	3,182 (25.0)	4,232 (33.3)	1,345 (10.6)	334 (2.6)	12,708 (100)

Sources: AIDXT trade statistics system at the Institute of Developing Economies, Tokyo.
Figures are based on statistics reported by importing countries.

billion in 1980 to $44 billion in 1987. The rapid increase of capital goods
imports is partly attributable to the increase of FDI inflow. Moreover, rapid
export expansion of manufactured products by these countries also contributed to
such development. More specifically, for the NIEs it was necessary to import
capital goods to expand exports, since these countries did not have a sufficient
amount of capital goods for export production. It is also important to point out
that importation of capital goods was possible because these countries did earn
foreign exchange through favorable export performance. By contrast, the amount
of capital goods imports by ASEAN countries did not show much increase
during 1980–87. But it is likely to have increased since 1987, because FDI
inflow started to grow remarkably around 1988.

Japan and the United States have been major suppliers of capital goods in the
region. In 1987 the share of Japan in total imports of capital goods by the NIEs
and by ASEAN amounted respectively to 41.6 percent and 33.3 percent, while
corresponding shares for the United States were 21.6 percent and 25.0 percent.
The high share of Japan in the imports of capital goods for these Asian countries
is partly due to the rapid expansion of Japanese FDI in these countries, as foreign
affiliates of Japanese firms tend to purchase capital goods from Japan.[6] Taking into
account the relationship between FDI and capital goods imports, one would expect
capital goods imports from the NIEs to ASEAN to increase in the future, as FDI from
the NIEs to ASEAN started to increase notably toward the end of the 1980s.

We have presented some evidence that ITT has intensified in Pacific Asia in
the latter half of the 1980s, through various channels. We presented an overall

Table 14.4

Channels of Technology Transfer from Japan to Asia (in number of projects and percent)

Total Projects Surveyed	856	(100.0)
Foreign direct investment	477	(56.7)
Licensing arrangement	347	(40.5)
Others	32	(3.7)

Source: Survey by Nikkei Research Institute of Industry and Markets (October 1990). The survey covered only four machinery industries: general machinery, electric/electronic products, automobiles, and precision machinery.

picture of ITT in Pacific Asia. We turn now to ITT through FDI by focusing on FDI by Japanese as well as Korean and Taiwanese firms.

A Comparison of the Characteristics of Technology Transfer among the Pacific Rim Countries

The most important development in the economy of Pacific Asia since the mid-1980s may be the intensive flows of technology among the countries in the region. Moreover, technology transfer in the region since the mid-1980s has been characterized by the rapid expansion of technology flows from Japan, and the increasingly important role played by Taiwan, Korea, and other Asian NIEs as new suppliers of technologies and other managerial resources. Given many differences between Japan and Asian NIEs in terms of stage of economic development, such as their size and economic structure, we may expect that the characteristics of Japan's technology transfer have been quite different from those of the NIEs. This section compares those characteristics. We first discuss the pattern of Japan's technology transfer in the region since the mid-1980s; then we turn to the recent trends in the role of the NIEs as new transmitters of technology. Due to data constraints, in the discussion on the NIEs we focus on FDI, the major channel of technology transfer.

Pattern of Japan's Technology Transfer in Pacific Asia

Let us start with a general picture of the technology transfer projects conducted so far in Asia by Japanese firms. Table 14.1 presents the results of a survey of 474 Japanese manufacturers in four machinery-related industries (general machinery, electric/electronics, transport equipment, and precision machinery). According to the survey, 342 firms had conducted a total of 856 projects involving technology transfer in Asian countries (including NIEs, ASEAN, China, India,

and Pakistan) by October 1990. The table shows that both foreign direct investment (FDI) and licensing arrangements (LA) have been important channels of
technology transfer by Japanese machinery-related producers to Asian countries.
"Other" channels include production cooperation and OEM (original equipment
manufacturing).

Table 14.5 breaks down all projects according to the recipient and timing of
the transfer. Three notable observations emerge from this table. First, Korea,
Taiwan, Thailand, and Malaysia have been the major markets for Japan's machinery-related technologies, followed by China and Indonesia. Second, for most
countries, about 40 percent or more of the projects were conducted during the
latest five-year period, 1986–90. This shows the aggressive behavior of Japanese firm regarding technology transfer to Asia following the sharp rise in the
value of the yen since the mid-1980s. Third, the concentration of technology
transfer in that period was more pronounced in ASEAN countries like Thailand
and Malaysia than in the NIEs such as Taiwan and Korea. This indicates that
Japanese firms have increasingly emphasized ASEAN as markets for their technologies. Since machinery-related technologies can be considered more sophisticated than those found in other industries, such as textiles and foodstuffs, the
figures in Table 14.5 suggest that Japanese firms have an increasingly strong
interest in exporting high technologies to ASEAN's growing economies.

Japanese firms seem to adopt different channels of technology transfer depending on the general technological level as well as the degree of political or
economic risk in host countries. Table 14.6 provides some evidence supporting
this point. The table summarizes the findings on the channels of technology
transfer by Japanese firms during the first two and a half years since the value of
the yen started its sharp rise. The table suggests that FDI is important in the NIEs
and ASEAN, while licensing and production cooperation have been mainly chosen for the Chinese market. OEM has so far appeared only in the NIEs. This may
be explained by the relatively high technological levels of firms in the NIEs,
compared with those in other Asian developing countries. Along with the accumulation of managerial resources, many firms in the NIEs have preferred OEM-
type technology transfers over FDI, which results in management control by
multinational corporations.[7] In terms of the cost of buying technology, OEM is also
much cheaper than licensing. From the point of view of Japanese firms, the attainment of a high technological level by NIE firms is a precondition for transfer
through the OEM channel because the products made by NIE firms as a result of
technology transfer will be sold under the brand name of the technology suppliers.
The reason why licensing has been the most important channel of technology transfer for China may be that Japanese firm consider China much riskier than the NIEs
or ASEAN countries because of the possibility of changes in foreign and domestic
economic policies as a result of changes in the political situation (Simon, 1995).

So far we have examined the type of ITT involving only two parties, or
bilateral international arrangements. However, the number of international ar-

Table 14.5

Technology Transfer from Japan to Asia

	Total no. of projects		Before 1970		1971–80		1981–85		1986-October 1990	
Korea	195	(100.0)	9	(4.6?)	44	(22.6)	53	(27.2)	87	(44.6)
Taiwan	155	(100.0)	25	(16.1)	28	(18.1)	40	(25.8)	59	(38.1)
Hong Kong	14	(100.0)	4	(28.6)	3	(21.4)	2	(14.2)	5	(35.7)
Singapore	47	(100.0)	0	(0.0)	28	(59.6)	9	(19.1)	10	(21.3)
Thailand	109	(100.0)	11	(10.1)	21	(19.3)	8	(7.3)	63	(57.8)
Malaysia	89	(100.0)	3	(3.4)	21	(23.6)	17	(19.1)	43	(48.3)
Indonesia	63	(100.0)	3	(4.8)	21	(33.3)	19	(30.2)	18	(28.6)
Philippines	31	(100.0)	2	(6.5)	10	(32.3)	6	(19.4)	11	(35.5)
China	68	(100.0)	0	(0.0)	2	(2.9)	26	(52.9)	29	(42.6)
Asia Total	856	(100.0)	59	(6.9)	187	(21.8)	229	(26.8)	357	(41.7)

Source: See Table 14.4.

Asia total includes India and Pakistan, which do not appear in the table individually. Total number of projects include some which will be conducted in 1991 and some for which the time of transfer was unknown. Figures in parentheses show percentage share in total number of projects.

rangements involving more than three parties is increasing as the economic as well as the political environment has been changing quite rapidly. For example, in the automobile industry, Mazda (Japan), Ford (USA) and Kia (Korea) have formed a cooperative arrangement, under which a car is produced in Korea with a Mazda design, and a large portion of production is shipped to and sold in the United States through the Ford sales network. This type of arrangement is pursued to maximize profit, given differences in cost conditions in different countries and given market accessibility. In the remainder of this section we look more closely at Japanese FDI for which the data are more abundant than for other channels of technology transfer.

Since late 1985, when the value of the yen started to increase sharply, Japan's FDI has expanded rapidly. Japan's manufacturing firms have actively undertaken FDI. On a reporting basis, Japanese FDI in manufacturing industries reached US$3.8 billion in fiscal 1986, an expansion of 62 percent over the previous fiscal year. The corresponding figures for fiscal 1987 were US$7.8 billion, or 106 percent. In fiscal 1988 and 1989, FDI by Japanese manufacturers increased even more significantly to US$13.8 billion and US$16.3 billion, respectively.

Along with this overall trend, Japanese FDI in Asia has also expanded rapidly since 1986. For all manufacturing industries as a whole, in nominal terms the cumulative FDI in the four years over 1986–89 exceeded the cumulative FDI over 1951–85 (Table 14.7). The rapid appreciation of the yen significantly changed the pattern of Japan's international competitiveness. Wages and other

Table 14.6

**Channels of Technology Transfer to Asia by Japanese Firms
1986–June 1988** (number of cases)

	Local Production (FDI)	Licensing Arrangements	Production Cooperation	OEM
Korea	127	98	44	9
Taiwan	209	51	43	8
Hong Kong	39	5	9	1
Singapore	113	3	4	0
Asian NIEs (A)	488	158	100	18
Thailand	129	21	6	0
Malaysia	62	5	2	0
Philippines	28	5	2	0
Indonesia	45	16	8	0
ASEAN (B)	264	47	18	0
China (C)	86	107	38	1
Asian Pacific (A+B+C)	837	312	156	19

Source: Compiled from NEEDS system of *The Japan Economic Journal* (*Nikkei Shimbun*).

factor costs in Japan, in dollar terms, rose rapidly due to the drastic change in the value of the yen. In 1986, Japanese wages, for instance, were about four times higher than the average level in the NIEs, and about thirteen times higher than in ASEAN (MITI, 1988). Given the even higher value of the yen in subsequent years, factor costs in Japan are now much higher than in 1986. As a result, many industries have had to venture overseas in order to achieve lower production costs. Until mid-1986 the NIEs, particularly Taiwan and Korea, were the major recipients absorbing new FDI. Since mid-1986 the waves have spread to ASEAN, especially Thailand and Malaysia. Since 1987, Japanese FDI in Indonesia has also risen substantially. These investments include not only the establishment of wholly owned subsidiaries or joint ventures, but also the expansion of productive capabilities (including the addition of new product lines) by existing overseas subsidiaries.

A number of notable characteristics of Japanese manufacturing FDI in Asia since the mid-1980s may be noted. First, the industrial structure of Japanese FDI in the region has been significantly upgraded in the sense that the share of technologically sophisticated industries has risen considerably. This is partially reflected in the increasingly strong presence of the electrical and electronics industries. In the four years between 1986 and 1989, they accounted for more than 30 percent of total Japanese manufacturing direct investment in Asia, compared with 11 percent in the preceding period (Table 14.7). In contrast, labor-intensive

Table 14.7

Japan's Manufacturing FDI in Asia

	Asia		ASEAN		Asian NIEs	
	1951–85	1986–89	1951–85	1986–89	1951–85	1886–89
All manufacturing	7,517 (100.0)	8,074 (100.0)	4,014 (100.0)	3,811 (100.0)	3,318 (100.0)	3,574 (100.0)
Foodstuffs	256 (3.4)	795 (9.8)	152 (3.8)	149 (3.9)	79 (2.4)	606 (17.0)
Textiles	1,182 (15.7)	387 (4.8)	818 (20.4)	183 (4.8)	356 (10.7)	77 (2.2)
Pulp & Paper	191 (2.5)	260 (3.2)	157 (3.9)	229 (6.0)	29 (0.9)	23 (0.7)
Chemicals	1,292 (17.2)	786 (9.7)	431 (10.7)	283 (7.4)	844 (25.4)	464 (13.4)
Steel and non-ferrous metals	1,697 (22.6)	881 (10.9)	1,474 (36.7)	599 (15.7)	192 (5.8)	259 (7.2)
General machinery	580 (7.7)	806 (10.0)	95 (2.4)	447 (11.7)	478 (14.8)	296 (8.3)
Electrical machinery	833 (11.1)	2,515 (31.1)	190 (4.7)	1,255 (32.9)	628 (18.9)	1,008 (28.2)
Transport machinery	692 (9.2)	633 (7.8)	368 (9.2)	254 (6.7)	285 (8.6)	340 (9.5)
Others	796 (10.6)	1,010 (12.5)	328 (8.2)	411 (10.8)	427 (12.9)	502 (14.0)

Source: Calculated from data released by the Ministry of Finance, Japan.
Note: Figures in parentheses are share of each industry in all manufacturing.

industries, typically textiles, and resource-intensive industries, such as chemicals, and steel and nonferrous metals, have shown a sharp decline in their shares. The exceptional case is foodstuffs, an industry that is considered labor-intensive. Its share rose sharply in the second period. This was due, however, to the merger and acquisition of a large firm in Singapore by a Japanese manufacturer of alcoholic beverages in 1989. This case has biased, in terms of statistical data, the structure of Japanese manufacturing FDI in the NIEs (Table 14.7).

The steady expansion of FDI by Japan's electrical/electronics industry has been increasingly accompanied by the transfer of high technology. Until the early 1980s, firms tended to transfer standardized or low-level technologies such as those related to the assembly of black-and-white television sets or those related to simple electronics parts. In recent years, however, Japanese firms have increased the transfer of technologies related to sophisticated electronic parts, production of color TVs, VCRs, and other areas.

FDI from other industries has also been characterized by the transfer of high technologies. As for the Japanese FDI in Korea's chemical industry, for example, there have increasingly appeared such high-tech projects as biotechnology and pharmaceuticals (JETRO, 1991). Tambunlertchai (1991) also documented the fact that Japanese FDI in Thailand has markedly increased in the fields of capital goods and intermediate electronic and electrical products.

A second characteristic of Japan's manufacturing FDI in Asia in recent years has been the increasing export orientation of investment projects. The rapid appreciation of the yen has forced Japanese firms to locate their manufacturing production activities overseas as a substitute for exports, on the one hand, and for sourcing cheaper products to serve their home markets on the other. According to a survey by MITI (1990) on the markets for products of Japan's manufacturing subsidiaries in Asia, in 1988, 15.2 percent of the sales of those firms were shipped back to the Japanese market, compared with 10.8 percent in 1983, and 26.5 percent were exported to third countries, compared with 22.3 percent in 1983. For electric and electronic products, third-country markets have been much more important than for manufacturing industries as a whole. According to the same MITI survey, for the Asian affiliates of Japanese firms in electric and electronics, 19.4 percent of outputs were shipped back to the Japanese market, another 37.4 percent were exported to third countries, and only 43.1 percent were sold in the local markets. The statistics from the side of recipient countries such as Thailand (Tambunlertchai, 1991) and Indonesia (Thee, 1991) also show the same trends.

In sum, since the mid-1980s, technology transfer by Japanese firms to the Pacific Asia region has been upgraded as well as actively conducted through various channels. Technologies transferred through FDI have been increasingly used to export products to Japanese and third-country markets. Among the technologies transferred, sophisticated technologies such as those relating to electric and electronic products have played an increasingly important role.

The Pattern of Technology Transfer by Asian NIEs

Since the mid-1980s the Pacific Asia region has witnessed the emergence of the NIEs as new transmitters of technologies. To provide a simple picture of this phenomenon, we review the pattern of FDI, which is a major channel of technology transfer, from Taiwan and Korea to ASEAN countries.

The Pattern of Taiwan's Direct Investment in ASEAN

Taiwan started to undertake FDI as early as 1959, but until around 1980 the annual FDI level was very low. Substantial FDI occurred in the early 1980s, and annual FDI flow expanded rapidly after the middle of the decade. The cumulative FDI for the two decades between 1959 and 1980 was only US$100 million, while the corresponding figure for the 1981–85 period was US$114 million. The sum of FDI undertaken during the two subsequent years, 1986 and 1987, was even higher, at US$160 million. Toward the end of the 1980s, annual FDI from Taiwan experienced a great leap: US$219 million in 1988, and US$931 million and US$1.6 billion in 1989 and 1990, respectively.[8]

A number of factors have pushed Taiwan firms to expand investment abroad in recent years, including the rapid rise in wages and other factor costs in Taiwan, the increase in the value of the New Taiwan dollar, and trade friction with the United States. For these reasons, Taiwan FDI so far has been conducted mainly by manufacturing firms. In terms of stock at the end of 1990, approximately two-thirds of Taiwan FDI was accounted for by manufacturing industries.

The United States has been the most important recipient of Taiwan FDI, but in recent years there has been a shift from the United States to ASEAN countries (Table 14.8). Up until 1987, the United States was particularly important for Taiwan's electric and electronics industry. However, in the area of light manufacturing (labor-intensive industries), such as textiles, apparel, wooden products, foodstuffs, and beverages, ASEAN has been much more important. As the table shows, light manufacturing industries accounted for about half of Taiwan FDI in ASEAN. In particular, Taiwan's FDI in labor-intensive industries in Thailand, Malaysia, and the Philippines has shown a remarkable rate of expansion. In 1988–89, Taiwan electric and electronics firms undertook substantial FDI in ASEAN. However, Taiwan electronics firms' FDI in Thailand and other ASEAN countries seemed to be involved primarily in the production of highly standardized products such as lamps, transformers, and washing machine motors (Ramstetter, 1988; and JETRO, 1991). This is quite different from FDI by Japanese electronics firms.

Recently, Taiwan light manufacturers have also been active in undertaking FDI in Vietnam, which promulgated a new foreign investment law in January 1988.[9]

The Pattern of Korea's FDI in ASEAN

Korea first undertook FDI in 1968 when it conducted a project for procuring lumber in Indonesia. Until 1985, however, the level of Korean FDI was small and its investments tended to be concentrated in resource development and in commerce and other service sectors aimed at facilitating export activities.

Since the mid-1980s, Korean FDI expanded rapidly and there has been an increase in the share of manufacturing industries. The cumulative FDI for the latest four years (1986–89) amounted to US$968 million, which was twice the cumulative FDI from 1968 to 1985 (US$476 million). The manufacturing sector accounted for only 17 percent of investment stock at the end of 1985, but the share rose to 39 percent in the period of 1987–89. As shown below, the share of the manufacturing sector has been even higher for Korean FDI in ASEAN countries.

The factors accounting for the expansion of manufacturing FDI since the second half of the 1980s are almost the same as those in the case of Taiwan: a sharp rise in real wages, a revaluation of local currency against the U.S. dollar, and trade conflict with the most important export market, the United States.

The recent patterns of Korean FDI in ASEAN are summarized in Tables 14.9 and 14.10. These statistics illustrate the following characteristics: first, for most ASEAN countries, substantial Korean FDI began in 1988–89. In particular, Korean FDI in Thailand and Indonesia was marginal before 1987. Second, with the exception of Indonesia, almost all FDI in ASEAN has been in manufacturing industries (Table 14.9). Third, within the manufacturing sector, Korean firms tend to invest either in labor-intensive industries such as foodstuffs, textiles and apparel, footwear and leather, wood and furniture, and "other" (which includes miscellaneous products), or in resource-intensive products such as chemicals, nonferrous products, and fabricated metals (Table 14.10). The first group of industries accounts for about 54 percent of the investment in Thailand, 81 percent in Indonesia, and 60 percent in the Philippines. The share of the second group of industries is high in resource-rich Malaysia. None of the ASEAN countries has received substantial FDI from Korea's electric and electronics industry.

These observations suggest that the pattern of Korean FDI in ASEAN has been almost the same as that of Taiwan: expansion in recent years and concentration in labor-intensive and technologically standardized industries. Such structure of FDI by these NIE firms contrasts sharply with that of Japan, which appears to transfer more sophisticated technologies to ASEAN.

Another difference in the pattern of NIEs and that of Japan is that the average size of investment projects undertaken in ASEAN by Taiwan, Korea, and other Asian NIEs has been much smaller than those of Japan (Ramstetter, 1988; Thee, 1990). This difference may be attributable to differences in the type of industries or technologies just mentioned.

Table 14.8

Structure of Taiwan's Foreign Direct Investment (in US$ thousands)

	ASEAN		U.S.		Other Regions		Total	
	1959–87	1988–90	1959–87	1988–90	1959–87	1988–90	1959–87	1988–90
Primary Industries	638	5,738	0	0	4,659	300	5,297	6,038
	(0.7)	(0.6)	(0.0)	(0.0)	(8.4)	(0.0)	(1.4)	(0.2)
All manufacturing	78,199	855,778	180,608	712,253	31,931	82,766	290,738	1,651,092
	(90.8)	(94.2)	(77.4)	(67.2)	(57.8)	(11.4)	(77.6)	(61.1)
Light industries	42,421	151,656	24,151	189,500	12,706	11,512	79,278	352,668
	(29.2)	(16.7)	(10.4)	(17.9)	(23.0)	(1.6)	(21.2)	(13.1)
Electric and electronic products	8,738	356,150	116,406	173,067	6,293	56,031	132,437	585,259
	(11.3)	(39.2)	(49.9)	(16.3)	(11.4)	(7.7)	(35.4)	(21.7)
Other manufacturing	26,040	347,972	40,051	349,970	12,932	15,223	79,023	713,165
	(30.2)	(38.3)	(17.2)	(33.0)	(23.4)	(2.1)	(21.1)	(26.4)
Construction and tertiary sector	7,306	46,649	52,606	348,220	18,636	644,623	78,548	1,044,799
	(8.5)	(5.1)	(22.6)	(32.8)	(33.7)	(88.6)	(21.0)	(38.7)
Total others	86,143	908,626	233,214	1,060,757	55,226	727,689	374,583	2,701,929
	(100.0)	(100.0)	(100.0)	(100.0)	(100.0)	(100.0)	(100.0)	(100.0)

Source: Compiled from *Statistics on Overseas Chinese & Foreign Investment, Technical Cooperation, Outward Investment, Outward Technical Cooperation.* Investment Commission, Ministry of Foreign Affairs, Republic of China, December issues for 1988, 1989, and 1990.

Note: Figures in parentheses are industry shares in total investment within each region. ASEAN excludes Brunei. Light industries include food and beverages, textiles, garment and footwear, lumber and bamboo products, pulp and paper products, leather and fur products, and plastics and rubber products.

Table 14.9

Korea's Manufacturing FDI in ASEAN (in US$ thousands)

	Thailand	Indonesia	Malaysia	Philippines
1973–85	1,981	11,993	26,488	2,009
1986	45	—	588	—
1987	997	2,349	240	2,062
1988	16,098	23,744	3,301	4,529
1989	13,363	76,383	33,858	8,758
1973–89	21,374	114,469	64,475	17,358
(% of total)*	(99.1)	(33.0)	(97.1)	(98.8)

Source: Compiled from data released by the Bank of Korea.
*% of total means the share of manufacturing in total FDI in all industries.

Table 14.10

Industry Composition of Korea's Manufacturing FDI in ASEAN
(outstanding investment stock as of the end of 1989 in US$ thousands)

	Thailand	Indonesia	Malaysia	Philippines
Foodstuffs	—	25,685	—	—
Textiles and apparel	2,903	22,432	—	6,723
Footwear and leather	3,684	22,840	—	2,809
Wood and furniture	—	8,120	2,754	—
Paper	—	1,520	—	—
Chemicals	2,118	10,190	10,383	—
Nonferrous products	—	—	25,062	1,000
Primary metals	45	1,278	565	—
Fabricated medals	12,770	8,852	25,145	5,894
Others	10,854	13,552	566	932
Total	32,374	114,469	64,475	17,358

Source: Compiled from data released by the Bank of Korea.

Conclusions

Pacific Asia has been one of the fastest-growing regions in the world since the 1970s. After a short setback in the early 1980s, the region's economic activities regained momentum in the latter half of that decade. As the rest of the world has experienced rather bleak economic performance, Pacific Asia is often characterized as a growth pole of the world economy.

The rapid economic expansion in the region in the mid-1980s is attributable to a number of factors, including expansion in FDI, exports, and fixed investment, all of which have worked together to result in economic growth. Expansion in exports, FDI, and fixed investment were precipitated by structural changes, which were in turn induced by the major currency realignment. The appreciation of the yen and of the NIEs' currencies promoted imports to Japan and the NIEs, thereby contributing to the expansion of exports from other countries. Exports from Pacific Asia to Japan were also promoted by Japanese FDI and the region, which was due mainly to the yen appreciation, as Japanese FDI established a link between the producers in the recipient countries to the Japanese market. Albeit at a lesser degree, a similar development is underway for the NIEs and ASEAN, as the appreciation of the NIEs' currencies promoted the NIEs' FDI to ASEAN countries.

Through active FDI and foreign trade, which resulted mainly from market forces, intraregional linkages among the countries in Pacific Asia have been intensified. Unlike state-led regionalization in North America and in Western Europe, regionalization in Pacific Asia is driven mainly by the private sector (Simon, 1995). As a growing region attracts private firms, growth momentum snowballs. Furthermore, we should point out that state-led regionalization in North America and in Western Europe accelerates market-led regionalization in Pacific Asia because expansion of exports to North America and Western Europe by outsiders has become difficult.

Rapid economic expansion in Pacific Asia was made possible by active transfer of foreign technology. The channel of technology transfer has been diversified. Some of the channels frequently used are foreign direct investment and new forms of investment such as licensing, production cooperation, and OEM. One of the most notable developments is the emergence of the NIEs as technology suppliers to the technology market in Asia, which was once dominated by the United States and Japan. As for the type of technology being transferred, it is manufacturing technologies that have been most actively transferred, but it is not clear if developmental technologies or managerial know-how have been effectively transferred. Estimation of the extent and the effectiveness of technology transfer is quite difficult due to the intangible nature of technology, but there is some evidence that there are obstacles to technology transfer. Some of the criticisms often voiced by the recipients against the technology suppliers are: inappropriate technology, unwillingness to transfer technology, high cost of equipment and materials necessary for the use of technology, and inability to communicate with the recipient. On the other hand, technology suppliers complain of a lack of effort for improvement, expectation of immediate return from imported technology, and job-hopping as obstacles to technology transfer.

To facilitate technology transfer and effectively to absorb foreign technologies, we present several policy recommendations. Since the international technology transfer we have studied here involves two private parties with a profit-making motive, there is not much that the governments of technology suppliers can do. The following policy recommendations therefore are directed at recipient countries. First, an environment under which intellectual property rights are protected has to be established; this is to address the appropriability problem associated with technology. Second, policies to improve the technological level of local people have to be pursued. Specifically, education, especially engineering education, has to be promoted. Improved technological capability through engineering education may not only facilitate the absorption of imported technologies but also allow local firms to acquire the ability to select appropriate technology. To promote education, economic assistance from developed countries may be used. Finally, for improving technological capability, one cannot overemphasize the importance of well-functioning markets, which provide the profit-making opportunity for an entrepreneur, because profit seeking gives rise to technological improvement.

Notes

The authors appreciate helpful comments from Professor Denis Fred Simon and other participants of the conference.

1. See, for example, Baumol, Blackman, and Wolf (1989) for empirical evidence.

2. For the importance of imported technology in economic development in Japan, see Urata (1990).

3. Throughout this chapter NIEs denote the group of countries including Hong Kong, Korea, Singapore, and Taiwan, while ASEAN denotes the group of countries consisting of Indonesia, Malaysia, the Philippines, and Thailand.

4. For detailed discussion on NFI, see Oman (1989).

5. For the United States, the world's largest exporter of technology, the nominal value of technology exports increased at an average annual rate of 17.7 percent between 1986 and 1989, while for Japan, the world's second largest exporter of technology, the corresponding growth rate was 14.4 percent between 1985 and 1990. World capital goods exports appear to have increased at about the same rate. This may be seen from the statistics on machinery exports (SITC 7), which may be used as a proxy for capital exports. World exports of machinery registered an average annual growth rate of 18.3 percent between 1985 and 1988.

6. Kreinin (1988) found that among foreign subsidiaries in Australia, Japanese subsidiaries rely substantially more on home country for the supply of capital goods. Urata (1991) also reports a high dependence of Japanese subsidiaries for the procurement of capital goods.

7. Approximately 30 percent of the firms surveyed by MITI (1989) have conducted OEM in Asia and other regions. The most important reason for choosing this channel of technology transfer is said to be "requests" from recipient firms.

8. FDI data released by the Taiwan authorities have usually been underestimated. This was in part because government approval was not sought for some investments. The government review process is usually time-consuming, so that in order to avoid possible delays of the investment schedule, firms do not apply to the government, if possible. This data problem, however, does not significantly affect our analysis here unless the unreported FDI has had a pattern quite different from what we describe.

9. Direct investment into Vietnam from Asian NIEs and other sources is analyzed in Tran (1991).

References

Baumol, W. J., Blackman, S. B., and Wolf, E. N. *Productivity and American Leadership*. Cambridge, MA: MIT Press, 1989.

JETRO. *Sekai to Nihon no Chokusetsu Toshi* [Direct Investment by Japan and the World]. JETRO White Paper on Investment. Tokyo, 1991.

Kreinin, M. "How Closed Is the Japanese Market? Additional Evidence." *The World Economy*, *11*, 4 (December, 1988).

MITI. *Tsusho Hakusho* [White Paper on International Trade]. Tokyo: MITI, 1987, 1988, 1989.

————. *Wagakuni Kigyo no Kaigai Jigyo Katsudo* [Survey on Overseas Activities by Japanese Companies], no. 19. Tokyo: MITI, 1990.

Oman, C. *New Forms of Investment In Developing Countries*. Paris: OECD, 1989.

Ramstetter, E. D. "Taiwan's Direct Foreign Investment in Thailand: The Potential for Technology Transfer." *Development and South-South Cooperation* (December 1988).

Simon, Denis Fred. *The Technology of Japanese Firms Toward the Pacific Rim*. Cambridge University Press, 1995, forthcoming.

Tambunlertchai, S. "The Changing Pattern of Japanese Direct Investment in Thailand." In V. T. Tran (ed.), *Japan's Direct Investment in Thailand*. The Japan Center for Economic Research, 1991.

Thee, K. W. "The Investment Surge from the East Asian Newly-Industrializing Countries into Indonesia." Paper for Economics of Trade and Development Seminars, Research School of Pacific Studies, Australian Studies, Australian National University, 1990.

Tran, V. T., ed. *Betonamu Keizai to Ajia-Taiheiyou* [Vietnamese Economy and the Asian Pacific Region]. The Japan Center for Economic Research, 1991.

Urata, S. "The Impact of Imported Technologies in Japan's Economic Development." In C. H. Lee and I. Yamazawa (eds.), *The Economic Development of Japan and Korea*. New York: Praeger, 1990.

————. "Japanese Foreign Direct Investment and its Impact on Foreign Trade in Asia." Presented at the Second Annual East Asian Seminar on Economics sponsored by the National Bureau of Economic Research, Korea Development Institute, and Chung-Hua Institution for Economic Research, Taipei, June 19–21, 1991.

15

Science and Technology Cooperation in the Pacific Rim: Bilateral and Multilateral Perspectives

Karen Minden

As the commercial importance of science and technology in the international market has grown, economic forces have driven increased cooperative activity among scientists, producers, and policy makers across national boundaries. The economic benefits of cooperation in science and technology are motivating countries to seek ways to expand cooperation with each other. This chapter examines some of the patterns of cooperation that have emerged in the Pacific Rim. The first section describes the major bilateral trends that have developed, followed by some observations about multilateral cooperation in the region. A discussion of these cooperation trends presents a framework for examining the issues of science and technology interaction. Beginning with a historical perspective of the transfer of technology and ideas in the region, the discussion then presents a matrix of interaction. This matrix categorizes cooperative activity into four domains: business, domestic policy formation, development assistance, and international policy coordination. Woven into this matrix are three central issues that have emerged as a *leit motif* of discussions of regional cooperation: the training and distribution of human resources, the parameters and recognition of intellectual property rights, and the need for international policy coordination. This interlocking grid of domains and issues will provide a reference point for the concluding discussion of regional patterns of bilateral and multilateral cooperation.

A Pacific regional consciousness has emerged in the last decade, often characterized by the optimistic forecast that the next century will be the "Pacific

Table 15.1

Japan's Investment in Asia, 1979–89 (US$ billion)

	Direct investment	Foreign aid	Tourism spending	Total
1979	$1.0	$1.3	$2.4	$4.7
1980	1.2	1.4	2.3	4.9
1981	3.3	1.6	2.4	7.3
1982	1.4	1.6	2.5	5.5
1983	1.8	1.6	2.5	6.0
1984	1.6	1.6	2.7	6.0
1985	1.4	1.7	2.5	5.6
1986	2.3	2.5	2.8	7.6
1987	4.9	3.4	5.8	14.1
1988	5.6	4.0	7.5	17.1
1989*	7.8	7.6	10.0	25.4

Source: Ministry of Finance, Foreign Ministry, Japanese Immigration Bureau, in the *Globe and Mail,* February 26, 1990 (Toronto).
Total for 1979 to 1989 $104.2 billion.
*1989 (estimate).

Century." One analyst refers to the Pacific Rim's "growing economic integration, with an interregional, interfirm division of labour. Neighbours are less competitors for market share in the industrialized countries and are more markets for exports and sources of imports."[1]

Bilateral Trends

During the last decade, Japan has clearly emerged as the key player in Asia Pacific trade, and in the development of science and technology. Media references to the new Japanese empire abound. The business section of a major North American newspaper reported that "for the most part, Japan is creating its community of interest with a simple yet potent catalyst—cash."[2] In the decade from 1979 to 1989, Japan invested more than US$100 billion through aid, tourism, and direct investment in Asia (see Table 15.1.) The Asian response has been characterized on the one hand by the historical experience of Japan's brutal occupation during the Second World War, and on the other, by a recognition of the opportunity for growth and prosperity offered by Japanese investment. Although there is an underlying fear that Japanese economic power translates to powerful geopolitical influence, most nations embrace Japan's contribution to their growth.

During the 1980s the Japanese government established science and technology agreements with ten countries, including China (1980), Australia (1980),

Indonesia (1981), Korea (1985), Canada (1986) and the United States (1988).[3] They ranged from agreements to hold scientific conferences, to detailed accords on cooperative research projects and joint data bases. The 1985 agreement with Korea, for example, states that cooperation in strategic sectors, including materials, biotechnology, and computer and information science, would be based "on the principle of equality and mutual benefit."[4] Exchange would be in the areas of policy issues, data, personnel, and joint research. In 1988, the original agreement with the United States was renewed. It is considerably more legalistic than other bilateral S&T agreements. It stresses the principles of "shared responsibilities and equitable contributions and benefits, commensurate with the two nations respective scientific and technological strengths and resources."[5] This agreement has a substantial annex on intellectual property rights, stipulating that cooperation will occur within a framework of mutually agreed definitions of confidentiality and copyright law.

Much of the bilateral cooperation between Japan and its Pacific Rim neighbors is conducted through business ventures, which often involve government agreements and programs to facilitate the relationship. The government of the Republic of Korea recently granted US$2.1 billion to Korean companies to increase their technical capability in manufacturing. Seven of these projects involved joint research with Japanese companies.[6] In the same vein, Japan's MITI has expanded its financial support for cooperative R&D to companies outside of Japan.[7]

Perhaps the second most cogent characteristic of science and technology relations in the Pacific Rim, after Japan's dominance, is the rivalry between the United States and Japan. Of the US$400 million in Asian investments to American universities and think tanks, 75 percent of the total came from Japan.[8] In an attempt to redress American accusations of unfair advantage, Japanese electronics firms have agreed to give American semiconductor makers a greater share of the Japanese market. As one Sanyo executive stated, "We didn't ask for LSI Logic because we couldn't do it in-house."[9] Strategic alliances between American and Japanese companies are likened to "David and Goliath," according to the *Far Eastern Economic Review*'s analyst of Japanese S&T relations.[10] While the United States has innovative capability and manufacturing and marketing strengths, Japan has both the venture capital and long-term perspective that make R&D possible. The United States laments the structural impediments to fair competition with Japan, while the Japanese criticize the United States' failure to bolster its competitiveness in high technology because of its neglect of international markets, business-government coooperation and intraindustry alliances.[11]

This competition is reinforced by the patterns of FDI in the region. Asian investment in Asia has surpassed American investment,[12] along with intra-Asian trade, which overtook Asian trade with North America and the European community in 1989.[13] While there is increasing investment by Taiwan and Korea in Pacific Rim economies, science and technology cooperation is dominated by the technology transfer associated with offshore production and joint ventures. Investment by the NIEs in southeast Asia tends to be in low-technology, labor-intensive industries, while investment in North America is often associated with technology acquisition. The ASEAN countries are largely the recipients of investment and aid, and tend to operate through multilateral forums in the area of S&T cooperation. In the case of China, there is limited trade with ASEAN countries, and it is predicted that they are more likely to be competitors than to experience economic integration with each other.[14] Although China and Indonesia recently negotiated a cooperative agreement on satellite launching, it is interpreted more as "rocket diplomacy" than significant S&T cooperation.[15] Here again, S&T cooperation is more probable within a multilateral framework.

Multilateral Cooperation

The Pacific region is increasingly characterized by subregions of trade and cooperative activity. Regional and subregional groups, if superimposed on a map of the Pacific Rim, would appear as a series of overlapping circles. Beginning with the smallest, we would see what *Business Week* calls "Asia's hot new growth zones," including "Greater China" (Hong Kong, Taiwan, and Guangdong), "Greater Korea" (North Korea, South Korea, and the "Soviet" Far East), Indochina (Thailand, Vietnam, Cambodia, Southwest China), and the "Northern/Growth Triangle" of Singapore, Malaysia's Johor state (Penang), and Indonesia's Riau province.[16] The increasing economic links within these subregions have been a catalyst for political cooperation, as in the case of the Northern Triangle. Here, the strategic alliance between Singapore's service sector and Penang's human resources and industrial infrastructure has led to interstate cooperation at the local ministerial level.

The Association of Southeast Asian Nations (ASEAN) comprises a larger circle encompassing Malaysia, Singapore, Indonesia, Thailand, the Philippines, and Brunei. It is primarily a political grouping characterized by senior ministerial meetings. Although Asean has been slow to develop viable economic integration, members have been reluctant to accept Malaysia's recent proposal to form a subregional East Asia Economic Group or Caucus, which would exclude the EC and North America.[17]

ASEAN's Committee on Science and Technology (COST) (supported in part by the Fund for Science and Technology) focuses on projects of regional significance in mutually beneficial areas such as environment, energy, and food and agriculture technology (see chapter 6). The cooperative activities are characterized not so much by intra-ASEAN cooperation as by interaction with ASEAN's dialogue partners: Australia, New Zealand, Canada, the United States, Japan, the EC, and the United Nations. A survey of the programs sponsored by COST[18] reveals that for the most part, cooperation means foreign aid. Joint projects with Australia in food protein research have been funded by Australia; energy research with the United States is funded by the United States; cooperation in marine sciences is funded by Canada; and materials science research has been funded by Japan. In the latter case, Japan is providing the coordinator for the project, as well as equipment and training in Japan.[19] It is interesting to note that outside partners tend to serve as a catalyst for intra-ASEAN cooperation. Germany, for example, signed a technical cooperation agreement with ASEAN which includes the provision of assistance in intra-ASEAN cooperation in technology transfer and vocational training. It is expected that the EC will play an increasing role in ASEAN's science and technology development. In 1991, the EC Council of Ministers adopted "New Guidelines" regarding relations with Asean, which include a focus on venture capital, human resource development, and science and technology programs.[20] Although ASEAN trade patterns have been relatively stable for the past fifteen years, there seems to be growing international interest in science and technology development.

Despite the number of organizations dedicated to the expansion of regional cooperation in science and technology, there continues to be interest in expanding opportunities for further participation. The Pacific Economic Cooperation Conference (PECC) is a multilateral, regional, nongovernmental organization established in 1980 to promote economic development through the tripartite participation of business, government, and academic representatives. In 1988, when Japan hosted the PECC plenary conference in Osaka, it urged the creation of a "Pacific OECD."[21] It was envisaged that trade and investment data and analysis, and the coordination of cooperative programmes would contribute to regional economic growth. In 1989, the PECC inaugurated a Science and Technology Task Force, cochaired by China and the United States, which stated its objectives as follows:

> to provide a forum where consensus can be reached and actions taken on programs and policy recommendations that foster Pacific Basin science and technology cooperation. This in turn will foster greater and more equitable economic and social development.[22]

Task Force members include representatives of twenty Pacific Rim economies, including China, Taiwan, and Hong Kong, and most recently the Russian Federation. Because members participate in their unofficial capacity, PECC forums allow the participation of government representatives from countries that do not normally have official relations with each other. This provides more opportunities for cooperative activity than a governmental organization such as the Asia Pacific Economic Cooperation. In addition, each member economy of PECC's S&T Task Force has a science and technology advisory committee, thus creating a Pacific Rim network of business, academic, and government experts in S&T. In November 1993, a major conference emphasizing the "tripartite" dimensions of technology transfer was held in Hong Kong under PECC auspices.

Science and technology subcommittees, led by various member countries, are responsible for developing programs in technology transfer, human resource development, and cooperative R&D. The task force is engaged in compiling OECD-compatible data bases on science and technology policies, indicators, investment flows, and human resource development programmes. It is involved in the organization of workshops to share "best practices" in the mechanisms for science and technology development, such as science and technology research parks. The task force also serves as a catalyst for bringing together a consortium for cooperative research and development on problems of regional concern. The most current project involves the effects of global warming on the region. PECC's work is best characterized as an attempt to build regional networks to augment bilateral cooperation with multilateral programs.

The recently established Asia Pacific Economic Cooperation (APEC), at its first senior officials' meeting in March 1990, identified a series of strategic issues to be addressed by working groups. Each group is led by a "shepherd," who is a country representative designated as the group's coordinator. Although APEC began as a relatively small group, it is expanding, and most recently admitted the "three Chinas" based on a formula worked out in PECC whereby Taiwan is referred to as Chinese-Taipei. Some analysts see the emergence of APEC as evidence of a tripolar trading system including North America, Europe, and East Asia. Japan's interest in APEC has been identified as promoting a regional division of labor, increased intraregional trade, and the gradual development of Japan's industrial infrastructure throughout Asia.[23]

Japan serves as the dominant "shepherd" of the working group on the expansion of investment and technology transfer. This organization, also led by Indonesia and the Philippines, hopes to cooperate with government, the private sector, and the academic community to identify investment patterns and needs, and to develop mechanisms to enhance technology cooperation and growth in the region.[24] At the present time, the agenda is said to be dominated by MITI's interest in developing technoparks in Asia. The current work programme could be characterized as a series of bilateral aid projects under the auspices of APEC.

A working group titled "Multilateral Human Resource Development Initiative" is also shepherded by Japan, with Thailand, Indonesia, South Korea, Malaysia, and Canada.[25] In this project, members identify lead institutions in their country to participate in strategic networks in the area of business management, economic development policy management, and industrial technical training. These three networks are led by Japan, Korea, and Australia respectively. The object of working group research and programs is to make recommendations to APEC ministers on trade and development policy, and regional cooperation.

These regional organizations, ASEAN, PECC, and APEC, have overlapping memberships and goals. Their development is indicative of regional interest in pursuing a variety of opportunities for cooperative activity in science and technology.

International Organizations

Prior to the development of regional forums, the United Nations was the key agency for promoting cooperative activity in Pacific Rim science and technology. Increasingly over the past three decades, the United Nations has focused on science and technology as a critical component of socioeconomic development. In 1976, the U.N. General Assembly adopted a proposal to highlight science and technology for development. In 1978 the Department of Technical Cooperation for Development advocated increased regional cooperation, with Asia Pacific identified as a key region. The Vienna Conference convened representatives from each of five regions to discuss a program of action for developing both indigenous science and technology capability and international cooperation in this area. By 1989 technical cooperation for development was identified as a UNDP priority. There has been a proliferation of organizations and programs to provide funding for infrastructural development, to enhance communication among the international science and technology community, and to develop national policies to support S&T development. Among them are the U.N. Fund for S&T Development (now incorporated within UNDP), UNIDO programs for S&T policy development, World Bank programs, The U.N. Center for Science and Technology Development, UNESCO's CASTASIA conferences, and ESCAP (Economic and Social Commission for Asia and Pacific) conferences and projects, including the Technology Atlas project.[26] In the area of policy development, the Science and Technology Policy Network (STEPAN), based in Australia and initially funded by UNESCO, provides support for national S&T policy development and management. STEPAN serves as both a research and a training facility.

In addition to the United Nations' interest in science and technology cooperation, OECD has developed a technology/economy program with regional implications. The recognition that a technoeconomic network affects social, marketing, and financial conditions beyond the borders of a firm or industry has led to an examination of the globalization of science and technology. The Tokyo Conference, "Towards Techno-Globalism," held in 1990, underlined the changes from the relatively simple technology transfer mechanisms of the 1980s (licensing, subcontracting) to a system of transnational interfirm cooperation in research and development, design, production, and marketing. In the 1990s, the barriers to cooperation in technological development and exchange have been identified as "technonationalism," whereby governments attempt to protect technology for national use. OECD documents promote the concept that positive synergy is created by technical cooperation and is a factor promoting the social and economic integration of technological progress.[27]

Although international programs were the first to address the issues of S&T cooperation and development in Asia Pacific, regional organizations have become the focus of cooperative activity in the last decade.

Framework for Assessing S&T Cooperation

This section provides an initial framework within which one can analyze the critical issues and domains of science and technology cooperation. It suggests

Figure 15.1. **Framework for Science and Technology Cooperation**

S&T COOPERATION
Problems

ISSUES: DOMAINS:	Human Resources	Intellectual Property	Policy Cooperation
Business	• mobility of high-tech personnel	• licensing agreements • copyright protection	• conflicting values: profit vs. public good
Domestic Policy-making	• emigration of professionals	• copyright laws • national security	• incomplete data • inadequate consultation mechanisms
Development Assistance	• students stay abroad	• ownership of science: "commercial"/ "precommercial"	• duplication • conflicting goals • cross-cultural communication
Internal Policy Coordination	• regional personnel "market"	• inconsistent rules • inconsistent definitions	• incomplete data • conflicting goals

ISSUES: DOMAINS:	Human Resources	Intellectual Property	Policy Cooperation
Business	• MNCs keep human resources within company • competitive recruitment	• litigation • innovation • management of hi-tech	• government-business consultation • participation in international organizations
Domestic Policy-making	• restrict mobility • create hospitable environment for S&T professionals	• facilitate R&D innovation	• comparative data • sharing best results
Development Assistance	• local training programs • long-term horizon	• cooperative R&D • restrict technology transfer	• inventory of programs • consultation for consensus on mutual benefit
Internal Policy Coordination	• cooperative HRD programs	• IPR agreements • international arbitration	• inventory of policies • participation in a regional fora

that cooperation occurs in four domains: business, domestic policy, development assistance, and international policy coordination. These domains intersect with three key issues in S&T interaction: human resource development, intellectual property rights, and international policy cooperation (see Figure 15.1). The following discussion examines the problems and responses in science and technology cooperation using this matrix as a framework.

Historical Perspective

The debate over the last four centuries of technology transfer has been characterized by a persistent set of questions: What are the social and economic consequences of introducing foreign ideas and technology? What is the most effective strategy for the diffusion of new knowledge? What is the balance between self-interest and equitable development? Who owns and controls the sources and products of knowledge?

The transfer of technology and ideas within the Asia Pacific region goes back thousands of years, and includes the transmission of science knowledge and techniques, language, religion, art, and music. Business trade has always been an avenue for the movement of technology from one place to another. Military conquest has been another. These avenues allowed the introduction of paper, navigation techniques, gunpowder, and other inventions within Asia and from East Asia to Europe. A significant transfer occurred when missionaries from the West took the ideas and techniques of Western science and philosophy to Asia, as part of their evangelical mission. The Jesuits attempted to introduce European science to the Ming court in China, to demonstrate the superiority of Western science and religion. Two centuries later, in the mid-1800s, European and North American Protestant missionaries introduced Western medicine, and eventually established universities that taught modern science and Western languages to the intellectual elite of urban China. Toward the end of the Qing dynasty, Chinese reformers themselves sought Western scientific knowledge in the search for means to strengthen the nation and promote economic prosperity.

In Meiji Japan in the late nineteenth century, government reformers sought Western technology and administrative structures which they adapted to the Japanese environment as they transformed their country into a modern nation.[28] Western imperialist governments from Britain, Germany, France, and the Netherlands also influenced the introduction of science and technology into Asia, through their universities, transportation and communication systems, and administrative and commercial institutions. The Japanese imperial government followed a similar pattern in the Asian countries which it occupied before the Second World War. Prior to the war, students from Asia pursued the study of Western science in transplanted foreign universities in their own countries, in universities in Europe and North America, and in

Japan, the most rapidly modernizing of the Asian economies in the first half of the twentieth century.

After the Second World War, United States foreign aid was directed to the restoration of the international trading system, and to the promotion of political stability through economic prosperity. The shattered industrial systems of Europe and Japan, and the emerging but impoverished postcolonial countries of the Third World were the recipients of American technology and training. From 1945 until the present, the United States, through government channels and nongovernment organizations, has been the major donor of international foreign assistance. In recent years, Japan, now a world economic power, has begun to undertake a role in providing foreign aid.

Governments of industrialized economies, motivated in part by humanitarian goals, also provide aid to developing economies to prepare the field for future business. They contribute to the building of infrastructure which supports economic development. They share risks with entrepreneurs from their own countries, organizing trade missions, subsidizing research and development, and adopting policies that promote trade. Governments of developing economies cooperate with foreign business and governments in order to facilitate the acquisition of foreign technology and know-how. Some transnational companies provide production skill training for local employees in developing economies, and some have begun to promote local capabilities in research and development. The issues that arise in the interaction between donor and recipient, investor and developing economy, are issues of conflicting values and goals, mutual benefit, and equitability. Regional forums for the promotion of science and technology cooperation in the 1980s and 1990s devote much of their energy to seeking mechanisms to enhance mutuality and effectiveness in designing strategies for increased interaction and trade.

S & T Policy Development

Given the historical development of S&T cooperation, it is useful to consider the four domains in which such activity occurs: business, domestic policymaking, development assistance, and international policy coordination.

Business

In the private sector, the last two decades have witnessed increasing cooperation in R&D, technology transfer, and training across national boundaries, but usually within the confines of transnational enterprises. This trend has shifted toward "strategic alliances" between or among firms, whereby technology, R&D, marketing, and production are shared for perceived mutual benefit. This kind of cooperation may be enhanced by government policies through trade and tax incentives, or domestic policies that favor the development of technological and productive capability.

Domestic Policy Making

The development of national policies for science and technology development, viewed as an essential component of S&T growth, has been aided by cross-national collaboration and assistance, both directly and indirectly. In some cases, national governments are inspired by policy approaches in other countries, and attempt to emulate these policies. In other cases, government-to-government aid, in the form of funding or expert consultation, is provided for the development of policy strategies. This kind of assistance is also provided by several multilateral organizations such as STEPAN.

Development Assistance.

Government-to-government assistance has been provided both bilaterally and multilaterally. Government aid agencies may offer capital, technology, or expertise to develop the prerequisite industrial infrastructure, human resources, research and development capability, and production facilities. The trend over the last several years has been an increase in the provision of human resource development through training programs, the exchange of students, and the exchange of researchers.

International Policy Coordination

Finally, there has been an emerging movement among Pacific Rim nations to facilitate regional trade by coordinating science and technology policy, and concomitant technology transfer policies. In addition, there has been the beginning of an attempt to avoid redundancy and maximize the use of resources by coordinating programs in research and in human resource development.

Numerous issues arise in the discussion of Pacific Rim science and technology cooperation, but there are three that serve as an effective catchment for a broad range of problems. These are (1) the distribution and training of human resources; (2) the definition and scope of intellectual property; and (3) the coordination of national policies as a component of international cooperation.

Human Resources

The most dramatic changes in science and technology capability in the Pacific region have undoubtedly taken place in the newly industrialized economies over the last two decades. Although UNCTAD figures for S&T development indicators are aggregated under the category "developing countries in Asia," they are nonetheless indicative of regional growth in this area. The number of scientists and engineers per 10,000 population has increased by almost 400 percent.[29]

Technology-related flows in capital goods and direct foreign investment during the period 1970 to 1987 increased 1400 percent and 940 percent respectively, while technical assistance decreased by 30 percent.[30] The identification of human resource development as a key factor in economic development is apparent in the S&T strategies of the Asia Pacific countries.

There are four issues that characterize human resource development interaction in the Pacific Rim in the early 1990s. They are the competitive relationship between Japan and the United States; Japan's emerging role as a leader in HRD, through both its private sector and overseas development assistance (ODA); increasing regionalism and nationalism in response to the predominance of English-language and Japanese influence; and the migration of skilled labor, often referred to as "brain drain."

United States Senator Jay Rockefeller is quoted as saying "Young people learning technology are tomorrow's trade statistics."[31] He was speaking on behalf of the U.S. lobby to restrict Japanese access to American research laboratories. In response to the U.S. loss of technological preeminence, some Americans have demanded either restriction of Japanese access to American S&T expertise, or at least reciprocal access to Japanese facilities. The problem has been that U.S. research is primarily concentrated in the public sector. It is located in military establishments, and in universities such as M.I.T., which are open to foreign students and scholars. Japanese research on the other hand is concentrated in the private sector, where 80 percent of research labs are located.[32] By the end of the 1980s, the United States began demanding that Japan contribute to the international pool of scientific knowledge and that American students and researchers be allowed entry to Japan's research facilities. A National Science Foundation survey of 270 Japanese companies with R&D facilities reported a favorable response to admitting foreign researchers.[33] The obvious obstacles to American participation in Japanese research is the language barrier, and the unwillingness of American scientists to leave the mainstream of research and potential funding sources. While U.S. scientists in 1988 were reportedly not interested in learning Japanese, working in Japan, or reading Japanese science publications,[34] U.S. trade analysts declared that asymmetrical access was a nontariff barrier to fair trade (see Figure 15.2).

At the same time as American critics were encouraging Japan to take a more prominent role in science and technology research and training, Japan's role in Asia expanded steadily. There has been a relatively long tradition of sending students abroad to study in the universities of Europe and North America, and since the turn of the century, to Japan. In the last few years, Japan has played an increasingly important role in the training of S&T personnel in Asia. Japanese subsidiary plants and joint venture companies train local experts in production and R&D. Within Asia Pacific, Japanese programs have already established a network for human resource development. Funded jointly by government and private enterprise, these programs address both development assistance and busi-

Figure 15.2. **Flow of Scientists between the U.S. and Japan, 1988**

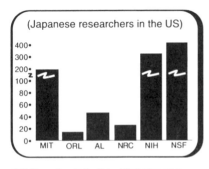 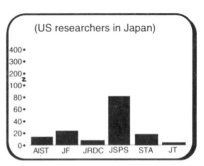

MIT: Massachusetts Institute of Technology (visits per year)
ORL: Oak Ridge Laboratory
AL: Ardonne Laboratory
NRC: National Research Council
NIH: National Institute of Health
NSF: National Science Foundation

AIST: Agency of Industrial Science and Technology
JF: Japan Foundation
JRDC: Japan Research Development Corp.
JSPS: Japan Society for the Promotion of Science
STA: Science and Technology Agency
JT: Japan Trust

Source: U.S. National Science Foundation, *Far Eastern Economic Review* (March 31, 1988) p. 63.

ness agendas. The experience of the Nippon Telephone and Telegraph Corporation (NTT) illustrates this trend. NTT is involved in a variety of international activities that allow it to build a regional network of technical infrastructure and expertise. Through the Japan International Cooperation Agency (JICA), the government's ODA organization, NTT participates in training experts in Singapore, Indonesia and the Philippines. A description of these efforts points out that each program is tailored to the development needs and policies of the host country in the effort to provide appropriate technology and training.[35] An advertisement for NEC in a recent issue of the *Far Eastern Economic Review* illustrates the Japanese attitude toward Japan's role in human resource development in Asia. The ad features an NEC engineer and his wife from Singapore, playing in the snow . Commenting that this was their first experience with snow, the text indicates that they would be returning to Singapore with more than the happy memory of one's first snowfall: "They'll be carrying a lasting wealth of experience and know-how to help NEC Electronics Singapore Pte Ltd. make better products." The ad goes on to explain that NEC brings 1,600 individuals to Japan each year for advanced training.[36]

In addition to private sector programs for technical upgrading, there has been a significant development of Japanese programs for foreign students, particularly from Asia Pacific. Of 30,000 foreign students in 1989, 70 percent were from

China, Korea, and Taiwan,[37] where most students have knowledge of the character base of the Japanese language, *kanji.* The next decade will see an increase in the number of students who do not have the advantage of being able to recognize *kanji,* as many Asian students do. A fledgling bilingual program at Tokyo University has already admitted eighty students who take their coursework in English.[38] The expansion of such programs will contribute to the already reversing trend whereby North American students will seek training in engineering and research in Japanese institutions.

Cooperative programs for HRD are beginning to shift away from the foreign aid model, in which industrialized nations provide funding and expertise to developing nations, toward a joint venture approach. This process addresses the ambivalent sentiments of Asians who seek foreign assistance but wish to maintain national identity. An example of such a program is the International Aviation Management Training Institute in Montreal, Canada. This organization's faculty is international, and funding is shared between government and the private sector. Although the funding sources are predominantly Canadian, other sources include participant fees and international sponsors.[39] A further example of a "joint venture" HRD program is the Thai APEC proposal for the development of telecommunication inservice training. This project includes participants and funding from APEC members, with primary input from Thailand and Canada. Participants include private sector consultants from Canada (with some government subsidy for expenses) and the United States, and government-funded experts from the Asean countries.[40] Although some of the funding from developing countries may be rechanneled aid money, it signifies a trend toward joint planning and administration of projects.

A related issue is the emergence of linguistic nationalism, particularly in Malaysia. With 40,000 Malaysians studying in universities abroad, and the need for English proficiency in international trade, there has been a strong push for English language study. At the same time, there have been campaigns to promote the Malay language. As one Malaysian observer comments: "The less English they [government officials] use the better it is. The more English they know the better it is."[41] Similar issues have arisen in Hong Kong and Singapore, where there is some conflict over the primacy of English or Chinese. These language controversies are not central to HRD planning, but they have the potential to be a barrier to international cooperative programs.

Another more difficult issue is the emigration of students and researchers from the developing economies who have studied or worked in industrialized countries, and choose to stay there. At the intersection of the "brain drain" issue and business, the primary problem is the mobility of highly skilled personnel. Although this movement is predominantly from developing to industrialized economies, it also occurs within the industrialized community. The response of businesses in the region includes the transfer of personnel across national borders but within transnational corporations. Smaller enterprises have to adopt competitive hiring practices, but it must be added that local companies are subject to the conditions imposed by local policies and conditions. Some government policy makers approach this problem by imposing restrictions on the mobility of scientists and engineers. Others attempt to create a more hospitable environment for S&T professionals through favorable economic development policies.

Local S&T policy in the developing countries is closely linked to international development assistance programs. While these programs augment local ability to provide human resource development, they add the risk of losing students, faculty, and researchers who study abroad to seek better opportunities to use and be remunerated for their skills than they would have in a developing economy. The immediate response to this problem is the design of locally administered programs, where visiting faculty from industrialized countries deliver training in local companies or institutes. From a historical perspective, we have seen a reversal of migration patterns at various times, as local opportunities change and expatriates return home. This occurred in 1950, as many Chinese students returned to the newly founded People's Republic to contribute to national self-strengthening. It is occurring in Korea, where U.S.-trained scientists and engineers are returning to participate in Korea's technological development. This approach requires a long-term view of the mobility of professionals; their foreign sojourn can be viewed as an incubation period, allowing them to flourish until their home environment becomes more hospitable. One way of approaching this problem is to adopt a long-term horizon. What in the short term is "brain drain," may in the long term be seen as a reservoir of personnel who can return to their home country when the environment is more conducive to their ability to make a contribution to science and technology development. The example of U.S.-trained Korean engineers illustrates this approach.

Denis Simon has argued that human resources in the Asia-Pacific region may more appropriately be considered as a regional rather than a national resource. Scientists and engineers are increasingly part of "a regional and even a global labor pool."[42] The mobility of highly skilled personnel, through government exchanges, interfirm contracts, and international consulting firms, diminishes the significance of national boundaries in the use of these resources. In the realm of international policy coordination, the challenge of an emerging "regional personnel market" requires collaboration on the design and implementation of human resource development programs that adopt a regional rather than a national perspective.

Intellectual Property

There is increasing concern in the scientific and business community about the privatization of scientific knowledge. This is evidenced by the high priority given to intellectual property rights in the Uruguay Round of the GATT negotiations. Although there is a philosophical conviction that science is international, access to scientific knowledge is in fact subject to competition. It is viewed as a key to military and economic strength. As the border between precompetitive and competitive science becomes blurred, and access to technology is inhibited by restrictive legislation, developing nations in particular protest the barriers to the free flow of science and technology. The two major issues associated with intellectual property rights are the definition of intellectual property, and equitable access to scientific research and innovation.

At the 1990 Seoul Symposium of the PECC Science and Technology Task Force, Zhu Lilan, a distinguished scientist from the People's Republic of China State Science and Technology Commission, described the cumulative and interdependent nature of science research. She postulated that the "development of science and technology invariably transcends national boundaries."[43] This argument suggests that there must be a balance between protecting industrial assets and furthering global scientific knowledge which serves to benefit from cooperative research and sharing of information.

For a business that exposes its leading-edge technology through licensing agreements or other mechanisms of transfer, the issue of copyright protection is higher on the agenda than equitable access to scientific knowledge. The response to violation of written and unwritten agreements about intellectual property has led to the pursuit of mechanisms for effective litigation and arbitration. Such mechanisms would have to be based on common definitions. An example of differing perceptions is the Japanese government's view of IPR, which contrasts with the view of European and American companies in the aerospace industry. The Japanese government, through MITI, provided much of the funding for Japanese private sector R&D, and Japanese law stipulates that the government owns all patents on technological development achieved with the use of government money. Companies must apply to use patents, and pay royalty fees. In the United States, the company that carries out the research owns the patent. This dispute affected an aerospace technology agreement among seven aircraft companies in Japan, the United States, and Europe, leading to negotiations to integrate patent law across national boundaries.[44] Another example of differing perception is illustrated by Hong Kong's proposal to decriminalize copyright violations. With 70 percent of software piracy cases occurring in private companies, Hong Kong wants to try these cases in civil court. The U.S. software lobby, which is most affected by these violations, is arguing to keep copyright protection a matter for the criminal courts. A third example of cultural differences is found in Japanese and American practices in publishing scientific research data. The United States has argued for restricting publication of joint Japanese–American research which, if accessed by a third country, could have potential security implications. The Japanese argue that U.S. publication is already restricted, since 40 percent of American research is military-funded; they have refused to negotiate on restricting Japanese publication of joint research.[45] In Thailand, debate over U.S. pressure to revise patent laws has raised the question of whether these demands are in the best interests of Thailand's S&T development.[46]

Another approach that is promoted by those who do not believe litigation is the answer is to accelerate the innovation process. Some managers of R&D facilities have argued that, particularly in small and medium-sized enterprises, firms do not have the resources to pursue copyright and litigation routes; they have opted to use their resources to stay at the cutting edge of innovation. This is one approach to the management of high-technology industry which may balance the preoccupation with intellectual property rights.[47] The role of domestic policy makers in negotiating this issue is both to develop copyright mechanisms and legislation that allow for international comparability, and at the same time to enact policy that facilitates innovation.

Development assistance in R&D and the transfer of technology is often restricted by national security and self-interest restrictions on sensitive technologies. The question of the ownership of science has led to a distinction between commercial and precommercial science and technology. Governments may respond by restricting technology transfer. Another response is to collaborate on strategic research and development which serves the needs of both donor and recipient. International policy cooperation must address the obstacles to arbitration where there are inconsistent rules, and inconsistent perceptions of the parameters of both "intellectual property" and "rights." These are as much philosophical as political and economic issues, and will likely require considerable negotiation before satisfactory agreements are reached.

International Policy Cooperation

If it is agreed that international cooperation is indeed beneficial to the regional development of economic strength, then it is important to address the problems of uncoordinated cooperative efforts. The proliferation of programs and policies for S&T cooperation often results in inefficient, redundant, and inappropriate use of resources. As a senior Korean scientist and policy maker explains, planning of international technical cooperation should be viewed as an effective "policy instrument" to promote development.[48] There is an expanding awareness of the important role of public policy in S&T development, and by extension, to the coordination of public policies across national boundaries to facilitate bilateral and multilateral efforts to develop regional S&T capability.

There is also an important role for consultation between business and the private sector. Because business and government operate on different principles, the former primarily motivated by "profit" and the latter by "public good," they tend to respond differently to the challenge of solving problems in the public domain. Many examples of business–government consultation in the development of economic and trade policies attest to the benefit of such exchange. In the area of S&T policy, high-technology industry can inform policy makers about the realities of the industry, and at the same time exert some influence in the formulation of policy.

Domestic policy making is hampered by inadequate data on the policies of trade partners. While there are numerous bilateral and some multilateral agreements in science and technology, there are relatively few mechanisms for *regular* consultation or sharing of information among policy makers in the Pacific region. Organizations like PECC and APEC offer some opportunities for establishing comparable data bases and "sharing best practices."

Among those domains that would benefit from coordination is development assistance programs. These have proliferated in the area of S&T, with much duplication among organizations. Obstacles to successful assistance include conflicting goals, and the barrier of cross-cultural communication. An inventory of programs would minimize duplication of efforts, and mechanisms for consultation to achieve consensus regarding "mutual benefit" would enhance the effectiveness of regional assistance projects.

Finally, the sharing of information about domestic policies, and participation in regional forums would contribute to the development of more compatible policies for S&T cooperation. In the area of technology transfer for example, the primary goal of developing economies has been and continues to be the acquisition of technology. Recent changes in approach, however, suggest that there has been a shift in emphasis toward the absorption and diffusion of technology. In response to tariff and nontariff barriers to the flow of technology across national boundaries, both industrialized and developing countries are shifting their focus to the enhancement of domestic capabilities in research and development, and developing a skills infrastructure to absorb imported technology more effectively. Linked to this is the recognition that indiscriminate acquisition of foreign technology is not as productive as technology transfer within the context of a carefully planned overall development policy. Indeed, such acquisition may be destabilizing to the socioeconomic system of a country. China in particular experienced this dislocation during the rapid expansion of technology transfer in the early 1980s.[49] Malaysia's National Science and Technology Policy (1986) is based on the premise that technology transfer must be linked to clearly identified national goals for economic development. Malaysia's policy is to seek international partnerships in priority sectors for development.[50] (This plan is also an example of international cooperation in policy making, as it was funded in part by the Canadian International Development Research Council.) Korea has also reacted to the need to develop endogenous capability to integrate technology imports. In his analysis of Korea's pattern of technology transfer, Choong Yong Ahn refers to the role of government policy. He argues that although technology transfer in a market economy is almost entirely market-mediated, government has a role in indirectly facilitating this process by encouraging and supporting local S&T capabilities.[51] What emerges in these examples is a trend toward recognizing the role of government in developing policy that facilitates private sector acquisition and diffusion of technology.

Cooperation in research and development has traditionally taken place through exchanges within the international scientific community. This occurs through publication, conferences, sabbaticals, and the like. In this regard, it is noteworthy that Korean engineers must learn to read Japanese or English in order to maintain their knowledge of state-of-the-art scientific and technical developments. Strategic alliances between research institutes is a trend that allows cost sharing and augmented talent pools, and this trend is beginning to cross national borders. As outlined in the discussion of bilateral relationships, Pacific Rim countries are entering into government-to-government agreements to encourage the exchange of scientists and the development of cooperative research efforts.

The PECC Science and Technology Task Force, in consultation with experts from twelve countries and economies in the Pacific region, has attempted to identify research areas of mutual interest. These include research in "enabling technologies," which are of equal importance to economies at all levels of development, specifically energy, environment systems, hazard mitigation, and ocean resources.[52] In response to this recommendation, a cooperative regional research program in the study of environmental warming is in the planning stages for implementation in 1992. The programme is based on common interests within the public domain, and will work with existing organizations to bring them into a cooperative venture.

Conclusion

This chapter has discussed the notion that the Pacific Rim is undergoing an increase in regional consciousness, and that the importance of integration is recognized as a benefit to all members of the region. The initial framework suggested here, based on issues (human resources, intellectual property, policy cooperation) and domains (business, domestic policy, development assistance, international policy coordination) may prove useful in assessing the patterns of cooperation in regional science and technology. The importance of establishing a data base cannot be overstated. Tabulating the bilateral and multilateral S&T cooperative agreements in the Pacific region is an overwhelming task because the data are scattered, incomplete, and not easily comparable. Establishing a data base of this information would make an invaluable contribution toward S&T policy coordination. It is the ideal project for a regional cooperative effort. In the interim, we can surmise from individual country reports and the few comparative data bases that are being developed,[53] some of the patterns that have emerged.

The common agenda for regional cooperation stresses the need for the following: development of comprehensive data bases on policies, programs, and investment; fostering of endogenous capabilities for science and technology growth; collaboration on the development of human resource development programs that take into account the cultural, social, and economic dimensions of the participants; and the establishment of mechanisms for cooperative research in areas of mutual interest and concern. While issues that characterized technology transfer in Qing China, Meiji Japan, and postwar Asia have taken on different dimensions, the fundamental goals of cooperative efforts in the Pacific region today echo those of the past: to achieve a balance between self-interest and more equitable, mutually beneficial relations in the search of economic prosperity.

Notes

This research was supported by the Social Science and Humanities Research Council of Canada, Canada Research Fellowship. The author also ackowledges Veronique Soubry for her capable research assistance, and Dr. Marie Sickmeier (University of Manitoba, Faculty of Management) for her helpful comments and suggestions.

1. Stuart Harris, "International Technology Transfer: National Policies among Countries in the Asia Pacific Region," in Karen Minden, ed., *Pacific Cooperation in Science and Technology*, Honolulu: East West-Center, 1991, p. 116.

2. Edith Terry, "New Empire Created as Tokyo Moves South." *Globe and Mail,* 26 February 1990, p. B1 (Toronto, Canada).

3. I would like to thank Ms. Peggy Tsang, North Asia Science and Technology Relations, External Affairs and International Trade Canada, for her assistance in supplying information on bilateral agreements in science and technology.

4. Agreement between the Government of Japan and the Government of the Republic of Korea on cooperation in the field of science and technology. Article 1. 1985.

5. Agreement between the Government of Japan and the Government of the United States of America on cooperation in research and development in science and technology. Preamble. 1988.

6. *Asian Wall Street Journal,* 4 February 1991.

7. *Asian Wall Street Journal,* 25 February 1991.

8. Bob Johnstone, "Bucks from Bugs." *Far Eastern Economic Review,* 26 April 1990, p. 24.

9. Jacob Schlesinger, "LSI and Sanyo Join to Develop HDTV Chips." *Asian Wall Street Journal,* 22 July 1991.

10. Johnstone, "Bucks from Bugs," p. 78.

11. Susumu Awanohara, "Just a Memory." *Far Eastern Economic Review,* 1 February 1990, pp. 34–5.

12. Urban Lehner, "Asians Overshadow U.S. as Source of Foreign Direct Investment in the Region." *Asian Wall Street Journal,* 15 April 1991, p. 3.

13. Steven Levington, "Asian Industrialization Enters Its Second Phase." *Asian Wall Street Journal,* 3 June 1991, pp. 1 and 22.

14. Fred Herschede, "Trade Relations between China and ASEAN: The Impact of the Pacific Rim Era." *Pacific Affairs* 64:2 (Summer 1991): 179–193.

15. Adam Schwarz, "Rocket Diplomacy." *Far Eastern Economic Review,* 14 February 1991.

16. *Business Week,* 11 November 1991, pp. 57–58, and N. Balakrishnan, "Logical Linkage." *Far Eastern Economic Review,* 3 January 1991.

17. Michael Vatikiotis et al., "Building Blocs." *Far Eastern Economic Review,* 31 January, 1991, pp. 32–33; and *Business Week,* 11 December 1991, p. 59.

18. ASEAN Secretariat, *Annual Report of the Standing Committee,* 1987–88, 1988–89, 1989–90; and *Asean Cooperation in Science and Technology,* No. 2, October 1985.

19. ASEAN Secretariat, *Annual Report of the Asean Standing Committee*, 1988–89.
20. "EC and ASEAN." *Far Eastern Economic Review,* 7 February 1991, p. 32. This article also reports that the EC's DFI in Malaysia, Indonesia, Singapore, the Philippines and Thailand has surpassed that of the United States.
21. Bob Johnstone, "Growth of the Theory of 'Symmetrical Access.' " *Far Eastern Economic Review,* 31 March 1988, pp. 48–64
22. *The Eighth Pacific Economic Cooperation Conference, Science and Technology Task Force Report.* Singapore, 20–22 May 1991, p. 1.
23. Charles Smith and Louise deRosario, "Empire of the Sun." *Far Eastern Economic Review,* 3 May 1990, pp. 46–48.
24. Summary and Conclusions of the First Asia-Pacific Economic Cooperation Senior Officials' Meeting (APEC-SOM), Singapore, 7–8 March 1990. Annex 5.
25. Ibid., Annex 6.
26. Yao Erxin, *Science and Technology for Development in Developing Asia/Pacific Countries; a Regional Report for Science and Technology for Development.* Draft. April 1988. Chapters 1 and 8 passim.
27. OECD Technology/Economy Programme. International Conference Cycle. Paris: OECD, 1991.
28. See D. Eleanor Westney, *Imitation and Innovation; The Transfer of Western Organizational Patterns to Meiji Japan.* Cambridge: Harvard University Press, 1987.
29. United Nations, *UNCTAD Statistical Pocketbook,* 1989, Table 4.39.
30. Ibid., Table 4.40.
31. Bob Johnstone, "Obstacles to Free-Flow of Scientists." *Far Eastern Economic Review,* 31 March 1988, pp. 62.
32. Bob Johnstone, "Rise of Techno-nationalism." *Far Eastern Economic Review,* 31 March 1988, p. 59.
33. Johnstone, "Growth of the Theory of 'Symmetrical Access,' " p. 60.
34. Johnstone, "Obstacles to Free-Flow of Scientists," p. 65.
35. Satoru Hashimoto, "NTT's International Cooperation in the Field of Telecommunications: Human Resource Development in the Asian Region," in Karen Minden, ed., *Pacific Cooperation in Science and Technology,* Honolulu: East-West Center, 1991, pp. 75–80.
36. NEC advertisement in the *Far Eastern Economic Review,* 12 December 1991, p. 68.
37. Fumio Nishino, "Japanese Cooperation with Developing Countries for Human Resource Development," in Minden, *Pacific Cooperation in Science and Technology,* p. 89.
38. Ibid., p. 89–90.
39. Michel Desjardins, "The Role of Specialized Training Institutes: A Case Study of the Canadian Experience," in Minden, *Pacific Cooperation in Science and Technology,* pp. 65–69.
40. Thai Rapporteur, "Paper for the APEC Working Group on Telecommunications," Kuala Lumpur, Malaysia, January 10–11, 1991. Update on this project provided by Robert Tritt, Director, Trade Policy, Department of Communications, Government of Canada (October 1991).
41. Michael Vatikiotis, "A Question of Priorities," *Far Eastern Economic Review,* 17 January 1991, p. 30
42. Denis Fred Simon, "High Technology, Human Resources, and the Globalization of the Pacific Region," in Minden, *Pacific Cooperation in Science and Technology,* p. 29.
43. Zhu Lilan, "An Introduction to the PECC Symposium Objectives," in Minden, *Pacific Cooperation in Science and Technology,* p. 3.

44. Jacob Schlesinger, "U.S., European Firms Sign Pact in Japan on Jet Engine," *Asian Wall Street Journal,* 25 February 1991, p. 14.

45. Johnstone, "Growth of the Theory of 'Symmetrical Access,' " p. 61.

46. Mingsarn Santikarn Kaosa-Ard, "Patent Issues in Thailand," *TDRI Quarterly Review,* 1991.

47. At a meeting entitled "Global Rivalry and Intellectual Property," an eminent Canadian scientist coined the phrase: "Innovate, Don't Litigate." Geraldine Kenney-Wallace, Institute for Research on Public Policy, Toronto, Canada, April 24–25, 1990.

48. Hyung Sup Choi, "International Technical Cooperation in the Socioeconomic Development of Developing Countries," in Minden, *Pacific Cooperation in Science and Technology,* p. 1.

49. See Zhang Ceyi, "Follow-up on Technology Transfer Projects: Digestion, Absorption and Assimilation," in Minden, *Pacific Cooperation in Science and Technology,* pp. 127–132.

50. See "Committee to Formulate and Action Plan for Industrial Technology and Development, Industrial Technology Development; A National Plan of Action." Kuala Lumpur, February 1990. Also, Omar Abdul Rahman and Michaela Smith, "Science and Technology Planning: With Special Reference to the Malaysian Planning Experience," in Minden, *Pacific Cooperation in Science and Technology,* pp. 155–160.

51. Choon Yong Ahn, "Technology Transfer and Economic Development: The Case of South Korea," in Minden, *Pacific Cooperation in Science and Technology,* p. 97.

52. Mike A. Collins, "Cooperative Research and Development Programme," PECC Science and Technology Task Force Meeting, position paper, 20–21 February 1991, Vancouver, Canada.

53. For example, the PECC S&T Task Force Pacific Science and Technology Profiles, a project led by the Japan National Committee for Pacific Economic Cooperation.

Bibliography

Canada-Japan Committee. *Canada-Japan Complementarity Study. A Joint Study for Enhanced Cooperation in the Field of Science and Technology between Canada and Japan.* Ottawa: Science Council of Canada, 1989.

Committee to Formulate an Action Plan for Industrial Technology Development. *Industrial Technology Development—A National Plan of Action; A Report of the Council for the Coordination and Transfer of Industrial Technology, Ministry of Science, Technology and Environment, Malaysia.* Kuala Lumpur: 1990.

Ernst, Dieter, and O'Connor, David. *Technology and Global Competition: The Challenge for Newly Industrialising Economies* Paris: Development Centre of the OECD, 1989.

Harris, Stuart, and Science & Technology Task Force, Pacific Economic Cooperation Conference. *Pacific Economic Cooperation on Technology Transfer: Policy Issues and Work Proposals.* Canberra: PECC, 1991.

Industry, Science and Technology Canada, Science Sector. *A Comparative Study of Science and Technology in Selected Countries: Canada.* Draft document, 1989.

International High Technology Industry Group, KPMG. *The Development of High Technology in the Asia Pacific Region.* Singapore Investec (Taiwan) Ltd.. 1990.

Kirk, Michael K. "Intellectual Property in the New GATT Round: Progress and Prospects." San Francisco: The Asia Foundation, Center for Asian Pacific Affairs, 1989.

The Technology/Economy Programme (TEP). *International Conference Cycle.* Paris: OECD, 1991.

United Nations Conference on Trade and Development. *Joint Ventures as a Channel for the Transfer of Technology.* Proceedings of a Workshop organized by UNCTAD in collaboration with the Chamber of Commerce and Industry (Consultation Centre) and Ministry of External Economic Relations of the USSR. New York: United Nations, 1990.

————. *The Implementation of Laws and Regulations on Transfer of Technology.* Study prepared by the UNCTAD Secretariat in collaboration with Jinjoo Lee, Korean Advanced Institute of Science and Technology. New York: United Nations, n.d. (ca. 1987).

————. *Transfer and Development of Technology in Developing Countries: A Compendium of Policy Issues.* New York: United Nations, 1990.

United Nations Industrial Development Organization. *National Approaches to the Acquisition of Technology.* Development and Transfer of Technology Series No. 1. New York: United Nations, 1977.

————. *Technological Self-Reliance of the Developing Countries: Towards Operational Strategies.* Development and Transfer of Technology Series No. 15. New York: United Nations, 1981.

Zaleski, Eugene, and Wienert, Helgard. *Technology Transfer between East and West.* Paris: OECD, 1990.

16

Japan's Role as a Regional Technological Integrator and the Black Box Phenomenon in the Process of Technology Transfer

Shoichi Yamashita

Japanese Influences in East and Southeast Asia

Recent economic development in East and Southeast Asia is remarkable. The Asian NIEs—South Korea, Taiwan, Hong Kong, and Singapore—and ASEAN member countries—Thailand, Malaysia, Indonesia, and the Philippines—are notable for their continuous economic growth.

Table 16.1 shows that the economic growth rates of the NIEs and ASEAN countries have accelerated since 1986. The NIEs first achieved double-digit growth rates in 1986–88, and the ASEAN countries followed with rapid growth in 1988–90. These economies have also shown fairly good economic performance for these years, with lower inflation rates and lower unemployment rates even during such a high-growth period.

The recent economic growth in the NIEs and ASEAN countries has taken place since the G–5 Plaza Agreement of September 1985. Growth was led mainly by the export of manufactured goods. In Korea and Taiwan, the growth rate of exports exceeded 30 percent per annum in 1986–87. Hong Kong and Singapore experienced similar increases in 1987. Thailand, Malaysia, and even Indonesia also achieved a 30 percent increase in exports. Thus, a double-digit growth rate was realized in these countries.

The expansion of NIE and ASEAN exports is related to the reduction of

Table 16.1

Economic Growth Rate and Export Dependency

	Economic Growth Rate (%)						Export Dependency (1989) (%)	GNP per capita (1989) (US$)
	1985	1986	1987	1988	1989	1990		
NIEs:								
Korea	6.9	12.4	12.0	11.5	6.1	9.4	29.7	4,958
Taiwan	5.0	11.6	12.3	7.3	7.6	5.2	45.2	7,292
Hong Kong	−0.1	11.9	13.9	7.9	2.3	2.4	45.6	10,843
Singapore	−1.6	1.8	9.5	11.1	9.2	8.3	98.1	10,759
ASEAN:								
Thailand	3.5	4.9	9.5	13.2	12.0	10.0	29.1	1,240
Malaysia	−1.0	1.2	5.4	8.9	8.5	10.0	70.2	2,054
Indonesia	2.5	5.9	4.9	5.7	7.4	7.0	24.5	499
Philippines	−4.4	1.7	4.6	6.3	5.6	2.6	17.5	736
Japan	5.2	2.6	4.3	6.2	4.7	5.6	9.7	23,016

Source: Institute of Developing Economies (Tokyo), based on reports by each government.
Figures before 1989 are actual. 1990 figures are estimated. Export dependency is measured as exports divided by GNP.

Japan's exports due to the appreciation of the yen after 1985. Thanks to advantageous exchange rates, exports from the NIEs increased substantially, especially to the United States and the EC, in markets previously held mostly by the Japanese (see Yamashita, 1991, ch. 1).

Observing the export drive of the NIEs and ASEAN countries, the role of foreign direct investment (FDI) must be recognized; that is, exports of manufactured commodities are, in most cases, produced by foreign-affiliated companies. In ASEAN countries Japanese joint ventures have played a major role in producing export commodities. In Thailand and Indonesia the biggest export commodity is garments. The materials from which the garments are made are mostly produced by Japanese joint ventures such as Teijin, Toray, and many other Japanese affiliated textile companies. Malaysia became the largest exporter of air conditioners due to the inflow of Japanese joint ventures or wholly owned Japanese electric and electronics companies, such as Matsushita, Sanyo, Toshiba, and Hitachi.

Such higher growth has been strongly supported by these foreign factors. The NIE and ASEAN economies heavily depend on export (see the level of export dependency in Table 16.1), foreign direct investment (FDI), official development assistance, and foreign borrowing, among other factors. Thailand, for example, achieved double-digit growth rates during 1988–90. The main factors that led rapid growth were increases in (1) exports, (2) inflow of FDI, and (3) the number of tourists from abroad.

Japan has played an important role in the process of economic development of the East and Southeast Asian nations. The expansion of the Japanese economy led the economic development of NIEs and ASEAN through bilateral and multilateral trade, private direct investment, official development assistance, and noneconomic interrelationships. Japan has had a continuous economic and technological impact on these nations, while the Japanese economy has also gained from trade and investment in the NIEs and ASEAN countries.

The NIEs and ASEAN nations aim at export-oriented industrialization by inviting foreign direct investment, mainly from Japan. Japan is now the biggest investor in East and Southeast Asia (Table 16.2 shows the trends and the scale of Japanese direct investment in Asian countries). Companies there import not only machines, parts, and materials, but also the management style from Japan. Japan has become a model of economic development, especially for Korea and Taiwan at the first stage. Then, after the success of Korea and Taiwan, the ASEAN countries are now following.

We can thus observe the group of high-economic-growth countries in this region. The pattern of economic development has been described as a "wild-geese-flying pattern" (see Akamatsu, 1956). The wave of dynamic economic growth has spread from Japan to the NIEs and then to the ASEAN countries. Although this hypothesis is based on the long-term observation of Japanese industrial development, it seems also to have been a valid model for the economic

Table 16.2

Japanese Direct Investment to Asia (in US$ million)

	1985	1986	1987	1988	1989	1990	1951–90 total	Japanese Share of Foreign Investment
Korea	134	436	647	483	606	284	4,138	54.3
Taiwan	114	291	367	372	494	446	2,731	30.4
Hong Kong	131	502	1,072	1,662	1,898	1,785	9,850	26.6
Singapore	339	302	494	747	1,902	840	6,555	24.0
Thailand	48	124	250	859	1,276	1,154	4,422	39.0*
Malaysia	79	158	163	387	673	725	3,231	31.1*
Indonesia	408	250	545	586	631	1,105	11,540	15.5*
Philippines	61	21	72	134	202	258	1,580	19.7*
China	100	226	1,226	296	438	349	2,823	16.1
Other Asia	21	17	32	41	118	108	646	—
Asia Total	1,435	2,327	4,868	5,569	8,238	7,054	47,519	—

Source: Export-Import Bank of Japan (1989).

Reported figures of FDI to Ministry of Finance (Fiscal year: April-March).

*Approved figures by each country.

development taking place in the East and Southeast Asian countries for most of the postwar period. At the next stage, the growth dynamism will spread to Asian socialist countries.

At present, the East and Southeast Asian economies have very strong connections with the Japanese economy but the nature of the relationship is different for each country. The structure of bilateral trade and the fields of Japanese investment are different for each country, depending on each country's stage of economic development, technological levels, scales, and policies. But when we observe the whole region, the East and Southeast Asian nations are going to be integrated under the Japanese umbrella, economically and technologically, although the market for their commodities still depends heavily on the United States and Europe. The relationship among Japan, the NIEs, and ASEAN may be an enlargement of the parent-subcontract industrial relation which strongly propelled the rapid economic growth of Japan. By strengthening these relations, Japan gains more than the NIEs and ASEAN countries through trade and investment, but the NIEs and ASEAN also gain and grow. Thus, Japan's central role as an economic and technological integrator in this region will continue.

The Importance of Technology Absorption Capacity and the Japanese Way of Technology Transfer

The Recognition Gap in Technology Transfer

Although technology transfer is highly recommended and valued by local governments, a recognition gap between the donors and recipients at times causes misunderstandings. A typical case arises when local government officials and some ASEAN economists believe that Japanese-affiliated companies are unwilling to carry out technology transfer. Their impression is based on comparison of the practices of Japanese companies and of U.S. or European companies in ASEAN regions.

The ASEAN authorities seem to understand that technology transfer will proceed when the foreign technical advisors have gone home. But Japanese technical advisors do not go home quickly—they stay for longer periods. This is seen as evidence that the Japanese-affiliated companies are unwilling to give technical training. In contrast, U.S. and European companies send their technical advisors home quickly, and the promotion of local staff is speedy.

It is important at this point to understand what real technology transfer is. Japanese-affiliated manufacturing companies confidently base their production management methods, and especially their technical training, on on-the-job training. European and American companies, on the other hand, basically utilize written manuals and detailed job descriptions. Since it is easy for workers to see and follow the manual, local people seem to be happier working at U.S. and European companies than at Japanese ones. At Japanese-affiliated companies the workers' job content is ambiguous: Japanese companies do not give workers a clear, detailed job description and work standards. They rely instead on OJT or on the technician's experience, which sometimes leads to misconceptions and misunderstanding between workers and managers. Some local people, including government officials, still consider Japanese companies unwilling to teach any technology to the local people.

The real attitude of the Japanese-affiliated companies toward technology transfer is as follows. At the first stage, technical advisors train the employees for the operation. There is no difference at this point between the practices of the Japanese and those of Euro-American companies except for the use of manuals.

The difference appears in the second stage of technology transfer. Most Euro-American companies withdraw their technical advisors when the factory is operating well, after which the local employees just follow the manuals without any modification. But in the Japanese companies the technical advisors stay even after smooth operation has been achieved. They continue to train the workers step by step in maintenance and repair, quality control, introduction of new production methods and new technology, and so forth.

When trouble occurs in Euro-American companies, technicians are flown to the factory to perform repairs, after which they go home. They do not trust the local workers in the repair and R&D fields. Japanese technical advisors, on the other hand, generally stay longer and train workers beyond the level of basic operations because they place great emphasis on the ability to respond quickly to changes in model design, production methods, materials, and new product development.

The local plants of Japanese and Euro-American enterprises are thus established on different premises, and this is reflected in their attitudes toward technology transfer and personnel training. Government officials and ASEAN economists should understand the differences between the practices and attitudes held by Japanese and Euro-American companies.

Japanese Managers' Perceptions of Technology Transfer—Nine-Stages Hypothesis of Technological Development

In order to learn about Japanese managers' perceptions of technology transfer, a questionnaire survey and interview were conducted in Southeast Asia concurrently with the survey on Japanese-style management (see Yamashita et al., 1989).[1]

One area of this questionnaire survey pertains to technology transfer in Thailand, Malaysia, and Singapore (Figure 16.1). This survey is distinguished from others in that "technology transfer" was divided into the nine stages shown in Figure 16.1. Naturally, technology transfer consists of different stages: the first stage is the transfer of operational technology; the second is repair and maintenance technology; the third, quality control (small group activities) technology; next is process management and procurement technology, and so on as the degree of technological content increases.

Figure 16.1. **Stage of Technology Transfer**

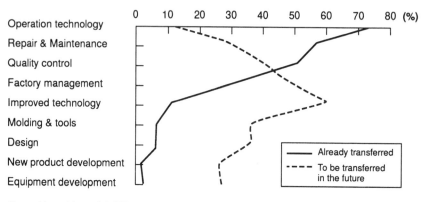

Source: Yamashita et al. (1989).

Note: Figures are based on a questionnaire survey of Japanese managers of Japan-affiliated companies in Thailand, Singapore, and Malaysia. The percentages are the proportion of total respondents who indicated that the technology in question had "already been transferred" or "would be transferred" in the future. The above figures are the average for three countries.

We asked the Japanese managers to indicate which stage of technology transfer they had completed by that time and which stage they planned to reach in the future. Seventy-four percent answered that they had completed the first stage, the transfer of operational technology. The figure for repair and maintenance and quality control were 57 percent and 50 percent, respectively. For production management the figure dropped to about 28 percent, for technology improvement it dropped further to 11 percent, and almost no enterprises had yet done anything about design and new product development.

For the sake of convenience we will call the first five stages of technology transfer the "early stages," which include technological development of new designs, molding, and tools, and development of new products and equipment. The early stages are technologies related to equipment that has already been set up and the affiliated production processes. Japanese enterprises have been teaching these stages to local employees, whereas the Euro-American companies seem to limit their technology transfer to the stage of operational technology.

The attitude and consideration shown by Japanese managers to the later stages of technology transfer differ from manager to manager. In the areas of development of new design, molding, tools, new products, and production lines, which seem to relate to so-called research and development (R&D), only a few managers responded that they are proceeding with technology transfer. Such negative responses are based on the managers' evaluation of the technical standards and research environment of the region. The managers have not yet placed their full confidence in the local employees, and consider it to be more efficient at this time to design and develop new products at the headquarters research centers in Japan.

Japanese enterprises should not, however, underestimate the abilities of the local employees; they need to better understand the local educational and economic environments. Local employees will soon bridge the technology gap. Thorough personnel training takes more time. Japanese managers, especially at the headquarters, should consider technology transfer in the longer term, and continuously train technical experts and managers.

Importance of Technology Absorption Capacity

The ASEAN countries are learning from the development experiences of the NIEs. The newly industrializing economies have achieved high economic growth through the strategic policy of export-oriented industrialization. Then the ASEAN countries seem to follow the NIEs' strategies.

However, the NIEs' experiences demonstrate that only a country with a high capacity for absorbing technology can promote export-oriented industrialization and make the best use of foreign capital and know-how. An export-oriented policy should be applied carefully and with attention to fulfilling a number of prerequisites. For instance, a certain level of industrial base and the presence of adequate numbers of entrepreneurial managers, technicians, and educated workers are necessary.

In view of the successes of the Asian NIEs, the ASEAN members and other developing countries have tried to apply the policy of export-oriented industrialization. But most have not been successful in exporting their manufactured commodities, and instead have been faced with trade deficits due to increases in imports of the materials, intermediate goods, and capital goods needed for domestic production. As the governments of the ASEAN countries came to recognize the importance of technology, they requested that foreign capital projects extend to technology transfer. At present it is common for local governments to provide various incentives to foreign capital projects that can produce exportable commodities through technology transfer. In addition, the recent ASEAN deregulation policies were also based on the NIEs' experiences.

Technical Training at Japanese-Affiliated Companies in ASEAN Countries

Japanese managers have long trained their workers and personnel at their overseas factories, but their evaluation of the technology transfer at the factories is not so high. At present they are satisfied with the transfer of operational technology (see Figure 16.1), but not with the technological level of repairs and maintenance and quality control. They are rather pessimistic about the transfer of total production management of the factory, the introduction of new models and new materials, and further stages. Nevertheless, they have made constant efforts to promote further technological and managerial transfer at the level of operation and maintenance because they believe that training at these earlier stages is crucial for further technological improvement.

To examine the actual training practices at Japanese-affiliated companies, we also carried out a questionnaire survey on the training of workers and personnel (see Yamashita et al., 1989). We examined four different job categories: worker, foreman, manager (section chief), and department manager (factory manager). The methods of training are classified into eight types as shown in Figure 16.2. Our concerns are the practices of OJT and training manuals.

Figure 16.2 shows the results by country. Some of our findings are as follows:

1. In Singapore and Malaysia, English manuals are used to a greater extent than in Indonesia and Thailand. The cultural and language characteristics are different among the two groups. In Indonesia and Thailand, manuals in local languages are used more often, though the share is decreasing as the job ranking becomes higher (see Figure 16.2, parts 1 and 2 on page 348).

2. The share of OJT is quite high for every country. OJT is a typical characteristic of Japanese companies in training personnel. Again, Indonesia's and Thailand's shares of OJT are higher than those in Singapore and Malaysia, especially OJT by locals at the workers' level. There is a tendency for the share of the OJT by locals to decrease as the job ranking is higher (Singapore is an exception). On the other hand, the share of OJT by Japan is increasing for higher ranking, typically in Thailand and Malaysia (see Figure 16.2, parts 3 and 4).

3. There are many differences among the four countries in the number of technicians and personnel sent to Japan for training. In Indonesia and Thailand the percentage of personnel sent to Japan is very high (see Figure 16.2, part 8). In Indonesia in particular, 71 percent of the companies have sent their department managers and/or factory managers to Japan for training. In Singapore sending personnel is not as high for any job category.

Based on these findings, we may say that Japanese-affiliated companies do not simply apply the same training method to each ASEAN country. They have tried to find appropriate ways for locals and have trained local personnel by different methods at different degrees. In this point the Japanese method differs from the training of U.S. and European-affiliated companies abroad. The U.S. and European companies use detailed manuals. They sometimes apply the same manual to all local factories and do not allow locals to make changes. The Japanese training method is more flexible, adapting to conditions in each country. The manuals the Japanese companies use are not so detailed; sometimes they are just job descriptions. One reason why Japanese companies do not have the detailed manuals is to cope with their model changes. In Japan it is common to change the model of the commodity, materials, and even the production line. At the factories abroad they need to adapt new or modified production methods.

The Japanese companies seem to be able to avoid the complicated revision of manuals.

Technological Black Box in Recent FDI Development in Southeast Asian Countries

Recent economic development in the ASEAN countries has been led strongly by foreign direct investment from Japan and the NIEs. The governments of the ASEAN countries are changing their policies more actively to attract export-oriented foreign investment, offering such incentives as exemption from corporate taxes and import duties. The export-oriented industrialization policies of the ASEAN countries coincide with the global strategies of Japanese and also NIE corporations. Thus we have seen a continuing increase in Japanese and NIE firms' investment in Southeast Asia over the past few years.

We should also note that the change of focus of Japanese ASEAN investment, from a local-market-orientation to an export orientation, has brought with it major changes not only in management style but also in production control and technology transfer.

One of the important changes is in the production system of Japanese-affiliated companies that recently established factories in ASEAN countries as part of an ASEAN export-oriented strategy. With an import-substitution industrialization policy, the market for products can be limited to the domestic market. The local government protects these domestic products by taxes and duties. The quality of the products is just high enough to fit the local standard. Thus, there is no need to equip a modern production line and no need to use high-tech machines.

However, once they aim at exporting their commodities, these countries need to improve quality to the level of international competition. In most cases, they will change their production systems to improve quality, by introducing automatic machines and importing qualified parts from advanced counties like Japan. We can see the changes in the recent Japanese investment in ASEAN countries.

Many Japanese electric and electronics manufacturing companies have rushed to establish factories in Thailand, Malaysia, and Singapore since the Plaza Agreement in 1985, responding to their own global strategies and the incentives offered by local governments. Those include makers of semiconductors, TV sets, and electronics parts. Their ultimate aim is to establish an export base in this region.

In Malaysia, for example, Matsushita Co. has established eleven factories that produce color TV sets, videocassette recorders, compressors, and other products. Many subcontractor plants followed Matsushita to supply parts and materials. Surprisingly, ten of the eleven Matsushita factories specialize in export or produce the parts for export commodities. Most of them have been established since 1985. Only one factory, which was built in 1960, supplies products to the domestic market.

Figure 16.2. **Japanese Technology Transfer Practices**

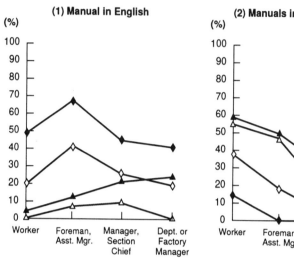

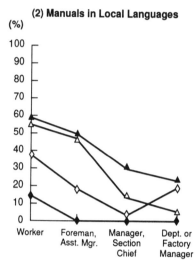

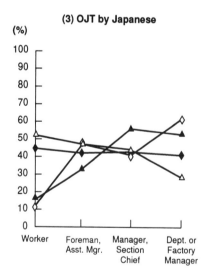

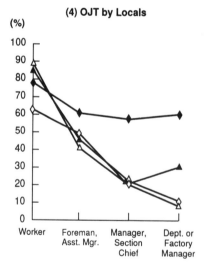

- ▲ Thailand
- △ Indonesia
- ◆ Singapore
- ◇ Malaysia

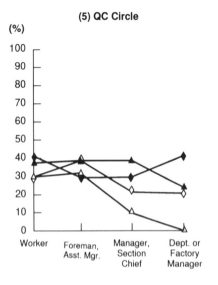

(5) QC Circle

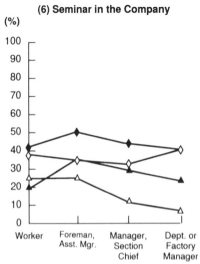

(6) Seminar in the Company

(7) Seminar Outside the Company

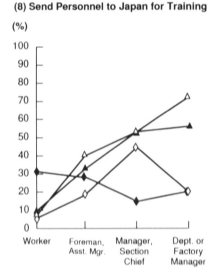

(8) Send Personnel to Japan for Training

- Thailand
- Indonesia
- Singapore
- Malaysia

Note: The percentage share shows the answers among the total companies.

Source: Yamashita (1989).

Naturally, the production systems of the two types of factory are different. The one for the domestic market has a history of almost 30 years of operation, and its production system is based on the original labor-intensive, local-market orientation. Production management and the ways of thinking in technological training at the factory are those typical Japanese styles as described earlier.

The system of the newly established factories is based on a different idea: these factories have introduced automatic and robot-controlled machines, high-tech inspection machines, and the like, to fill the technological gap between local staff and the requirements of Japanese companies. To improve the quality of their product, and maintain their international competitiveness, they need to introduce high-tech machines, instead of relying on unskilled labor forces. The original strategy of Matsushita was to train workers and technicians to match the required quality level. But this would take time. They could not wait because they need to export their products now and to compete with their rivals. Hitachi, Sanyo, NEC, Sony, and other Japanese electronics companies were involved in the same activities. Matsushita, as well as its market rivals, needed to equip the factories with high-tech machines and to import qualified parts from Japan and the NIEs.

What are the results of changing the production system? First, the local Matsushita factory has become capable of producing high-quality color TV sets and videocassette recorders, and of exporting. The method of production relies mostly on automatic machines, less on the skill of the labor force. The situation of technology transfer may differ from the original, local-labor-intensive, model. This is what we need to discuss here.

The automatic and sophisticated factory that is producing products for export may cut off the high-technology transfer process. This is rather paradoxical. Local governments ask the advanced countries to transfer higher technology, and as a result, the electronics industry—say, of Japan—in response comes to establish factories in Malaysia. However, because of the great technological gaps between local employees and Japanese requirements, Japanese electronics companies introduce automatic machines equipped with high technology. When the high-tech machines are installed, it is difficult to train technicians and workers at the factory, because their initial absorption capacities are low and training takes time.

There must be a discontinuity of technology transfer in this new system of production management. We call it a "technological black box" in the production process, which is shown in Figure 16.3 as a hypothetical figure.

Figure 16.3 illustrates the case of a typical electronics industry assembly line. In Malaysia the electronics industry relies heavily on imported materials and components from the same group of companies in Singapore, Korea, and Japan. The production activities by locals are limited to preliminary processing, assembling, and packing.[2] The important aspects of processing and testing that ensure high quality are performed by automatic machines. So local workers and technicians do not learn the technology of these processes, and the learning process is limited.

Figure 16.3. **Technological Black Box in the Production Process**

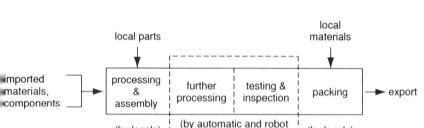

Local factories could produce high-quality products more efficiently by automatic and robot controlled machines. The technical training for local workers was simplified and shortened the training period. Jobs at the factory are divided into small portions. Thus the Japanese managers corresponded to the introduction of automatic and robot-controlled machines and the quick establishment of their export base in the Southeast Asian countries. This simplification of the work and training of locals also corresponded to their job-hopping or high rate of separation, especially in Singapore and Malaysia.

These practices have had one important result. Malaysia has become a strong exporter of high-tech products, such as color TV sets, CD players, videocassette recorders, and other electronic products and components. It is said that Malaysia will be the top exporter of color TV sets in the world in the very near future. It relies, however, on imported components, automatic assembly equipment, and Japanese-style management, and will continue to do so in the future.

In this context, the learning process is limited. But, it is also true that, if the local government refuses the introduction of high-tech production systems, they may not be able to learn such high-tech production methods or they may not develop new technology by themselves.They have been able to become exporters of high-tech commodities to the world market mostly because of assistance from foreign-affiliated companies. If it is possible to reduce the black box in the future, they should do so.

There are similar technological relations between Japan and ASEAN countries in many sectors. These are probably the result of the "short-cut" style of industrialization of the ASEAN countries. When the goal is export-oriented industrialization in the fields of higher technology, it is natural to adopt such a "black box" production process and to depend on foreign technology for a certain period.

The Japanese ways of technology transfer have been evaluated in ASEAN countries as they train local staff not only at the level of operational technology,

Figure 16.4. **Trade Specialization Coefficient of High-Tech Products**

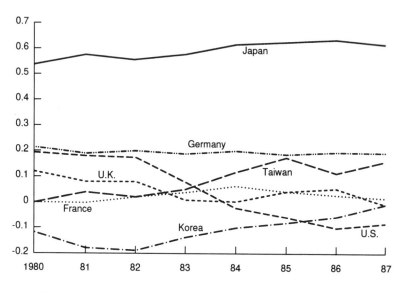

Source: Economic Planning Agency, *Annual Economic Report* of FY1991.

but also in terms of further technologies and know-how, such as repairs and maintenance, quality control, new model documentation, production of molding, design, development of new products, and so on. These, however, were typical practices at Japanese-affiliated companies before the recent yen appreciation. Since 1985, production control and management have changed drastically. We need to observe the results and implications of these drastic changes.

The Role of the Private Sector and Government Coordination

Technological Development in Japan

The strength of the Japanese economy is derived from the competitiveness of its high-tech commodities, which supports prolonged high growth and economic prosperity.

Figure 16.4 compares the trends of the specialization coefficients of high-tech commodities for seven important countries. Japan shows extremely high competitiveness in high-tech trade. The specialization coefficient is measured here as the difference between the export and import of high-tech commodities, divided by the total high-tech trade.[3]

The durability of Japanese competitiveness in high-tech commodities will determine whether Japan can take the role of technological integrator in Asia and the Pacific Rim. Noboru Makino, Director Counselor of the Mitsubishi Research Institute, takes a rather optimistic view of the continuation of technological innovation in Japan. He explains that technological innovation is divided into three stages: basic research (science), new product development (development), and industrial production (engineering) (*Nihon Keizai Shimbun*, August 30, 1991). He says that Japanese technologies are superior at the stages of development and engineering, and that at the stage of basic research, Japan is now in the catching-up process, which is mainly promoted by the efforts of the private research institutes. He cites the numbers and the share of the patents given by the U.S. Patent Office; the Japanese share is 21.2 percent.[4] Furthermore, he notes that the number of citations of Japanese patents among them is more than that of U.S. patents.

In the stage of new product development and industrial engineering, Japan has shown its superiority, especially in the development of the transistor radio, super LSI, laser disk, and similar technologies that were originally invented in the United States but were improved and developed in the process of production engineering in Japan. According to Makino, no country can compete with Japanese-made automobiles, color TV, facsimiles, or the like. The level of Japanese high-tech engineering is still very high, and he estimates that Japan will continue to develop new products and maintain its strong competitiveness in the future.

Japan's Position as Technological Integrator

Japan's level of high technology will determine whether it takes on technological leadership in Asia and the Pacific Rim in the future. So far it has maintained its strong competitiveness in high-tech commodities, through whose export Japan has enjoyed huge trade surpluses, making it one of the biggest sources of official development assistance and private foreign investment in the world. One of the foundations of Japanese strength was the trade surplus based on the export of high-tech commodities.

In the future the international competitiveness of Japanese commodities will be weakened as increased production costs continue to surpass the speed of technological improvement. In the field of new product development and production engineering, continuous technological innovation will be expected.

Although the pace of the increasing trend of Japanese foreign direct investment will slow down, Japan can still play an important role as technological leader and regional integrator in Asia. For one thing, the private sector, which led the technological development in Japan and has accumulated most of the high technologies and know-how, is still active and will play this role within and outside the country. Second, the NIEs and ASEAN countries are showing themselves highly capable of filling the technological gaps. The Japanese-affiliated

companies can work together in their catching-up process. Third, the Japanese government and official agencies, which are very slow to take action and
hesitate to take a leadership position, can be involved in providing the yen
credits through the Overseas Economic Cooperation Fund (OECF) and official technical assistance by the Japan International Cooperation Agencies
(JICA).

The Necessities of Government Coordination

In technological innovation and transfer of technology, the superiority of the
private sector will continue in Japan. As Makino predicts, the private sector is
still a strong competitor in technological innovation. So far, Japanese companies
have pursued better quality, new product development, and efficient production
engineering. But, because of the yen appreciation, trade frictions, and increases
of production costs in Japan, they have been forced to move their factories to
Asian countries as well as to the United States and EC.

At present, private companies in Japan are gradually strengthening research
and development as they invest in more efficient machines and facilities for their
survival. Although the international trade competitiveness of Japanese commodities will be weakened, private companies will compete with each other to develop new commodities and to generate technological innovation. In this sense,
the Japanese private sector is still active in the field of research and development
and will take a leadership position as the innovator and technological integrator
in the world.

The problem, however, with private research and development is that efforts
have been concentrated in the development of private and commercial goods,
which directly affect profit making. It may be the role of the public sector to
promote further development and innovation in a wider arena, including environmental studies and medical science.

In the transfer of technology, Japanese private companies play an increasingly
important role in the East and Southeast Asian nations. As long as the black box
of production technology exists at the local factories, and as long as Japanese
parent companies are unwilling to transfer the "latter stage" of technologies[5] to
the Asian countries, the technological gaps between Japan and locals may not be
closed—that is, the East and Southeast Asian nations will continue to rely on
Japanese higher technologies. The private sector should recognize that it is when
these countries develop that Japan will enjoy a high living standard. Thus Japan
can play a leading role in promoting the technological progress and transferring
technologies in this region.

At the same time, the Japanese government and public research institutes,
including universities, should support the promotion of science and technology
both within and outside Japan from the long and broader points of view. The
Japanese government should reexamine the distribution of Official Development

Assistance (ODA). Japanese ODA are provided mostly for constructing the infrastructure of developing countries by yen credit. Although the construction of infrastructure is crucial for economic development, the government should grant more technical assistance for human resource development. The share of technical assistance among total Japanese ODA was only 12 percent in 1989.

The Japanese government should be aware of the importance of human resource development—improving education systems, training technicians and middle-level managers, and supporting the science and technology of developing countries. For this purpose, the Japanese government should examine the following directions.

First, the activities of JICA (Japan International Cooperation Agency) should be opened up to train employees in the private sector. So far, the JICA training programs have mostly been offered to government officials, but the training demand of developing countries is changing. The present demand for technical and managerial training is increasing, because this training is important and useful for industrialization. The Japanese government should expand JICA's technical assistance activities in this field with the cooperation of the private sector.

Second, the government should invite more foreign students and scholars. In 1990 Japan accepted more than 40,000 foreign students. Only one-fifth of them received Monbusho (government) scholarships. Young students and scholars have a great potential as promoters of technological development and innovation. In addition, Japan's education system lags behind current needs of students and is not well organized for the foreign students. The government should reform the education system, especially at the graduate level.

Third, it is necessary to establish a new center in Japan for international cooperation in promoting the development of science and technology and international technology transfer. Such a center should be able to coordinate public and private activities in technological training, promotion of science and technology, and international joint research programs, as well as organizing financial funding for these activities.

Notes

1. Most of the sample was from automobile and electric (electronics) industries, in which Japanese companies are concentrated in these countries.

2. Prayoon Shiowattana (1991) has studied the technology transfer problem of the electronics industry in Thailand.

3. Our definition of high-tech commodities follows the criteria of the U.S. Department of Commerce, "DOC-2."

4. The U.S. Patent Office granted 95,500 patent rights in 1989; the U.S. share was 52.5%.

5. See the nine-stages hypothesis of technological development in Figure 16.2.

References

Akamatsu, K. "Wagakuni sangyo hatten no ganko keitai: Kikai kigu kogyo ni tsuite" [A wild-geese flying pattern of Japanese industrial development: Machine and tool industries]. *Hitotsubashi Ronso* [Hitotsubashi Review], *6*, 5 (1956).

Export-Import Bank of Japan. "Ajia NIEs to ASEAN no seizogyo ni taisuru Nihon no chokusetu toshi" [Japan's direct investment to manufacturing sectors in Asian NIEs and ASEAN]. *Monthly Report of Research Institute of Overseas Investment* (May 1989).

Koike, K., ed. *Skill Formation in Japan and Southeast Asia.* Tokyo: University of Tokyo Press, 1991.

Shiowattana, Prayoon. "Technology Transfer in Thailand's Electronic Industry." In S. Yamashita (ed.), *Transfer of Japanese Technology and Management to the ASEAN Countries.* Tokyo: University of Tokyo Press, 1991.

Yamashita, S., ed. "ASEAN shokoku no kaihatsu katei to nihon no kakawarikata ni kansuru kenkyu" [A study of Japanese involvement in the development process of ASEAN countries]. Hiroshima University, unpublished, 1988.

———. "Nihon no kaigai chokusetsu toshi to Ajia no keizai hatten" [Japanese direct investment and economic development in Asia]. In T. Taniura (ed.), *Ajia no Kogyoka to Chokusetsu toshi* [Industrialization in Asia and Direct Investment]. Tokyo: IDE, 1989.

———. *Transfer of Japanese Technology and Management to the ASEAN Countries.* Tokyo: University of Tokyo Press, 1991.

Yamashita, S.; Takeuchi, J.; Kawabe, N.; and Takehana, S. "ASEAN shokoku ni okeru nihonteki keiei to gijyutsuiten ni kansuru keieisha no ishiki chosa" [Japanese managers' consciousness on the Japanese type management and technology transfer in ASEAN countries]. *Hiroshima Economic Studies, 10* (March 1989).

17

The Technological Emergence of the Pacific Rim: Threat or Opportunity to the United States?

Richard P. Suttmeier

"[T]he best technology may not all be in the U.S."
—*Sematech spokesman, Buddy Price*

Introduction

"Sematech Turns to Japan for Chip Insight" read the headline of a small article on the front page of the January 25, 1992 issue of *The Nikkei Weekly* (Inoue, 1992).[1] In many ways, this brief headline goes to the heart of the complex questions concerning the challenges and opportunities facing the United States as a result of the rapidly improving Asian capabilities in technology and science.

With Department of Defense encouragement and with $500 million of government financial support, the Sematech consortium was established in 1986 to facilitate precompetitive corporate research cooperation to help assure U.S. preeminence in microelectronic technology. Its mode of organization was inspired by government-orchestrated research consortia in Japan, and represented a rare, and somewhat reluctant, acquiescence by the Reagan administration to demands for an industrial policy to bolster U.S. competitiveness.

That Sematech should now seek to cooperate with the country widely seen as the greatest threat to American technology is thus worthy of note. But how we interpret this decision is by no means obvious. Does it mean that the "best of the U.S." (Sematech's members include most of the leaders of American industry) can't "cut it" after all? Has the center of technological greatness shifted to Japan, as some would suggest (see Kodama, 1991)? Does it mean that the United States is finally putting to rest the "NIH" ("not invented here") hubris that may have blinded the American technical community to the rapid development of technical capabilities in Japan over the past three decades?[2] Does it mean that the globalization of technology has gone further than we sometimes think, and that talk of *national* competitive strength is increasingly misplaced? Or does it mean all of the above?

The growing, though still inadequate, awareness in the United States of Asian technological strengths, not only in Japan, but in the Asia Pacific region as a whole, comes at a time of great international change and uncertainty. It also comes at a paradoxical period in the American experience. With the end of the Cold War and the *tour de force* of American technology in the war against Iraq, U.S. international power and influence is in many ways unchallenged. Yet, Americans are profoundly concerned about the future of their country. Social problems abound, but, as the first years of the Clinton administration have revealed, consensus on the financial and institutional means to solve them is elusive. Sensible ways to manage public finances seem to escape the grasp of political leaders, and a chronic trade deficit seems to point to a lost ability to compete in both domestic and international markets. The growth of foreign direct investment (FDI) in the United States over the past decade—partially as a consequence of the above two factors—is taken by some as the beginnings of a slide toward a loss of control over national assets. The United States thus approaches the post-Cold War world with considerably less confidence than one might expect from a "victorious" power.

As the United States begins to plumb the causes of its collective malaise, issues involved with the trade deficit have become central to the thinking of many. With so much of the deficit resulting from trade with Asia and, of course, with Japan in particular, much attention has been focused on the causes of the imbalance. Hypotheses identifying low production costs, especially cheap labor, as keys to Asian competitiveness, no longer suffice as causal explanations for imbalances in high-value-added industrial sectors. Asian industrial policy and restrictive trading practices enjoy special favor with many Americans seeking explanations, but these increasingly must be understood with reference to a growing technological excellence—already evident in Japan and developing elsewhere in the region—which goes beyond industrial policy *per se*.

Under these conditions, the development and enhancement of scientific and technological capabilities in Asia might understandably be viewed in the United States with concern, if not alarm, and lead to perceptions of threat rather than opportunity. The replication of Japanese successes in technological development by other nations in Asia conjures visions of competitive threats to American industry in frightening multiples, as does an Asian "technological system" controlled and directed by Japan. Moreover, this is occurring at a time when we have yet to experience the full impact of China's modernization on global economic and technological affairs.

The challenges and opportunities faced by the United States as a result of Asian technological development are considerably more complex than an alarmist reaction would allow, however. To understand the complexity requires that the various strands of the U.S. technical relationship with Asia be parsed out, and that these be seen in light of both trends in the region and global developments. The S&T ties which the United States has with countries of the region are already extensive, and the U.S. shares many common interests with these countries—in commercial technology, and in "public" science and technologies—through complex relationships involving government agencies, universities, and private companies. As assets in commercial and political relations with the region, these are likely to be of increasing importance. How these assets are approached and used, however, depends on a number of factors. Chief among these is how science and technology are seen by the United States in defining its overall political relationship with the region, our assessments of the patterns of Asian technological development, and the ability of the United States to find a consensus on how to respond to the globalization of economic life.

The United States in Asia—Of Fans and Flying Geese

While the role of science and technology in U.S. political relations is of increasing importance, the problem of defining U.S. interests in Asian technological development is complicated by the fact that the latter is highly differentiated, and U.S. interests vis à vis different countries, or groups of countries, are not identical. The enormous stakes the United States has in technological competition and cooperation with Japan, for instance, are a qualitatively different matter from U.S. concerns about the use of China's technical capabilities to support destabilizing strategic exports, also a matter of great importance. U.S.-Japan cooperation in promoting the dissemination of environmentally benign technologies to China and Southeast Asia has a legitimate and compelling rationale, but it is one that springs from a very different set of concerns than those inducing U.S. commercial strategic partnering with Korean, Chinese, and Southeast Asian firms to compete with Japan.

A second source of complexity is the mix of policy concerns involved. Trade, security, environment, human rights, educational, and research policies are very much intermeshed with general foreign policy in dealing with the region. This makes it difficult conceptually to segregate issues, and leads to a policy-making process that is crowded with actors having a variety of agendas. Whereas it was once possible, for instance, to segregate positive sum political/military relations with the region from contentious, zero sum commercial relations, this is becoming more difficult, as the FSX controversy so nicely illustrates.[3]

Some observers wonder whether mastery of these complexities may not be eluding the United States. In spite of the well-known figures attesting to the commercial significance of Asia for the United States,[4] many Asians, and many Americans attentive to Asian affairs, have the impression that American interest in Asia in recent years has waned, and that with U.S. policy and business attention focused on other areas of the world, critical opportunities for forging a new relationship with the region for the post-Cold War era have been missed (e.g., Katz, 1992). Former President Bush's awkward, embarrassing, and arguably counterproductive trip to the region in January 1992 might very well be taken by some as further strong evidence that the United States is out of touch with trends in Asia.

Writing in the Winter 1991–92 issue of *Foreign Affairs*, then-Secretary of State Baker sought to dispel such ideas by presenting the administration's vision of an "emerging architecture" for a post-Cold War world Pacific community (Baker, 1991). In this vision, the objectives of U.S. policy are seen as the achievement of a framework for free trade, the promotion of democratization, and the modernization of the region's defense structure:

> Given the challenges and opportunities we now face in Asia, a viable architecture for a stable and prosperous Pacific community needs to be founded on three pillars. First, we need a framework for economic integration that will support an open global trading system in order to sustain the region's economic dynamism and avoid regional economic fragmentation. Second, we must foster the trend toward democratization so as to deepen the shared values that will reinforce a sense of community, enhance economic vitality and minimize prospects for dictatorial adventures. Third, we need to define a renewed defense structure for the Asia-Pacific theater that reflects the region's diverse security concerns and mitigates intra-regional fears and suspicions—a prerequisite for maintaining the stability required for continuing economic and political progress. [Baker, 1991, p. 3]

Baker likens U.S. involvement in the region to an unfolded fan, "spread wide" across the Pacific from Australia to Northeast Asia. The staves of the fan are bilateral relations emanating out from the United States as pivot point, the most important of which are those connecting the United States with Japan, Korea, ASEAN, and Australia. Connecting the staves is the fabric of the fan, the "shared economic interests now given form by the Asia Pacific Economic Cooperation (APEC) process."

While oriented to the future, the "emerging architecture" clearly also reflects assumptions from the past. Continuity with America's post–World War II international mission of sustaining regimes of security and commerce is especially evident in the vigor with which Baker's discussion projects an image of the United States as the internationally responsible hegemon, interested in providing the infrastructure for the common good in response to changed international conditions. The fan metaphor *does* attempt to capture the sense of the regional interactions that are so central to contemporary Asian Pacific dynamics, but the image as presented also conveys a belief that the structuring principles for these interactions emanate from the United States.

While Baker's "emerging architecture" fits current realities in many respects, it fails to address some of the fundamental issues being raised about the United

States role in the region. And, despite the Clinton administration's willlingness to embrace APEC, the U.S. role in Asia continues to be ambiguous. There is, first, the issue of Asian perceptions of the U.S. role. While the weight of Asian elite opinion seems to favor active U.S. engagement in the region, some voices clearly do not. Malaysian Prime Minister Mahathir Mohamad's proposal for an East Asian Economic Caucus that excludes U.S. participation is well known and is a source of concern to the United States. The extent of quiet support in high places in other parts of Asia, especially Japan, for the Malaysian proposal is less known, but it certainly exists (Takagi, 1991).

Similarly, the imagery of Secretary Baker's fan metaphor may be neither acceptable nor accurate to others in the region. While the United States may see the structuring principles for an Asia Pacific community emanating from North America, others see regional realities in terms of images that are Asia-centered and exclusive of the United States. Japan's "flying geese" model (with Japan as the lead goose) is clearly one alternative, as would be the still inchoate image of "Greater China" (Howe, 1990), discussed further below.

More fundamentally, there is the question of the availability of American resources for the kinds of U.S. leadership being proposed, and Asian perceptions of those resources. While the United States does seem to recognize that it will need help (especially from Japan) in getting the "architecture" in place, it seems to presume that the resources it brings are indispensable to the task. We need a better accounting of these resources if the U.S. role is to be fully understood, and such an accounting inescapably brings us back to the technology factor in U.S.-Asian relations.

While U.S. resources would clearly include military power and diplomatic muscle, the relative importance of these must be seen in an context where other factors—including economic performance and science and technology capabilities—have assumed greater weight. As Michael Mastanduno has recently put it,

> To a considerable degree, the struggle for national security in the post-cold war era, defined broadly in terms of both economic welfare and defense capabilities, will be a struggle over the mastery of a cluster of technologies generally associated with the information revolution, including computers, microelectronics, telecommunications, and flexible manufacturing systems. . . . Given its remarkable performance during the 1980s, only Japan currently poses a serious challenge to the ability of the United States to hold its own, much less dominate, in that competition. [Mastanduno, forthcoming]

Thus, some of the most critical resources needed for the United States to play a leadership role in Asia are in fact contested by another country in Asia and, as implied by the report on Sematech noted at the outset, may not be for the United States in secure supply. This ambiguity about the availability of leadership resources, and Japan's role in creating the ambiguity, suggest that the two axial relationships for understanding the challenges and opportunities for the United States in Asian technological development are the U.S.-Japan technological competition and Japan's technological relations with other countries in the region, two issues not discussed by the secretary. As a first cut into understanding these relationships, let us reflect briefly on the dynamics of Asian technological development.

Getting to Tomorrow—The New Asian Development Strategy

The scientific and technological development in Asia which is our concern is occurring in a larger context of dramatic change within the international political economy. Assumptions that underpinned the earlier successes of Japan and the "newly industrializing economies" (NIEs), about an international free trade regime, and especially about a virtually unlimited U.S. market, can no longer be made with assurance. Concerns about the competitive challenges from the NIEs thus also make the latters' access to the advanced technologies of the OECD countries increasingly uncertain, and changes in the climate for international business are altering traditional assumptions about international technology flows. Increasingly, one must have technology to get technology.[5] Thus, the context in which the current quest for S&T mastery in East and Southeast Asia is occurring makes it imperative that we rethink technological development strategies for the countries in the region.[6] Countries in the Asian region, with varying emphases, are responding by pursuing a five-part strategy for the enhancement of technical capabilities. Taken together, these constitute part of a "New Asian Development Model," the understanding of which is essential for any discussion of U.S. options.

First, Asian countries are trying to position themselves to benefit from the globalization of industry and to gain access to the advanced technologies they require. Symbolizing the new approaches to technology acquisition (and restructuring more generally) has been the creation of high-technology industrial zones throughout the region as loci for the meeting of foreign and domestic technical communities. Where once the export processing zone served as a "signature" of East Asian development, now Korea's Daeduk Science City, Singapore's Science Park, China's thirty-odd new high-technology zones, as well as Taiwan's Hsinchu Science Park, have become emblematic of the new strategic orientations.[7]

Second, as other chapters in this volume document, the countries of the region have significantly accelerated investments in domestic R&D and advanced education, and have seen a steady growth in their stocks of R&D manpower.[8] As part of these efforts, an increasing number of students are going abroad for advanced study in technical fields. Foreign study in the United States, for instance, helps meet the strategic goal of improving qualitatively their human resource bases to enhance capabilities in science and technology. While the data in Table 17.1 do not differentiate among fields of study, they do reflect the extent to which students from Asia dominate foreign student enrollments in U.S. universities.

Table 17.1

Countries with the Largest Number of Students in the United States

	1989–90	1988–89	1987–88
China, PRC	33,390	29,040	n/a
Taiwan	30,960	28,760	23,770
Japan	29,840	24,000	13,360
India	26,240	23,350	16,070
Korea	21,710	20,610	18,660
Canada	17,870	16,030	15,410
Malaysia	14,110	16,170	23,020
Hong Kong	11,230	10,560	10,710
Indonesia	9,390	8,720	n/a
Iran	7,440	8,940	14,210

Source: Institute of International Education.

A third element of strategy, especially important for South Korea and Taiwan, but with less success for Singapore, is to induce scientists and engineers (those who constituted the "brain drains" of the past) to return from abroad. In Taiwan, returning scientists and engineers have been instrumental in the rapid development of the electronics industry, and have played key entrepreneurial roles in starting high technology firms in the Hsinchu Science Park. In Korea, more than 1,200 scientists and engineers have been recruited back to serve in government laboratories and universities during the mid-1980s, with more going to industry. It has been estimated that returnees to Korea have helped the semiconductor industry save five years of development time (Yoder, 1989).

Fourth, the countries of the region are actively promoting the establishment of technology "outposts" abroad. The commercial manifestations of "outposting" include the establishment of companies or offices in centers of high technology, such as Silicon Valley, or the taking of equity positions in companies already established in such locations. Investment of this sort from Taiwan, much of it focused on Silicon Valley, was expected to reach some US$1.5 billion in 1991, while investments by Singapore's government-controlled companies, such as Singapore Technologies Holdings, are thought to total at least US$300 million (Balakrishno, Awanohara, and Burton, 1992). Imaginative staffing of diplomatic posts—embassies and consulates—is also used to monitor, and, where possible, to capture new technologies in the advanced countries.

Finally, in an era of uncertainty about access to established markets, about the meaning of the North American Free Trade Agreement, about the shape of economic integration in Europe after the collapse of the Soviet empire, and about sources of technology and modes of technology transfer, attention has turned to the desirability and feasibility of new forms of regional cooperation, and for some countries, the development of ambitious new relations with centers of technical expertise in the Russian Republic (see, for instance, Lee, 1992).

As this brief review of key steps taken by Asian countries to enhance techno-logical capabilities indicates, the United States involvement with the region in science and technology has been extensive, and certain aspects of the Asian development strategy would have been unthinkable without ready access to American S&T resources. Yet, however important the United States is, and has been, the S&T of other industrialized countries is also playing a role. Put some-what differently, the technological growth of the countries of the region has a strong global dimension to it.

A Regional Technological System?

The increasing concern for intraregional cooperation noted above has called attention to the extensive role Japan is playing in regional technological integra-tion, as earlier chapters have shown. In terms of its wealth, economic size, and technical capabilities, Japan dwarfs its regional neighbors, and there is consider-able evidence that the economies of the countries of the region are becoming increasingly integrated with Japan's (Sterngold, 1990). However, such integra-tion also poses problems and questions, not the least of which is whether eco-nomic integration will also be accompanied by new forms of technological cooperation.

With Japan's large R&D community, commitment to innovation, ready cash, and low rate of inflation, the impacts of Japanese R&D investments are expected to grow. With them, and absent a more open orientation toward technical cooper-ation, Japan's technology gap with its neighbors would likely widen. Thus, Jap-anese behavior with regard to technology transfer and S&T cooperation becomes an important variable in the calculations of its neighbors as they seek to devise new technological strategies. Japan is often perceived by its neighbors as a reluctant transferrer of technology in spite of the fact that its commercial partners believe they need much greater access to Japanese technology if further economic integration is to proceed. Change is beginning to occur, however. In 1987, for instance, more than half of Japan's receipts for patents and other forms of intellectual property came from Asia (*The Economist*, 1989). More significant, perhaps, is the decision by Japanese firms to establish new R&D facilities in the region.[9]

While Japanese investments and technology transfers have certainly created new wealth in a number of Asian countries, questions about their long-term viability continue to arise. At certain levels of development of the host countries, for instance, the current patterns of Japanese technology transfer are non-problematic as long as jobs are created and wealth is generated. As host coun-tries seek to develop their own technological capacities, however, and seek greater technological independence, will Japan be as reliable a source of knowl-edge and skill transfers as the United States has been? From the Japanese point of view, will the maturing of technological capacity, as one sees in Korea for instance, generate concerns for new competitors, and thus reduce incentives for expanded technology transfer? More generally, in light of the widespread distrust of Japanese long-term intentions for the region, and the existence of global technical ties noted above, should predictions about the emergence of a regional technological system, characterized by both Japanese leadership and shared, or mutual, interests, be accepted without qualification?

There is considerable evidence that past patterns of Japanese technology transfer have created a continuing dependence on Japan for high-value-added components needed to operate the plant and equipment that constituted the original transfer. The bill for these components is high, and can create a trade deficit with Japan for countries in the region which is structural, and seemingly antithetical to regional integration based on principles of mutuality (*Free China Journal*, 1992; Seow, 1992).

Further complicating predictions about the structure of regional S&T cooperation is the vision of a "Greater China." While a Japan-led Asian technological system is already in the process of emerging, in recent years we have also seen a growing involvement of mainland China in the economic and technological affairs of the region, and signs that the region's three Chinese territories—the mainland, Hong Kong, and Taiwan—are moving toward more integrative relations. Taiwan investment in the mainland continues to grow and, of course, there is already a very high level of integration between the economies of Hong Kong and Guangdong province.

The technological potential of a "Greater China" is gradually coming into view (Suttmeier, 1993). At a recent conference on technical cooperation held in Amoy, Fujian province, Taiwan investors reportedly were offered access to ninety items of Chinese mainland developed technology, valued at US$46 billion (Song, 1991). For Hong Kong, Taiwan, and other countries in the region, such as Singapore (Levingston, 1991), mainland China's extensive R&D system (according to Young [1989], Shanghai alone has "50,000 more scientists and engineers than Singapore, and 30,000 more researchers than South Korea") offers opportunities to marry China's scientific resources with the financial, production, and marketing skills that have contributed to the rapid economic development of the NIEs.[10] China's stated intent to set up an advanced semiconductor plant in Hong Kong, reportedly with American technology, provides a new spin on the "Greater China" theme (Taylor, 1992).

Thus, no discussion of the prospects for the region would be complete without an assessment of the emergence of a reformist China into the international political economy. What remains to be seen (assuming current political developments are transitory) is whether China becomes solely an arena for competition among Japan and the NIEs, or whether by virtue of its size and leadership potential (thus far not exercised), China will become a force for further integration. The mainland itself would seem to lack the financial resources, skills, and experience to play such a role in the near future, but when seen in cooperation with Hong Kong and Taiwan, China becomes a major international economic force, and the regional significance of its large technical community and resources for research, which have been seriously overlooked in assessments of the prospects for regional technoeconomic cooperation, begin to take on considerable importance. While it is likely to be some time before "Greater China" can compete with Japan in setting the standards for Asian regional technological development, it does, nevertheless, represent an alternative subsystem that adds to the texture of the regional system, and further illustrates the enormous synergistic potential resident in Asian technological development.

The Context for U.S. Choices

The discussion above points to an image of Asian technological development as part of a highly complex and highly dynamic system. Individual countries are pursuing strategies to enhance technical capabilities, but they are increasingly linked to both global trends and patterns of regional cooperation. Japan looms large as both a global force and as a regional technological integrator. The United States faces special bilateral challenges and opportunities with Japan, confronts Japan in a regional context, but also engages the region—minus Japan—in a variety of ways on its own terms.

To better appreciate the range of choices the United States has in responding to Asian scientific and technological development, it is first necessary to recognize that different sectors of American society have different interests in what happens in Asia; interests in Asia within the United States technical community (and its subsectors) are themselves not monolithic, and the presence within that community of large numbers of Asian-American scientists and engineers creates its own subset of challenges and opportunities. These differences are best seen when we recognize that the United States engages Asia on issues of technological development in three areas: those involving the quality and mobility of human resources and U.S. access to these resources, those falling under the rubric of "public" science and technology, and those relating to commercial technologies. While analytically distinguishable, it is also important to recognize that the totality of these relationships is more than the sum of the parts. Let us examine the challenges to and opportunities for the United States in each of these areas.

Human Resources

While human resource issues are central to both commercial and public technology relations with Asia, their importance extends to other areas as well, especially education. American universities have long been major forces for S&T development in Asia and beneficiaries of Asian interest in S&T. University-based scientists and engineers have traveled and lectured throughout Asia, shar-ing knowledge, helping to build programs, and recruiting students for study in the United States.

As noted above, over the last fifteen years, an increasing number of students in science and engineering from the Asia/Pacific region have been coming to the United States for various forms of higher education. Foreign study in the United States for their students is for most countries in the region a part of a strategic orientation to improve qualitatively their human resource bases and to enhance capabilities in science and technology. Asian students have enriched the lives of American universities, and they have become increasingly important factors in the health of the U.S. science and technology enterprises. Many have stayed on in the United States, assuming positions in universities, industry, and government.

While the quest for educational opportunities in the United States continues, efforts by nations in East and Southeast Asia to actively promote their own science and technology systems have led to the establishment of graduate pro-grams in science and engineering and to the strengthening of national research and development infrastructure. Research in industry is taking on new import-ance as many of the economies in the region experience a transition to more knowledge-intensive production. Not surprisingly, with new research and sci-ence-based economic opportunities becoming available in their home countries, Asian scientists and engineers who have studied, and in some cases worked, in the United States, are participating in a reverse brain drain by returning to the lands of their birth.

This enhancement of scientific and technological capabilities in Asia raises many interesting and important questions for the future health and leadership of U.S. academic science. At first glance, concerns about the continuing vigor of the U.S. research enterprise would seem misplaced. The United States continues to dominate the publication of scientific papers, and American universities and research institutes continue to be magnets for technical talent from all over the world. Yet, it is also true that U.S. science is increasingly dependent on foreign-born personnel, with scientists and engineers from Asia being an especially large group. In addition, many American universities are facing serious financial prob-lems and have become quite receptive to financial support from Asia.

With declining interest in studying science on the part of Americans, the U.S. strategy of "importing" S&T talent to overcome shortfalls in "domestic supply" has proven to be viable thus far. However, its future will depend on the continu-ing satisfaction of a number of conditions: the continuation of English as the language of international science, welcoming immigration policies, financial support, the continuation of American institutions—especially universities—as excellent environments for advanced training and research (which involves a series of factors ranging from the condition of facilities and instrumentation to institutional cultures), *and* the absence of competition from other countries.

It is the latter that is of greatest interest to us here. A number of developments may hold the possibility for the diminution of Asian preferences for the United States as the scientific destination of choice. While no one of them is likely to have a major impact over the medium term, in combination they could gradually erode the privileged position enjoyed by U.S. institutions. Of perhaps the greatest long-term importance is the changing role of Japan as a scientific center. Until recently, Japan has not been, quantitatively, an important destination for advanced education and research. The Japanese language has been a major obstacle, and Japanese universities and research institutes were ill prepared to receive large numbers of foreigners. In addition, rightly or wrongly, Japan was not known as a great center for basic science.

Important changes are now underway. Due to both foreign pressures for it to provide more international "collective goods," and out of a sense of national interest, Japan is enhancing its commitment to basic research. It is making a concerted effort to "internationalize" its institutions to make them more accessible to foreigners, and it is also actively promoting the study of the Japanese language throughout the Asia Pacific region. This is beginning to have the effect of attracting an increasing number of students and scholars to Japanese institutions. As Japan's Official Development Assistance (ODA) programs continue to expand, it is likely that there will be ample resources to make study in an internationalizing, scientifically and technologically advanced Japan quite attractive.

Nevertheless, it is likely that the American university will continue to be a magnet for aspiring scientists and engineers from Asia for some time. Strong traditions of basic science and advanced, doctoral-level education are still relatively rare in Asia. It is clear, however, that serious efforts are now being made by a number of countries in the region to develop such programs, and the consequences of these need to be monitored. Over the medium term, the success of indigenous programs is likely to reduce the numbers of highly talented recruits for opportunities in the United States. Quality education and rewarding research opportunities in the region are likely to increase (thus altering incentives for study abroad), and challenging careers in industry are becoming more numerous (again, with incentive effects for overseas study). Some of these industrial opportunities will be with U.S. firms, thus indirectly putting the latter in competition with American universities for Asian technical manpower.

Access to S&T talent from Asia has served the United States extremely well in the past. The terms by which that access is secured in the future remain somewhat uncertain, but they are likely to change as the region's own scientific and technological development proceeds. We should recognize that the enhancement of S&T in the Asian region not only leads to an expansion of the supply of qualified scientists and engineers, but it also creates new demand for technical personnel. Japan is facing a shortage of qualified scientists and engineers, and will increasingly be competing with the United States for talent in other countries in the region, including China. But, in addition to such competition for Asian talent, we should expect increased competition with Asian countries for access to talented technical manpower from elsewhere. The most intriguing pos-sibility, of course, is the exploitation of Russian technical talent, especially that found in the Russian Far East, by the countries of the region. Taiwan, reportedly, has been negotiating with the Russian Academy of Sciences on some eighty projects (Song, 1991), and has reached agreement with the academy to establish reciprocal offices in Moscow and Taipei to facilitate scientific and technological exchanges, with Russian aerospace technology being of particular interest to Taiwan (Lee, 1992). Interest in Soviet technical expertise is evident in Japan and Korea as well.

"Public" Science and Technology

A second area of engagement is in what might be called public science and technologies. Included here would be basic research as well as technologies pertinent to health, climate, pollution control, aspects of natural resources, en-ergy, communications and transportation, and defense and security. The public science and technology area is one where S&T issues often merge with policy and institutional issues. This both challenges the United States to learn more about Asian policy models in these areas of concern, and provides opportunities to promote U.S. institutional norms for the management of these public goods.

Government agencies, typically, are the lead players in public science and technology, and the already extensive governmental S&T programs with coun-tries in the region indicate how science and technology cooperation might be used as an instrument of foreign policy in U.S. relations with a number of Asian countries.[11] It also serves the missions of U.S. government agencies in such diverse fields as defense, earth sciences, medicine, space, energy, agriculture, and environmental protection. Cooperative activities in these areas have usually been driven by concerns for capturing good research being done in Asia that relates to agency missions, for taking advantage of unique ecosystems or other conditions necessary for enhanced scientific understanding of phenomena ger-mane to agency missions, or in some areas—especially with Japan—for sharing costs of particularly expensive projects. Cooperative programs of these kinds have also been useful for monitoring developments in Asian S&T, and as bridges to Asia for university-based science and, to a lesser extent, for commercial activities.

One of the causes for uncertainty about the shape and direction of a post-Cold War international order is the rise of new issues. Of these, international concern over global environmental quality is becoming central. The Asia Pacific region figures prominently in efforts to understand transborder ecological issues and many countries of the region have severe pollution problems. While in many cases, the near-term consequences of environmental degradation are local; in others, they are regional and global. China's degraded environment, in particular, looms large as a regional and global problem.

One can expect that a growing share of the developing S&T capabilities in the region will be devoted to attacks on environmental problems. Questions of sustainable development already loom large for countries of the region, and one can expect to see innovative technologies emerging from this mix of concerns and capabilities. The rise of environmental issues, in short, opens up a spectrum of new challenges and opportunities for the United States, ranging from new scientific understanding (the rich variability of the region's flora, fauna, topography, and geomorphology are of great scientific interest), to trade and technology-transfer possibilities, to opportunities to participate in and benefit from innovative approaches to the management of environmental insults.

Science, politics, and economics often merge in environmental affairs. International environmental issues have already introduced new fault lines in international politics, and these are sure to be widened during the coming decade. At the same time, new possibilities for international cooperation are called for, and are beginning to occur. North-South relations take on new meaning in the face of environmental issues, and China is staking out a claim for itself as the voice of the South in the developing dialogue over aid and technology transfer to ameliorate environmental harms. Active U.S. engagement with Asia on environmental issues is necessary if the United States is to establish a position of proactive leadership in international environmental affairs, and cooperation with Japan on regional environmental issues is the key to that engagement.

As a country that has mounted effective campaigns against some of its own environmental problems, as one with financial resources available for regional environmental problems, and as a source of technologies for pollution abatement and environmental management, Japan has the potential to play a very significant role in regional environmental affairs. The rise of environmental concerns in Asia offers the United States and Japan an opportunity to form a partnership of common purpose vis à vis the region on environmental problems that would help offset the tension in the commercial arena. (Commission on U.S.-Japan Relations in the Twenty-First Century, 1991). A variety of specific suggestions for cooperation have recently been advanced. One is the formation of an American counterpart to work with Japan's recently established Research Institute of Innovative Technologies for the Earth (RITE) on its proposed New Earth 21—Action Program for the 21st Century, a program that calls for the development of environmentally sustainable new technologies for international dissemination. Other opportunities include the establishment of a joint Asian regional environmental center (modeled on the recently established Regional Environmental Center for Central and Eastern Europe), and joint research and assistance to third countries on environmentally benign energy technologies (Colglazier, 1991).

Environmental problems do not exhaust the possibilities for mutually beneficial technical relations between the United States and Asia in the area of public science and technology. Nor is there a guarantee that interactions in this area would necessarily be more cooperative or conflict-free. The recent discussions between Japan and the United States over cooperation in the construction of the superconducting supercollider illustrate how interests can diverge, and how frictions can develop. However, in our preoccupations with Asian technological threats. to U.S. commercial competitiveness, we should not lose sight of the extensive ties in areas of public science and technology. These constitute an important part of the complex fabric of U.S. technical relations with Asia. In the face of challenging new global issues, such as those of the environment, these ties are likely to become considerably more salient.

Commercial Technologies

In spite of the importance of public science and technology, and of the deep and complex interests the United States has in Asian scientific and engineering manpower, in American public discourse the development of Asian S&T poses the greatest challenge for U.S. interests in the area of commercial technologies. As concerns about American competitiveness have turned to issues of technological capabilities, the U.S. stance toward Asian technological development has been seen increasingly in terms of trade and investment; it has also led to a reexamination of assumptions about international trade and the relationships between technology and economic growth. By demonstrating the feasibility of "creating" comparative advantage through focused government policies, the technological development strategies of Japan and the "Four Tigers," or Asian NIEs, have forced a rethinking of the dynamics of international technological development, of international technology flows, and especially of product cycle logic as a guide to international business strategy.

Many factors—both institutional and technological—combine to make the world of international business especially fluid and unpredictable. Through all the fluidity and unpredictability, however, runs the widespread assumption that technological innovation and prowess in technology more generally (understood as the ability to capture value from technological innovations) are the keys to commercial competitiveness. Finding the financial resources for increasingly expensive new product development, finding markets to recapture those development costs, and having access to high-level technical manpower have become central requirements for successful business operations.

The difficulties individual firms from all countries have in meeting these requirements account in part for the new patterns of business partnerships and "strategic alliances" that are daily reported in the business press. With its market potential, the "deep pockets" enjoyed by many Asian companies, and the enhancement of Asian technical resources—R&D manpower and institutions—Asia increasingly can be seen as an enormous reservoir of capabilities to be factored into the development of the business strategies of American firms. This fact is recognized by many U.S. companies who have availed themselves—through aggressive marketing, though joint ventures and strategic alliances, and increasingly, through the location of R&D facilities in Japan (NSF, 1991; Nihon Keizai Shimbun, 1992) and elsewhere in the region—of the rich opportunities that Asian technological development affords. Yet, in the eyes of many others, the overriding lesson to be learned from the enhancement of Asian capabilities in commercial technology is in the threats it poses to American industrial competitiveness, to the American industrial base, and ultimately to American national security.

These differing perceptions of what Asian technological development means in commercial terms have prevented the formation of any kind of consensus in the United States on the nature of the challenge and how to respond to it. The concept of competitiveness, for instance, can lead—and often has led—to confusion when used in policy discourse. As Paul Krugman has recently argued, an important part of the confusion stems from the indiscriminate use of the term for both companies and countries (Krugman, 1991). While the meaning of "competitiveness" with reference to firms is relatively clear, when applied to countries, *and* assuming principles of international comparative advantage hold, it can produce serious economic misunderstandings and political mischief.

Central to the competitiveness issue, of course, is whether or not principles of comparative advantage *do* hold in light of the great virtuosity in industrial policies shown by Japan and the Asian NIEs. As seen by Krugman and others, comparative advantage (as exogenously given) often gives way to "created" comparative advantage in areas of high-technology manufacturing; successful industrial activity of this sort can generate external economies in the form of knowledge spillovers among firms (thus creating a strong national knowledge base) and a large market (thus creating a national pool of skilled manpower and abundant, high-quality suppliers) (Krugman, 1991; Itoh, 1990). For some Americans, Asian experience demonstrates that government-sponsored industrial policy can enhance the scope and value of these external economies, leading to international specialization which is more a function of external economies than of exogenously given comparative advantage. Under such circumstances, the idea of a *country*'s competitiveness, or of a *nation*'s industries being more or less competitive, becomes more understandable and may warrant offsetting non-market governmental responses (see Office of Technology Assessment [hereafter OTA], 1991, ch. 1).

With the development of technological capabilities in Asia, we have seen also an expansion of Asian investment in the United States. The meaning or significance of this investment has been the subject of controversy as well (Graham, 1991). For some, it has been a welcomed business decision that helps create jobs, pay local taxes, and produce products that are in demand. Others have argued that the jobs created are qualitatively inferior, and that Asian investments in small high-technology U.S. firms can be seen as strategies of predatory acquisition of American advanced technology (see OTA, 1991; Press, 1990; Harris, 1990).

The United States clearly has an interest in seeing that the quality of jobs in the economy remains high, and that American firms can compete internationally on the basis of high productivity and quality products, rather than low wages. While foreign investment in the United States might be thought of as threatening to these objectives, it is probably not a principle threat that would warrant the development of defensive or excessively restrictive investment policies (Graham, 1991). What does seem to be lacking, however, is a sense that Asian investment represents opportunities for technology enhancement. Needed is a sense of strategy for extracting know-how from such investments, in much the same ways as Asian countries have extracted know-how from American investments. While the conditions and means may differ, the underlying importance of having a strategy seems essential (see Mastanduno, forthcoming).

What constitutes a strategy for responding to the challenges of competitiveness, however, is at the center of the broad debate in the United States over industrial policy, a debate (I argue below) that is strongly conditioned by differing views over principles of political economy. While the debate over industrial policy continues, the *range* of strategic policy choices is known. As usefully outlined in a report by the Congressional Office of Technology Assessment, these choices extend from the relatively uncontroversial to the highly contested, and from actions the United States could take domestically, on its own, to steps in the area of trade policy directed at changing behavior in other countries (OTA, 1991, ch. 2).

For instance, the partisans of different positions on industrial policy are likely to find common ground in the proposition that there is a need in the United States for more of what OTA has called a "technology-friendly environment" (OTA, 1991). Such an environment would include a more supportive financial climate (e.g., with regard to the cost of capital for technological innovation), the solution of problems inhibiting education and training for human resource upgrading, and a far more aggressive and imaginative approach to domestic technology diffusion.

In the area of trade policy, consensus might be found for the idea that active market-opening pressures from the United States are called for when Asian industrial policies have kept U.S. firms from markets where they enjoyed comparative advantage, as with cellular phones, satellites, and supercomputers. Consensus is considerably less assured for other strategic options, such as the use of protection against selected Asian exports to the United States, domestic content requirements for foreign-invested firms operating in the United States, more aggressive export promotion measures, including a more expansive approach to export financing, and further relaxations of export controls (OTA, 1991). Clearly, which of these tools is used and how they are used range from the currently accepted to the far more controversial.

A third area of choice identified by OTA—and one on which there may be even less consensus—pertains to options for government-industry partnerships.

These include cooperation in the setting and implementation of a national strategic technology policy (e.g., an expanded version of the recently initiated Advanced Technology Program run by the Department of Commerce), financial risk sharing—through tax expenditures and other means—on the development of key technologies, and a more targeted, U.S.-focused, use of government procurement (OTA, 1991).

While technologically progressive Asian firms do pose threats for some U.S. interests, they have also made available to American consumers attractive products at affordable prices, and for those who have invested in the United States, they have provided jobs. Many Americans have made welfare gains from Asian technological development even as some American firms have ceased to be competitive. Thus, it is not surprising that after more than a decade of study, analysis, rhetoric, and attempts at legislation, it has been very difficult for the United States to develop a strategic response.

Countries in Asia have demonstrated that effective strategies for wealth production and technological enhancement can be forged under conditions of unfavorable competitive pressures, and that they can go hand in hand with foreign participation in their economies. These strategies have included sound domestic policies, have been informed by knowledge of what the opportunities abroad are all about, *and* have been based on a more coherent sense of political economy than one finds in the United States. While the importance of having a sense of strategy of some sort for addressing the issues of commercial competitiveness may be becoming more widely accepted in the United States, were there a broader consensus on principles of political economy, the fashioning of a strategy would be easier. Such a consensus does not exist, however, with the result that "strategy" can only emerge slowly from the pulling and hauling of American politics. A better understanding of the grounds for dissensus may help illuminate the broader, long-term challenges and opportunities occasioned by Asian technological development.

Of Borders and Orders—Cultural Pluralism and Political Economy

The more manifest signs of dissensus in the United States about the challenges of a new global economy and the role of a dynamic Asia in a new international order are seen in differing views about the relative reliability of market mechanisms and governmental action for dealing with the problems of America's economic and technological standing in the world, and relations with Asia. The ongoing debate about industrial policy provides a visible forum for the proponents and opponents of intervention to contest this central issue of political economy. This central issue of market efficacy, of course, extends to other areas as well, including academic and policy debates about the dynamics of international trade, the desirability of trade blocs and "managed trade," and other issues of trade policy (Krugman, 1991; Heiduk and Yamamura, 1990; Mastanduno, forthcoming).

However, rapid international change in the waning years of the twentieth century is also introducing new issues furthering the trend toward dissensus. Central among these is the question of the changing meaning of national identity. Functional and/or affective bases of inherited political identification are becoming blurred throughout the world, whether in the new Europe, Kazahkistan, South China, or the West Coast of the United States. While obituaries for the nation state may be premature, challenges to its powers and prerogatives—from a number of different directions—are increasing. Some come from problems of domestic governance in many countries, resulting from new forms of domestic political mobilization and the questioning of the terms of political legitimacy. Some come from new actors in the international arena who compete with states in increasingly efficacious ways. In addition to multinational corporations, these would include international organizations and regimes, and transnational networks of nongovernmental organizations (Rosenau, 1990).

The business of defining "national interests" and of fashioning coherent "national" responses to the kinds of challenges we are discussing here has become ambiguous if not inherently self-contradictory. How does one understand and protect national competitiveness (based on assumptions about "borders") when the firms one seeks to protect are engaged in global commercial dealings ("orders") which often involve cooperation with foreign competitors? How does national purpose get expressed when one nation's citizens are in policy alliances with groups in other nations pursuing agendas that may be at odds with national governments, as happens increasingly in international environmental affairs?

When issues of national political identity, along with attitudes toward markets, are seen as structuring our debates about political economy, we have a clearer sense of the shape of dissensus. As Figure 17.1 illustrates, it is possible to map contemporary orientations toward political economy according to market attitude and state identification variables, and to postulate ideal-type "cultures"[12] of political economy occupying each of the four cells.

The culture of cell A in Figure 17.1 might best be described as *traditional internationalism*, and is perhaps best represented by Reagan-Bush Republicanism of the late 1980s. This culture places great faith in the operation of markets, domestically and internationally, but also emphasizes the importance of political order for market operation, an order (as we have seen in former Secretary of State Baker's discussion, above) which is seen as depending on U.S. power. Interventions in markets for national security reasons—as in export controls—are justified.

Industrial policyism might best describe the culture of cell B. While committed to the market in principle, this culture is considerably more sensitive than A to market imperfections, and to the extent to which the rules for market opera-

Figure 17.1. **Competing Cultures of Political Economy**

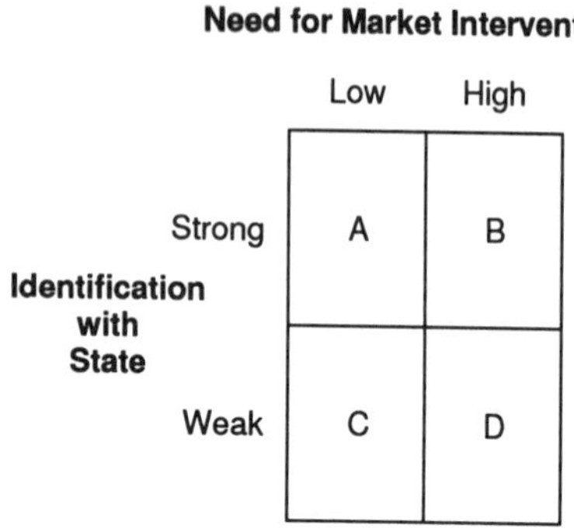

Need for Market Interventions

	Low	High
Strong	A	B
Weak	C	D

Identification with State

tions are followed ("level playing field" concerns). This cell reflects many perspectives of the Clinton administration. "National security" is increasingly seen in economic as well as in military terms, and thus state action to advance international economic position is warranted. Many adherents of this culture, though not all, exhibit strong strains of economic nationalism, and distance themselves from the neoclassical tradition of "economic science."

The cultures in cells C and D are somewhat less widely noted. Culture C might best be described as *global entrepreneurialism*. While not entirely forsaking affective commitments to the nation-state, those participating in this culture are drawn to powerful transnational forces (commercial and career opportunities, research grants, forms of artistic expression, etc.) which, functionally, make identifications with nation states peripheral or incidental. Clearly, multinational corporations partake of this culture, but so do many small entrepreneurial firms as well as many scientists and engineers, artists, journalists, and the like.

Distinguishing global entrpreneurialism from the *new ageism* of cell D is the strong commitment to the market of the former in comparison with the ambivalence—often bordering on hostility—toward market mechanisms shown by the latter. Those embracing new ageism have a profound distrust of national governments, seek solutions to human problems through forms of decentralized collective action by communities of believers, and take comfort in transnational relations with the like-minded. Concerns for the efficacy of internationally linked nongovernmental organizations (NGOs), as with some environmental groups, figure prominently in the world view of new ageism.

Implications

The discussion above has attempted to make a number of points that are germane to the fashioning of a U.S. response to the challenges and opportunities resulting from Asian technological development. These include, first, that S&T relations with Asia are multifaceted, and that in our responses we should not become fixated on any one of them. Mutually beneficial relations with Asia exist in areas of human resources, science, in public technologies, *and* in commercial technologies. A preoccupation with trade frictions should not be allowed to sour the extensive, healthy ties that exist in other areas, especially in light of the growing need for international cooperation on environmental issues. In the face of the considerable dissensus in the United States over fact and principle in the competitiveness debate, it is particularly important for the United States to see developments in Asian science and technology as a fabric, or complex web, that binds different U.S. interests in the region's technical future to Asia in multiple ways.

Second, in spite of the growing expansion of Japanese influence over the processes of development and integration of technologies in the region, Asian S&T are not likely to fall totally under a new Japanese technological hegemony. A variety of political factors argue against regional technological integration under Japanese hegemonic influence, and regional integration itself is by no means assured (Clad, 1992). The dynamism of the Chinese economies also points to a considerably more complex regional system than the Japan-dominated model would suggest. And finally, however strong the forces for regional cooperation, they in no way cancel the strong forces for globalization to which the countries of the region are subject.

There is thus no reason, inherent in the dynamics of the region, for the United States to be excluded from beneficial participation in Asian S&T development. Indeed, when we consider the strategies of technological development being followed by countries in the region, as discussed above, it is clear that close relations with the United States have been necessary for them to succeed. However, the United States does not enjoy a monopoly on the resources necessary for Asian technological success, and as successes are realized, the United States faces the possibility of being considerably less relevant for the launching of new technological trajectories.

We have seen that how one reacts to the major gains in Asian technological development of the recent past depends on the kinds of assumptions about a rapidly changing world one brings to the assessment. Americans are differentially affected by Asian technological development. Some industries, some sectors of the technical community, and some regions of the country have much more to gain from it than others. More generally, the rise of technically dynamic, vigorous industrial economies in Asia is part of a wider economic globalization, and it is becoming increasingly clear that U.S. society is differentially prepared for, and perhaps divided over, responses to a new international technological order. Some sectors of society have the skills, literacy, tastes, and experience to benefit from the enhancement of technological capabilities in Asia; for others, global economic and technical change, of the sort we see in Asia, can only be seen as threatening. A major challenge for the United States, as the Clinton administration has realized, is to see that the gap between these two parts of the society is narrowed, a challenge that calls for imaginative new domestic structural adjustment policies focused on education, retraining, and repairing the social fabric.

Managing the problems caused by differential levels of preparedness for the global economy has been made easier for the United States in the past by the privileged access it has enjoyed to S&T talent from throughout the world. As the discussion above has indicated, the American university has been an especially important magnet for this talent, and continues to be an extremely important national asset in international S&T. As Asian S&T capabilities expand, the United States will gradually find itself in competition with Asia for technical expertise, located both in Asia and in other parts of the world. The most reliable strategy for the United States in maintaining its competitive edge in the quest for this talent will be to insure the continued vitality of the American university, the quality of American education more generally, and the freedoms and opportunities afforded by U.S. society.

The development of Asian technology challenges the United States to become considerably more informed about developments in science and industry in the region. The information needs occur at different levels, and although different tasks will necessarily devolve to government, industry, and the university, the monitoring, analysis, and digestion of information about the region needs to become a way of life. Though attitudes have changed—especially toward Japan—the effects of the "NIH" mentality linger.

Industry, of course, should have the incentive to seek out information on the technological trajectories of competitors, and the growing interest in locating R&D facilities in Asia is in part a response to this incentive (see NSF, 1991; Nihon Keizai Shimbun, 1992). But there is also much government can do in helping to lower the costs of becoming informed. The science and technology reporting responsibilities of U.S. embassies in the region should be expanded, the staffing of positions having those responsibilities with qualified personnel should be accorded a high priority, and information tasks should be defined to include both high-quality technical assessments and policy reviews. Inattention to Asian government planning documents and to the interactions between Asian bureaucrats and Asian technical communities (i.e., those responsible for "creating" comparative advantage) has too often left Americans behind, rather than ahead of the curve, on critical developments (see Harris, 1990). In a very different area, the United States needs to assure itself that it is acquainted with important technical literature from Asia. While government-sponsored translation services are important, there is also a need for a new generation of scientists and engineers who can work comfortably in Asian environments in Asian languages.

The emerging new world of global technology of which Asian technological development is a part points to the need for according science and technology, especially international S&T, a higher status within the United States government, especially in the foreign policy establishment. Throughout the Cold War period, American foreign policy, including policy toward Asia, was driven by political and military concerns. Political/military specialists tended to dominate policy processes, and careers were made by being such specialists. With the growing importance of international economic and environmental issues for national security, and the key role of S&T in these issues, new kinds of competencies are required at the center of foreign policy making, and new kinds of institutional arrangements supportive of these competencies are required.

Conclusion

Fumio Kodama has recently argued that the growing excellence of Japanese high technology should be understood as a "techno-paradigm shift" (Kodama, 1991). For Kodama, the requirements for innovation in high technology are different from those in earlier forms of industrial technology. Japanese institutions and values, organizational forms, and management practices are seen as inherently more conducive to high-technology industrialization than those in the West and, in an age of high technology, this is leading to a shift in the world's technological center of gravity to Asia. One need not agree with all of the implications of Kodama's analysis to recognize nevertheless that in the efficiency and creativity of Japanese R&D (NSF, 1991) and in Japanese effectiveness in linking R&D to the production of new products, the "Japanese system of manufacturing" has emerged as a new international standard.

Americans have much to learn from this standard, as many are belatedly realizing (see Westney, 1990; NSF, 1991). The central lesson has less to do with issues of an underlying inventiveness or creativity, however, than with the provision of conditions for "capturing value" from inventiveness (Teece, 1987; Ergas, 1987). It is unlikely that the United States could, or should, attempt to replicate in the United States those conditions that work so well in Japan. It must find its own approach, one that would view as a necessary condition closing the gap between the society's globally oriented cosmopolitans and those who are at risk from trends in the global economy. U.S. "cultural pluralism" can accommodate this need, and indeed, in the diversity of views about national interests and international opportunities it offers, it can be seen as an advantage in creating conditions for capturing value from innovation. The challenges and opportunities arising from Asian technological development should be seen in this light.

By keeping a focus on the multidimensionality of technological dynamism in today's Asia, the "threat perception" theme which lies so close to the surface of contemporary U.S. thinking about Asia loses some of its edge. This is not to say that perceptions of threat are unwarranted. The vigorous trends in the development of commercial technologies in Japan, and selectively, in other Asian countries have demonstrably affected U.S. competitiveness, and should force the United States to think long and hard about strategies of response. Strategies that ignore the full range of possibilities for mutual benefit from S&T cooperation with Asia, however, are likely to be self-defeating.

Notes

This paper builds on research made possible by assistance from the National Science Foundation (grant nos. SRS–8719232 and SRS–8813941).

1. The report featured Sematech's recent decision to expand relations with the Japanese technical community, including a decision to take membership in the Ultraclean Society, a consortium of 235 Japanese and 20 foreign firms led by Professor Tadahiro Ohmi of Tohoku University, a leading authority on semiconductor manufacturing.

2. See the epigram above.

3. The complex mixture of commercial competitiveness and military cooperation issues and interests in the FSX case has been further complicated by a dispute over illegal transfers of sensitive avionic technology to Iran by Japan Aviation Electronics Ltd., a firm that had been participating in the FSX project (Usui, 1991).

4. For example, two-way trade with the region has now surpassed $300 billion annually, and is almost one-third larger than that with Europe (Baker, 1991).

5. The uncertainties in the international trading system are reflected in the behavior of international corporations, as they adapt to the globalization of industry and technology (Miller, 1988; Castells and Tyson, 1988; Guile and Brooks, 1987; Muroyama and Stever, 1988). The high costs of new product development, highly efficient international communications, and the reduced labor content of manufacturing resulting from new technologies are having revolutionary effects on international business. Of greatest interest here are the new patterns of cooperation between firms ("strategic alliances"), and an altered calculus for industrial location decisions pertaining to foreign operations more generally. As the labor component of production decreases, the appeals of offshore, low-cost manufacturing sites may be declining for many companies from the OECD countries. For some industries, the benefits of maintaining R&D, design, and manufacturing in close proximity result in "home country" advantages which outweigh lower-cost overseas production. Foreign operations thus become driven less by cost considerations than by the size of the foreign market and by the availability of technical talent abroad. Countries wishing access to the technologies of the companies of the OECD world must have technological assets to bring to cooperative schemes. Whether these global changes represent a trend toward greater international industrial concentration, or not, remains to be seen (see Ernst and O'Connor, 1989), but they do have important implications for the S&T development strategies of the countries of the East/Southeast Asian region.

6. These had been based largely on the transfer of technology from the advanced countries, the need for which continues. However, the terms of such transfers are changing. The advanced countries fear competition from the NIEs in many industries, and thus have become especially cautious in transferring technology. At the same time, the international business operations—and thus, the rationales for transferring technology—of the firms that own much of the desired technology are changing. The globalization of markets, the uncertainties of the international political economy, and technological change itself have led to the alteration of business strategies, of which technology transfer is part. (See Ernst and O'Connor, 1989; Miller, 1988; Castells and Tyson, 1988; Guile and Brooks, 1987; Muroyama and Stever, 1988).

7. From these efforts, a series of new technical links with firms from the OECD countries are being forged. Japanese companies are establishing an R&D presence in Taiwan and Singapore; Matsushita, for instance, has recently set up an R&D unit in Singapore for work on audiovisual equipment and information technology. Matsushita, Hitachi, and Sharp now have an R&D presence in Taiwan's Hsinchu Science Park. IBM, Wang Labs, and GTE also have established R&D facilities in Hsinchu, Motorola has established a state-of-the-art semiconductor manufacturing plant in Taiwan, and Acer has

joined forces with Texas Instruments to produce memory chips. Korea has also been active in new technical tie-ups. TI has joined with Hyundai to assist the latter in its DRAM business, while Hitachi has done the same for Lucky Goldstar. Hewlett-Packard has joined with Samsung to produce high-powered work stations at a cost intended to be well below the market leaders. Samsung is also involved with General Electric for the production of medical equipment intended to compete with Japanese products. In a dramatic effort to enter the commercial aviation business, Taiwan Aerospace has offered to pay US$2 billion for a 40 percent share of the commercial business of McDonnell Douglas. The list could go on.

8. The average annual growth in R&D spending in Korea between 1980 and 1987 was approximately 14.3 percent, for instance, while that of Taiwan was approximately 12.1 percent. By contrast, Japan's was 4.1 percent.

9. See note 7. Fumio Kodama's (1991) recent work on Japanese high technology can be usefully read in conjunction with chapters 14 and 16 in this volume to get a sense of the dynamic Japanese system for innovation at home and diffusion abroad. As these so clearly document, the technology transfer accompanying the surge of Japanese investments in Asia over the past decade has often been advanced, but also has been very much embodied in the capital equipment brought in to start new factories. Actual transfers of know-how proceed more slowly, and very much according to a model that is *sui generis*. Taken together, Kodama, Yamashita (ch. 16), and Tho and Urata (ch. 14) offer an account of what might usefully be called "the Japanese system" of technological innovation and diffusion. Describing things in these terms is meant to convey the weight, systemic character, importance, and power of Japanese technological virtuosity in much the same way as the term "the American system of manufacturing" once conveyed the wonders of an American industrial economy of an earlier period.

10. In Hong Kong, for instance, the textile industry has taken advantage of CAD/CAM technology which relies on the talents of software engineers from Shanghai. The New Technology Corporation PTE Ltd. of Singapore has joined forces with the Satellite Communications Technology Corporation of the Chinese Academy of Sciences to produce satellite TV receivers (Stoltenberg, 1990, p. 35), and the academy has also joined with Singapore interests to establish the Kexin Corporation, a firm intended to promote the export of products and saleable ideas from the academy's laboratories. New companies affiliated with the Chinese Academy of Sciences have developed joint ventures with Hong Kong (e.g., Legend Computers), with Korean, with Japanese, and with Thai firms.

11. S&T occupied an important place in the deliberations leading to normalization of relations with China. Programs with Korea, going back to the establishment of KIST, have served to advance U.S. interests in Korean development. Current interest in responding to the S&T aspirations of ASEAN are used to signal ongoing U.S. support for the ASEAN process.

12. As used here, "culture" is understood as a collection of empirical and normative beliefs about how the world does and should work. "Cultural pluralism" results from the paucity of common rules, or metaprinciples, for resolving disagreements over normative and empirical beliefs from group to group. See Schwarz and Thompson (1990).

References

Baker, James A. "America in Asia: Emerging Architecture for a Pacific Community." *Foreign Affairs*, 70, 5 (Winter 1991): 1–18.
Balakrishno, N.; Awanohara, Susumu; and Burton, Jonathon. "Silicon Implants: Singapore Gambles of U.S. Technology Ventures." *Far Eastern Economic Review* (February 6, 1992): 45–46.

Castells, Manuel, and Tyson, Laura D'Andrea. "High Technology Choices Ahead: Restructuring Interdependence." In Overseas Development Council, *Growth, Exports, & Jobs in a Changing World Economy*. New Brunswick, NJ: Transaction Books, 1988.

Clad, James Clovis. "The Half-Empty Basin." *The Wilson Quarterly*. (Winter, 1992): 74–84.

Colglazier, E. William. "Four Ideas for U.S.-Japan Cooperation in the Energy/Environment Field." In Commission on U.S.-Japan Relations in the Twenty First Century, *Adding an Energy/Environmental Dimension to the United States-Japan Alliance*. Washington, DC: Commission on U.S.-Japan Relations in the Twenty-First Century, 1991.

Commission on U.S.-Japan Relations in the Twenty First Century. *Adding an Energy/Environmental Dimension to the United States-Japan Alliance*. Washington, DC: Commission on U.S.-Japan Relations in the Twenty First Century, 1991.

Dollar, David. "South Korea-China Trade Relations." *Asian Survey, 29*, 12 (December 1989): 1167–76.

Ergas, Henry. "Does Technology Policy Matter?" In Bruce R. Guile and Harvey Brooks (eds.), *Technology and Global Industry: Companies and Nations in the World Economy*. Washington, DC: National Academy Press, 1987.

Ernst, Dieter, and O'Connor, David. *Technology and Global Competition: The Challenges for Newly Industrialising Economies*. Paris: OECD, 1989.

Free China Journal. "High-Tech Program to Cut Trade Deficit with Japan." *Free China Journal* (January 31, 1992): 3.

Graham, Edward M. "Foreign Direct Investment in the United States and U.S. Interests." *Science 254* (December 20, 1991): 1740–45.

Guile, Bruce R., and Brooks, Harvey, eds. *Technology and Global Industry*. Washington, DC: National Academy Press, 1987.

Haggard, Stephan, and Moon, Chung-in, eds. *Pacific Dynamics: The International Politics of Industrial Change*. Boulder, CO: Westview Press, 1989.

Harris, Martha Caldwell. "Asymmetries and Potential Complementarities: Scientific and Technological Relations between the United States and Japan." In Frank Press (ed.), *Scientific and Technological Relations Between the United States and Japan: Issues and Recommendations*. Washington, DC: Commission on U.S.-Japan Relations in the Twenty-First Century, 1990.

Heiduk, Gunter, and Yamamura, Kozo, eds. *Technological Competition and Interdependence*. Seattle: University of Washington Press, 1990.

Howe, Christopher. "China, Japan and Economic Interdependence in the Asia Pacific Region." *The China Quarterly, 124* (December 1990): 662–93.

Inoue, Yuko. "Sematech Turns to Japan for Chip Insight." *The Nikkei Weekly* (January 25, 1992): 1.

Itoh, Motoshige. "The Impact of Industrial Structure and Industrial Policy on International Trade." In Gunter Heiduk and Kozo Yamamura (eds.), *Technological Competition and Interdependence*. Seattle: University of Washington Press, 1990, pp. 87–107.

Katz, Richard. "U.S. Business Urged to Invest More in Region." *The Nikkei Weekly* (January 11, 1992): 19, 20.

Kodama, Fumio. *Analyzing Japanese High Technology: The Techno-Paradigm Shift*. London: Pinter Publishers, 1991.

Krugman, Paul A. "Myths and Realities of U.S. Competitiveness." *Science, 254* (November 8, 1991): 811–15.

Lee, Rachel F.F. "Handshakes More Firm as Sci-Tech Relations with Russia Strengthen." *The Free China Journal* (January 17, 1992): 4.

Levingston, Steven E. "Singapore's CSA Sets Lead in Tapping Asian Labor Pool for Software Work." *The Asian Wall Street Journal* (December 16, 1991): 2.

Lim, Linda Y.C., and Stoltenberg, Clyde D. "Becoming a Region." *The China Business Review* (May-June 1990): 24–32.

Linder, Staffan Burenstam. *The Pacific Century*. Stanford, CA: Stanford University Press, 1986.

Mastanduno, Michael. "American Trade Policy: Fashioning A Strategy for the 1990's." In Robert Art and Seyom Brown (eds.), *American Foreign Policy: Toward the Year 2000*. Forthcoming.

Miller, Arnold. "Critical Factors in the Development of an Electronics Industry." Technology Strategy Group, unpublished paper, 1988.

Moon, Chung-in. "Conclusion: A Dissenting View on the Pacific Future." In Stephan Haggard and Chung-in Moon (eds.), *Pacific Dynamics: The International Politics of Industrial Change*. Boulder, CO: Westview Press, 1989, pp. 359–74.

Muroyama, Janet H., and Stever, H. Guyford, eds. *Globalization of Technology*. Washington, DC: National Academy Press, 1988.

National Science Foundation. *International Science and Technology Data Update: 1988*. Washington, DC: Directorate for Scientific, Technological and International Affairs, Division of Science Resource Studies, NSF 89–307, 1989.

———. *Survey of Direct U.S. Private Capital Investment in Research and Development Facilities in Japan*. Report prepared by the Global Competitiveness Corporation and Technology International, Inc. for the Science and Technology Indicators Program. Washington, DC: NSF, Grant No. SRS–8912547, 1991.

Nihon Keizai Shimbun. "Bi Rise Seen in Foreign-linked Research." *The Nikkei Weekly* (February 8, 1992): 10.

Office of Technology Assessment. *Competing Economies: America, Europe and the Pacific Rim*. Washington, DC: Congress of the United States, 1991.

Press, Frank. *Scientific and Technological Relations Between the United States and Japan: Issues and Recommendations*. Washington, DC: Commission on U.S.-Japan Relations in the Twenty-First Century, 1990.

Rosenau, James M. "Turbulence in World Politics: A Theory of Change and Continuity." Princeton, NJ: Princeton University Press, 1990.

Schwarz, Michiel, and Thompson, Michael. *Divided We Stand: Redefining Politics, Technology and Social Choice*. Philadelphia: University of Pennsylvania Press, 1990.

Seow, Shaun. "ASEAN Calls for a Better Deal." *The Nikkei Weekly* (February 8, 1992): 1, 19.

Song, Su-feng. "High-tech Transfers in Spotlight." *The Free China Journal* (December 24, 1991): 8.

Sterngold, James. "Japan Builds East Asia Links, Gaining Labor and Markets." *The New York Times* (May 8, 1990): D1.

Stoltenberg, Clyde D. "China's Links to Southeast Asia." *The China Business Review* (May-June 1990): 33–38.

Suttmeier, Richard P. "In Brothers' Shadows: Implications of the 'Greater China' for the Development of Chinese Science and Technology." In American Enterprise Institute, *The Chinese and Their Future*, 1993.

Takagi, Hisao. "Similar Ends, Different Means." *The Nikkei Weekly* (December 7, 1991): 2.

Taylor, Michael. "Role Reversal: China Firm to Establish Chip Plant in Hong Kong." *Far Eastern Economic Review* (January 16, 1992): 49.

Teece, David J. "Capturing Value from Technological Innovations: Integration, Strategic Partnering, and Licensing Decisions." In Bruce R. Guile and Harvey Brooks (eds.),

Technology and Global Industry: Companies and Nations in the World Economy. Washington, DC: National Academy Press, 1987.

Usui, Naoki. "Japan Protests License Embargo." *Defense News* (December 23, 1991): 1, 20.

Westney, D. Eleanor. "U.S. Industrial Culture and the Japanese Competitive Challenge." In Alan D. Romberg and Tadashi Yamamoto (eds.), *Same Bed Different Dreams.* New York: Council on Foreign Relations, 1990.

Yoder, Stephen Kreider. "Reverse 'Brain Drain' Benefits Asia but Robs U.S. of Scarce Talent." *The Asian Wall Street Journal Weekly* (April 24, 1989): 1.

Young, Charles. "Fifth 'Tiger' in Asia May be Shanghai, Experts Bet." *China Daily* (March 20, 1989): 1.

18

An Analytic Framework for Measuring Technological Development

Greg B. Felker and Charles Weiss, Jr.

Introduction

Many of the contributors in this volume hold different implicit definitions of technological development. For some, the essential aspect of technological development is that the productive sector of the country should achieve competitive manufacturing efficiency as rapidly as possible. For this purpose, multinational corporations (MNCs) are seen as effective means of advancing technological development and transferring technical capabilities to local personnel and firms. For others, the essence of technological development is that local people master production technology and rapidly deepen their technical contribution through adaptation, development and research. From this point of view, MNCs are seen as displacing indigenous learning and mastery.

This difference of approach leads to the use of different indices of technological development. If technological development consists of rapid advance toward the technological frontier, then revealed comparative advantage scores may be taken as a proxy for technological development. Indeed, if MNCs are thought to be the most important means of this advance, then direct foreign investment (DFI) may be used as a proxy for technological development! If, on the other hand, the essence of technological development is the indigenous capacity to adapt and innovate, then the technological autonomy of locally owned firms and the technological sophistication of their management become the critical considerations, so that indigenous R&D budgets and the stock of employed scientists and engineers become preferred measures of technological development.

These alternative conceptions often parallel disciplinary divisions, with economists emphasizing the advantages of liberal investment and trade policies in fostering technological development, and political scientists and engineers stressing the need for policy interventions to promote indigenous command over technology. Frequently (though certainly not always), scholars from developing countries tend to focus on the obstacles confronting local efforts to master and deploy advanced production technology in pursuit of national development goals, while developed-country scholars depict international flows of technology as the natural way to stimulate technological development among the NIEs (newly industrializing economies).

More recently, the literature on technology transfer has recognized the wide variability of MNC performance in the level and types of technological capacities transferred to local personnel.

In other words, the issue is not local ownership *per se*, but the deepening of the technological capabilities of firms located within the country, whatever their ownership, and the deepening of the technological activities of local nationals working in these firms.

This chapter proposes a framework that facilitates the discussion of alternative strategies of technological development at firm, sector, or country levels, by distinguishing between indigenization and technological advance, and by distinguishing between local activities carried out by foreigners and by local people. It does not treat the difference between locally and foreign-owned firms, but could be easily extended to do so.

Technological Trajectory

The metaphor of *technological trajectory* serves as a useful way of depicting alternative paths for the technological development of a firm, an industry or a country. For this purpose, we define such a trajectory as a path traced through a multidimensional space whose dimensions represent the major variables of technological development.[1] In the case of the newly industrializing economies we observe three critical dimensions: technological deepening, proximity to the technological frontier, and indigenization of the capacity to manage technology. We define each of these *critical dimensions of technological development* below. The relative weights assigned to them define the *technological development strategy* associated with a given path.

The choice of strategies for technological development confronts important trade-offs among these three variables. For example, indigenization of management and engineering capabilities may require slower advance toward the technological frontier. By distinguishing among these variables, we make it possible to analyze alternative strategies for technological development, and to reconcile the competing definitions on which these strategies are based. We also provide an analytical framework within which to interpret the various indices used for measuring progress in technological development.

Deepening

The first basic dimension of technological development is the *depth of technological capabilities* possessed by a firm, an industry, or a country. Technological deepening is defined as the performance within the country of progressively more demanding technological functions related to the production process. The hierarchy of technological deepening begins with production capabilities, and includes maintenance and repair of production systems, technology evaluation and selection, production engineering, and product and process engineering and design, and ends with the capability to carry out process or product innovations, and eventually research. These capabilities may be those of local people or of foreigners permanently resident in the country; for example, the expatriate technical staff of the subsidiary of a multinational corporation or the providers of long-term technical assistance financed by a development assistance agency.

Many of the chapters in this book show concern with the depth of technological capabilities. The most thorough of these discussions of technological deepening is that of Yamashita (see chapter 16), who constructs a nine-layer framework of capabilities and surveys Japanese MNCs to document the depth of capabilities they transfer to their overseas subsidiaries. The nine layers are operation of technology, maintenance, quality control, production management, improved technology, molding, design, new product development, and equipment development. Yamashita asserts that the first four capabilities are easier to transfer, while transferring the latter five functions requires a high level of local absorption capacity in the form of high technical standards and a supportive research environment. This framework is somewhat similar to the schema developed by Dahlman et al., which distinguishes three main categories of functional capabilities, namely those involved in production, new investment, and innovation.[2]

To these nine levels of capability should be added one that lies beyond product and process development, namely the concept of strategic management, called "demand articulation" by Fumio Kodama.[3] Strategic management entails the ability to commercialize innovations through an integrated strategy for product design, manufacturing, and market development. This capability is essential if maximum value added is to be extracted from innovative capabilities, since the most profitable and most difficult step in innovation is usually the commercialization of one's own product under one's own brand name.

For an independent company, this capability is essential to the critical transition from original equipment manufacturer to producer of brand-name products. Several Taiwan and Korean companies have developed strategic management capability in this way as part of their overall commercial and technological strategies. In principle, an MNC affiliate in an industrializing country may also be given sufficient autonomy to participate in the strategic decision making of its global corporate network, and to organize and deploy its technological capabilities in support of its own product strategies. However, ownership by nationals is often a prerequisite.

Proximity to the Technological Frontier

The second basic dimension of technological development is *proximity to the technological frontier*, by which we mean the distance of a firm or industry's product and process technology from that industry's most productive or sophisticated technology. Moving closer to the frontier frequently means changing production processes and equipment, and often involves changing product design in order to move "upmarket."

For economies engaged in rapid, export-oriented industrialization in quality-sensitive sectors like electronics, this typically means adopting newer, more capital-intensive vintages, rather than employing the depth of one's technological capabilities to stretch older vintages by extracting maximum efficiency.[4] Competitive pressures tend to force upgrading, even at the cost of some depth of technological capabilities. For example, there is limited advantage in being able to make innovations in the hand-soldering assembly of integrated circuits if semiautomated circuit production dominates and drives the more labor-intensive assembly process out of the market. In this volume, the discussion by Ding (chapter 11) of the efforts of the PRC to upgrade its technology base addresses this dimension most clearly and explicitly. Liang and Denny (chapter 12) discuss the need to upgrade the technological base as a central element of Hong Kong's effort to transform its industrial structure toward higher-value-added industries.

Indigenization

The third basic dimension of technological development is the *indigenization of technological capability*. Indigenization is the degree to which indigenous personnel (as opposed to foreign technical experts located in the country) have mastered the production, management, design, and innovative tasks within productive enterprises located in the country. The growing role of MNC subsidiaries in the industrialization of the Pacific Rim makes it particularly important to isolate this dimension. In sectors with no MNC presence and no permanent expatriate staff, all technological capabilities are by definition indigenized. Technology transfer studies often conclude that investment regulations that are designed to ensure indigenous control (e.g., by limiting the role of foreign experts through immigration restrictions, and by controlling terms of technology contracts) in fact reduce the incentive of MNCs to transfer their most modern technology. This suggests a trade-off between indigenization and proximity to the frontier, at least when that indigenization is brought about in response to legal requirements.

In the short run, at least, there may also be a trade-off between deepening and indigenization of technology development. MNCs increasingly transfer a substantial depth of functional responsibilities and the most modern process technologies to their subsidiaries. Local personnel, however, may not fully participate in the more demanding technical operations of these subsidiary firms, and specific sophisticated subcomponents close to the technological frontier may continue to be imported from the parent company. In discussing the record of Japanese MNC subsidiaries in indigenizing technological capabilities within their operations, Yamashita describes a process whereby their increasing technological depth and proximity to the technological frontier contributes to a lag in indigenization, which he calls technological "black boxes."

Measuring Technological Development

Generally available indicators of science and technology input and output offer only imperfect measures of the technological trends critical to development in the Pacific Rim. First of all, detailed data are frequently lacking or are of questionable reliability. The important work of the PECC Science and Technology Task Force, reported by Kodama and Minden, respectively, seeks to improve the collection and comparison of standard S&T indicators among the Pacific Rim economies.

Second, and equally important, the standard indicators, even when available, often aggregate different elements of technological development. For example, statistics on expenditures on R&D do not distinguish between research performed by local and foreign personnel. Similarly, statistics on FDI, licensing fees and royalty payments do not illuminate the productivity or efficiency of the technology or the depth of the technological capabilities transferred.

While much can be done to disaggregate and systematize standard indicators, the interpretation of these data must be guided by a clearer conception of the overall context and of the specific aspects of technological development that they measure. Moreover, evidence cited in this volume suggests that better indicators could in fact provide direct measures of the three critical variables incorporated in this trajectory model.

Classifying Indicators

Measuring the Depth of Technological Capabilities

Input indicators are often used to measure the depth of technological capabilities on both the national and the firm level: R&D expenditures as a percentage of sales or GDP, employment of research scientists and engineers, or counts of R&D labs operating (or of R&D projects being undertaken) in a country. Technological trade figures may also be used to indicate the depth of capabilities in the importing countries, as in the chapter by Tho and Urata (chapter 14), which interprets capital goods import, technology licensing, and FDI as indicating increasing depth in terms of technology transfer.[5]

However, these standard S&T indicators offer only a limited picture of the depth of technological capabilities in the newly industrializing countries of the Pacific Rim. First, input indicators such as R&D and RSE figures do not measure innovative capacities directly, and the efficiency of the R&D process in generating innovations may generally be lower in developing countries. More fundamentally, as Poh-Kam Wong observes (chapter 15), standard S&T indicators do not register capabilities for production and adaptation that do not involve significant innovations but which may be of critical importance to NIEs.

Without a specific context, technology trade indicators are even more ambiguous. A high ratio of licensing fees to capital goods imports may, as Ding (chapter 11) suggests, reflect insufficient technology absorption in the PRC; on the other hand, however, it may provide evidence of significant reverse engineering and innovative capacities, as in the South Korean capital goods sector.

Another approach to the measurement of technological depth is to survey firm activities directly in order to document the functions actually performed. As the Yamashita paper (chapter 16) illustrates, this approach allows for the quantification and comparison or aggregation of technological deepening across firms and industries. If this approach is to be widely pursued, researchers need to refine and standardize categories of technological capabilities similar to those of Dahlman, Westphal, and others, and to develop experience in how these ideas can be adapted to the particular characteristics of different manufacturing and service industries. It should be possible systematically to survey the performance of these functions to generate empirical data on the value of public and private investment in each of these functions.

Measuring Proximity to the Frontier

Improvements in specific technical performance and economic or cost variables mark progress toward the technological frontier. Such progress can be differentiated into ordinary, incremental efficiency improvements and more discrete changes in the set of production techniques, which constitute a new "vintage" of process or product technology. Such a vintage comprises both machine-embodied technology and the managerial systems that surround it, which together define best-practice production technology for a given industry.

For individual manufacturing industries, the basic vintage process technologies available "on the shelf" are usually apparent and amenable to survey. Several chapters refer to the diffusion of information technologies in the service sector, such as CAD/CAM/CIM and EDI systems, or the computerization of service and public sector enterprises. Statistics on the number of such systems in use can in principle be systematically gathered. Ding (chapter 11) offers several statistics which are claimed to measure proximity to the frontier: the number and value of capital-upgrading investments; the percentage of such upgrading expenditures in gross fixed capital formation; and the percentage of capital equipment of recent vintage. Ministries of finance or other tax authorities already collect such firm-level investment data in many countries.

By using capital investment by firms as a proxy for technological upgrading, we recognize that new technology embodied in specific production equipment must be introduced by replacing the old capital stock. However, capital investment figures are input indicators that are only indirectly related to the relation of the capital stock to the technological frontier. The imperfections of the international technology market and the different cost conditions that developing-country firms face create variations in the marginal yield to investments in modernization of capital stock. Moreover, the gains from improving the management of the technology are not captured by these investment figures.

Two output-focused approaches to measuring progress toward the technological frontier are the comparison of growth rates in total factor productivity (TFP) and the analysis of revealed comparative advantage. Total factor productivity growth is defined as the difference between the rate of growth of output and the growth rate of weighted inputs. Technological development within protected or non-market economies often scores high on deepening and indigenization scales, while lagging productivity scores reveal an economy which is falling further and further behind the technological frontier.[6]

TFP statistics have several limitations in the measurement of proximity to the frontier of production technology. Lack of TFP data and formidable methodological problems confront any effort to aggregate TFP scores across industries and to compare them across countries.[7] Noncompetitive factor markets distort the weighting of inputs by marginal value output, while distorted price regimes bias output values themselves. Beyond these measurement considerations, TFP comparisons reflect a range of factors wider than just technological vintage or upgrading. These include scale economies and the efficiency of resource allocation.[8] If TFP could be disaggregated into its determinants, one could then control for productivity-reducing factors not related to the sophistication of the technology employed. These drawbacks notwithstanding, comparisons of trends in TFP scores may be the likeliest approach to measuring proximity to the frontier in the absence of specific technical information on the vintage of technology employed.

Revealed comparative advantage (RCA) statistics offer similar advantages and drawbacks as an indicator of progress toward the technological frontier. Like TFP statistics, RCA figures constitute output measures of competitiveness in production, and thereby register improvements in mastery of both the hardware and managerial aspects of technology. Furthermore, success in export markets denotes competitiveness in terms of product quality, which in turn reflects significant technological capabilities not easily measured by other indicators. To be sure, an economy's trade performance is a function of many more factors than its relation to the frontier of technological capabilities in production. Macroeconomic conditions, variable levels of real effective protection, and changes in factor markets and other cost variables all impact RCA scores. Furthermore, RCA analysis will not capture significant upgrading of production technology in nontradeable sectors or within industries with low export ratios. Nevertheless, given the increasingly trade-dependent nature of industrialization in the Pacific Rim, trends in RCA provide an important, if rough, indicator of an industry's movement relative to the frontier of production technology.

Measuring Indigenization

Efforts to measure indigenization often begin with the assumption that MNC subsidiaries constitute manufacturing platforms with little local technological participation, so that the degree of MNC presence in an industry is taken as a limiting measure of indigenization. In principle, however, an MNC, especially when staffed by local managers and technicians, may make significant contributions both to local technological capacity and to indigenization. The point here is not to defend the actual performance of the MNCs in this area, but to point out that their activities should be disaggregated, measured and judged according to explicit criteria of technological development.

In practice, however, modes of industrialization that allow MNCs to dominate the most dynamic sectors carry several risks: relocation of footloose industries; adverse effects on local industrial activity as a result of the global profitability of the parent company; and, of more direct concern here, structural limitations on the extent of the deepening and indigenization of technological capabilities. Poh-Kam Wong (chapter 5) discusses a lack of technological depth in Singapore resulting from its heavy reliance on MNCs to keep it close to the global frontier of production technology.

Standard S&T indicators are often used to give a broad picture of the overall state of indigenous capabilities. Since the public R&D budget generally does not support R&D performed in the MNC sector, but flows nearly entirely to local researchers, this indicator is often used as a broad measure of indigenization of R&D. For example, Sripaipan views the relatively low ratio of government expenditure on R&D to GDP in Thailand as pointing to insufficient indigenous technological development.

Technology trade statistics may also be used to provide indirect evidence of the stock of indigenous technological capabilities. This indicator is useful only in special circumstances, however, particularly when there are low overall levels of MNC penetration and hence less likelihood that the data will be distorted by intrafirm transactions motivated by overall tax minimization. Such evidence was used, for example, in a 1987 UNCTAD study of Korean industrialization, which, in discussing indigenous technological development, focuses on the high ratio of arm's-length modes of technology transfer to FDI.[9] However, the significant role of MNCs in many Pacific Rim economies clouds the relationship between standard R&D and technology-trade indicators, on the one hand, and indigenization on the other.[10]

It seems clear, therefore, that adequate measurements must look inside the firm to discern the extent to which indigenous personnel participate in the various levels of technological activity. Concern with indigenization has driven the discussion regarding the relative merits of Japanese, U.S., and European FDI and management practices for the technological development of host countries. Several chapters use anecdotal and case study evidence to discuss the degree of indigenization of technological skills and knowledge among MNC subsidiaries. Going beyond these anecdotes, Yamashita (chapter 16) analyzes quantitative measures of the transfer of technology to indigenous personnel at various ranks and according to the mode of training used. Baba and Suzuki (chapter 13) report data on the numbers of foreign RSEs employed by Japanese corporations, both in Japan and in the host country. To be sure, such personnel data do not directly measure the degree to which these functions could be performed by indigenous personnel alone, but they are the closest practicable measure of this dimension of technological development, and lend themselves to general, standardized collection.

Indexes and Technological Trajectories

With this variety of partial and imperfect indicators of progress along the three dimensions, comparative analysis of technological trajectories across industries, sectors, and countries will remain imprecise. Actually plotting technology development trajectories requires the use of some index for each of the three dimensions. For the foreseeable future, however, the construction of such indexes out of available indicators will remain the work of individual analysts and will be tailored more to specific research questions than to general comparative efforts.[11]

However, progress along each of the three dimensions of technological development is a matter of degree, even if a single common index cannot be constructed for all firms and industries. Given the construction of even very approximate indexes, a rough trajectory might be plotted in order to frame discussions of the theoretical issues raised in the conference papers.

Technological Development Strategies

Technological Trajectories and Strategies

The path traced by a technological trajectory represents the relative progress of a firm, industry, or country over time along the three dimensions of technological development. Given likely short-run tradeoffs among these dimensions, a country's particular trajectory largely reflects a choice among policy goals, as expressed through public investments in technological development, regulation of FDI and technology transfer, and the impact of broader economic policies on the technological decisions of private firms. These decisions must be made under conditions of substantial uncertainty. Market signals do not give an unambiguous indication as to whether emphasis on indigenization, deepening, or upgrading of technology will pay off most over time.

The key strategic imperative facing developing-country governments, then, is to minimize the trade-offs between these dimensions over time. As Yu (chapter 4) shows, while a less restrictive stance vis-à-vis FDI might have accelerated Korea's advance toward the technology frontier in heavy and high-tech sectors, its reliance on a protected domestic market to achieve indigenization and (to a lesser extent) deepening did not prevent a progressive advance toward world-competitive levels of productivity. On the other hand, a developing-country government may calculate that emphasizing proximity to the frontier through FDI will establish an industry in the global markets and yield more short-run economic returns and production experience, and that this will in turn make subsequent deepening and indigenization, or the "opening of black boxes," far easier and more successful over time. Malaysia's or Singapore's technology strategy might be interpreted in this way.

Technological Trajectories, Industrial Development Sequences, and Global Trends

The success of a particular technological trajectory in supporting rapid industrial development depends on the broader industrial development strategy or sequence pursued by a country, and on global technological trends, particularly the rate of innovation in a given industry. Certain industrialization sequences may be more compatible than others with an emphasis on indigenization and deepening. South Korea, for example, moved from light consumer goods, to intermediate goods, to heavy industry, and finally to technology-intensive sectors of production. This sequence corresponds to the dictates of product-cycle theory: that developing countries begin industrialization in technologically mature industries such as textiles and footwear, and gradually move into progressively more technologically sophisticated industries. Indigenizing in a technologically mature industry costs less in terms of lags behind the technological frontier.

The Southeast Asian near-NIEs, by contrast, have experienced rapid growth in technology-intensive electronics sectors relatively early in the development of their manufacturing sectors. Developing the industrial structure in this way may put a high premium on proximity to the frontier, given the rapid pace of global technological change in these industries. This would seem to imply a large MNC role, with consequently lower levels of indigenization.[12]

However, as Simon (chapter 1) implies, several global trends may be making it more difficult to pursue a trajectory that stresses indigenization and deepening above proximity to the frontier, even when a product-cycle industrialization sequence is followed. First, the pace of technological change has increased dramatically even in mature industries. Microelectronics-based process innovations like CAD/CIM systems and numerically-controlled machine tools increasingly affect best-practice production technology in mature industries, such as textiles, while advances in materials science have led to many new product innovations. Quality standards in mature industries also continue to rise fairly quickly. This means that technological upgrading is important if market share is to be retained even in mature industries.

Second, the entry of new labor-surplus countries into export markets means that the advantages of low-cost labor are quickly eroded, as the East Asian NIEs have experienced and the Southeast Asian second-tier NIEs are discovering. The speed with which the product cycle takes mature industries out of the scope of comparative advantage of a rapidly industrializing economy is increasing, thereby forcing an emphasis on upgrading the industrial structure of all manufacturing exporters toward technology-intensive production.

National Technological Trajectories and International Technology Systems

Technoliberalism and Technonationalism

The differences in industrial development sequences and technological trajectories between Japan and East Asian NIEs on the one hand, and the Southeast Asian second-tier NIEs on the other, raise important questions about the optimal strategy for technological development.[13] A central concern of the chapters is the proper balance between efforts to accelerate indigenous and indigenously controlled technological development, and the advantages of integration into the international technological economy. Broadly speaking, the conference participants divide between "technoliberals," who rely on integration with regional and global markets (especially through FDI) to make it possible to approach the world technological frontier quickly, and "technonationalists," who stress investments in indigenous scientific and technological capability and the avoidance of overreliance on FDI for technology acquisition, even at the expense of delay in achieving the technological frontier.

Both the "internationalists" and the "nationalists" agree on the necessity of indigenous technological effort or capacity creation via human resource development, supporting public technological infrastructure, and adaptive R&D. They disagree, however, about the advisability of strong government intervention in specific industrial sectors to promote indigenous technological development and to control technology transfer.

If the proponents of the two types of argument are to yield better understanding of what causes technological development, each must seek to address the other's theoretical concerns. Programs of discretionary "targeting" of national technology, such as the Indonesian EVIT program analyzed by Alam, need to measure the impact of these policies in deepening and indigenization over time to document the actual success of the policies in achieving their intended goals. Moreover, they must document the direct costs of such programs, as well as the cost of possible lags behind the technological frontier induced by these policies and programs.

The internationalist approach is reflected in the majority of the chapters in this volume. This approach sees technological development within the Pacific Rim as fundamentally shaped by transnational dynamics expressed in trends in multinational business and flows of human resources. From this perspective, decisive advantages accrue to those countries able to take advantage of, in Minden's words, "the positive synergy created by technical cooperation . . . promoting the [transnational] social and economic integration of technological progress" (chapter 15). Greater integration with regional or global technological trends will foster progress along the three dimensions of technological progress.

In confronting developing-country skeptics, advocates of technoliberalism must do more than demonstrate the volume and progress of global and regional technological trends. They must also show that growing interdependence will not lock developing countries into unequal technological relationships that inhibit deepening or indigenization. Indices of the integration of local firms with those of the larger region or of the world economy, such as the flow of FDI or strategic alliances, must be evaluated according to their contribution to deepening and indigenization, as well as introducing more advanced technology per se.

Even so, the prospects for national technological development are decisively influenced by the global technological environment, as the conference papers make clear. The accelerating integration of national production systems through FDI, and the trend toward an integrated global strategic orientation (or "denationalization") among MNCs, has spurred the creation of a global technological economy. Participation in transnational technology networks appears increasingly critical to technological development in the context of an export-led industrialization strategy. Greater attention to transnational technology flows is needed to discern the implications of different trends for national technological development.

Measuring International Technological Integration

Three dynamic transnational forces of technological development are analyzed in the chapters in this volume: the internationalization of R&D and product design operations; the development of a regional market in human resources; and the integration of technological complementarities through the formation of strategic corporate alliances.

The first of these trends has been documented in the papers primarily by reporting counts of the R&D operations established by Japanese and other MNCs overseas. The survey data presented in the Baba and Suzuki paper, for example, suggest that it might be possible to collect data not only on the number of R&D centers sited overseas, but also on the expenditure value and percentage share of R&D undertaken overseas to total firm R&D expenditures. A variety of data are either available, or could in principle be measured, to document the trends in human resource flows, including numbers of foreign students, visits of scientists and engineers, etc. Statistics on employment of foreign research scientists and engineers by multinationals in the region would be a more direct measure of the pooling of regional human resources, and thus should be an area for more systematic data gathering. Finally, the chapters discuss the rise of strategic alliances, though primarily from anecdotal evidence. These examples depict OEM relations developing in the most technologically sophisticated industries, technology swaps, and joint R&D undertakings in industries such as high-definition television.

The challenge in documenting these trends is to distinguish them according to their impact upon the technological trajectory of particular countries. The multinationalization of R&D and design clearly advances deepening among MNC subsidiaries, but says little in and of itself about indigenization. The general surge in FDI within the Pacific Rim may be presumed to bring developing-country industries closer to the technological frontier and may also be contributing to deepening, though this assertion requires specific data on the technological content of FDI agreements.

While significant amounts of technology flow appear to be involved in strategic, "other-than-market" alliances, the precise nature and degree of technology transfer involved remains relatively obscure. The first step toward measuring this trend should be to develop an adequate general typology of the various forms of these contractual agreements according to their technological components, and then to generate simple counts of their frequencies. For example, it would be of great interest to register the number of joint research, joint product development, technology swap, and OEM agreements. Do such agreements simply involve the transfer of more modern technologies to developing-country firms (upgrading) in exchange for that firm's added production capacities, or do they have an impact on their depth of capabilities?

More difficult would be to move beyond simple counts to a "shadow" valuation of the technology flows contained within the contract agreements. Clearly the firms involved calculate the values of agreements into which they enter, but these numbers are usually proprietary information. If technological development increasingly involves the integration of technological assets from foreign environments, then ". . . one should be able to measure how the national institutions are rounding up the needed inputs in a framework where the ideal condition is no longer self-sufficiency but the ability to exploit world knowledge."[14]

Conclusion

Plotting technological development trajectories will neither substitute for nor resolve the broader ongoing theoretical debate over the causes and appropriate policy strategies to foster technological development. It will, however, serve to organize comparative inquiry into the different technological development strategies and experiences of rapidly industrializing economies. The importance of progress on this level lies in organizing theoretical debate about the determinants of technological development in newly industrializing economies, its dynamics and appropriate strategies to promote it, and in influencing the gathering of data for analysis.

It will take many years to define, validate, and agree on new indicators for measuring technological development that can illuminate the situation in the more advanced developing countries. By defining a better methodology now, we can lay the groundwork for a better understanding not only of the technological trajectories of the current generation of NIEs, but also of their successors in the coming decades.

Notes

The authors would like to thank Professor Denis Fred Simon for his comments.

1. The notion of a technological trajectory was first elaborated at the micro-level by Nelson and Winter (1977, 1982) and by Dosi (1982) to represent the pathway of innovation activity at the frontier of technology. This pathway results from the perception of engineers and scientists of the most fruitful avenues of technological advance, combined with policy, institutional, and market factors that influence the demand for the innovation and its profitability. In this model, the trajectory of a given technology results from strategic choices undertaken in the face of major uncertainties regarding both the supply and demand for the particular innovation. These strategic choices are analogous to those faced by government and firms in developing countries in formulating the strategies for technology development discussed here.

2. See Carl Dahlman, Bruce Ross-Larson, and Larry Westphal, *Managing Technological Development: Lessons from the Newly Industrialized Countries*, World Bank Staff Working Paper No. 717 (1985). An elaboration and empirical application is given in Westphal et al., "The Development of Technological Capability in Manufacturing: A Macroscopic Approach to Policy Research," in Evenson and Ranis, *Science and Technology: Lessons for Development Policy* (Boulder: Westview Press, 1990), pp. 84–86; see esp. Table 5.1.

3. Fumio Kodama, *Analyzing Japanese High Technologies* (London: Pinter, 1991.)

4. The significance of proximity to the frontier raises the economic debate about the degree of factor substitutability within manufacturing technology. Pack's work in the textile industry (1988, 1990) shows that productivity can often be raised significantly through improved management and other measures. This implies that newer, more capital-intensive technologies do not necessarily dominate the older, labor-intensive processes. In such a case, LDC firms can enhance their competitiveness by improving their production or management capabilities without upgrading their capital stock.

In contrast, the emphasis here on upgrading toward the most sophisticated products and technologies reflects three pressures specific to the NIEs. First, the cost of labor for manufacturing typically rises rather quickly, changing the optimal factor mix. Second, in many industries, quality control standards are critical to success in export markets, and this exerts a bias toward automated techniques. Third, producers in countries with lower labor costs enter the export market using the same standard technologies and factor ratios (even though they are therefore not optimizing). Thus, while different factor costs and correctable factors depressing productivity may make labor-intensive technologies temporarily optimal, NIE economies face the pressure to upgrade. The length of time during which an industry may retain competitiveness with a particular vintage of technology is limited.

5. Output indicators, such as patent data and bibliometric data, are given little attention in this volume. In an environment where technological development consists primarily of "learning" processes, these indicators capture little of the innovative activities occurring on the firm level. The usefulness of these output indicators may be higher in countries like India, where there is significant basic research activity that is captured by statistics on scientific publication.

6. See, for example, Sanjaya Lall, "Trade in Technology by a Slowly Industrializing Country: India," in Nathan Rosenberg and Claudio Frischtak, *International Technology Transfer: Concepts, Methods, and Comparisons* (New York: Praeger, 1985), pp. 45–76.

7. See Anne O. Krueger and Baran Tuncer, *Estimating Total Factor Productivity Growth in a Developing Country*, World Bank Staff Working Paper No. 442 (October 1980); and Howard Pack, "Total Factor Productivity and Its Determinants: Some International Comparisons," in Ranis, West, Leiserson, and Morris, *Comparative Development Perspectives* (Boulder: Westview Press, 1984).

8. See Howard Pack, "Industrial Efficiency and Technology Choice," in Evenson and Ranis, *Science and Technology: Lessons for Development Policy.*

9. UNCTAD, "The Implementation of Laws and Regulations on Transfer of Technology: The Experience of the Republic of Korea," New York, UNCTAD, 1987.

10. See also "The Technological Balance of Payments: An Indicator of Technology Transfer," OECD *STI Indicators Newsletter* No. 11, 1988.

11. See OECD Technology/Economy Program, *Technology and the Economy: The Key Relationships* (Paris: OECD, 1992), especially the Annex "Consequences of the TEP for the Development of Indicators," pp. 283–295 and Box 56.

12. An alternative for those countries that wish to enter into technology-intensive production immediately, and that are willing to accept high costs, is to indigenize and deepen beyond import-substituting barriers in the manner of Indonesia's EVIT program of promotion of high-technology industry and Malaysia's push for heavy industries. This approach risks lagging behind the technological frontier, as measured in both technology vintage and factor productivity.

13. The important variations in industrial development sequencing and technological development strategies within each of these groups are here noted only in passing.

14. Giorgio Sirilli, "Conceptual and Methodological Problems in the Development of Science and Technology Indicators," in Morita-Lou, *Science and Technology Indicators for Development* (Boulder: Westview Press, 1985), p. 194.

References

Dahlman, Carl J.; Ross-Larson, Bruce; and Westphal, Larry E. *Managing Technological Development: Lessons from the Newly Industrializing Countries.* Washington, DC: The World Bank, 1985.

Dosi, Giovanni. "Technological Paradigms and Technological Trajectories: A Suggested Interpretation of the Determinants and Directions of Technical Change," *Research Policy 11* (1982).

Ernst, Dieter, and O'Connor, David. *Technology and Global Competition.* Paris: OECD, 1989.

Evenson and Ranis, eds. *Science and Technology: Lessons for Development Policy.* Boulder, CO: Westview Press, 1990.

Fransman, Martin, and King, Kenneth, eds. *Technological Capability in the Third World.* New York: St. Martin's Press, 1984.

Freeman, Christopher. *Technology Policy and Economic Performance.* London: Pinter, 1987.

Kaplinsky, Raphael, and Cooper, Charles, eds. *Technology and Development in the Third Industrial Revolution.* London: Frank Cass, 1989.

Nelson, Richard R., and Winter, Sidney G. *An Evolutionary Theory of Economic Change.* Cambridge: Belknap Press of Harvard University, 1982.

————. "In Search of a Useful Theory of Innovation." *Research Policy, 6* (1977), pp. 36–76.

Pack, Howard. "Industrial Efficiency and Technology Choice." In Evenson and Ranis, eds., *Science and Technology: Lessons for Development Policy.* Boulder, CO: Westview Press, 1990.

————. *Productivity, Technology, and Industrial Development: A Case Study in Textiles.* New York: Oxford University Press, 1987.

————. "Total Factor Productivity and Its Determinants: Some International Comparisons," in Ranis, Leiserson, and Morris, eds., *Comparative Development Perspectives.* Boulder, CO: Westview Press, 1984.

Rosenberg, N., and Frischtak, C., eds. *International Technology Transfer: Concepts, Measures and Comparisons.* New York: Praeger, 1985.

Weiss, Charles. "Scientific and Technological Constraints to Economic Growth and Equity," in Evenson and Ranis, eds., *Science and Technology: Lessons for Development Policy.* Boulder, CO: Westview Press, 1990.

Index

European Space Agency (ESA),
    49–50
Exchange rate policy (Indonesia),
    195
External demand articulation,
    47–48

F

Fairchild Industries, 16
Food industry (Thailand), 167
Food science and technology, ASEAN
    cooperation in, 139–40
Ford, 11, 304
Ford Escort, 8
Foreign direct investment
    by Japan, 303–7, 340, 341
    by South Korea, 309–11
    in South Korea, 70
    by Taiwan, 308
    technology transfer by, 296–300
    in United States, 358
Formosa Plastics, 9
Four dragons, 3–4
FSX fighter aircraft, 50
Fujitsu, 16, 288

G

GATT, 149
GE, 281
Gemmell, Norman, 58
Gems and jewelry industry (Thailand), 167
General Dynamics, 18
Geophysics, ASEAN cooperation in,
    140–41
Germany, 319
Global entrepreneurialism, 376
Globalization of Pacific Rim, 4, 7–15
    responses to, 9–15
    trends, 18–23
Goh Chok Thong, 108
Goldstar, 9, 14, 15, 69
Government role
    China, 243–44, 250–51, 254
    Hong Kong, 266–67
    Japan, 354–55
    Malaysia, 175–76
    in NIEs, 55–56
    South Korea, 94–95
Guangdong, 257, 259

H

Habibie, B.J., 190–92
HAN Project, 93–95
Hewlett Packard, 121
High-definition TV (HDTV), 45–47,
    287–88
High technologies. See also South Korea
    definitions of, 87–89
    transfer mechanism of, 36–37
Hitachi Ltd., 11, 14–15, 22, 283, 288,
    350
Holistic technology, 43–45
Homogenization of demand, 7
Honda, 286
Hong Kong, 256–74
    and China, 20–21, 267–68
    decriminalization of copyright violations
        in, 330
    early industrial development of, 60, 61
    economic shifts in, 256–58
    economic strengths of
        China, proximity to, 259
        entrepreneurial business climate in, 258
        telecommunications infrastructure of,
            259–60
    export manufacturing during 1970s in,
        63–64
    governmental environment, 258
    government policy trends in, 76
    impediments to growth of science and
        technology in, 260–61
    key technologies for, 261–64
        advanced manufacturing technology,
            263
        biotechnology, 264
        information technology, 262–63
        materials technology, 263–64
        technology management, 261–62
    mechanisms for upgrading science and
        technology in, 264–67
        governmental support, 266–67
        higher education institutions, 264–66
        science and technology centers, 266
    science and technology policy in, 74
    trends of science and technology in,
        268–71
        China, closer links with, 268–69
        government/industry/education
            cooperation, 269
        infrastructure development, 269–70

Research and development (R&D)
  (continued)
  Russia, 10
  Singapore, 115–16, 118–23, 125–29
  South Korea, 69–70, 91, 96, 99–100
  Taiwan, 75–76
  targeting of, by governments, 68
  Thailand, 152–60
    expenditures, 152–54
    funding for, 154, 155–57
    outputs, 154, 157–58
    private sector, 158–60
  transnationalization of, 5–6
  United States, 10, 276–77
Research Institute of Innovative
  Technologies for the Earth (Japan),
  370
Resource allocation, 105
Rho Tae Woo, 93
Rockefeller, Jay, 326
Rolls Royce, 281
Rosenberg, N., 29

S

Samsung, 9, 10, 14
Samsung Aerospace, 17
Sanyo, 287, 288, 350
Science and Technology Agency (Japan),
  280–81
Science and Technology Policy Network
  (STEPAN), 321
Science and technology (S&T) policies.
  See also ASEAN countries; China;
  Indonesia;
  Malaysia; Singapore
  Hong Kong, 74
  Korea, 69–71
  in NIEs, 56–57, 68–69
  Taiwan, 71–73
  Thailand, 163–68
Scientific cooperation, international,
  48–51
Seiko, 21
Sematech, 357
Semiconductors (South Korea), 14–15
Semitech, HK, 260
Shanghai Jiaotong University, 20
Sharp, 22, 287
Shin-Kansen bullet train, 46
Simon, Denis, 329

Singapore
  aggregate economic growth performance
    (table), 124
  early industrial development of, 60–62
  export manufacturing during 1970s in,
    64–65
  GDP distribution by sectors (table), 124
  government policy trends in, 76–77
  phases of economic development in,
    106–8
  R&D expenditures (tables), 125–30
  science and technology policy in, 73–74,
    103–6, 108–23
    creative and design skills, promotion
      of, 120
    foreign talent, attraction of, 121–22
    government sector, deployment of
      technology in, 114–15
    infrastructure development, 113–14
    innovation, need for investment in,
      117–18
    international acquisition of
      technology-based companies, 121
    MNC operations, upgrading of, 109–10
    MNCs, partnership with, 121
    MNC technology transfer, promotion
      of, 110–13
    new National Technology Plan, 118–20
    and performance, 116–17
    R&D, promotion of, 115–16
  training at Japananese-affiliated
    companies in, 346
Singapore Airlines, 18
Singapore Institute for Standards and
  Industrial Research, 108
Singapore Semiconductor, 18
Singer, 260
Solar battery, 44
Sony, 21, 22, 286–88, 350
Sony Precision Engineering Corporation,
  121
South Korea
  early industrial development of, 60,
    62–63
  and Eastern Europe/former USSR, 10
  electronics exports, 67
  export manufacturing during 1970s in,
    65–66
  high-technology development in, 81–100
    current challenges, 83–84
    definitions of high technology, 87–89